HABITUATION

VOLUME I

Behavioral Studies

CONTRIBUTORS TO THIS VOLUME

DAVID A. GOODMAN

FRANCES K. GRAHAM

PHILIP M. GROVES

MICHAEL J. HERZ

HERBERT D. KIMMEL

HARMAN V. S. PEEKE

SHIRLEY C. PEEKE

LEWIS PETRINOVICH

RICHARD A. ROEMER

TIMOTHY J. TEYLER

RICHARD F. THOMPSON

NORMAN M. WEINBERGER

EVERETT J. WYERS

HABITUATION

Edited by

HARMAN V. S. PEEKE
Langley Porter Neuropsychiatric Institute
University of California
San Francisco, California

MICHAEL J. HERZ
Langley Porter Neuropsychiatric Institute
University of California
San Francisco, California

VOLUME I

BEHAVIORAL STUDIES

ACADEMIC PRESS   New York and London   1973

A Subsidiary of Harcourt Brace Jovanovich, Publishers

ACADEMIC PRESS, INC.
111 Fifth Avenue, New York, New York 10003

United Kingdom Edition published by
ACADEMIC PRESS, INC. (LONDON) LTD.
24/28 Oval Road, London NW1

LIBRARY OF CONGRESS CATALOG CARD NUMBER: 72-88370

PRINTED IN THE UNITED STATES OF AMERICA

Contents

Chapter 1.   Behavioral Habituation in Invertebrates

Everett J. Wyers, Harman V. S. Peeke, and Michael J. Herz

Chapter 2.   Habituation in Fish with Special Reference to Intraspecific Aggressive Behavior

Harman V. S. Peeke and Shirley C. Peeke

Chapter 3.   Habituation in "Lower" Tetrapod Vertebrates: Amphibia as Vertebrate Model Systems

David A. Goodman and Norman M. Weinberger

List of Contributors

Numbers in parentheses indicate the pages on which the authors' contributions begin.

DAVID A. GOODMAN (85), Newport Neuroscience Center, Culver City, California

FRANCES K. GRAHAM (163), Departments of Psychology and Pediatrics, University of Wisconsin, Madison, Wisconsin

PHILIP M. GROVES (239), Department of Psychology, University of Colorado, Boulder, Colorado

MICHAEL J. HERZ(1), Langley Porter Neuropsychiatric Institute and Department of Psychology, University of California, San Francisco, California

HERBERT D. KIMMEL (129), Department of Psychology, University of South Florida, Tampa, Florida

HARMAN V. S. PEEKE (1, 59), Langley Porter Neuropsychiatric Institute, and Department of Psychiatry, University of California, San Francisco, California

SHIRLEY C. PEEKE (59), Langley Porter Neuropsychiatric Institute, University of California, San Francisco, California

LEWIS PETRINOVICH (141), Department of Psychology, University of California, Riverside, California

RICHARD A. ROEMER (239), Department of Psychobiology, University of California, Irvine, California

TIMOTHY J. TEYLER (239), Department of Psychobiology, University of California, Irvine, California

RICHARD F. THOMPSON (239), Department of Psychobiology, University of California, Irvine, California

NORMAN M. WEINBERGER (85), Department of Psychobiology, School of Biological Sciences, University of California, Irvine, California

EVERETT J. WYERS (1), State University of New York, Stony Brook, New York

Preface

The phenomenon of habituation, the waning of responsiveness to repeated or constant stimulation, has received much recent attention. Although historically dismissed as a functionally insignificant form of behavior, most contemporary scientists view habituation as a form of adaptive modification of behavior (learning). The research and theory presented in these volumes reflect the fact that habituation has recently achieved a position of prominence among investigators concerned with the neurobiology of behavior. The current interest appears to have evolved from two previously somewhat separate lines of research which have converged upon a common goal, i.e., the understanding of both the behavioral and physiological bases of habituation.

Early biologists working in apparent isolation provided a foundation of empirical studies of behavioral response waning in many species, mostly invertebrates. Later, habituation was accorded a central role in the organism's adaptive capacity by the inclusion of a chapter on habituation in Humphrey's "The Nature of Learning" (1933), a source still frequently referenced and quoted today. Hinde, an ethologist, studying the waning of predator-mobbing behavior in birds, has demonstrated the field relevance of the phenomenon in a quasi-natural situation in a series of papers published between 1954 and 1961. More recently, Thorpe's "Learning and Instinct in Animals" (1963) placed habituation on a par with classical conditioning and instrumental learning as an important form of learning. All of these influences have contributed to the contemporary interest in behavioral habituation, much of which is reviewed and discussed in the first volume of this two-volume treatise.

The second major influence on the study of habituation, reflected in the second volume, has come from the laboratories of neurobiologists who have demonstrated the plasticity of the nervous system utilizing repeated presentation of stimuli that have resulted in decrement or cessation of neuronal activity. While habituation in neurophysiological experiments often is a much shorter term phenomenon than that observed with behavioral responses, Thompson and Spencer's (1966) properties of habituation appear to occur even when responses of single neurons are examined. This similarity between the neuron and the whole organism has led many investigators to seek the physiological basis of habituation in terms of neurophysiological and neurochemical consequences of repeated stimulation in partial organism preparations and then to attempt to relate these results to intact, behaving animals.

In assembling these volumes we have attempted to cover a good portion of the literature on behavioral habituation and its substrates by choosing representatives from the many investigators concerned with this phenomenon. While we feel that the work presented represents much of the best available, many additional chapters could have been added. It is our hope that this selection of papers presents a fair and representative sample of the large body of literature available on this subject.

The chapter by Drs. Pakula and Sokolov requires special mention. To our knowledge, this is the first exposure of some of this Soviet research to Western readers. The authors gave us permission to edit the chapter in order to clarify points and to make it more readable. Dr. Bertram Peretz spent many additional hours on this contribution attempting to clarify points from his perspective as an expert in the behavior and neurophysiology of Mollusca. We hope that our efforts have improved understanding and apologize for any inaccuracies which we may have introduced into the chapter. We would also like to thank Dr. David Galin who was also particularly helpful in the editing of one of the chapters, and Dr. Shirley Peeke who was of immeasurable help in assembling the Subject Index.

We would like to express our appreciation to Dr. Alex Simon, Director of Langley Porter Neuropsychiatric Institute and University of California, Chairman, Department of Psychiatry who has actively supported our scholarly and basic research activities. Finally, we would like to especially thank Dr. Enoch Callaway III, Professor and Chief of Research, for his personal encouragement as well as for his having created a scientific and scholastic atmosphere conducive to free inquiry in the bio-behavioral sciences. Finally, we would like to express our appreciation to Professor Everett Wyers, who kindled our interest in habituation and inhibitory processes while we were still impressionable graduate students and with whom we have argued for many years about the topics covered in these volumes.

HARMAN V. S. PEEKE
MICHAEL J. HERZ

Contents of Volume II

Chapter 1
Behavioral Habituation in Invertebrates[1]

EVERETT J. WYERS, HARMAN V. S. PEEKE,
AND MICHAEL J. HERZ

I. Introduction

A young, laboratory-reared chimpanzee moving around its cage encounters a novel object. It is startled, assumes a preferred posture, and freezes. It may scream or whimper. Often it covers its eyes and turns its back to the object, sometimes assuming a prone or supine posture (Menzel, 1964).

[1] This chapter was written while the authors were receiving the following grant support: Everett J. Wyers, National Science Foundation Grant GB-5634; Harman V. S. Peeke, USPHS Research Grants MH18636 and MH19978, and Training Grant MH7082; Michael J. Herz, USPHS Research Grants MH18636 and MH19978, and Training Grants MH7082 and MH6992.

1

Gradually this withdrawal response gives way to more and more changes in posture, and a quadrupedal position is assumed. Picking at the cage then alternates with self-directed responses while the animal often looks away from the object. After a time, it begins to jump up and down and "threaten" the object. This is interspersed with racing around the cage. As yet the object has not been touched; the stimulus situation remains unchanged. With repeated visual exposure to the object, the chimpanzee's responses to it have changed markedly.

Now definite but tentative approaches are made. The animal leans over and brings its eyes and nose almost, but not quite, within touching distance. It might even straddle the object, making pelvic thrusts or spitting at it, but all without touching. These approaches are followed by sudden backward jumps and brief assumption of a stereotyped swaying posture. Still the stimulus situation remains unchanged, but approach responses have replaced withdrawal responses. Have the latter "habituated"? Certainly a characteristic pattern of response to a repeated stimulus has undergone decrement. Is it now "inhibited"?

Gradually the chimpanzee does come to touch the object. At first very cautiously, with a finger, the back of the wrist, or an extended lower lip, or even the forehead. This is followed by brief hand contacts, rapidly withdrawn with subsequent sniffing of the fingers, and ultimately grasping and manipulation. Up to the point of grasping and manipulation, a change in the visual stimulus configuration still has not occurred; although response to it (approach), after touching begins, may be said to be followed (reinforced) by tactile stimulation. Nevertheless, it is clear that decrement of a major response pattern has been succeeded by emergence of another. This has happened through repeated exposure to the object, without a change in the stimulus consequences of response to that object.

It should be emphasized that only a very few young chimpanzees demonstrate the sequence of events noted, completely during their initial testing session with a novel object. Most require repeated tests and remember their previous experience from test to test, always demonstrating clear-cut discrimination of novel from familiar objects. The animals learn and remember, clearly so, but does their pre-grasp learning and remembering differ in any way from their post-grasp learning and remembering? What role does the post-touch introduction of response-induced sensory change play, if any? Were such changes covertly present even during pre-touch learning and remembering?

In the analysis of any complex problem an advantage inheres in considering its simplest instances. Learning and memory involve discriminative control of behavior through differential inhibition and excitation of specific responses. Every animal lives embedded in a stream of constantly shifting and changing sensory inputs. The momentary mosaic of current and recently past sensory inputs provides the impetus for discriminative control of behavior. To understand learning and memory the mosaic is frequently simplified, and perhaps its simplest instance is that of habituation. Only one element of the mosaic is made to vary systematically over time, while all others are held constant or permitted only "random" variation between set limits.

This simplification of the mosaic frequently takes the form of the use of a simpler organism in a behavioral abstration often making use of partial organism preparations. Such approaches are called model systems (see Abraham *et al.*, 1972, for a detailed description of current approaches and directions to be taken in model systems analyses of the neurobiology of learning).

A marine gastropod mollusk of the genus *Aplysia* lies clamped and immobilized in a small aquarium, the dorsal edge of its mantle shelf pinned to a substage, cooled and aerated seawater circulates around it, and periodically a constant and quantifiable jet of seawater is briefly directed against the edge of its mantle shelf (Pinsker *et al.*, 1970). At first it reacts by withdrawing its gill, normally part of a complex defensive response, withdrawing it from potentially noxious tactile stimulation. After a few repetitions of the seawater jet, it withdraws its gill only slightly and after many repetitions hardly at all. The magnitude of its gill withdrawal response has decreased as a function of increased repetition of an unchanging stimulus. This is habituation—almost.

Then, a strong stroke of a soft brush is applied to another part of the animal, or, alternatively, the mantle shelf is briefly stimulated electrically, or a stronger jet of seawater is directed against it, and the magnitude of gill withdrawal response is increased markedly. Thereafter, response to the periodic jet of seawater is at first increased and then decreases rapidly with its next few repetitions. This is habituation—certainly.

Certainly, the magnitude of *Aplysia*'s gill withdrawal response did not decrease because the repeated exposure to jets of seawater had injured it. Certainly, the repeated exercise of gill withdrawal had not fatigued it, nor had its continued immobilization somehow weakened it. Certainly, its sensitivity to the impact of the seawater jet had not weakened or adapted with the repeated impacts; *Aplysia* can still react strongly, and does so, when afforded the opportunity. It discriminates jets of seawater from stronger ones and from other forms of stimulation. Yet it reacts alike to all on initial presentation: Its experience has taught it; it has learned to discriminate these stimuli.

Certainly, the decrement in magnitude of *Aplysia*'s gill withdrawal response results from integration over time of the central neural influence of the repeated sensory impact of the unchanging jet of seawater. It is this influence which has taught *Aplysia* to discriminate. An influence whose temporally integrated consequences can be instantly and temporarily removed behaviorally by altering the stimulus engendering it. An influence from whose temporally integrated consequences *Aplysia* recovers with sufficient "rest": The periodic jet of seawater ceases for 122 minutes and *Aplysia* again withdraws its gill with near initial magnitude.

Certainly, the central neural influence of the repeated sensory impact of the jet of seawater is an inhibitory one, temporarily suppressing gill withdrawal. It is an inhibitory influence resulting from the unchanging nature of that repeated stimulus. Or is it?

The sufficient condition for habituation is the repeated elicitation of a response. Under this condition, the response weakens. In its absence, the response strengthens. The restoration of response strength with rest (and changing stimulation) makes it apparent that an active process is responsible for the weakening. Thus, habituation is frequently seen as a manifestation of some type of inhibition; i.e., response reduction resulting from some sort of positive stimulation. The repetition of an unchanging stimulus is but one sort of positive stimulation. Viewing habituation as an active inhibitory process then implies that: (1) positive stimulation is involved, (2) the same stimulus originally evoking the response in strength becomes its inhibitor, and (3) the response is not obliterated but somehow simply suppressed. It is *not* implied that the suppression of response need necessarily flow uniquely from repetition of an unchanging stimulus. Neither is the nature of the active response suppressive process specifically implied.

The idea of studying learning and memory by repeated presentation of a single unchanging stimulus in a constant setting provides a useful simplification. The idea that the stimulus uniquely produces an inhibition specific to it and its response does not. It draws attention away from other sources of inhibition and response change, rendering the conception of habituation insular.

Habituation is a "central" process and a discriminative one. The repetitive stimulus occurs in a relatively constant setting of other stimuli. Apparently selective suppression and facilitation of competing input–output processes is the functional essence of central neural integrative mechanisms. This being the case, conditions other than the parameters of single stimulus presentation may be expected to facilitate and/or hinder exactly those mechanisms mediating the single stimulus case.

The presence and timing of competing inputs must be critical in facilitating or hindering habituation. It must also be that with the progress of habituating the weighting of other inputs into the "integrative mix," including those generated by the animal's own responses, alters radically. Thus, response dominance in the ongoing situation can be thought of as shifting, and progressively so.

Whatever the nature of the underlying neural mechanisms of habituation may be, these considerations suggest their relationships to more molar descriptions of habituation can well be sought in their discriminative function; i.e., in their influence on response selection under diverse stimulus concatenations. At another level, one may ask, is there value to the organism in habituation-induced alterations in discriminative control of behavior?

This approach does not beg the question of mechanism. It does not restrict the functional properties of habituation. Conception of habituation as inhibitory decrement in a repeatedly elicited response occurring as a result of repeated or continuous stimulation does so. It emphasizes stimulus-response-specific inhibitory mechanisms and focuses attention on response suppressive, rather than response selective, properties of such mechanisms. One aim of this chapter is to inquire whether the properties of habituation are adequately characterized by this conception of habituation and its consequences. They may well be, but the conception carries its own consequences.

One consequence is in the design of experiments on habituation. Usually these are designed to permit the occurrence and evaluation of only one response: the response of immediate interest. Frequently, only one aspect of the response, such as latency, frequency, or amplitude, is measured, and in the interests of objectivity this is done automatically. The constant stimulus setting in which the response eliciting stimulus occurs is usually simplified to an extreme, and changes are introduced often only for control testing. The result is, that in the interests of detecting stimulus-response-specific inhibition (response decrement) related to the parameters of single stimulus presentation, opportunity to detect sequential changes in the patterning of variable response components and the occurrence of different responses is sacrificed. Thus, it may well be that the properties of habituation and their import are seriously underestimated.

Recently, Thompson and Spencer (1966) proposed that a detailed list of nine widespread and generally agreed upon characteristics serves as the specific operational specifications of habituation. In examining these characteristics, Hinde (1970b) was led to question the generality of most of them. He singled out cases of response decrement based on complex interactive effects of incrementing and decrementing processes with varying time constants of decay. In these cases, the precise results obtained depended on the particular dependent variable selected for study. Therefore, he recommended studying more than one dependent variable at a time. Such a procedure enhances opportunity to detect the existence of properties of habituation other than response suppressive characteristics of parametric variation of the repetitive or continous single eliciting stimulus. The inconsistent results Hinde reported as occurring across species and experimental setting of parametric variation of the single eliciting stimulus also suggest limiting habituation to refer to the empirical single stimulus learning situation without reference to possible underlying processes or to characteristic properties engendered.

Habituation in invertebrate animals is examined here because the behavior of invertebrate animals has received relatively little systematic attention. By and large, they are strange and little known to anthropocentric man, foreign to the apparatus and methodology of mammalian behavior study, and therefore more apt to have their behavior described more completely and in more representative detail rather than as an automatically recorded measure of one aspect of a single response. Also, habituation is said to occur in literally all species of animal. Another aim of this chapter is to inquire how far the properties of habituation differ from one instance to another. It is expected that they will differ with the discriminative abilities of the species studied and opportunities for discrimination provided it in that study.

II. Methodological Notes

Hinde (1970a,b), Ratner (1970), and Denny and Ratner (1970) have discussed in detail analysis of response suppression resulting from parametric variation of the habituation stimulus. Consequently, this subject is not treated systematically here. Our comments concern a few considerations conducive to description of the discriminative properties of habituation.

A. Recovery and Retention

Given that habituation refers to response decrement resulting from repetitive stimulation in the single stimulus learning situation, there should be no difficulty in separating short-term and long-term effects other than practical ones specific to the experimental setting. The distinction is an important and useful one. Even though, as Hinde (1970a) pointed out, "the distinction is by no means clear-cut, especially when cross-species comparisons are being made," it should be drawn. The duration of all such effects is measured in terms of standard untis of time. It is the specification of persistence over time as the criterion which constitutes the difficulty. Time-independent behavioral criteria avoid it.

Given recognition of this consideration, the problem of distinguishing short- and long-term effects is as easily resolved as the distinction between spontaneous recovery and extinction in animal conditioning and forgetting and retention in memory studies. This is implicitly recognized in many studies, such as in the delineation by Groves and Thompson (1970) and Thompson *et al.* (1973) of a sensitization process independent of habituation in the spinal cat, but it is seldom made explicit. The occurrence of recovery provides an objective behavioral criterion giving meaning to the short- vs. long-term distinction and differentiates the meaning of the concept of habituation. In so doing, it provides for those effects that persist in spite of recovery as in the usage of Thorpe (1956, 1963) and Hinde (1954a,b, 1961). Long-term effects appear as retention (potentiation) of habituation and short-term effects as complete or less than complete recovery after rest. Recovery is measured in terms of restoration (completeness) of initial response. Ideally, it is evaluated during the very first trial (stimulus presentation) of the post-rest session. Recovery assessed on the basis of a series of early trials may reflect incremental contributions from sensitization and hence not truly reflect recovery of response strength. An asymptote of first trial responsiveness would better reflect recovery from habituation.

Retention is evaluated as savings in trials to a criterion of response decrement. Even when recovery is incomplete and reaches an asymptotic level, retention is in this manner separable from it and, incidentally, from difficulties in the evaluation of rate of response decrement (Hinde, 1970a). Finally, there appears to be no *a priori* reason for neuronal processes underlying recovery and retention, or their biochemical substrate, to gear themselves to the lifetime, or the life style, of the organism they exist in. If such is indeed the case, it will appear from cross-species comparisons correlating the effects of habituation with lifetime and life style.

B. Stimulus Specificity and Generalization

As with recovery and retention, the conception of stimulus specificity and stimulus generalization need not necessarily be tied together. Stimulus specificity is indicated when, after response has waned during habituation, a different stimulus is presented and response recurs. Stimulus generalization of habituation may, or may not, accompany such an event. Ascertainment of its presence depends upon the presentation of further exposures to the "novel" stimulus. If habituation of response to it is facilitated, in comparison with its habituation without prior habituation to the original stimulus, generalization is clearly present; if not, it is absent. If stimulus specificity is not indicated, i.e., response does not recur on presentation of a different stimulus, generalization of habituation may be inferred but should be checked in the manner indicated.

C. Dishabituation and Sensitization

Dishabituation refers to the removal, or cancellation, of habituation by interpolation of an extraneous stimulus differing from the habituation stimulus. Its occurrence can only be detected by following the extraneous stimulus with further presentations of the habituation stimulus in regular order. Ideally, the progress of response waning should match that obtained from trial one to interpolation of the extraneous stimulus. Sensitization refers to the masking, or blocking, of habituation by the interpolation of the extraneous stimulus. As Groves and Thompson (1970) have shown in the spinal cat, and Wolda (1961) with the water bug *Notonecta*, it is detectable by resuming presentations of the habituation stimulus after increasing rest intervals following the interpolation of the extraneous stimulus. In the absence of response sensitization, the assumption is that response restoration indicates the presence of dishabituation, but again, this is best checked in the manner indicated.

D. Response Measures

Changes in the topography of response, in the sequence of response elicited, and the emergence of new responses may well serve to delineate the discriminative properties of habituation. However, even if only a single element of response is used (e.g., gill withdrawal of *Aplysia* defensive response; chink call of chaffinch mobbing), it is well to measure as many facets of it as possible; i.e., latency, frequency, amplitude, form, duration, rise time, and fall time. Hinde (1970b, p. 13) commented; "It must be noted that the strength of a behavioral response may be the consequence of diverse processes within the organism. If, even when the response wanes, incremental effects may be present but concealed, the term 'habituation' is best restricted to the measured change in response strength, and not used for the underlying process or processes." This statement emphasizes the point that short-term and long-term response decrements measured as above may be determined by complex interactions of underlying incremental and decremental processes of different time-decay constants. To unravel this complex causation, comparison of measures of several facets of response can be helpful as Hinde's (1954a,b, 1961) analysis of the chink-call component during habituation of the mobbing response in chaffinches indicates. Such analysis may serve investigations of mechanism best but can also indicate dimensions reflecting discriminative response control; i.e., the question "Do particular components of stimulation relate more strongly to specific facets of response?" deserves more attention than it has received. This is especially true with invertebrate animals, whose points of sensory contact with environment are presumably limited by "simpler" receptive systems and whose response systems are frequently organized within segmental ganglia (Roeder, 1963).

E. Response Topography

Another measure of response change during habituation has been emphasized by Ratner (1970) and by Denny and Ratner (1970). They point to cases in which repeated presentation of a stimulus results in alterations in the topography of response to that stimulus. For example, simultaneous components of response can decay at different rates as in the withdrawal and hooking reactions of earthworms to vibration (Gardner, 1968). Balderrama and Maldonado's (1971) studies on the deimatic response of mantids (consisting of seven components) provide another case in point.

By definition habituation refers to stimulus—response relationships of significance to the organism studied, in that the concept applies to responses the subject brings to the test situation without special training. Analysis of this significance is essential. Its analysis can be facilitated by comparison of topographic change in response to different stimuli. An absence of such changes, indicative of simple decay of strength of the response as a whole, may relate directly to stimulus significance and its control of resistance to habituation. In Balderrama and Maldonado's work topographic changes were found most prominent in response to the stimuli of least effectiveness (canary and Java finch), even though subjects were preselected for equal levels of initial response to all stimuli. It was to the stimulus (cowbird) of direct ecologic significance, a natural predator of mantids, that the total deimatic response remained most intact as its strength decayed. It is also notable that although recovery was most complete with this stimulus, a high degree of retention was found even after a 6-day rest interval when a savings score was computed.

What can such results mean? Perhaps for the cowbird stimulus the response mobilizing effects (sensitization effects) of stimulus onset remained unchanged as habituation proceeded, but the affective consequences of such response arousal decayed; i.e., the information provided by the stimulus was integrated and evaluated more quickly.

F. Response Substitution

Another effect of habituation indicative of increased capacity to integrate information is that of response substitution. As the negative phototaxic response of Zanforlin's (1969) fly larvae declined, new orientation and locomotory responses appeared which removed the animals from culs-de-sac more and more readily. Such results focus attention on the consequences of response in habituation experiments and suggest associative learning. Few experiments permit the evaluation of stimulus significance in terms of response substitution by reason of rigid confinement of their subjects and a focus on but one measure of a single dependent variable. In those studies where freedom of action is permitted, systematic changes in response to the stimulus can be expected to appear. These need not involve a shift in stimulus control of behavior to other "contextual" elements of the stimulus situation (Zanforlin's larvae continued to show an altered response to light); rather, the development of a new response to the habituation stimulus can frequently occur. Thus, habituation may involve more than a decline in probability of occurrence of the original response. Increased probability of other responses can also be involved.

G. Response Sequence

Such changes in response as alterations in topography and shifts to other response modes imply alteration of structure in a central integrating mechanism. Quicker integration of information provided by the stimulus (quicker appreciation of its significance) and alterations of significance as a function of the habituation procedure are mediated by this structural alteration. These changes are perhaps most clearly seen where a behavioral action composed of a sequence of responses is initially elicited by the stimulus. Barass' (1961) studies of habituation of courtship response sequences in Hymenoptera and Szlep's (1966) studies of prey catching in arachnids are cases in point. In both, terminal response components decayed faster than earlier ones, with orientation responses being slowest. Clearly, a change in central structure took place during habituation reflecting in behavior a change in the specific significance of the stimulus.

H. Individual Differences

Although the course of response waning may be progressive, its rate is seldom constant. Even with grouped data, curves plotting response strength against stimulus repetition show many variations and irregularities. When individual data are examined, frequently virtually all indication of a smooth and continuous course of response weakening is lost.

Concerning the withdrawal reaction to sudden stimuli, Clark (1960b) reported results which may well be typical. Individual *Nereis pelagica* differ from one another and from one occasion to the next in strength and pattern of reactivity to repeated stimuli. The majority react to the first stimulus, reextend within 1 minute and thereafter react only sporadically to the subsequent stimuli. Thus, even when responses are grouped across blocks of trials, the curves of individual subjects are more often variable and irregular than smooth and continuous in nature.

In spite of the individual fluctuations in responsiveness, almost all subjects in reported studies of invertebrate habituation eventually reach a stage of prolonged nonresponsiveness. In many cases, this stage bridges long time intervals and, in addition, may be reflected in a major curtailment of response recovery. Individual difference in the number of stimulus repetitions required to reach this state, plus the aforementioned fluctuations in responsiveness over trials, may well account for the smooth, continuous, exponential functions frequently seen in appropriately grouped data.

Wolda (1961) found that the more rapidly prolonged suppression of prey-catching responses in the water bug *Notonecta glauca* was reached, the more rapid the rate of response waning. The more slowly such a criterion was achieved, the slower the rate of response waning *and* the later the onset of response decrement terminated the initial asymptotic level of high responsiveness. In addition, the animals who were poorest at response suppression also were more variable and irregular in its achievement. These relationships were highlighted by grouping data backward across trials from criterion achievement (less than 25 responses of a possible 100) for animals who took 100–199 trials, 200–299 trials, 300–399 trials, etc., to reach it. Grouping data for all animals together across trials from trial one would have produced a rather flat negative exponential curve, obscuring the relationships noted. Such a curve suggests a continuous graded course of response waning, whereas the abrupt transitions from responsiveness to nonresponsiveness evident in the backward curves suggest a nongraded discontinuous course, more in keeping with the individual data of Clark (1960b) and others. Such transitions can be viewed as manifestations of extreme quantitative variation of rate of change in a continuous graded process. If this point of view is taken, the occurrence in individual subjects of scattered responses, singly or in bouts (whose duration also appear in discontinuous function), remains a source of annoyance.

If the source of habituation cannot be assumed to be a simple and unitary underlying process; if, in fact, habituation is multiply determined, and differently so for different species, response systems, and environmental situations, then why not for individuals? The view that the transition from responsiveness to nonresponsiveness is a rapid positively accelerated process, if not an abrupt discontinuous one, deserves more attention. Examination of the behavior of individual subjects, taken one at a time, may offer insight into background and contextual factors affecting the "state" of the organism and shifts from one to another state.

I. A Note on Definition

The studies reviewed below are all concerned with habituation in a narrow sense. Habituation is defined as stimulus specific response decrement resulting from repeated or constant exposure to the response eliciting stimulus. However, only those cases of constant stimulation are considered where the stimulus acts on receptors of the organism *only* when they are appropriately oriented. In such situations the animal is able to control his own inter-exposure interval. In this context, habituation, by definition, requires repeated shifts from the stimulated state to the nonstimulated state and vice versa, although no necessary limit on the duration of each state is prescribed. Specifically eliminated by this definition are studies of acclimatization, where acclimatization refers to constant, continuing stimulation; e.g., amoeba stop streaming and cease movement at the onset of a weak electric current (Verworn, 1889) or a light intensity increase (Folger, 1925), but they shortly resume their usual movements and continue as though no change had occurred as the stimulus continues.

Repeated exposure, as a limiting condition, automatically requires three as a minimum; a third to test for the effect of the single repetition. Thus, single stimulus and paired stimulus studies designed to measure the temporal decay of short-term residues of single stimuli are excluded. Such studies generally involve the use of intertrial intervals of a duration sufficient to preclude the development of response decrement during their course; thus, one cannot say whether habituation was possible or not under their stimulus conditions.

The definition, as is usual, also excludes response decrement resulting from other causes requiring specification in terms other than the number and manner of stimulus exposures. Thus, decrement resulting from diurnal environmental changes, is excluded; as is that resulting from circadian rhythms or simply aging and maturation. All these classes of events are worthy of consideration, especially when dealing with invertebrates. In addition, decrement resulting from sensory adaptation (sensory-process change), fatigue (effector-process change), illness, injury, and so forth, is excluded.

III. Nature of Habituation

In the following sections the characteristics and discriminative properties of habituation in various species of invertebreate animals are examined. The literature of the past 30 years was given precedence and the behavior of the whole animal emphasized throughout. Harris (1943) and Thorpe (1963) provided general reviews of the earlier literature, and the behavior of partial organism preparations was reviewed by Horn and Hinde (1970); it is also reviewed in several chapters of the present volumes. The species are arranged by phyla, the number of species studied at each phyletic level represented being too small to justify finer taxonomic subdivision. Classification by response systems was considered but rejected for a similar reason: too few represented in the literature. This arrangement is for classificatory convenience only; inferences as to the evolution of habituation, or its relation to structural complexity of the nervous system, are *not* intended.

A. Protozoa

Many of the studies referenced in the earlier literature as indicating habituation in protozoa (Harris, 1943; Thorpe, 1963) are acclimatization and single or paired stimulus studies aimed at determining differential stimulus sensitivity. Although in some instances these bear upon discriminative capacity, they are not reviewed here. Those studies that are reviewed are all concerned with cessation of movement and contraction responses to various forms of mechanically induced stimulation in ciliated forms.

The contraction response of the protozoan *Spirostomum ambiguum* was studied by dropping a solenoid on a deep-well depression slide containing a drop of culture medium. The number of protozoa contracting to each stimulus was photographically recorded. With repetition of the stimulus fewer and fewer animals contracted in response to it. Control experiments ruled out changes in the medium as responsible (Applewhite and Gardner, 1971). The absence of an effect of temperature on rate of habituation (Gardner and Applewhite, 1970) suggested a nonenergy consuming process such as diffusion might be involved. Inward diffusion of substances was ruled out by habituating animals in deionized water. No evidence of outward leakage of protein and RNA from *Spirostomum* during habituation could be found (Applewhite *et al.*, 1969), and outward diffusion of other substances was eliminated by habituating animals in supernatant media obtained from habituated and resting control groups (Applewhite and Gardner, 1971). Protozoa receiving medium from habituated animals, either themselves or independent groups, did not differ in habituation rate from those receiving media from quiet groups or those receiving untreated deionized water. It was concluded that changes occurring solely within *Spirostomum* are responsible for the acquisition of habituation.

Such changes are relatively short-lived. With a 5-second interstimulus interval 60 animals tested individually required a mean of 3.6 trials to a criterion of two successive trials without response (Applewhite and Morowitz. 1966). Higher intensity stimuli required more trials, and recovery of response was slowed. With the lower intensity, stimulus recovery was complete within 30–60 seconds and no savings on rehabituation was obtained. With the more intense stimulus 10 trials to criterion were required and significant savings were still obtainable after 60 seconds. A distinction between recovery of response and retention of habituation was not evident;

"after the organism returns to its 'normal' state, it takes just as many stimuli to habituate again as it did the first time" (Applewhite and Morowitz, 1966, p. 93).

Other control experiments permitted elimination of receptor-process or effector-process changes (adaptation, fatigue, and injury) as responsible for the response decrement. *Spirostomum* exhibits dishabituation, or sensitization, in that more intense stimuli restore the contraction response, as do touch and electrical stimulation (Applewhite, 1968a). In no case were tests differentiating dishabituation and sensitization conducted. As with rats (Davis and Wagner, 1969) animals given a series of stimuli gradually increasing in intensity are habituated as readily to a high intensity stimulus as though they had received it as a constant stimulus all along (Applewhte *et al.*, 1969). In this study, for two cultures of approximately 100 animals each, the solenoid was dropped at constant and maximal intensity every 4 seconds a total of 65 times. One additional stimulus was presented 45 seconds later to test recovery of response. (see Table I). The same two cultures received a

TABLE I

PERCENTAGE OF ORGANISMS CONTRACTING TO STIMULI OF
CONSTANT OR GRADUALLY INCREASING INTENSITY[a]

Stimulus (sec)	Percentage of organisms contracting	
	Gradual	Constant
1	0	69
10	9	—
20	16	53
30	20	—
40	22	31
50	22	—
Maximal Intensity for Both Groups		
59	18	18
60	23	22
65	20	18
+45	29	37
Total % of contractions[b]	1000	2500

[a]From Applewhite *et al.* (1969).

[b]Area under curve when percentage of organisms contracting is plotted against stimulus number.

series of stimuli gradually increasing to maximal intensity from trial 59 on; after a rest interval of 30 minutes permitting recovery of normal responsiveness. Two other cultures were treated in the reverse order. Three other cultures received constant stimuli at two different lesser intensity levels, in separate series, and one random intensity series. These were all presented to each of the three cultures in random order and separated by rest intervals of 30 minutes. Maximal intensity stimuli were presented from trial 59 on in all series and during the single response recovery test 45 seconds later.

Tables I and II are adapted from Applewhite *et al.* (1969). Table I indicates that the gradually increasing stimulus group habituates to the same degree as the constant stimulus group with 60% fewer responses and with a much lower mean stimulus intensity. Table II indicates that exposure to the same number of stimuli as the constant group is not sufficient to produce the same amount of habituation. The intensity 70 (constant) condition is more effective than any of the others, which do not differ from each other. It is evident that the number of stimuli received and contractions produced do

TABLE II

PERCENTAGE OF ORGANISMS CONTRACTING TO STIMULUS OF
VARIABLE OR CONSTANT INTENSITY[a]

Stimulus (sec)	Percentage of organisms contracting			
	Intensity 20	Intensity 40	Random (mean intensity 40)	Intensity 70
1	3	16	33	63
10	3	11	12	—
20	3	9	42	35
30	4	7	6	—
40	2	9	27	15
58	2	6	19	12
Maximal Intensity for Both Groups				
59	25	23	22	11
60	29	26	29	8
65	27	23	23	10
+45	31	24	31	17
Total % of contractions [b]	160	534	1312	1657

[a]From Applewhite *et al.* (1969).
[b]Area under curve when percentage of organisms contracting is plotted against stimulus number.

not directly determine habituation. It is concluded that "the order of presentation of the stimuli and their intensity must jointly be the critical factors" (Applewhite *et al.*, 1969, p. 845).

Earlier work with *Spirostomum ambiguum* supports this conclusion (Wawrzynczyk, 1937). Frequency of stimulation was varied by dropping a 4-gm weight to a slide mount from a constant height. Regular 6 per minute or irregular 6–12 per minute stimulation both resulted in habituation of the contraction response. For 25 animals regular stimulation required a mean of 307.9 responses and 194 minutes of stimulation time before response ceased. Irregular stimulation required 322.5 responses and 156 minutes. Figure 1 summarizes the time course of response decrement for the two conditions. In spite of its greater absolute frequency of stimulation the irregular condition produced a higher level of responsivity and maintained it for the first 60 minutes of stimulation, although the rate of decline in responsivity was initially greater for this condition.

Response was restored by shifting a group habituated to regular 12 per minute stimulation to the 6 per minute condition. Recovery of responsivity was complete. Adaptation, fatigue, and injury are thus ruled out as primary causative factors by this observation. Change in the culture medium was controlled by changing the solution. After habituation the number of food vacuoles observed was the same as in resting unstimulated animals.

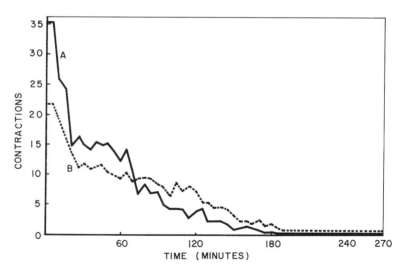

Fig. 1. Mean frequency of contraction as a function of time: A, irregular stimulation (6–12 times per minute); B, regular stimulation (6 times per minute). From Wawrzynczyk (1937).

The research of Kinastowski (1963a,b) also indicates the critical role of intensity and frequency of stimulation in habituation of the contraction response of *Spirostomum*. In this case a seemingly more naturalistic stimulus (analogous to raindrops) was used: a drop of culture medium falling into a relatively large (2 cm³) container housing the animal. Frequency and force of impact were controlled. Figure 2A (adapted from Kinastowski, 1963a) demonstrates the influence of stimulus intensity on habituation for 10 per minute stimulation. Response ceased after 8 minutes with stimulation of 400 and 800 ergs and after 15–20 minutes with 1600 ergs. The higher the level of stimulus intensity, the greater initial responsiveness and the greater its persistence. Similarly, as Fig. 2B shows, for a stimulus strength of 1600 ergs, initial responsivity and persistence of response decline steadily as frequency of stimulation increases from 1 to 20 per minute.

Control experiments verified the results of the experiments described above. Other stimuli, such as touch and vibration stemming from a tuning fork, resulted in response whether the animals were habituated or not. So also did use of stimuli both stronger and weaker than the habituation stimulus. It was not clear whether dishabituation was tested.

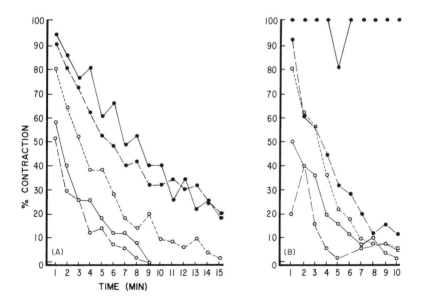

Fig. 2. (A) Mean frequency (percent) contraction as a function of stimulus intensity. Stimuli of 400 (O——O). 800 (O—O), 1600 (O---O), 3200 (●--●), or 4800 (●——●) ergs were administered 10 times per minute. (B) Mean frequency (percent) of contraction as a function of frequency of 1600 erg stimulation. Stimuli were presented 1 (●——●), 5 (●--●), 10 (O---O), 15 (O——O), or 20 (O—O) times per minute. Adapted from Kinastowski (1963a).

In the Warzynczyk (1937) experiments recovery from habituation pro- duced by regular 6 per minute stimulation via the shock produced by dropping a 4-gm weight 6 cm, typically took 40–50 minutes. Kinastowski(1963b) found that complete recovery (with no evidence of retention) required a rest interval of 25–30 minutes following 10 minutes of 10 per minute 1600-erg stimulation. This is shown in Table III (adapted from Kinastowski, 1963b). The time course of rehabituation following seven different rest periods, ranging from 1 to 30 minutes, is shown as a percentage of original habituation. In both experiments recovery of response was much slower than that observed by Applewhite and his associates (Applewhite and Morowitz, 1966). In the latter experiments recovery was complete in 1–2 minutes, even at their more intense levels of stimulation.

Results similar to those using *Spirostomun ambiguum* have been obtained with the contraction response of the trumpet-shaped ciliate *Stentor coerulus*. Harden (1972) placed approximately 100 animals in each of many dishes containing 20 ml of spring water. After the animals had attached themselves to the bottom, their dish was displaced through a known lateral excursion at an approximately constant velocity. Two seconds after each displacement the dish was photographed. Thirty such trials were given at 1-minute inter-

TABLE III

MEAN NUMBER (%) OF CONTRACTIONS TO 10 PER MINUTE 1600-ERG
STIMULATION FOLLOWING REST PERIODS OF 1–30 MINUTES[a]

Mean No. of contractions prior to pauses (comparable)	Time (min)	Duration of rest interval (min)						
		1	5	10	15	20	25	30
80	1	28	28	48	50	62	72	90
62	2	14	20	30	36	40	54	62
56	3	14	16	18	26	24	32	44
36	4	6	10	16	12	18	24	30
22	5	6	4	10	6	10	20	32
18	6	—	—	4	6	6	10	18
10	7	—	—	4	2	6	8	14
8	8	—	—	—	—	—	6	8
8	9	—	—	—	—	—	6	8
6	10	—	—	—	—	—	6	6
Mean No. of contractions for the first 5 min		13.6	15.6	24.4	26.0	30.8	41.8	51.6

[a]From Kinastowski (1963b).

vals. After the last one, a terminal photograph was taken following a 2-minute rest interval. This permitted identification of those animals who had remained attached through the whole procedure. The contraction responses of only these animals were counted from each frame of the developed film. Other dishes were subjected to variations of this basic procedure.

If left completely undisturbed, without subjection to displacement (5 dishes), approximately 5% of the animals were contracted in each of the 30 photographs taken. Typically, about 50% of the animals contracted to the first displacement. With successive trials the proportion contracted decreased, approaching 10% by trial 30 (9 dishes). If the flash of a strobe light replaced displacement on the thirty-first trial, the proportion increased to approximately 40% on that trial, indicating stimulus specificity of the response decrement. This observation also ruled out simple effector-process change (fatigue) as responsible for the decrement.

Dishabituation was not examined following strobe light stimulation. However, brief and partial restoration of response (to approximately 30%) followed by immediate decline (over two trials) occurred in two groups (6 dishes each) whose water was exchanged following trial 15, indicating sensitization rather than dishabituation followed interpolated extraneous stimulation. Both groups had most of their water removed following trial 15 and replaced following trial 16; one with its own water, the other with water from a dish of undisturbed animals. The sensitization effect was gone by trial 18.

Two other groups had most of their water removed prior to 30 trials of displacement stimulation; one (5 dishes) had its own water immediately replaced, the other (6 dishes) received immediate replacement with water taken from groups after their fifteenth displacement trial. Both groups began their trials approximately 30 minutes after having their water level replenished. The initial responsiveness *of both* was somewhat depressed (approximately 35% for each) and declined to approximately 10% by trial 15. These results indicated change, or accumulation, of something in the water was not responsible for either the habituation decrement obtained in other groups or the divergence in responsiveness of these last two from the others. (The water exchange dishes all contained 15 ml rather than 20 ml of water initially.)

Recovery of response was complete and there was no retention evident in a group (1 dish) given runs of thirty displacement stimulations at 24-hour intervals over 9 successive days. However, a group (1 dish) given four such runs each day at 1-hour intervals over 9 successive days, exhibited incomplete recovery (initially lower responsivity) and considerable retention (faster response decrement) over its hour-long rest intervals.

Like the experiments on *Spirostomum*, this study demonstrates a dramatic reduction in contractile responsiveness to repeated mechanically induced shock stimulation; a reduction clearly separable from simple fatiguelike alterations in the contractile effector process, and from "injury" of the animal. However, it does not clearly separate habituation from possible sensory-process changes, including sensory adaptation; although the persistence of response decrement over an hour's rest interval militates against the latter possibility. The classic studies of Jennings (1902, 1906) on modifiability in ciliates, including *Stentor*, suggest that such a separation might well be found. If *Stentor* can alter its response to a continuing stream of carmine, or series of touches, it may also do so in reaction to repeated mechanical shock. The occurrence of such response substitution, the development of a new response to the continuing stimulus, would separate habituation from sensory-process change. Restoration of the original contractile response, either before or after emergence of another response, through reduction of extent and velocity of displacement, thus reducing stimulus intensity, would serve the same end.

Wood (1970a,b,c) sought electrophysiological correlates of habituation of the contractile response in *Stentor coerulus*. His data suggest a sensory-process change (receptor adaptation) may well provide the basis for habituation of the contractile response to mechanical shock stimulation in *Stentor*, and, indeed, in all other acellular animals. He compared the behavioral properties of such animals to those of single cells in metazoan animals (specifically, neurons) and saw habituation in them as equivalent to postsynaptic chemoreceptor desensitization of surface areas of central neurons. His data indicate an action potential may trigger contraction (Wood, 1970b). Electrical and localized mechanical stimulation induced negative, all or nothing spikes in animals contracting 7–11 msec after stimulus onset. A negative prepotential was observed with mechanical stimulation. It could be dissociated from the spike. Mechanical stimulation occasionally produced prepotentials without spikes following. Electrical stimulation only produced spikes. In addition, the prepotential correlated well with stimulus magnitude. The prepotential also decreased in amplitude and increased in latency during habituation of contraction to a localized mechanical stimulus (Wood, 1970c). All other potentials remained essentially unchanged. He regarded the prepotential as representing a receptor (transduction) process, while the contractive process involves the spike potential; the former is seen as essentially analogous to an excitatory postsynaptic potential in the nerve cells of metazoan animals.

Wood also used displacement to elicit contraction responses in *Stentor coerulus* (Wood, 1970a). A negative exponential decrement in this response was clearly evident over sixty such stimulations presented at 1-minute intervals. Over 90% of his animals responded to an initial stimulus of sufficient intensity and 96.9% of them responded less frequently during the last 10 trials as compared to the first 10 trials. Weaker stimuli were less effective initially and response decrement was greater and more rapid over the 60 trials, reaching an asymptote of approximately 10% in trials 11 to 20 with the least intense stimulus used. In addition, an interstimulus interval of 2 or 3 minutes was less effective than a 1-minute interval.

Response recovery was nearly complete after a 6-hour rest, using a moderately intense stimulus; i.e., response over the first 10 trials of rehabituation was nonsignificantly less than over the first 10 trials of initial habituation. Longer rest intervals were not tested (the animals tended to alter their positions). Animals in this group also reached a 7 of 10 nonresponse trial criterion with fewer trials than were required initially. Thus, retention was still evident after recovery was essentially complete. In addition to this surprising result, dishabituation by a much more intense stimulus, or by interpolation of an electrical shock, proved totally ineffective. If such stimuli produced a sensitizing effect, and they seemed to, since response to them approximated 100%, it was a very brief one. Its effect was not detectable 1 minute later. Analysis of the effect of a prior habituation series of mechanical shocks on the threshold of response to an electrical stimulus indicated the essential independence of these two means of eliciting contraction; the electrical threshold was not altered.

Two types of displacement stimuli were used, vertical and horizontal. The initial response to either following 60 habituation trials with the other indicated the response decrement was not specfic to either of these two stimuli; they were not discriminable. However, generalization of habituation was not tested; it was presumably complete. Generalization of habituation with discriminably different stimuli was found when a very weak stimulus was compared with a stronger stimulus. Habituation of the low level of responsiveness (approximately 25%) found with the smallest displacement possible, over 30 trials, resulted in a more rapid decline in response to a following larger displacement, over 60 trials, although initial response level to that stimulus was not affected. Unfortunately, stimulus specificity and generalization of habituation were not tested in the opposite order; from prior stronger to following weaker stimulation. Similar results there, response restoration followed by faster response decrement, would have isolated, or eliminated, the contribution of sensory-process change.

That simple sensory-process change is *not* critical to habituation in *Stentor* may perhaps be seen in the finding that "... differences in probability of response can be produced by varying the pattern of stimulation while keeping the number and sequence of contractions roughly constant" (Wood, 1970a, p. 356). Here, appropriate distribution of 30 stimuli over an hour's time (initially more frequent, terminally less frequent) resulted in a number of contractions and time course of response decay matching those produced by 59 regular once-per-minute stimuli. However, response in the sixtieth minute (to the thirty-first stimulus and sixtieth stimulus, respectively) was much greater (69%) for the "patterned" animals than for the "regular" animals (23%). Only two mechanical shock stimuli were presented to the patterned group in the previous 10 minutes; however, the thirty-first followed the thirtieth stimulus at the same interval as the thirtieth followed the twenty-ninth stimulus. Interpretation of this result as a simple sensory-process change (e.g., sensory adaptation) and its decay is necessarily complicated by persistence of the effects of 60 once-per-minute stimuli over 6 hours (Wood, 1970a) and of 30 such stimuli over one hour (Harden, 1972).

In any case, though by what mechanism is not clear, these *Stentor* experiments (Wood, 1970a,b,c; Harden, 1972) and those on *Spirostomum* (Kinastowski, 1963a,b; Wawrzynczyk, 1937) make it clear that information regarding the temporal patterning of mechanically induced shock stimuli is encoded in these two ciliated protozoa.

B. Coelenterata

Among the coelenterates, the contraction response of *Hydra* (*H. pirardi* and *H. viridis*) is subject to habituation (Rushforth, 1965, 1967). As with the protozoan studies discussed above, mechanically induced displacement was the stimulus of choice. In this case rotary agitation of calibrated intensity (e.g., 130 rpm), duration (e.g., 3 seconds), and frequency (e.g., every 30 seconds) was used. Initially the proportion of a group of 100 *H. viridis* contracting increased with stimulus strength and duration but was independent of the interstimulus interval. After an hour of stimulation the proportion contracting was less with a short interstimulus interval (1 minute) than with a longer one (5 minutes). No habituation took place at the longer interstimulus interval, even with the strongest stimulus used. At the shorter interstimulus interval rate and extent of habituation were greater with the weaker stimulus strengths and shorter stimulus durations; results opposite to expectation if the process were one of a fatiguelike effector mechanism exhaustion. In addition *H. pirardi* responded promptly and fully to 1 minute exposures of a light stimulus, even as the periodic mechanical stimulus continued.

In both species, recovery was complete in 3–4 hours. Retention following complete recovery was not tested. Generalization of habituation to weaker stimuli appeared in both species during brief tests of sensitivity to stimuli graded in intensity, but the inverse relation was not tested. Thus, sensory-process change was not eliminated as a possible explanation of the effects obtained. In spite of incomplete recovery an hour after habituation and savings on rehabituation in one experiment with *H. pirardi* (Rushforth, 1965), the slow decay of a sensory-process change resulting in decreased sensitivity to mechanical displacement seems indicated. The experiment involved an 8-hour initial habituation session (approximately 5 hours to asymptotic response level) of frequent (e.g., every 16 seconds), prolonged (e.g., 2.5 seconds), and strong (e.g., 140 rpm) mechanical stimulation. If an internuncial integrative process, associated with the functioning of *Hydra*'s diffuse neural network, were responsible for such stimulus induced decrement in response, habituation of that same response to a weaker, briefer stimulus should be much more easily attained. Goldsmith (1927) reported that even a very slight tap to the substrate induced a complete contraction and reextension within a minute. Using such minimally effective stimuli both he and Wagner (1905) before him obtained no evidence of habituation if the interstimulus interval permitted reextension of the animal. Rushforth (1967) reported that habituation was obtainable in his experimental situation even when interstimulus extension was permitted.

Among the structurally more complex coelenterates, the *Scyphozoa* have yet to be represented in a habituation study, and studies of the contraction response in the *Actinozoa* are limited to those of Jennings (1905), Pieron (1908), and Kinoshita (1911). Although poorly controlled, these studies do agree in finding that waning of the contraction response to tactile stimulation induced by touch or mechanical displacement stimuli is prompt and limited to short interstimulus intervals (5 minutes or less). In addition, Kinoshita (1911) found the duration of contraction to decrease with successive stimuli. Of significance is the report by Jennings (1905) that as successive drops of water, falling from a height of 30 cm to the water surface just above the outspread disc of the anemone *Aiptasia annulata* continue periodically, a succession of responses occur. Contraction is usually limited to the first, or the first few, drops. Thereafter, following a period of no response, a gradual shrinking away from the water surface and the region where the drops fall, occurs. With stronger stimulation (as by touch), "the anemone reacts first by contraction, then by turning repeatedly into new positions, then by moving away." Similar results were noted by Wagner (1905) for *Hydra* and by Jennings (1902) for *Stentor*. It is of interest that even in Wood's (1970a,b,c) recent studies of *Stentor*'s contraction response, he found it necessary to exclude the data of a small percentage of his subjects under all conditions because they had moved away from their original site of attachment. This, even with a generalized, nonlocalizable, mechanical shock stimulus, was apparently a problem of sufficient magnitude to limit the length of the recovery intervals he found it practicable to test; too many animals tended to shift position of attachment as rest following stimulation sessions was prolonged.

The ingestion response of several species of anemone has also been studied in a series of early papers by several researchers. These have been reviewed by Maier and Schneirla (1935), Harris (1943), and Thorpe (1963). They will not be discussed in detail here. However, taken together they suggest the existence of a "centrally" mediated habituation of ingestive response to inadequate stimuli (filter paper) in these animals. Nagel (1892, 1894) first reported alternate presentation of food and filter paper to the tentacles resulted in continued acceptance of the former and progressive rejection of the latter. This result was confirmed by Parker (1896), but Jennings (1905) found that acceptance of both food and paper ceased together. Since nonstimulated tentacles also were affected, he concluded that loss of hunger was responsible. However, Allabach (1905) showed that ingestion of food was not necessary; among other conditions, she first provided paper (plain or soaked in meat juice), then meat (swallowing permitted or not permitted), and then paper again. Initially the paper was accepted; it was not accepted following the trials with meat, whether fully ingested, or not. She concluded, ". . . it is the reaction of the animal, not the precise character of the stimulus, that causes the fatigue." Fatigue was seen as exhaustion of the local capacity for production of mucus. Gee (1914) scraped the accumulated mucus off of "fatigued" tentacles and they remained fatigued thus excluding the covering of sensory cells as an explanation. He also ruled out muscular fatigue by showing that repetitively induced contractions through touching the tentacles did not affect their acceptance of food. Loss of sensitivity through a physiological change within the organism remained as an explanation. Parker (1917) identified this as a "sensory fatigue," pointing out that ". . . both Allabach and Gee have failed to recognize that there are several kinds of fatigue." As for the transfer of effect to nonstimulated tentacles, the transfusion of stimulating substances, ingested during food presentations (whether swallowed or not), from the cavities of such tentacles to their sensory mechanism, was seen as producing a similar sensory fatigue. Instances of perseveration of food ingestion after rejection of paper appear as response to stronger stimulation as sensory fatigue proceeds.

Since the duration of the sensory fatigue noted by Allabach and Parker is measured in minutes, provided the animal is hungry (Allabach, 1905), the casually reported findings of Fleure and Walton (1907) raise a question. They found that ingestion of plain filter paper pellets presented once a day to the same tentacles of *Actinia* or *Taelia* ceased in 2–5 days, and tentacular response stopped in 4–7 days. Thereafter, other unstimulated tentacles exhibited only one or two responses prior to rejection of the paper. Recovery of response was said to be complete in 6–10 days, ". . . though we incline to fancy that they 'learn' more quickly from a second set of experiments than they did from the first; i.e., it seems to be more easy to reinduce the persistence of a particular impression than it was to induce it originally." This report stands as the only indication in publication that "habituation" in a coelenterate may be other than sensory fatigue, and the quotation is the *only* evidence for retention of such habituation following recovery of response. It is indeed surprising that such interesting results have not been followed up (Thorpe, 1963). Ross (1965) reported that he tried to repeat them using *Actinia*, but his animals would not accept filter paper at all and he abandoned the effort. In discussion of this paper Horridge (1965) mentioned that *Taelia* responds well to clean filter paper and repeated application to the same tentacle results in response cessation which does not transfer to neighboring tentacles; a result accountable as exhaustion of local nematocyst supply. However, further information is not provided; so here, off the published record, the matter must stand.

C. Platyhelminthes

Applewhite (1971) studied habituation of contraction to touch in the rhabdocoel flatworm *Stenostomum*. Habituation was carried to three successive failures of response to touches occurring once every 4 seconds. Six or seven such stimuli were sufficient to reach this criterion. The response decrement to touches at one end of the organism transferred to touches at its other end, only one or two stimuli being required to reach criterion. Sensory-process change was thus, presumably, ruled out as responsible and somatotopic generalization of habituation established. That contractile process change was also not responsible was indicated by occurrence of contraction to an electrical stimulus following habituation. Successive habituation series to touch and electrical stimulation in both orders gave no evidence of transfer from one to the other. Habituation to these two stimuli was essentially independent, although responsivity to the electrical stimulus was greater (requiring 12–14 shocks to criterion). Dishabituation, recovery, and retention were not tested. In an essentially similar study, however, Applewhite and Morowitz (1966) found that the more intense the stimulus (mechanical shock) the longer it took to become habituated and the slower recovery took place. In this study recovery was complete in 4–8 minutes with a weak stimulus, and still incomplete after 8 minutes with a stronger one. A more intense stimulus following habituation produced the response, but again, dishabituation, generalization, and retention of habituation were not studied. Similar results were obtained with another species of flatworm, *Macrostomum*.

Qualitatively different results were obtained with the planarian *Dugesia dorotocephala* in response to increased illumination (Westerman, 1963). Light intensity was increased from 40 to 400 foot-lamberts in each of 25 3-

second trials presented daily at intervals of 30–60 seconds. Habituation was carried to a criterion of two successive days (50 trials) without response. Initial responsivity was probably much lower than in the previous studies, since 35 naive animals averaged only a little over 30% responses during the first 5 trials; although one cannot be certain since none of the studies reports the proportion of animals responding to the initial stimulus. In any case, a considerable degree of recovery between daily sessions is indicated by the mean of 386 trials (15.44 days) required to achieve criterion (zero response). In addition a clear-cut intra-day and inter-day decrement of response was noted. Even after 15 days, recovery was almost complete (as measured by percentage response during the first 5 trials) on the sixteenth day for the 16 of the original 35 animals still not having met the criterion. In spite of this, these 16 animals exhibited a high degree of retention of habituation on that day (see Fig. 3). Retention over rest intervals of 3 and 7 weeks was also evident. Finally, it was reported that habituated planarians would still respond to a qualitatively and quantitatively differing light intensity increase.

D. Annelida

Clark (1960a) studied habituation of the withdrawal response to mechanical vibration and photic stimuli in the tube dwelling "errant" polychaete *Nereis Pelagica*. Presentation of stimuli at 1-minute intervals resulted in rapid and complete waning of response. Vibration, light intensity decrease, and a moving shadow all failed to produce a response after fewer than twenty presentations. Complete waning of response to a sudden light increase proved more difficult, requiring sixty repetitions of a 9-second exposure. The light intensity used had a strong "arousing" effect upon the worms inasmuch as increases in its duration increased persistence of response up to a point. Beyond this point light adaptation presumably became an effective factor decreasing response persistence. This is one instance in which stimulus duration has proved an effective parameter in controlling rate of response waning in an invertebrate. The effect was not compensated by decreased frequency of trials; i.e., a 15-second exposure required as many trials to complete waning with a 1-minute as with a 5-min intertrial interval. Thus, duration and frequency of stimulation were separable at lower levels of light adaptation.

Recovery from habituation of response to a sudden increase in light intensity was separable from retention of such habituation. The initial percentage of animals reacting was the same after rest intervals of 1, 5, and 17 hours following previous complete habituation. However, savings in trials to complete absence of response was greatest after 1, less after 5, and non-existent after 17 hours of rest. Thus a distinction between short-term and long-term holding of habituation generated information can be drawn in this

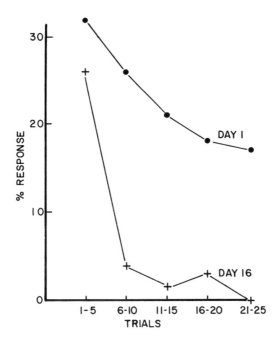

Fig. 3. Percent response to 3-second light stimulation by 5 trial blocks on first and sixteenth day of stimulation. Each point on day 1 represents the mean percent response of 35 planarians and each point on day 16 represents 16 animals. From Westerman (1963).

instance. As indexed by the degree of initial recovery obtained, it is clear that *Nereis pelagica* lacked the means to hold a habituatory response decrement to sudden light intensity increase in readiness for at least as long as an hour (the shortest rest interval tested). It is also clear that the effects of habituation were nevertheless still present and retrievable with repeated trials after rest intervals greatly exceeding one hour. That such long-term retention of habituation was held in a central, rather than a peripheral neuromuscular or sensory receptive, process was indicated by several ancillary results.

Repeated exposure to a weak stimulus (a light intensity increase) eliciting no visible response greatly reduced the number of exposures to a similar stimulus, presented immediately afterward, required to produce complete response waning. It is of interest that initial responsiveness to the strong stimulus was also reduced (from 80 to 60% of the worms tested) although the response had not previously been elicited. In addition, after habituation of response to one stimulus (mechanical shock), that response would again appear in full strength to another stimulus (moving shadow) and vice versa.

This result also indicates the independence of the habituation processes involving the two stimuli concerned.

The ancillary results above preclude persisting neuromuscular change (fatigue) as the basis of retention of habituation. Sensory receptive process change is precluded by reappearance of response following a slight change in the stimulus acting on the sense organs involved as in the results described in the following paragraphs. Both kinds of changes are precluded by the persistence of reduced responsiveness over relatively long rest intervals.

Perhaps the most interesting and significant results reported by Clark (1960a) stemmed from his study of the interaction of habituation to two similar stimuli. Worms previously habituated to a moving shadow required more trials than usual to habituate to a sudden decrease in light intensity although habituation to the shadow was maintained. Conversely, previous habituation to light intensity decrease prolonged habituation to a moving shadow, but habituation to the light intensity decrease was not maintained. If habituation is regarded as an active process, rather than a simple dropping out of response, this anomalous mutual interaction between two similar forms of stimulation, a "fast" darkening and a "slow" darkening, are interpretable. Habituation to one of these stimuli may well make habituation to the other more difficult if sensitivity to stimulus change is increased by habituation; i.e., the more habituation, the less its stimulus generalization and the greater discriminative control of response. That stimulus generalization, and therefore the development of discriminative control, is not symmetrical should not be surprising. As in Balderrama and Maldonado's (1971) study of the praying mantis, habituation of the withdrawal ("fright") reaction in *Nereis pelagica* to a more effective stimulus generalized to a less effective one more strongly than habituation of a less effective stimulus generalized to a more effective one. A similar function has been demonstrated in rats (Peeke and Zeiner, 1970). This is to be expected; the "intensity" of a stimulus is as much prescribed by the "nature of the beast" as its physically measured strength.

The nature of the beast depends in part upon its past experience either in natural habitat (Hargitt, 1909; Nicol, 1950) or in other circumstances (Hargitt, 1909; Bohn, 1902). Emphasis on genetic and developmental history can easily be overdone, even in such relatively "simple" creatures as the tubicuolous marine worms and other annelids. In *Nereis diversicolor* (an estuarine species) habituation to a sudden light intensity decrease and darkening under a moving shadow (each lasting 9 seconds) is equal, and immediately successive habituation series with each, in either order, show none of the complex interactive effects evident in *Nereis pelagica* (an intertidal species), where the two stimuli differ markedly in response elicitation effectiveness (Clark, 1960b). In the latter species, fast darkening and slow darkening could be discriminated. In the former species they were not responded to discriminatively and may not be discriminable. Clark (1960b) suggested the normal experience of the worm in its normal habitat may be related to this difference. However, working with wild-caught specimens, he found *N. pelagica* habituated to moving shadows at the same rate whether tested a few days after being collected or after 5 months in constantly dimly lit aquaria. (Unfortunately, *N. diversicolor* was not provided with special circumstances designed to modify its preexperimental experience.) On the other hand, working with species of *Hydroides dianthus*, Hargitt (1909) did find prolonged exposure to dim light over the winter months reduced his subjects' sensitivity to moving shadows. Recovery of sensitivity occurred as exposure to higher levels of illumination was prolonged. In another case, prolonged exposure to bright sunlight reduced sensitivity to moving shadows in *Hermella ascolata* (Bohn, 1902). Nicol (1950) also concluded that the previous history of the animal influences responsiveness to decreased light intensity. In the sabellid worm *Branchiomma vesigulosum*, he felt the relative frequency of stimulation by illumination decrease, and not the general level of light exposure, to be the critical factor. The significant structural differences between *N. pelagica* and *N. diversicolor* and their relative lack of difference in habit, aside from ecologic preference, further reinforce the suggestion that the circumstances of past experience are critical in habituation of withdrawal reflexes in these species.

The circumstances of past experience may well play a role in altering the significance of a stimulus during the course of habituation also. *Nereis pelagica* responds with withdrawal to the first few of a series of hard taps to its prostomium or tentacular cirri, but this response rapidly wanes and is replaced by attempts to grasp the object doing the tapping with its jaws. It may even emerge further from its tube. In his analysis of the habitat conditions of *N. pelagica*, Clark (1960b) noted that these worms are likely to always be in a state of partial habituation to such stimuli as moving shadows and mechanical shock. It is also likely that all their known predators (fish, birds, and crabs) signal their appearance by mechanical disturbance and a moving shadow. It seems likely that any treatment or circumstance imposed upon the worm, that reduces sensitivity to moving shadows, would also alter its response to other stimuli. Rapid short-term recovery ensures prompt withdrawal to stimuli typical of potential danger. Long-term retrieval of habituation ensures nearly as prompt a follow-up on the possible food tokenism of those typical stimuli.

Evans (1969a,b) related the supplanting of withdrawal responses by "attack" responses in *N. pelagica* with repeated tactile stimulation to the predominant carnivorous mode of existence of this worm. However, he noted that *N. diversicolor* and *Platyneresis dumerilii*, identified as primarily herbivorous, also demonstrate the same sequence of response change during tactile stimulus habituation, but only after a much longer series of trials. Thus, altered significance of repeated tactile stimulation flowing from the restriction of the habituation procedure appears general across three related species of polychaete worms.

Nereis diversicolor lives in U-shaped burrows, sometimes with ramifying galleries, in estuarine mud flats largely protected from wave action and its consequent mechanical shock stimulation of the animal. *Nereis pelagica* lives on rocky shores, in crevices and under stones, where dense growths of seaweeds abound, and is frequently, if not incessantly, exposed to the action of waves and the passing of errant shadows. *Platynereis dumerilii*, in contrast, lives in mucus tubes attached to seaweed and other objects at depths precluding much variation in the prevailing dim illumination and largely protected from the sorts of sudden mechanical shocks engendered by wave action. Evans (1969b) failed to find consistent differences in general reactivity and rates of habituation to different stimuli relating these species to their habitats.

He compared *N. diversicolor* and *N. pelagica* collected from shores exposed to wave action (an atypical locale for the former species) with *P. dumerilii* collected sublittorally, where it is not exposed to wave action. The two species exposed to wave action were more reactive to mechanical shocks and habituated more slowly to such stimuli than the latter species, a result opposite to that expected by Evans: "Species normally exposed to waves might be expected to habituate rapidly to mechanical shocks because this stimulus occurs innocuously with each incoming and out-going tide" (Evans, 1969b, pp. 110–111). In addition, response frequencies and rates of habituation to sudden illumination decrease and shadow passage did not differentiate the three species in his experiments. However, he did find substantial differences with sudden illumination increase as stimulus. *Platynereis dumerilii* hardly responded at all, *N. pelagica* was intermediate in responsiveness and differed significantly from both *P. dumerilii* and *N. diversicolor*, the most responsive of the three species. The species were ordered in like manner when mean extent of contraction and rate of habituation to sudden illumination increase were considered. Evans noted that like *P. dumerilii*, other sublittoral polychaetes, such as *Branchiomma vesiculosum* (Nicol, 1950), *Hydroides dianthus* (Yerkes, 1906), and *Serpula vermicularis* (Hess, 1914), respond little, if at all, to sudden illumination increase, and related this to the innocuousness of such stimulation in their normal environments.

Whatever its basis, and regardless of expectation, it is clear that a relationship to the state and past experience of the species observed is here demonstrated. A closer study and analysis of predator–prey relationships of the animal in its environmental niche is required for precise delineation of the relationship noted. The relative frequency with which simultaneous and successive pairing of various stimuli (e.g., mechanical shock, shadow, and tactile) and their further consequences occur appears critical for such analysis. *Mercierella enigmatica* (Rullier, 1948), *N. pelagica* (Clark, 1960b; Evans, 1969b), *N. diversicolor* (Evans, 1969b), and *P. dumerilii* (Evans, 1969b) all habituate more slowly to paired than to single presentation of the component stimuli. Evans (1969b) found that both *P. dumerilii* and *N. diversicolor* react more frequently, habituate more slowly, and contract more extensively to simultaneous illumination decrease and mechanical shock than to either alone, although *N. pelagica* did not show such differential effects.

A related point was made by Clark (1965), regarding the complexity of the neurophysiological mechanisms of habituation, in his review of the integrative activity of the polychaete brain. Response to a simple stimulus (e.g., shadow) is followed by mechanical stimulation of proprioceptors and bristle receptors as retraction into the worm's tube begins. This reminds us that successive compounding of stimuli is the rule, not the exception, and the effects of combining additional mechanical stimulation with illumination decrease exacerbates this condition. When, in addition, one considers, as did Clark, the continuing barrage of repeated, complex, and varied stimuli to which these animals are normally exposed, one cannot help but agree with him that "Probably they react to any change in the prevailing background of stimulation and this may involve a much more complicated neurophysiological process than any that has been envisaged so far" (Clark, 1965, p. 365).

Although little studied in tubiculous polychaetes, the occurrence of shifts in response topography and sequence (as well as the response substitution previously noted) may also indicate one extent of such neurophysiological complexity. Touching the anal cirri of an extended and intact *Nereis virens* results in contraction of the whole worm and orientation of the parapodia toward its hind end. An alternative response is bending of the tail away from the stimulated side. It is confined to the terminal segments and is slower than the contraction-parapodial response. "The tail-bending response may be elicited many times after the symmetrical total jerk has disappeared" (Horridge, 1959, p. 250). Thus, withdrawal by contraction from a posterior tactile stimulus is replaced by withdrawal by bending away from it. Withdrawal by contraction itself changes during habituation. The waning of the parapodial component has apparently not been studied in detail, but the initially extensive contractions are quickly replaced by slower incomplete ones. The former must almost certainly be giant axon responses, since giant axon potentials are recordable from ventral nerve cord only to the first few stimuli presented, while the latter contractions are associated with fine fiber activity in the cord (Horridge, 1959; Gwilliam, 1965). Apparently, inquiry into habituation would be well rewarded by detailed study of the components of initial responsiveness and succeeding alterations of response as repetition of stimuli evoking withdrawal response in tubiculous polychaete annelids continued.

The withdrawal response of the earthworm *Lumbricus terrestris* contains two easily distinguishable components. The animal contracts its anterior and posterior portions while simultaneously flattening and hooking approximately the last fifteen segments of its posterior portions. In nature the first component serves to withdraw the animal into its burrow, while the second provides an anchoring point by digging the worm's bristlelike locomotory appendages (setae) into the substrate. Gardner (1966, 1968) studied habituation of this response to vibratory stimulation presented for 0.25 seconds every 18 seconds. Its topography changed as habituation proceeded, the withdrawal component waning much more rapidly than the hooking component. Habituation was carried to a criterion of 10 successive trials without observable response. This criterion was achieved for the withdrawal component in less than 20 trials by 80% of the 60 animals tested, while 110 trials were required to habituate the hooking component to this criterion in 80% of the animals (Gardner, 1966).

Retention was followed by computation of a savings score on rehabituation to the same criterion. Retention of habituation of both components was statistically evident after a 4-day, but not an 8-day, rest interval. Apparently differential retention of habituation of the two response components was not statistically clear; however, five independent comparisons (at $\frac{1}{2}$, 1, 2, 4, and 8 days) showed mean retention of habituation of hooking to be less than that for the withdrawal component (Gardner, 1968). With regard to the evaluation of retention in this experiment it should be noted that the animals were housed and tested in what may well have amounted to an unchanging environmental situation for them. Initiation of a habituation session was signaled only by the onset of the first vibration stimulus trial.

No effect of below-zero habituation (overhabituation) was noted in two groups of animals given two and three times as many trials as required to reach criterion when they were rehabituated 24 hours later (Gardner, 1966, 1968). Overhabituation did not facilitate rehabituation of either response component. Attention was again focused on the difference in trials to criterion in habituation and rehabituation. Gardner (1966) suggested the effects of overhabituation may have dissipated within 24 hours. This may well be, but it may also be that the measure chosen was not sensitive to such effects. The literature on below-zero habituation in invertebrate animals is extremely limited, and what there is suggests that this phenomenon may be limited to recovery of response as distinct from retention of habituation

(Humphrey, 1930). The literature on vertebrate animals is also limited and suggests a similar conclusion (Wendt, 1936; Prosser and Hunter, 1936; Thompson and Spencer, 1966). In addition, it may be noted that following rehabituation all of Gardner's animals withdrew and hooked to a tactile stimulus and thereafter responded similarly to a single additional vibratory stimulus. Apparently overhabituation 24 hours earlier did not modify the response restorative effect of tactile stimulation. Whether this effect is a sensitizing or dishabituating one cannot be said from the data; however, its occurrence does rule out sensory adaptation and effector fatigue as responsible for the response decrements obtained.

E. Mollusca

Although there have been demonstrations of habituation in various immobilized, semiintact preparations of the sea hare *Aplysia californicus* (Pinsker *et al.*, 1970), such modifications appear only to last for minutes or, at the most, hours. More recently, Carew *et al.* (1972) have investigated the same response, the gill-withdrawal reflex, in the intact, freely moving *Aplysia* and have found that response decrements build up over 5 days and are retained for at least 3 weeks (see Fig. 4). Direct stimulation of a siphon with a jet of seawater elicits a "complex defensive reflex consisting of the withdrawal of the siphon into the mantle cavity, and the concomitant contraction of the gill and mantle shelf." Repeated elicitation of this response produces withdrawal for increasingly shorter periods of time until the response fails to occur. Using 800 msec jets of water at variable interstimulus intervals (each stimulus following the previous one 30 seconds after the termination of the previous response), 10 trials per day were administered for 4 days followed by 10 trial retention tests 1, 7, or 21 days later. The results indicate that the duration of each withdrawal response decreased reliably within each set of daily trials and that the degree of recovery between days also declined over the initial 4 days of stimulation. Recovery as tested 1 week after the 5 successive days of training was no greater than that observed between the fourth and fifth days, and although recovery was significantly greater 21 days after training, habituation was significantly faster than observed on day 1, indicating retention. Furthermore, animals administered spaced training (10 trials per day for 4 days) evidenced significantly greater retention when tested on successive days than did subjects given massed training (40 trials on 1 day, see Fig. 5).

The stimulus specificity of habituation of prey-catching behavior and its enhancement of the discriminability of the objects of such behavior is clearly evident in the molluskan cephalopods. Young (1958, 1959) exposed freshly caught octopuses to repeated presentations of novel objects under

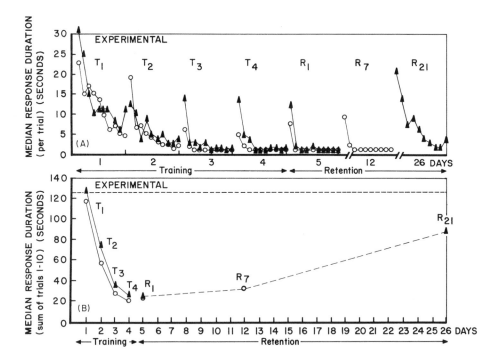

Fig. 4. (A) Long-term habituation. Buildup of habituation during training for 4 days (T_1 to T_4) and retention after 24 hours (R_1), 1 week (R_7), and 3 weeks (R_{21}). Data from three experiments are presented: two independent, identical replications in which retention was tested at 24 hours and 1 week have been pooled (O——O); in the third experiment, retention was tested at 24 hours and 3 weeks (Δ——Δ). Each data point is the median duration of siphon withdrawal for each of 10 habituation trials. (B) Time course of habituation. Habituation within each daily session is expressed as a single score, the sum of 10 trials (the net amount of time spent responding during the entire habituation training session). Compare retention tested at 24 hours and 1 week (O——O) and retention at 24 hours and 3 weeks (Δ——Δ) with control (day 1) habituation (upper dashed line). From Carew *et al.* (1972).

three conditions: while fasting, when fed outside the testing situation, and when fed for attacks on an object not used in the tests. The objects were made of plastic, moved slowly up and down, and were presented during 15-second (sometimes 30-second) trials at a distance of 80–90 cm from the animal.

Fasting animals (never fed in captivity) presented with a white vertical rectangle six times a day at intervals of at least 40 minutes for 6 successive days, at first increased the frequency of their attacks on the rectangular object. By the third day attack frequency stabilized at approximately 17% of

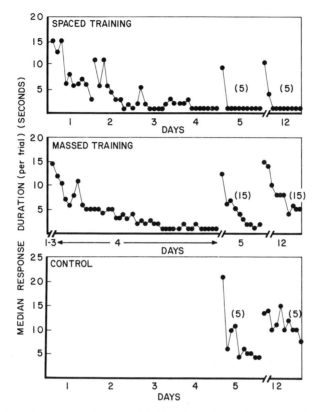

Fig. 5.   Spaced as compared to massed habituation training. Two groups of experimental animals were given either 4 days of habituation training (10 trials per day spaced training) or 1 day of habituation training (40 trails massed training). Both groups as well as a control group, which had received no training on days 1–4, were tested for retention after 24 hours (day 5) and 1 week (day 12). The spaced-training group was significantly lower than the massed-training group at both 24 hours ($P < 0.01$) and 1 week ($P < 0.01$), despite the fact that both groups had received the same number of training trials. The massed-training group was not significantly different from controls in either retention test. From Carew *et al.* (1972).

daily opportunity. No decrement from this figure was noted; however, a white circular object presented twice daily during the later days of the experiment initially evoked at least twice as many attacks. In another experiment, 20 animals were fasted for 4 days. On the third day the rectangular object was presented and response declined from 40% to less than 10% of opportunity over a period of 18 hours, a decline which persisted to the fourth day over a 23-hour rest interval. The same animals demonstrated marked responsiveness to a black circular object (75%) presented for the first time toward the end of the third day's session. Response to this object also waned rapidly and the decrement persisted into the fourth day. When live crabs were presented they "... were attacked by nearly all the octopuses, but even here there was a tendency to decrease when the attacks yielded no reward" (Young, 1959, p. 228). Unfortunately, data concerning the duration of these response decrements were not obtained, nor was the effect on them of subsequent feeding evaluated.

Similar results were obtained with wild-caught animals fed in their home-dens at night on the second through the sixth day of an 8-day experimental period. Six daily trials at hourly intervals produced no marked decrement in attack response to a plastic object. However, again, occasional presentation of two different objects demonstrated that novel objects were more readily attacked than the repetitively presented object. It was noted that after being brought from the sea and isolated, the learning of food collecting habits in the tank is preventable only by leaving the animals fasting and that giving food in the home-den increases the likelihood of attack on any moving object during a subsequent period. Thus, the effects of becoming acclimatized to the tank environment and feeding in the home-den antagonize those of habituation of response to a repetitively presented object.

Rewarding the animals for attack on an object also increases the likelihood of attack on any object, particularly one moving in the locale of previous reward. Yet, if the moving object is not one that was previously rewarded, the tendency to attack it is rapidly extinguished. Recovery occurs over 24 hours and retention of habituation (extinction) is evident in savings during the succeeding session (Young, 1959).

Even with previous reward or home-den feeding, attack responses to crabs slowly habituate when unrewarded. Systematic studies at long intertrial intervals were not conducted (Young, 1959), but even with frequent trials (every 5 minutes) the process is slow. For example, on the first day of showing a crab every 10 minutes, each of 5 animals attacked during all fifteen opportunities presented, and with only a slight increase in latency toward the end of the series. On the next day, each animal again attacked during the first ten opportunities. Thereafter, some animals stopped attacking and the latency of attack increased more than on the previous day. These effects were very slight, indeed virtually negligible, and it was not noted whether the animals were fed in their home-dens overnight.

Habituation of prey-catching response to a natural stimulus object is perhaps more clearly evident in the cuttlefish *Sepia officinalis* (Wells, 1962). Six newly hatched and six adult *Sepia* were individually exposed to prey animals, shrimps (adults) or mysids (young animals) inside a glass jar placed in their aquarium. Time spent attacking the prey was recorded for the first 5 minutes, and in sample 5-minute periods at intervals thereafter. At first the adults were somewhat more persistent (mean of 178 seconds) than the young animals (mean of 112 seconds), but thereafter grew more spasmodic in their attacks and ceased attacking entirely after hours. The young animals, in contrast, were still making intermittent attacks after 6 hours, although their attacking time per 5 minute period had dropped markedly (mean of approximately 22 seconds). The prey animals were then removed. When they were replaced for a 5-minute "retention" test the next day the adults attacked only once or twice and then stopped in contrast, the young animals showed much less retention (mean of more than 56 seconds time spent in attacking). Thus, both groups demonstrated retention of habituation, the young being less affected by habituation and showing more recovery of response. Unfortunately, a second 6-hour habituation session (rehabituation) was not carried out. Thus, meaningful comparison of amount of retention is not possible. In addition, difference in persistence of attacking, recovery, and retention may well stem from differential stimulative effectiveness of the prey animals used rather than age or some other organismic variable like hunger.

F. Arthropoda

From the point of view of detailed evaluation of all aspects of response change, Szlep's (1964) study of the prey-catching response in orb-weaving spiders is one of the most complete. The orb web of spiders of *Uloborus* is arranged in an almost horizontal plane. The spider sits at rest in its center, oriented in the direction of the decline of the web. The first and second pairs of legs are stretched forward resting on a single radius, while the third and fourth pairs stretch backward along the corresponding radius. Under stimulation the legs are first spread apart into contact with different radii, enabling more efficient discrimination of web vibrations. The spider then turns toward the vibration center and runs along a radius toward it. It hangs beneath the web plane as it does so, dragging an auxiliary thread behind it. Location of the vibration center is extremely accurate. Normally, if a fly is present, the spider circles it (trapping it with the trailing thread) and then attacks.

This response sequence (including circling but excepting attack) was elicited by touching a vibrating needle to a radius of the web (it was removed just before the spider was able to step on it). If it was removed and reapplied during a run, or just as the spider began to circle (spin) around the needle, flight was induced in most cases (unfortunately, habituation of this interesting phenomenon was not studied). Only spiders demonstrating prompt, strong, and complete response, which did not wane in the first few stimulus applications, were studied. Typically the needle was applied once every minute, with a 5-minute rest between groups of 10 applications, although more frequent and less frequent applications were tested in addition with another species of spider (*Araneus*) demonstrating a highly similar response sequence. Upon return to the hub, *Uloborus* turns backward, cuts the auxiliary thread with its forelegs, and then resumes its resting position.

Rhythmic periodic recurrence of the vibratory stimulus slows down the response and changes its nature. The movements of the animal come to resemble those in a slow motion film. Response initiation, turning, running, and return to resting position are all retarded. The interval preceding running after the turn is also lengthened. Waning (omission) of the run is the first alteration in the nature of the response. Then the turn disappears and only the opening of the legs indicates reception of the vibration. Thereafter, the leg opening becomes one-sided, and finally only one leg moves (twitches). The intensity of leg movements decreases progressively through these changes. The weakest sign of stimulus reception detectable was a feeble abdominal movement. As the response wanes, retarded and incomplete responses increase progressively in frequency, and complete lack of response begins to appear finally. On return to the hub the backward turn is more frequently omitted, and the auxiliary thread is cut by a posterior rather than an anterior leg.

Application of fewer trials per day (50 vs. 100), increasing their temporal spacing (15 seconds to 5 minutes for *Araneus* spiders), or varying the vibration place (every second or third radius) raised the level of response and slowed its rate of waning within and across days. Individual differences were large and consistent across days. These observations illustrate retention of habituation across days and its recovery between days. The number of complete responses is greatest during the initial series of 10 trials each day and response waning is progressively more rapid. Recovery is nearly complete during the first few days (even after many days most animals produce complete responses at the beginning of each daily session). The number of trials given per day decreased as complete extinction of response occurred more quickly; even so the recovery level declined. The vibratory stimulus lasted only 15 seconds during nonresponse trials and ranged between means of 3 and 5 seconds for response trials. These latter observations indicate that sensory and effector process changes cannot be responsible for the response decrements obtained. In addition, response returned upon shifting the radius vibrated, increasing vibration intensity, or placing a real fly on the web. The dishabituatory effects of these stimulus changes were not tested, and generalization of habituation to them was not ascertained. The results do indicate stimulus specificity of habituation.

In addition to the systematic changes noted above, repeated vibration resulted in a number of transitory and intermittent alterations of behavior.

As a rule, a stimulated spider does not pass beyond the vibration center once it is reached. During the first 10 trials of the first day, spiders frequently moved along the radius beyond the center after removal of the needle, passing on to the frame of the web or to adjacent radii, which were then plucked and shaken. This was rarely observed during later sessions. In contrast, another form of web plucking, occurring after return to the hub, was retained for a long time. This plucking response was similar to one shown by some spiders after turning to a vibrating radius but before the run—they pluck at the vibrating radius (a response also transitorily increased under recurrent stimulation). These aftereffects of vibratory stimulation suggest the growth and decline of a searching-for-prey response as habituation proceeds.

As the response to vibration waned, running was interrupted by return to the hub before cessation of the vibration in a few cases. As a rule the run was continuous, even as it became slower with repeated stimulation. In some spiders frequent pauses, during which the vibrating radius was plucked, came to interrupt running during later phases of habituation. In others this appeared only occasionally. Again, altering the normal resting position on return to the hub to face the vibration radius was observed to occur without regard to phase of habituation as recurrent stimulation continued. Turns under stimulation also changed in some cases to the opposite of normal. These turns were sporadic, occurring once, twice, or three times per series of 10 trials. "In all spiders, the turns in opposite direction occurred mainly during the later experimental phase. In the majority of cases, the spider stopped running after having turned away from the vibrating radius" (Szlep, 1964, pp. 231–232). These indications of developing avoidance of the vibrating radius are reinforced by several instances in which *Uloborus* ultimately tore down that "offending" strand of its web.

Both the systematic and "incidental" changes in behavior as habituation proceeded again indicate increased sensitivity to, and discrimination of, the habituation stimulus. Although apparently not frequent and systematic enough across individual spiders and progressive trials to warrant detailed analysis, the incidental observations strongly suggest the growth and development of new responses as the initial response to the habituation stimulus wanes. Again an associative learning process is suggested. In spite of constancy of experimental conditions (vibration amplitude was uniform and preselected according to the response of the individual spider) and absence of experimental manipulation of the significance of the stimulus, its significance did change, according to the individual spider and the vagaries of passing circumstance. Clearly, the recurrent rhythmic vibration supplied by the needle differed from the complex of stimuli produced by the impact of a fly: it differed from the vibrations, the weighting of the web, the irregular oscillations caused by the fly's movements, and undoubtedly in other ways.

In spite of such differences the needle vibration did not become simply a "neutral" stimulus, casually ignored and devoid of ability to elicit response. Certainly it became discriminable from a more natural stimulus, but in a "meaningful" way contingent upon the consequences of response to it, as indexed by the transitory "search" behavior and developing avoidance reactions observed. That these were not as frequent and as systematically related to the course of habituation as they might have been indubitably relates to the degree and manner in which individual animals are sensitive to the differences between artificial and natural stimulation. Some spiders easily discriminate regular needle vibrations from the complex stimuli provided by a fly, while for others they are equivalent. In the absence of experimental manipulation of response consequences the significance of a stimulus is left to such individual differences in sensitivity, however they are determined. It might be well if every habituation experiment contained an "associative" control.

That habituation involves more than the simple waning of a response as a result of the growth of an internal inhibitory process specific to it and its stimulus is again strikingly shown in the work of Zanforlin (1969, 1970) on inhibition of light orientation in insects. He concluded that attending to behavior that follows response waning "may give a very different classification to the 'known facts' that are now mixed together under the heading of reaction waning" (p. 90), and again, "when we consider the biological function of a particular 'adaptivity' mechanism, it becomes evident that the selective value is not given only by the possibility of a reaction being stopped, but also by the particular reaction or kind of behavior that follows the reaction once this has stopped" (p. 89). Two cases supporting these conclusions are examined.

The fly larvae *Sarcophaga barbata* crawl *away* from light in a straight path consistently and persistently. Upon entering a blind alley, after a short period of time at the end wall involving repeated attempts to crawl away from the light, they turn and crawl *toward* the light until they pass the entrance and then again crawl away from light. Zanforlin (1969) found that what happens at the end wall to enable this reversal of negative phototaxis is that the turning reaction (bending the body away from light) habituates after a few repetitions. This was demonstrated by putting the larva into an alley open at both ends with a light at one end. The alley was turned whenever the larva turned away from the light. After 8–10 turnings the response had waned and the larva continued crawling toward the light. Once the larva, in crawling along the walls of the alley toward the light, has passed the exit, it bends its head slightly more to one side than the other and moves in a wide and imprecise semicircle, described as a "wide turn," utterly unlike the bending of the body in a sharp turn as in the turning reaction. The persistence of this altered negative phototaxic response is not indicated.

However, that the straight path klinotaxic response returns in due course may be surmised from the observations on recovery.

The habituation was specific to the particular light and its intensity. Increased intensity or a different stimulus could restore the response shortly after it had waned. Without stimulation, recovery took 2–3 minutes; even with continuous stimulation the turning reaction can reappear in 5–10 minutes and apparently in full strength. Potentiation of habituation and reduction of recovery with repetition were not ascertained for either continuous or repeated stimulation. These observations exclude receptor change, adaptation, and effector process change as responsible for the response waning. An effect of general activity level was noted; the number of turnings to response extinction being low when activity level was low and high when it was high. However, this measure was not influenced by stimulus intensity and stimulus specificity was found; thus, reduced general arousal can be excluded as a factor in the waning.

The second case concerned Lymantridae *Lymantria dispar* caterpillars. These animals are attracted by light. When placed in a test tube with the closed end pointing toward light, they persist in trying to approach it until starved to death, even with food available at the other end of the tube. Zanforlin (1969, 1970) placed some animals inside and some on the outside of a test tube. They all crawled toward the light. Those on the inside continued crawling up and down the closed end wall until they died. Those on the outside, even when the tube they were on was encased in a larger one, turned (2 minutes and 30 second average time on a 1-cm-diam tube) and crawled away from the light.

When the caterpillars were placed in a glass tube between alternating lights they turned regularly as long as observed. On a stick they crawled on regardless of the light after an average of only 2.8 turns. In the tube they crawled along the side walls and always bent upward in turning; the stick presented opportunity only for horizontal or downward turns. It was the lack of upward going tactile stimuli that enabled the caterpillars on the outside of the tube to turn at its end. Again, on a vertical surface they turned regularly and consistently to alternative lights at the sides, averaging 122 turns in 30 minutes. A negative geotaxis prevented waning of the positive phototaxis as long as its stimuli were present, or alternatively "what inhibited the light orientating reaction was a 'lack of tactile stimuli in the upwards direction'" (p. 83); i.e., repeated extensions beyond the end of the tube produced waning of the phototaxic response for those on its outside surface. On the vertical surface the animals did not reach the top (the phototaxis being stronger than the geotaxis) but crawled horizontally toward the alternating lights, always bending upward as they turned with each alteration.

That the going away from light was not simply an inversion of the positive phototaxis was indicated by placing caterpillars on an elevated horizontal sheet of cardboard with a light to one side. They crawled toward the light in a straight path, but once having reached the edge of the sheet none simply reversed its direction. They either turned and wandered about the surface or kept to its edge. In addition they frequently stopped and raised their fore-parts while swinging their heads from side to side (1.7 times/cm on the average), an action rarely seen during initial approach toward the light. Thus, after habituation of the phototaxis, a kind of exploratory behavior super-vened. It did not last long. After crawling approximately 15 cm the average caterpillar turned and headed straight back toward the light. If left undis-turbed, subsequent crawlings away from the light lasted longer. The effect was cumulative, and the distance traveled increased proportionally. In normal life these *Lymantridae* caterpillars are led by their attraction to light to the tops of trees where food is plentiful. However, normally they do not starve at the end of leafless branches but do indeed turn back down again and eventually climb up other branches.

Thus, in the absence of simultaneous upward-going tactile stimuli, short-term habituation of the positive response to light takes place and becomes cumulatively stronger (unless dishabituation occurs through extraneous disturbance) until it leads to a survival-promoting event: opportunity to again go upward to food—this event being preceded by the emergence of a qualitatively different response as the positive phototaxis wanes, which progressively increases in strength. Clearly, the significance of the stimulus (light) changes as a function of the consequences of response to it (absence of upward-going tactile stimuli), and as a result avoidance of that stimulus and exploratory behavior ensue.

These observations do not credit the larvae of a butterfly with the long-term associative memory usually equated with learning, but they clearly indicate a short-term modification of response contingent upon its con-sequences; an effect generally considered a fundament to "operant" or "instrumental" conditioning rather than simple "single stimulus" habitua-tion. They also indicate that one must consider carefully the context of stimuli embodied by the experimental situation in which one presents a single stimulus in order to study "habituation" or response to it. The con-sideration can offer in no sense a guarantee that only a single stimulus is operative; thus, detailed analysis of response topography and its sequential change is a prerequisite to understanding of the processes occurring in any single instance of habituation.

Rilling *et al.* (1959) placed mantids *Parastagmatoptera unipunctata* and *Hierodulae* gen. at a fixed position in a cylindrical white arena for observa-tion of their prey-catching response. Live flies, dead ones, and various models were tested for their response-eliciting effectiveness. Response waning was studied by presenting a stimulus object continuously until all response ceased (response satiation). This procedure was continued, usually at 5 minute intervals, until 3 or 4 trials passed in succession with no response whatsoever. The number of strike responses to satiation was determined for each trial.

Optimal prey objects fell between certain size limits, had "legs" and "wings," and moved jerkily, with many stops and starts. When dummy prey objects were presented behind glass, response waned rapidly and ceased in 2 or 3 minutes. On the other hand, a live fly, moving behind glass, could elicit responses for hours. However, even in this situation, the response of hungry mantids wanes to zero, or nearly so, in 4–5 hours. Substitution of a fresh living fly partially restored response, suggesting a degree of stimulus specificity, although the effect of the fly substitution operation alone was not evaluated. Following substitution, waning was more rapid than initially, indicating a high degree of stimulus generalization of habituation.

Recovery of response was said to usually be complete after 30 minutes, occurring mostly during the first 5 minutes; a fact which prompted use of a 5-minute intertrial interval for most of the work. However, savings over trials (retention of habituation) was not checked at either of these, or longer, intervals. The effectiveness of the several models was tested in terms of responses to satiation, but again habituation rate was not studied in detail over repeated sessions. It was evident that waning was more rapid initially if a winged dummy was actually caught, carried to the mouth parts, and sometimes actually mouthed before being discarded, than if this sequence of events were prevented by the interposition of a glass pane. However, total response cessation (satiation) was reached earlier under the opposite condition; i.e., with the dummy behind glass. Considering the persistence of response to a live fly behind glass, repeated contact with the glass is not likely to be responsible for the difference. Since the stimulus is the same in both situations, the difference can be attributed to the nonidentity of the response sequences involved. When the dummy is caught, a sustained flexion of tibia on femur occurs, and it may be carried to the mouth prior to being discarded. In contrast, without a catch, the tibia opens within 40–50 msec and slowly closes over approximately 140 msec during resumption of the striking attitude. Thus, a pronounced change in stimulus consequences occurs in the former, which does not take place in the latter case. The consequences of the striking response are evidently critical in determining the difference.

If the strike response produces sensory inputs different from those prevailing before its occurrence, and ensuing responses further alter sensory input (return to the prestrike pattern of sensory input is thereby delayed), initial responsivity is lowered and striking persists longer. Whereas, if the strike response results in no change in, or a prompt restoration of, prestrike sensory input, initial responsivity is elevated and cessation of striking is hastened. This suggests that the stimulus situation initiating striking has both an incremental and a decremental effect upon that response. Alteration of sensory input consequent upon the response, with subsequent elicitation of other responses, curtails both effects so that initial responsivity is lower and response waning is slower.

Balderrama and Maldonado (1971) placed mantids *Stagmaoptera biocellata* in small bare isolation chambers under constant illumination, temperature, and humidity. Thirty times a day the animals were faced (through a transparent partition) with a living bird (confined in a facing compartment) for 3 minutes. This initially elicited a "fright response" from all animals during at least 3 of the first 15 trials (less responsive animals were discarded).

The fright response (deimatic reaction) consists of seven components: (1) oblique backward direction of the antennae, (2) opening of the mouth parts showing colored mandibles, (3) lateral extension of the forelegs, displaying a big black spot on each femur, as the prothorax is raised, (4) elevation of the wings displaying eyelike stigmas on the forewings, (5) tilting and twisting of the abdomen to the side, (6) abdominal rubbing against the wings making a rustling sound, and (7) violent swaying from side to side. Habituation of this response to three different species of bird was studied. In all cases response recovery (responsivity over first 15 trials) was not complete after either a 2- or a 6-day rest (in the isolation chamber) and retention (savings in trials to criterion) was clearly evident, although retention was less and recovery more after a 6-day than after a 2-day rest. Retention was least and recovery greatest for the initially most frightening bird species: the shiny cowbird (a natural predator of mantids). Since the mantids for the different groups were selected in terms of responsivity to different species of birds, which differed in stimulus strength, the groups differed in overall strength of reactivity.

Response topography changed during habituation to all three species, but least so to the shiny cowbird. This change was indexed by increased frequency of incomplete responses and decreasing response duration. The specific nature of the change (if there was a systematic change) was not reported. This measure reflected least recovery and most retention for the least frightening stimulus (a canary) and intermediate levels for the intermediately frightening stimulus (Java sparrow). These two stimuli did not differ in trials to criterion during either initial habituation or rehabituation following either recovery interval. Both bird species are seed eaters; the Java sparrow *Padda oryzivora* resembling the shiny cowbird *Molothrus bonariensis* more so than the canary *Serinus canarius*. However, the overall results showed habituation to be more rapid and more pronounced the weaker the stimulus.

The three stimuli wre also graded in the same manner in their "dishabit-uating" effect. Repeated presentation of a new and more frightening stimulus after habituation to a less frightening one resulted in response recovery, but number (frequency), completeness, and duration of response were all less than the same stimulus provoked in naive mantids. Trials to criterion with repeated presentation of the new stimulus was also reduced compared to presentation of the same stimulus to a naive mantid. No such effects were found when a less frightening stimulus was repeatedly presented following habituation to a more frightening one. There was no restoration of response in this case. These relationships indicate stimulus generalization of habituation. In addition, the response restorative effect of introducing a novel shiny cowbird stimulus following habituation to Java sparrows was much less than when it followed canary stimuli, reflecting a greater degree of generalization of habituation.

The persistence of response decrement over long time periods, together with the slow recovery of response and the response restorative effects noted above, rule out sensory adaptation or fatigue as causative agents. There appears little doubt that habituation of the deimatic response of mantids occurs. Considering the reduction in responsivity to a more frightening stimulus effected by generalization of habituation to a less frightening one, it would be interesting to examine the dishabituation effects of both novel more frightening stimuli and novel "neutral" stimuli (perhaps of other sense modalities than vision). Together with the asymmetric nature of generaliza-tion of habituation indicated by the results (generalization from more to less frightening stimuli was complete), the relationship noted above suggests that rather than dishabituation, the insertion of a more frightening stimulus into a series of less frightening ones (and vice versa) might well accentuate habituation. On the other hand, dishabituation proper should follow inter-polation of a neutral novel stimulus. In addition, the variety of response measures available might well differentiate sensitization (Groves and Thompson, 1970) from habituative effects of the same stimulus.

Similar results have been reported for the prey-catching responses of the water bug *Notonecta glauca* (Wolda, 1961). This interesting animal hangs upside down from the surface film with its legs extended laterally, the tarsi and the tip of its abdomen in contact with the surface. Small vibrations of the surface cause it to turn its body so the head is oriented to the source. It then swims toward the source and, given appropriate visual or tactile stimuli, the object causing vibration is seized. Then, after testing with the proboscis if it is suitable prey, it is eaten.

Touching the water surface repeatedly at 5-second intervals with a thin steel wire at a spot 2 cm to the left of *Notonecta* at first consistently elicits turning, swimming, and sometimes seizing. During habituation, the response sequence fractionates. Turning is most resistent to waning, its degree decreasing almost linearly with decreasing response frequency. Swimming wanes rapidly at first, but thereafter, if turning occurs at all, swimming follows 50–65% of the time. Response topography thus changes in both its simultaneous and sequential aspect as habituation proceeds.

Recovery of responsiveness is complete in 24 hours, but retention is evident in a sharply increased rate of response waning. Dishabituation (and stimulus specificity) was tested by interpolating a series of stimuli to the right side of the animal during a rest interval separating two series of left side stimuli. Responsiveness to left stimuli was augmented only if the right side stimuli immediately preceded the second series of left stimuli. If they were given at the beginning of the rest interval, no augmentation of response was observed. In no case was augmentation of responsiveness to left stimuli obtained by interpolating stimuli presented to the front, or to the left rear, of the animal, although response to these stimuli (and to right stimuli) themselves was clearly greater than to left stimuli.

Stimulus specificity is evident in these results but dishabituation was not obtained, rather, a rapidly decaying facilitation, or sensitization, like that indicated for the spinal cat by elicitation of contralateral responses (Groves and Thompson, 1970), is suggested. In addition to stimulus specificity, as indicated by immediate responsiveness to a new interpolated stimulus, no evidence for generalization was found with prolonged presentation of right immediately after left stimuli, or vice versa, nor with left–right following left stimuli and front following alternating right and left stimuli. In this context, it is of interest to note that strictly simultaneous right and left stimuli did not elicit a response of any sort. The data produced were consistent in indicating that habituation of response to each of the various stimuli used was largely, if not entirely, independent. Whether this independence was specific to the spatial localization of the stimuli was not determined; the influence of strength and frequency of stimulation was not investigated.

On the other hand, choice of two simultaneously presented spatially distinct stimuli was altered when one alone had previously undergone habituation. After habituation of response to stimuli placed to the right front of the animal, more left front responses were observed with both presented simultaneously. Without the prior habituation both were observed in equal numbers. So also, prior habituation to left front stimuli increased the proportion of choices of left rear stimuli when both were presented simultaneously. These results, the independence of habituation and its alteration of choice, are to be expected if, in fact, habituation increases the discriminability of stimuli. One should expect strong stimulus specificity and lack of generalization in such a case.

In addition to consistency with a discrimination model of habituation, the data from *Notonecta glauca* also bear upon another possible property of habituation which is most often overlooked. Although, unfortunately, the data are not definitive in this regard, they are worth mentioning for their suggestive value. Besides the alteration in direction of response evident in the choice experiments, there is also a reduction in overall level of responding. How much of this results from the interpolated single stimulus habituation and how much from the preceding simultaneous double stimulus series is not ascertainable; the appropriate controls were not run. The overall response level is lower, however, than what might be expected by inference from the data of the other experiments reported for successive series of the "nonhabituated" stimulus presented alone. If this is so, then the difference would be attributable to pairing the two stimuli. This suggests a generalized response suppressive effect of a habituated stimulus when paired with a response-eliciting one, akin to Pavlovian conditioned inhibition.

IV. Discussion

The literature reviewed does not permit definitive conclusions relating habituation to phyletic status. The organisms and experimental situations studied and the methods and procedures used in their study vary much too greatly. More systematic study may reveal, however, that the response system involved is as important a parameter of such a relation as the level of structural complexity of the organism. The apparent dependence of retention, as distinct from recovery, on bilateral symmetry and an anterior ganglion in the nervous system, which may be gleaned from the literature on the contraction and withdrawal response, could as well result from the type of stimuli used to elicit such response. Still, if a phyletic relation exists, this one comes closest to having been adequately evaluated over the years since the turn of the century. Other parameters of habituation do not differentiate the representatives of the different phyla studied.

Conclusions relating habituation to neurobiologic response systems are also premature; however, again, it is likely that recovery from, and retention of, habituation will ultimately be found to differentiate such systems in relation to selective pressures stemming from each species ecologically prescribed requirements for survival. Aside from these properties of habituation, its decay and its retention, none of the others appear likely to provide generally differentiable categories, although, of course parametric variation can be expected within narrow limits. For example, prey-catching and predator-escape may well prove generally differentiable across species and phyla in terms of characteristic patterns of recovery and retention functions; i.e., the present data suggested complete or partial recovery and a high degree of retention for predator-escape responses, and eventual complete recovery with little or no retention for prey-catching responses. Variation of the other parametric characteristics of habituation, such as frequency and intensity of stimulation, can be expected to result in a limited quantitative differentiation of such response systems rather than a major one bordering on the qualitative.

In any case, it is evident that discriminability of the stimulus habituated will prove an important parameter of the recovery and retention properties of habituation as well as those of stimulus specificity, generalization, and dishabituation. One might expect a strong relationship between these properties and discriminability as evidenced either in receptor structure function, or in response alteration during habituation, i.e., changes in topography and sequence and emergence of new response. The latter, indicative of shifts in stimulus significance as habituation proceeds, rather than simple waning or weakening thereof, necessarily reflect a high degree of discrimination of both habituation and contextual stimuli.

Instances of initial complete recovery of response followed by evidence of marked retention of habituation (savings on rehabituation) indicate a complexity of discriminative process, wherever it occurs, difficult to handle for a simple stimulus–response specific inhibitory view of habituation. Given that the habituation stimulus is discriminable (e.g., as evidenced by stimulus specificity of habituation) it is difficult to understand why complete recovery should ever occur in the presence of significant retention. One would think that the transition from excitatory to inhibitory control of response effected by habituation would be evident in *every* instance of stimulus presentation during its continued existence. The postulation of decay of a short-term inhibitory process supplementing response suppression by the developing inhibitory connectivity of the stimulus to its response does not help. After decay of such a short-term process the status of the retained inhibitory connectivity should be most accurately assessable and not assessed as zero. Postulation of a masking excitatory process elicited at initiation of rehabituation and decaying quickly thereafter also fails to help. Such a process suggests sensitization of the input–output channel utilized by the stimulus, either through a specific sensory facilitation effect or through a general arousal (startle) effect. In either case one must explain why all existing connectivities in that channel (including the inhibitory ones) are not equally activated. Clearly, a multiple-stage process of access of sensory input to the neural residues of its prior occurrences is required. Either redintegration (reestablishment) or retrieval (reactivation) or previous response suppressive influences is facilitated by stimulus repetition. If the latter, their storage other than in the input–output channel used would seem required.

Whatever one's approach, whether a molecular-mechanistic one or a molar-systematic one, a complex calculus of selection among competing centrally represented influences is necessary to an understanding of habituation and its properties. Clearly, an animal undergoing habituation discriminates the habituation stimulus from other stimuli, including those forming the situational context, but also it discriminates successive instances of presentation of the habituation stimulus, one from the other. It is not enough to assume that all else remains unchanged while the discrimination of succeeding from preceeding trials depends only on their distribution in time and other parametric facets of the habituation stimulus. Many of the research reports reviewed indicate that we must look to the influence of the contextual stimuli and to the influence of changing sensory feedback resulting from the animal's own response to successfully account for the nature and properties of the changes wrought in animals through application of the habituation procedure.

In several of the instances described (e.g., Zanforlin, 1969; Fleure and Walton, 1907; Rilling et al., 1959) response to the habituation stimulus led to a distinctive type of sensory feedback. When an octopus draws in a novel object and mouths it (Wells, 1961) and when a mantid strikes a prey object and encounters an intervening transparent partition (Rilling et al., 1959), one is tempted to ascribe response waning to negatively reinforcing properties of the distinctive character of such response-produced sensory feedback. Yet such instances are typically included as examples of habituation (Harris, 1943; Thorpe, 1963). Usually there is reason to believe that suppression of the response "punished" in such a manner cannot account for the waning. Even so, does this situation differ in any essential way from those where such characteristic response feedback is presumably absent? Does not the contracted state of the earthworm (Gardner, 1966) and the vibratory condition of the web with vibrating needle just removed (Szlep, 1964) constitute just such a distinctive response-induced sensory feedback? The situation differs from the typical learning one only in that the reinforcing properties of the feedback are not independently delineated. Who is to say whether or not the sensory consequences of nonreinforced responses are not in themselves reinforcing? Whatever one's view concerning the nature of learning and the role of reinforcement in it, would not a demonstration that habituation results in discrimination no different from when it is deliberately taught indicate that these processes are based on common events? Unfortunately, we have no such direct demonstration, but where behavioral constraints are minimal and descriptions of behavioral change relatively complete, evidence of the changing significance of a repeated stimulus abounds. With vertebrates habituation-induced deficit in leg flexion conditioning (Lubow, 1965) and CER conditioning (Carlton and Vogel, 1967) have been reported, and with repetition the CS does come to inhibit both the conditioned and unconditioned response in human GSR conditioning (Kimmel,

1966). We can only conclude that the inference embodied in our introduction has drawn ample supportive information from habituation of invertebrate animals and its direct investigation is well warranted.

Theories of the nature of habituation relate either to its function in the service of species survival or to its communality with associative learning. It is often said that associative learning begins with the platyhelminthes, while learning by "habituation" characterizes all animal phyla. In this view, the former depends on the presence of synaptic differentiation of neurons, the ganglionic congregation of interneurons, and bilateral symmetry of bodily and neuronal organization, or all three together. On the other hand, learning by habituation is seen as depending only on the presence of neuronal, or neuroid, differentiation of transmissive capacity. Thus, the evolution of learning capacity is seen as involving a discontinuity and "emergence" of new learning properties dependent upon a new organization of neural processes.

A less popular point of view denies the existence of a discontinuity and suggests a gradual and continuous evolution of learning capacity evident in comparisons of existing animal species (Harlow, 1958). According to this view, associative learning, and all "higher" learning capacities, can be seen as accountable by, or evolving from, the capacity for learning by habituation. The phyletic increase in size and complexity of central nervous systems is then interpreted in terms of increasing sensory contact channels with the environment and increasing capacity to process such environmental information simultaneously. It is the most complex interplay of such differentiated and multitudinous informational channels on neural output systems which accounts for "insight" and "thinking."

A third point of view regarding the evolution of learning capacity does not make the assumption, implicit in the two previously noted, that learning capacity has evolved as an independent adaptive process. Instead, learning is seen in the context of neurobehavioral systems evolved to adapt the species to specific aspects of its ecologic role in life. Thus, learning capacity and mechanism can be seen as differing in relation to such systems. Although this point of view is not directly concerned with the question of continuity vs. discontinuity in the relation of habituation to associative learning, the evidence related to it is, nevertheless, relevant to that question.

Functionally, habituation is seen as eliminating response to repeated biologically irrelevant stimulation (Lorenz, 1965; Thorpe, 1956). The resulting economy of energy, and direction of effort, enhances survival and reproductive probability. It does so in at least three ways:

1. Strong, disturbing, alarm and escape reactions are restricted to infrequently occurring novel stimulus patterns, more apt to characterize a

predator's approach (Thorpe, 1956). Thus, the animal is most often left to the normal course of its daily activities in its familiar environment.

2. Orienting and exploratory approach as well as alarm reactions to stimuli characterizing the familiar environment are eliminated. Thus, territorial limits are defined for the animal in terms of the presence and absence of such reactions, and thereby, behaviors enhancing reproductive probability (aggression, courting, etc.) are assured expression; strong and irrelevant competing reaction tendencies are absent.

3. Species-specific fixed patterns and individually acquired adaptive reactions are restricted to optimal stimulus situations (Thorpe, 1963). Thus, discrimination of sign and releasing stimuli sharpens and synchronization of social behavior is enhanced.

The seeming contradiction between the principle of selection and habituation to a predator has been repeatedly discussed (Hinde, 1954b; Thorpe, 1963; Lorenz, 1965; Balderrama and Maldonado, 1971). "The response to a predator could habituate without contradiction of the survival principle... because of the constancy in the environmental conditions in which the stimulus was repeatedly presented, whereas it is difficult to admit such an habituation to the same predator in *any* environment" (Balderrama and Maldonado, 1971; italics theirs). Actually, the contradiction is more apparent than real and one should expect habituation to the predator itself to make its evasion more efficient rather than less. Habituation to stimuli characterizing the predator in any situation permitting its occurrence should sharpen rather than dull discrimination of changes in such stimuli; i.e., distance (optical size), color and pattern differentiation, and type of movement. The contest between predator and prey which develops with increasing knowledge of each other is evident in many walks of life.

It is just this sharpening of discrimination which accounts for the asymmetry of generalization of habituation reported by Balderrama and Maldonado (1971); their reported "habituation of dishabituation" notwithstanding. After habituation to a less "threatening" (initially less effective) stimulus, a more threatening one elicited greater initial recovery of response. Whereas, after habituation to a more threatening stimulus, and shift to a less threatening one, response did not occur. This is exactly what one should expect if information about a predator is integrated more quickly as habituation proceeds; i.e., the response is tuned more finely to quantitative and qualitative variation in the stimulus characteristics of the predator.

While clearly evident in the presentation of Balderrama and Maldonado (1971), the relationship under discussion is there somewhat obscured, and in other reports totally obscured, by the manner of presenting data. Trials to criterion, mean latency or duration of response, frequency of response over trial blocks, and others are useful measures conveying selective information about the habituation process. However, they give misleading information about the nature of response recovery. Balderrama and Maldonado's percent of incomplete response is more informative in this regard, and report of percent of subjects showing complete response on the *first trial* of each habituation, recovery (rehabituation), and dishabituation session would have been most informative. As in Szlep (1964) and Wolda (1961), it would have made the relationship of response to initial stimulus change inescapable.

V. Conclusion

In the previous sections we have attempted to present a picture of the current status of research on the behavioral changes exhibited by intact invertebrate animals in habituation paradigms. It should be emphasized that we have made no attempt to exhaustively review the large body of data concerned with invertebrate habituation but rather have chosen to discuss in detail what we consider to be some of the more representative examples of detailed discriptions of waning of responsiveness across invertebrate phyla. In reviewing this literature our goal has been to convey the idea that habituation should not be viewed as primarily a distinct functional process or behavioral capacity characteristic of the animal's nervous system. Rather, habituation, like classical or instrumental conditioning, is merely a set of operations, an experimental paradigm within which an organism's behavior is assessed. However, contrary to other types of learning, where attempts have been made to view behavioral capacity as increasing as a function of the level of complexity of the organism (see Dethier and Stellar, 1961, for an example of this approach), habituation appears to be a more widespread and pervasive phenomenon. Throughout the invertebrate series detailed analyses of a variety of paradigms indicate that behavioral habituation can occur, meeting all of the requirements set by Thompson and Spencer (1966), although there is still some question concerning demonstration of dishabituation in protozoans.

In reviewing the literature on invertebrates we have been particularly impressed by the finding that with careful, detailed investigation habituation emerges as an extremely complex and subtle phenomenon, even with apparently simple organisms. The historical dismissal of such behavior as an important aspect of species and individual survivial, despite the early investigations of Jennings (1906) and Humphrey (1930), today appears to have been unjustified. The facts which emerge from our review, as well as from the other chapters in these volumes, are that habituation can be as long-lasting and as much under the influence of discriminative control as the other, more complex types of learning. The key to the demonstration of such characteristics in invertebrates as well as with vertebrates would appear to be the patience and throughness of the experimenter rather than the level of complexity of the organism.

Although our emphasis here has been on behavioral habituation in invertebrates, it should not be concluded that the waning of responsiveness occurs independent of a physiological substrate. In fact, the use of invertebrates or portions of them as model systems for investigations of the substrates of habituation has become widespread. But it should be noted that the more successful of these models have been based upon detailed descriptions of behavioral habituation with which changes in neural or biochemical activity have been related (e.g., Carew et al., 1972).

References

Abraham, F. D., Palka, J., Peeke, H. V. S., and Willows, A. O. D. (1972). Model neural systems and stratagies for the neurobiology of learning. Behav. Biol. 7, 1–24.

Allabach, L. F. (1905). Some points regarding the behavior of Metridium. Biol. Bull. 10, 35–43.

Applewhite, P. B. (1968a). Non-local nature of habituation in a rotifer and protozoan. Nature 217, 287–288.

Applewhite, P. B. (1968b). Temperature and habituation in a protozoan. Nature (London) 219, 91–92.

Applewhite, P. B. (1971). Similarities in protozoan and flatworm habituation behaviour. Nature (London), New Biol. 230, 284–285.

Applewhite, P. B., and Gardner, F. (1971). A theory of protozoan habituation learning. Nature (London) 230, 285–287.

Applewhite, P. B., and Morowitz, H. J. (1966). The micrometazoa as model systems for studying the physiology of memory. Yale J. Biol. Med. 39, 90–105.

Applewhite, P. B., Gardner, F. T., and Lapan, E. (1969). Physiology of habituation learning in a protozoan. Trans N.Y. Acad. Sci. [2] 31, 842–849.

Balderrama, N., and Maldonado, H. (1971). Habituation of the deimatic response in the mantid (Stagmatoptera biocellata). J. Physiol. Comp. Psychol. 75, 98–106.

Barrass, R. (1961). A quantitative study of the behavior of the male Mormoniella vitripennis (Walker) (Hymenoptera, Pteromalidae) towards two constant stimulus-situations. Behaviour 18, 288–312.

Bohn. G. (1902). Contribution à la psychologie des annelides. Bull. Inst. Gen. Psychol. 2, 317–325.

Carew, T. J., Pinsker, H. M., and Kandel, E. R. (1972). Long-term habituation of a defensive withdrawal reflex in Aplysia. Science 175, 451–454.

Carlton, P. L., and Vogel, J. R. (1967). Habituation and conditioning. J. Comp. Physiol. Psychol. 63, 348–351.

Clark, R. B. (1960a). Habituation of the polychaete Nereis to sudden stimuli. I. General properties of the habituation process. Anim. Behav. 8, 82–91.

Clark, R. B. (1960b). Habituation of the polychaete *Nereis* to sudden stimuli. II. Biological significance of habituation. *Anim. Behav.* **8**, 92–103.

Clark, R. B. (1965). The integrative action of a worm's brain. *Symys. Soc. Exp. Biol.* **20**, 345–379.

Davis, M., and Wagner, A. R. (1969). Habituation of startle response under incremental sequence of stimulus intensities. *J. Comp. Phsyiol. Psychol.* **67**, 486–492.

Denny, M. R., and Ratner, S. C. (1970). "Comparative Psychology; Research in Animal Behavior," rev. ed. Dorsey Press, Homewood, Illinois.

Dethier, V. G., and Stellar, E. (1961). "Animal Behavior." Prentice-Hall, Englewood Cliffs, New Jersey.

Evans, S, M. (1969a). Habituation of the withdrawal response in nereid polychaetes. 1. The habituation process in *Nereis diversicolor*. *Biol. Bull.* **137**, 95–104.

Evans, S. M. (1969b). Habituation of the withdrawal response in nereid polychaetes. 2. Rates of habituation in intact and decerebrate worms. *Biol. Bull.* **137**, 105–117.

Fleure, H. J., and Walton, C. L. (1907). Notes on habits of sea-anemones. *Zool. Anz.* **31**, 212–220.

Folger, H. T. (1925). The quantitative study of reactions to light in amoeba. *J. Exp. Zool.* **41**, 261–292.

Gardner, F. T., and Applewhite, P. B. (1970). Protein and RNA inhibitors and protozoan habituation. *Psychopharmacologia* **16**, 430–433.

Gardner, L. E. (1968). Retention and over-habituation of a dual-component response in *Lumbricus terrestris*. *J. Comp. Physiol. Psychol.* **66**, 315–318.

Gardiner, L. E. (1966). Habituation in the earthworm: Retention and overhabituation Ph. D. Thesis, Michigan State University, E. Lansing, Mich.

Gee, W. (1914). The behavior of leeches with special reference to its modificability. *Science* **39**, 364.

Goldsmith, M. (1927). Acquisition d'un habitude chez le poulpe. *C. R. Acad. Sci.* **164**, 737–738.

Groves, P. M., and Thompson, R. F. (1970). Habituation: A dual-process theory. *Psychol. Rev.* **77**, 419–450.

Gwilliam, G. F. (1965). The mechanism of the shadow reflex in cirripedia. II. Photoreceptor cell response, second order responses, and motor cell output. *Biol. Bull.* **129**, 244–256.

Harden, C. M. (1972) Behavior modification of *Stentor coeruleus*. Unpublished study appearing in corning, W. C., Dyal, J. A., and Willows, A.O.D. (Eds.) Invertebrate Learning." Plenum Press, New York (in press).

Hargitt, C. W. (1909). Further observations on the behavior of tubicolous annelids. *J. Exp. Zool.* **7**, 157–187.

Harlow, H. F. (1958). The evolution of learning. *In* "Behavior and Evolution" (G. G. Simpson and A. Roe, eds.), pp. 269–290. Yale Univ. Press, New Haven, Connecticut.

Harris, J. D. (1943). Habituatory response decrement in the intact organism. *Psychol. Bull.* **40**, 385–422.

Hess, C. (1914). Untersuchung Uber die Lichtsing mariner Wurmer und Kerbse. *Pfluger's Arch. ges. Physiol.* **155**, 421–435.

Hinde, R. A. (1954a). Factors governing the changes in strength of a partially inborn response, as shown by the mobbing behaviour of the chaffinch (*Fringilla coelebs*). I. The nature of the response, and an examination of its course. *Proc. Roy. Soc. Ser. B* **142**, 306–331.

Hinde, R. A. (1954b). Factors governing the changes in the strength of a partially inborn response, as shown by the mobbing behaviour of the chaffinch (*Fringilla coelebs*). II. The waning of the response. *Proc. Roy. Soc. Ser., B* **142**, 331–358.

Hinde, R. A. (1961). Factors governing the changes in the strength of a partially inborn response, as shown by the mobbing behaviour of the chaffiinch (*Fringilla coelebs*). III. The interaction of short term and long term incremental and decremental effects. *Proc. Roy. Soc., Ser. B.* **153**, 398–420.

Hinde, R. A. (1970a). "Animal Behaviour," 2nd ed. McGraw-Hill, New York.

Hinde, R. A. (1970b). Behavioural habituation. *In* "Short-term Changes in Neural Activity and Behaviour" (G. Horn and R. A. Hinde, eds.). p. 3–40 Cambridge Univ. Press, London and New York.

Horn, G., and Hinde, R. A. (1970). Short-term Changes in Neural Activity and Behaviour. Cambridge Univ. Press, London and New York.

Horridge, G. A. (1959). Analysis of the rapid responses of *Nereis* and *Harmothoë* (Annelida). *Proc. Roy. Soc., Ser. B* **150**, 245–262.

Horridge, G. A. (1965). The electrophysiological approach to learning in isolatable ganglia. *Anim. Behav., Suppl.* **1**, 163–182.

Humphrey, G. (1930). Le Chatelier's rule and the problem of habituation and dehabituation in *Helix albolabris. Psychol. Forsch.* **13**, 113–117.

Humphrey, G. (1933). "The Nature of Learning and its Relation to the Living System." Harcourt, New York.

Jennings, H. S. (1902). Studies on reactions to stimuli in unicellular organisms. IX. On the behavior of fixed infusoria. *Amer. J. Physiol.* **8**, 23–60.

Jennings, H. S. (1905). Sea anemones: Modifiability of behavior. *J. Exp. Biol.* **2**, 447.

Jennings, H. S. (1906). "Behavior of the Lower Organisms." Macmillan, New York.

Kimmel, H. D. (1966). Inhibition of the unconditioned response in classical conditioning. *Psychol. Rev.* **73**, 232–240.

Kinastowski, W. (1963a). Der einfluss der mechanischen reize auf die kontrakilitat von *Spirostomum ambiguum* Ehrbg. *Acta Protozool.* **1**, 201–222.

Kinatowski, W. (1963b). Das problem "des lernes" bei *Spirostomum ambiguum* Ehrbg. *Acta Protozool.* **1**, 223–236.

Kinoshita, T. (1911). Uber den einfluss mehrerer aufeinanderfolgender wirksamer reize auf den ablauf der reaktions bewegungen bei wirbellowen. II. Versuche an colenteraten. *Pfluegers Arch. Gesamte Physiol. Menschen Tiere* **57**, 493–552.

Lorenz, K. (1965). "Evolution and Modification of Behavior." Univ. of Chicago Press, Chicago, Illinois.

Lubow, R. E. (1965). Latent inhibition: Effects of frequency of nonreinforced preexposure of the CS. *J. Comp. Physiol. Psychol.* **60**, 454–457.

Maier, N. R. F., and Schneirla, T. C. (1935). "Principles of Animal Psychology." McGraw-Hill, New York.

Menzel, E. W., Jr. (1964). Patterns of responsiveness in chimpanzees reared through infancy under conditions of environmental restrictions *Psychol. Forsch.* **27**, 337–365.

Nagel, W. (1892). Das Geschmacksinn der Actinien *Zool Anz.* **15**, 334–338.

Nagel, W. A. (1894). Experimentelle sinnes physiologische untersuchungen an coelenteraten. *Arch. Gesamte Physiol. Menschen Tiere* **57**, 493–552.

Nicol, J. A. C. (1950). The responses of *Branchiomma vesiculosum* (Montagu) to photic stimulation. *J. Mar. Biol. Ass. U.K.* **29**, 303–320.

Parker, G. H. (1896). The reaction of *Metridium* to food and other substances. *Bull. Mus. Comp. Zool., Harvard Coll.* **29**, 102–119.

Parker, G. H. (1917). Actinian behavior. *J. Exp. Zool.* **22**, 193–230.

Peeke, H. V. S., and Zeiner, A. R. (1970). Habituation to environmental and specific auditory stimuli in the rat. *Commun. Behav. Biol.* **5**, 23–29.

Pieron, H. (1908). Contribution à l'étude des phénomènes sensoriels et du comportment des vertèbres inférieurs. *Bull. Inst. Gen. Psychol.* **8**, 321–327.

Pinsker, H., Kupfermann, I., Castellucci, V., Kandel, E. R. (1970). Habituation and dishabituation of the gill-withdrawal reflex in *Aplysia. Science* **167**, 1740–1742.

Prosser, C. L., and Hunter W. S. (1936). The extinction of startle responses and spinal reflexes in the white rat. *Amer. J. Physiol.* **117**, 609–618.

Ratner, S. C. (1970). Habituation: Research and Theory. *In* "Current Issues in Animal Learning" (J. Reynierse, ed.). p. 55–84. Univ. of Nebraska Press, Lincoln.

Rilling, S., Mittelstaedt, H., and Roeder, K. D. (1959). Prey-recognition in the praying mantis. *Behaviour* **14**, 164–184.

Roeder, K. (1963). "Nerve Cells and Insect Behavior." Harvard Univ. Press, Cambridge, Massachusetts.

Ross, D. M. (1965). The behaviour of sessile coelenterates in relation to some conditioning experiments. *Anim. Behav., Suppl.* **1**, 43–52.

Rullier, F. (1948). La vision et l'habituation chez *Mercierella enigmatica* Fauvel. *Bull. Lab. Mar. Dinard* **30**, 21–27.

Rushforth, N. B. (1965). Behavioural studies of the coelenterate *Hydra pirardi* Brien. *Anim. Behav., Suppl.* **1**, 30–42.

Rushforth, N. B. (1967). Chemical and physical factors affecting behavior in *Hydra*: Interactions among factors affecting behavior in *Hydra. In* "Chemistry and Learning" (W. C. Corning and S. C. Ratner, eds.), pp. 369–390. Plenum, New York.

Szlep, R. (1964). Change in the response of spiders to repeated web vibrations. *Behaviour.* **23**, 203–238.

Thompson, R. F., and Spencer, W. A. (1966). Habituation: A model phenomenon for the study of neuronal substrates of behavior. *Psychol. Rev.* **73**, 16–43.

Thompson, R. F., Groves, P. M., Tyler, T. J., and Roemer, R. A. (1973). A dual-process theory of habituation: Theory and behavior. *In* "Habituation: Behavioral Studies" (H. V. S. Peeke and M. J. Herz, eds.). Academic Press, New York (to be published).

Thrope, W. H. (1956). "Learning and Instinct in Animals." Methuen, London.

Thorpe, W. H. (1963). "Learning and Instinct in Animals." Harvard Univ. Press, Cambridge, Massachusetts.

Verworn, M. (1889). "Psycho-physiologische Protistenstudien." Fisher, Jena.

Wagner, G. (1905). On some movements and reactions on *Hydra. Quart. J. Microsc. Sci.* **48**, 585–622.

Wawrzynczyk. S. (1937). Badania and paiecia *Spirostomum ambiguum* major. *Acta Biol. Exp.* (*Warsaw*) **11**, 57–77.

Wells, M. J. (1961). Centres for tactile and visual learning in the brain of *Octopus. J. Exp. Biol.* **38**, 811–826.

Wells, M. J. (1962) "Brain and Behaviour in Cephalopods." Stanford Univ. Press, Palo Alto. California.

Wendt, G. R. (1936). An interpretation of inhibition and conditioned reflexes as competition between reaction systems. *Psychol. Rev.* **43**, 258–281.

Westerman, R. A. (1963). Somatic inheritance of habituation of responses to light in planarians. *Science* **140**, 676–677.

Wolda, H. (1961). Response decrement in the prey catching activity of *Notoneca glauca* (Heminoptera). *Arch. Neer. Zool.* **14**, 61–89.

Wood, D. C. (1970a). Parametric studies of the response decrement produced by mechanical stimuli in the protozoan, *Stentor coeruleus. J. Neurobiol.* **1**, 345–360.

Wood, D. C. (1970b). Electrophysiological studies of the protozoan *Stentor coeruleus. J. Neurobiol.* **1** 362–377.

Wood, D. C. (1970c). Electrophysiological correlates of the response decrement produced by mechanical stimuli in the protozoan *Stentor coeruleus. J. Neurobiol.* **2**, 1–11.

Yerkes, A. W. (1906). Modification of behavior in *Hydroides dianthus*. *J. Comp. Neurol. Psychol.* **16**, 441–450.

Young, J. Z. (1958). Responses of untrained octopuses to various figures and the effect of removal of the vertical lobe. *Proc. Roy. Soc., Ser. B* **149**, 463–483.

Young. J. Z. (1959). Extinction of unrewarded responses in *Octopus*. *Publ. Sta. Zool. Napoli* **31**, 225–247.

Zanforlin, M. (1969). The inhibition of the light orientating reaction in insects. *Accad. Patavina Sci. Lett. Atti Mem.* **82**, 79–94.

Zanforlin, M. (1970). The inhibition of light orienting reactions in caterpillars of Lymantriidae, *Lymantria dispar* (L.) and *Orgyia antiqua* (L.) (Lepidoptera). *Monitore Zool. Ital.* (N.S.) **4**, 1–19.

Chapter 2

Habituation in Fish with Special Reference to Intraspecific Aggressive Behavior

HARMAN V. S. PEEKE[1] AND SHIRLEY C. PEEKE

I. Introduction

Thorpe, in his phyletically organized review of learning and instinct in animals, found little evidence regarding habituation in fish (1963). The situation has changed in the 10 years since that review was completed. The study of habituation has become central in both behavioral and physiological aspects of psychobiology, and a portion of these studies have utilized fish as experimental preparations. Recent attempts at systematizing available habituation data into theoretical models have been provided by Groves and Thompson (1970; Chapter 6, Volume II), Thompson *et al.* (Chapter 7, this volume), and Ratner (1970). Attempts at providing categorizations of char-

[1] One of the authors (H.V.S.P.) is supported by Mental Health Training Grant No. MH-7082. The research of the author's reported herein was supported in part by NIMH Grant No. MH 19978 and in part by a General Research Support Grant No. FR-05550.

acteristics of habituation have been presented (e.g., Harris, 1943; Thompson and Spencer, 1966), and they have been criticized for being not inclusive enough and, hence, premature and oversimplified (Hinde, 1970). In the hopes of aiding future efforts at systematizing, we have, in the first section of the present paper, attempted to describe studies of habituation in fish by considering four basic characteristics that emerge upon review of the available literature: (1) the ubiquity of demonstrations of habituation in fish, (2) a discussion of the relationship between stimulus parameters and habituation rate, (3) the evidence regarding the recovery of habituated responses, and (4) a discussion of behavioral patterns that covary with responses that wane.

Two different approaches might be followed in a survey of the available literature on habituation in fish. The first emphasizes the effects of varying certain experimental parameters such as interstimulus interval, stimulus intensity, and recovery interval on the rate and amount of habituation across various situational, stimulus and response systems. This approach provides information of the kind discussed in Section II of the present paper. The second approach emphasizes the functional significance of habituation in the natural behavior of the organism; for example, the role of habituation in predatory behavior, or the role in intraspecific aggression and the maintenance of territory. The present paper, in Section III, takes this approach, where studies of habituation of aggressive behavior are assessed as to their consistency with the hypothesis that habituation plays a major role in the modification and maintenance of lowered levels of aggression among adjacently territorial conspecific fish. This functional approach is also seen, to a lesser extent, in the discussions of the characteristics of habituation in Section II.

It is hoped that the two approaches may prove complementary in providing some basic understanding of the roles habituation may play in the behavior of fish.

A. Definitional Considerations

For the purposes of the present chapter, Thorpe's definition of habituation as "... the relatively permanent waning of a response as a result of repeated stimulation which is not followed by any kind of reinforcement..." (1963, p. 61) has been adopted. Thorpe pointed out that the additional characteristics of stimulus specificity and relative permanence are sufficient (at least provisionally) to differentiate habituation from sensory adaptation and fatigue processes. To Thorpe's term "repeated stimulation" should be added "constant stimulation" to allow inclusion of those studies in which the stimulus is presented for fixed periods of time. It has been suggested that the phrase regarding reinforcement is superfluous (Lorenz, 1965); however, this aspect of the definition is of secondary importance. The important features of the definition are the characteristics of permanence and stimulus specificity with regard to the waning of the response. Other definitions, more specific and clearly more operational, may be defended, particularly where the subject matter is more circumscribed such as when the behavior of interest is at the neuronal level, reflex level, or concerns restricted classes of behavior compared across species. However, as Hinde (1970) pointed out, studies of habituation in simple preparations are still lacking in sufficient detail to allow generalizations to be made between simple and complex levels of behavior. Often relationships discovered from spinal studies appear overly simplified when the attempt is made to apply them to behavioral habituation of intact organisms.

Finally, no assumption is necessarily made in this chapter that habituation as we speak of it is a unitary phenomenon. It is likely, as Hinde (1970) pointed out, that habituation is a term reflecting many processes. We use the term in its broadest meaning, leaving the task of enumerating classes and kinds of decremental phenomena we now subsume under the term habituation to a time when there is more data available.

II. Characteristics of Habituation in Fish

A. *Ubiquity of Habituation in Fish*

Insofar as the main purpose of this section is to provide some overview of the range of situations in which habituation may be the underlying behavioral mechanism, we have taken the liberty of referring to work that is, in some cases, too briefly or too poorly described, to clearly differentiate the process described as habituation from some other decremental process. Often, important control groups have been left out, leaving the best interpretation unclear. In any case, we have included them to provide the most complete overview possible.

Habituation to the general environmental situation, where the specific stimuli to which the fish is responding are either unclear or unspecified, is reported by both professional and hobby aquariasts. Welker and Welker (1958) have described initial flight, hiding, and freezing (motionless behavior) when individuals of the marine species *Eucinostomus gula* were introduced to a strange aquarium. This behavior habituated but was easily reinstated. Habituation to disturbances in the general environment such as the introduction of novel objects has been studied by Russell (1967a) where reactions to a novel stimulus were studied with fish having varying degrees of familiarity with their environment. She assumed that more familiarity (habituation) to the general environment would make a novel object more salient and hence would increase exploration of it. Her hypothesis was confirmed. Fish that school (*Brachydania rerio*) and are housed together will school when first introduced into a strange aquarium; this response wanes but is reinstated by introduction of a novel and/or strong stimulus (Breder and Halpern, 1946). These studies, taken together, provide modest experimental substantiation of the common observation that introduction of sudden strong or novel stimuli stops or modifies ongoing behavior and that response to such disruptive stimuli wanes and can be reinstated by repetition of the stimulus.

Habituation to specific stimuli which are assumed to signify the presence of nonaquatic predators has been demonstrated in two studies. Rodgers *et al.* (1963) studied the tail-flip response, which propels the fish rapidly away from the locus of stimulation, in the goldfish *Carassius auratus*. They found that the response could be evoked by either a shadow stimulus or, more effectively, by tapping the side of the aquarium, and that habituation was more easily obtained when the fish were at the bottom than near the surface (presumably where the "predator" was more of a threat). Reinstatement of the response was provided by a harder tap. Russell (1967a) observed that components of the response of the guppy *Lebistes reticulatus* to a shadow stimulus waned with repetition. Such studies provoke the question of the adaptive value of habituation in some situations. However, several points must be made in this regard. First, in neither study did the "escape" response reach zero, and in neither study did the orienting response show much decrement. Also, recovery occurred rather rapidly. In neither case was the stimulus particularly natural and in the case of the study by Rodgers *et al.* (1963), the stimulus elicited responding in only 50% of the administrations before habituation, thus raising the question of the initial adequacy of the stimulus. Further, in nature it may be that suboptimum predatory stimuli occur sufficiently often that some habituation to them is necessary if the fish is to engage in the other activities necessary to survival.

Two unquantified reports and one experimental study indicate that responses to food or prey wane if the food is found to be worthless or the prey unobtainable. Herrick (1924, p. 197) observed that catfish will take in a cotton ball the first few times it is presented but later reject it as food. Triplett (1901) reported that perch *Marone americanus* cease to attack minnows which are protected by a glass plate and removal of the barrier does not imperil the minnows. The goldfish *Carassius auratus* and the paradise fish *Macropodus opercularis* will gradually cease attempting to bite at brine shrimp which are confined in a clear plastic tube (Peeke and Peeke, 1972). As is clear from Fig. 1, such responses show decrements persisting over days and are quite resistant to reinstatement through sensitization and

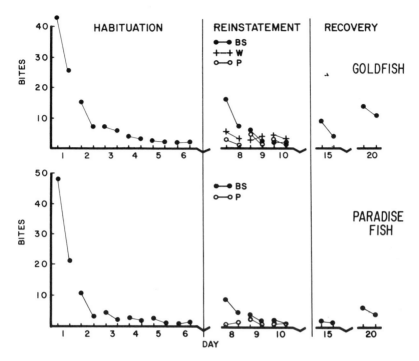

Fig. 1. Frequency of bites at live brine shrimp confined to a clear glass tube during initial habituation over 6 days (panel 1), during reinstatement provided by presenting either live brine shrimp (BS), tubifex worms (W), or pebbles (P) on day 7, testing for responsiveness on days 8, 9, and 10 (panel 2), and during recovery on either day 15 or day 20 (panel 3). Data are presented separately for the goldfish *Carassius auratus* and the paradise fish *Macropodus opercularis*. Connected points are the first and last 5-minute period for each daily 10-minute session (from Peeke and Peeke, 1972).

recovery. They relate their findings to a means whereby the experiental basis of a reward expectancy or search image may be provided.

There is a dearth of information regarding habituation of sexual behavior. Baerends (1957, p. 250) reported that if the male guppy *Lebistes reticulatus* does not elicit a positive sexual response in the female during prolonged courtship, the courtship behavior wanes. There is little additional information concerning the role that habituation may play in the natural sexual behavior of fish.

Although there are a great many studies of the waning of intraspecific aggressive behavior, only a few species have been studied. The Siamese fighting fish *Betta splendens*, while bred by aquariasts for colorful and bountiful plummage, remains as hardy a fighter as its drabber wild forebears in

Southeast Asia where it is used in "sporting" contests in which large sums of money are wagered on the outcome. Baenninger (1966) demonstrated that a *Betta* will avoid confrontation with either a conspecific or a mirror image after being left with these two alternatives for 32 consecutive hours. He interpreted this avoidance as habituation. Clayton and Hinde (1968) recorded several response components in *Bettas* attacking their mirror image, two of which waned over time: frequency of gill cover erection and frequency of tail beats. However, the use of the mirror image as an aggression-eliciting stimulus for this species has been criticized by Peeke and Peeke (1970), who pointed out that the reflected behavior provides aggressive postures not often found in "real" two-fish encounters (Simpson, 1968).

Peeke and Peeke (1970), in a subsequent study with *Betta*, used a live male confined to a clear plastic tube as the aggression-eliciting stimulus. They found more complete waning of both display and biting than was found by Clayton and Hinde. In a more recent study it was found that *Bettas* placed in a large, 128-liter aquarium will reduce the number of attacks on each other over the first 3 hours after initial introduction and will frequently establish "territories" at either end of the aquarium (Johnson and Peeke, 1970). Figler (1970) has contributed data regarding habituation rate (of a short-term variety, showing little retention between days) as a function of elicitation strength of the stimulus in *Betta*. Details of this relationship will be explored below, but his study did provide more evidence for habituation of aggressive responses in *Betta*.

Many of the principles upon which classic ethology is based have arisen from studies of a small, usually anadromous, widely distributed fish, the three-spined stickleback *Gasterosteus aculeatus*. In an early study using crude wooden models as "releasers" for aggressive responses, Peeke, *et al.* (1969) found that biting by territorial males waned over days. The level of initial responding was less than to a natural stimulus as shown in another study (see Fig. 2) which compared rate of waning between a wooden model and a live conspecific confined in a clear plastic tube (Peeke, 1969). This study demonstrated that "charges" at the stimulus and bites waned both between and over days, but that "orientations" toward the stimulus showed somewhat less waning. Van den Assem and van der Molen (1969) studied waning of aggressive behavior in adjacently territorial sticklebacks, some of which were separated by a transparent barrier and others were not. They found that such exposure did result in lowering of the aggressive tendency in both conditions as measured by the resident fish's response to a "standard test" (a male confined to a clear glass tube presented in the territory for 3 minutes). This method is somewhat indirect, and no direct measures of the behavior between the two adjacently territorial fish were provided.

Recently we have begun a series of studies of habituation of aggressive

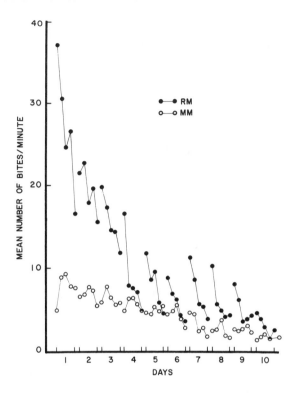

Fig. 2. Mean number of bites per minute delivered at the stimulus by a male three-spined stickleback, *Gasterosteus aculeatus*, for a group presented with a real, male conspecific confined to a glass tube (RM) and a group presented with a crude wood model male (MM) moved in a circular path in the territory of the subject fish. Each point represents the average of 3 successive minutes (from Peeke, 1969).

behavior using the convict cichlid *Cichlasoma nigrofasciatum*. It has been demonstrated that convict cichlid males, placed in a large tank divided by parallel opaque and transparent partitions, will habituate their mutual aggressive behavior when the opaque partition is removed, and that such waning occurs both when the partition is removed completely or is removed for only 20 minutes/day (Peeke *et al.*, 1971). Furthermore, both display and biting behavior wanes, but at differential rates. In a further study (Gallagher *et al.*, 1972) it was found that the preexperimental isolation imposed upon the fish in the Peeke *et al.* study was not a factor in either the initial level or the rate of waning of the aggressive responses. Gallagher *et al.* (1972) demonstrated that placing a conspecific (male or female), a paradise fish, or any other fish in a separate but transparent section of the experimental compartments did not affect the rate of waning, but it did reduce the initial timidity toward an adjacently territorial conspecific. Further, unpublished work in our laboratory has shown that male–female pairs of convict cichlids will maintain a territory and breed in the laboratory as they do in the wild (Meral and Barlow, 1971) and that, housed in this fashion, they also habituate their aggressive behavior to adjacently territorial pairs.

In summary, it is clear that in a wide variety of situations there is ample evidence that the response to various stimuli can be lowered by repeated or continuous exposure to those stimuli. This process is characteristically called habituation. It is by no means clear whether or not habituation or some similar decremental process plays an important role in the behavior of some or all fish, or, if it does, in what kind of behavior it is important. However, in the laboratory, certain operations can be performed under which waning of a variety of responses occurs and these operations appear to be consistent with the operational specifications of habituation.

B. Stimulus Parameters and Habituation Rate

I. Measurement Problems

Several authors have noted the measurement problems encountered in comparing the effects of differing intensities, frequencies, and schedules of stimuli on amount of habituation (Groves and Thompson, 1970; Hinde, 1970; Figler, 1970; Davis and Wagner, 1968, 1969). Such problems are frequently definitional ones since the amount of decrement can be assessed by referring to (1) the absolute amount of decline of response, (2) the relative amount of decline, or (3) other measures such as the number of presentations of the stimulus required for the response to reach zero. An illustration of how the method of assessment can produce opposing results is seen in Groves and Thompson's position that "... relative habituation (habituation measured under constant stimulus intensity conditions) is inversely related to the habituation stimulus intensity, but that absolute degree of habituation (determined by varying the test stimulus relative to the habituation stimulus) is directly related to the habituation intensity..." (1970, p. 425).

Figler (1970), concerned that the use of absolute amount of habituation does not make allowance for the different initial levels of responding, suggested use of a proportional measure of decrement with the initial response level as the anchor point.

Hinde (1970), while discussing at length the relationship between rate of waning and method of assessment, was also concerned about another measurement problem, the applicability to individuals of generalizations drawn from group data. Hinde maintained that although data grouped across time intervals or individuals result in a smooth curve, individual records commonly show oscillations and patterns of bursts. Such fluctuations may reveal information about underlying processes that are obscured by grouping.

Until these measurement problems are clarified and perhaps until some formal or informal conventions are adopted, few parametric studies are likely to be done. This restriction may be reflected in the relatively few studies of habituation in fish which are parametric in nature. Figler (1970), studying the effect of stimulus intensity on rate of waning, reported that the strength of the initial eliciting stimulus is inversely related to the proportion of across-session-decrement (i.e., the stronger the initial response, the smaller the decrement). Peeke (1969), however, found that both within and between days response decrement was greater for the strong stimulus than for the weak one (for both absolute and relative measures). This difference in results may be because of differences in schedules of stimulus presentation, species or type of response recorded. Whatever the case, such differences indicate that the relationship between stimulus intensity and rate of waning is not simple and universal even when method of assessment is held constant.

2. STRENGTH AND NATURALNESS OF THE STIMULUS

Thompson and Spencer (1966) suggested that a relatively simple relationship exists between stimulus strength and elicitation and waning of the response where the weaker the stimulus, the more rapid the habituation. Their observations were based primarily on waning of behavior at the reflex level. Examination of more complex forms of behavior suggests that strong stimuli may produce qualitatively different effects than weak stimuli. For example, in the study of aggressive responses, the use of models of male fish has been found to produce lower levels of responding and faster habituation than presentation of confined live male fish stimuli (Peeke, 1969); however, the number of sexual responses directed toward a female in daily sex tests increased in the group receiving a live male stimulus and showed no change in the model group. Such an interaction between waning of aggressive responses and increase in sexuality could only be observed with a live male stimulus although the model stimulus had been adequate to elicit aggressive attacks.

A stimulus used more often than models to elicit aggression is the mirror image of the subject fish. Baenninger (1966), Clayton and Hinde (1968), and Figler (1970) reported waning of aggressive responses displayed to such a stimulus; however, Clayton and Hinde reported that while the aggressive display showed significant waning the bite frequency did not. Peeke and Peeke (1970), working with the same species (*Betta splendens*), used a live male fish confined to a tube as the stimulus and found significant waning with both aggressive display and bite frequency. Such differences can perhaps be attributed to the unnaturalness of the mirror image stimulus.

If such differences (both quantitative and qualitative) are found with models, mirror images, and live male fish confined to a tube, we must likewise expect to find differences when live males are allowed to interact freely rather than through a barrier such as a transparent tube. So far, few studies of freely interacting fish have been reported. Van den Assem and van der Molen (1969) report that sticklebacks allowed to freely interact with a rival neighbor showed a slightly slower waning of aggression during the standard aggression test (where a male fish is confined to a tube and introduced into the subject's territory for 3 minutes/day) than those who could interact with the rival only through a transparent barrier. However, this study does not report the level of aggression directed toward the rival neighbor in the two situations and whether or not it has waned. Such information would be more useful in determining the role of the naturalness of the stimulus on elicitation and waning of aggression since it would not require the assumption of generalization of habituation from the rival to the confined male.

Finally, in the study of the tail-flip response to a predatory stimulus by Rodgers et al. (1963), a tap on the aquarium wall alone was sufficient to elicit the response, as was a visual shadow stimulus, and habituation occurred readily in both cases; however, when the two stimuli were presented together (presumably providing a much more convincing portrayal of a large predatory bird striking the surface of the water) many more responses were elicited and there was little evidence of habituation in 10 days. The two stimuli together provided a markedly different effect than either stimulus alone.

These reports suggest that while some information is gained by the use of a stimulus consisting of some prominent feature of a natural stimulus, the results of such studies must be interpreted with caution since they might not be applicable to a more natural situation. Also relevant here is Lorenz (1965, p. 52) suggestion that the ease with which habituation is attained in the laboratory as compared with the field situation is the result of relative constancy of the experimental situation.

Another dimension of the relationship between strength and naturalness of the stimulus and rate of habituation derives from Seligman's recent paper (1970) regarding the basic assumption that has previously permeated studies of associative learning, i.e., that all stimuli are qualitatively equally capable of being associated. Instead, Seligman suggested, stimuli may be ordered on a continuum from those very "prepared" to be associated to those "contra-prepared", the assumption being that concepts such as meaningfulness of the stimuli to the organism imply differential conditionability in the service of individual and species survival. A similar notion is suggested here. It may be that some stimulus—response units are prepared to habituate while others are located at the other end of the continuum (contraprepared). This would complicate the notion of what produces faster or slower habituation and would likely require some specification of stimuli along both an intensity and preparedness continuum.

It seems clear that the relationship between strength and/or naturalness of the eliciting stimulus and the rate of waning of the response must take into account both quantitative and qualitative aspects of both the stimuli and the responses as well as the rate of waning.

3. STIMULUS PRESENTATION SCHEDULES

Studies comparing the effect of different rates of stimulus presentation report varying results with some responses being affected differently from others. Russell (1967b), studying the jerk response to a shadow stimulus in guppies, presented the stimulus at intervals of 15 seconds, 2 minutes and 4 minutes. The 15-second interval resulted in a more complete and rapid decrease in jerk frequency than the 2- and 4-minute intervals which gave very similar results. However, the freezing response to the shadow was relatively independent of stimulus frequency and, in fact, persisted longer with the 15-second group than with the 2- and 4-minute groups. This result suggests that even though the jerk response had habituated, the level of fear to the shadow stimulus remained high. This is a strong argument for the measurement of multiple response components in the analysis of any response system.

Massed and distributed rates of presentation were compared by Peeke and Peeke (1970), who studied waning of aggression by presenting one group with a 15-minute presentation of a rival male each day for 20 days and a second group with a 1-hour presentation per day for 5 days. The total duration of stimulus presentation was the same for both groups (5 hours) but distributed experience led to more rapid habituation than massed experience, an effect contrary to the usual result with experimental extinction of learned responses. Furthermore, biting and two aspects of display (gill covers erect and fin extension) showed different patterns of waning in the two groups, suggesting that multiple processes underlie the rate of habituation.

Peeke et al. (1971) also studied waning of aggression to a rival male by exposing one group of cichlids to the rival for 20 minutes/day for 38–44 days and by exposing another group continuously for 24–28 hours. They found that both biting and display measures waned at a faster rate in the massed exposure group than in the distributed exposure group, a result contrary to that found by Peeke and Peeke (1970) in *Bettas*. Since the "massed" exposure group was 1 hour in the Peeke and Peeke study, it falls between the two exposure periods used by Peeke et al. and might indicate that the effect is a reflection of a U-shaped function; i.e., very short and very long periods produce faster habituation. The use of a larger number of exposure periods in the same species would help to answer this question.

4. Additional Factors Affecting Habituation

It was pointed out earlier that the initial response to a new environment is fear in the form of flight, hiding, or freezing responses which habituate but are readily reinstated by sudden or novel stimuli. Since many of the predatory, aggressive, or sexual stimuli to which fish are exposed during habituation studies are sudden or novel stimuli, it is clear that the sort of response elicited by those stimuli depends in part on the degree of adaptation to the environment. When the environment is strange, the rate of habituation to a stimulus must represent an interaction between the natural course of the response to the stimulus and residual fear of the environment.

A related factor, isolation, seems to prolong the occurrence of fear responses to environmental change. Barlow (1968) has designed a technique to reduce such fear responses called "dither" which consists of placing small, active fish of a different species in a transparent compartment of the experimental tank. Another method, also suggested by Barlow, consists of applying vibratory stimulation to the aquarium at irregular intervals during weekends when normal laboratory stimulation is lacking. Fish treated this way appear to be less skittish on Monday mornings and respond to stimuli at more representative levels. Barlow's report illustrates the disrupting effect of changes in level of environmental stimulation and serves as a reminder that the fish's environment includes visual and vibratory stimuli outside the aquarium.

The effect of social isolation on aggressiveness toward a neighbor was studied by Gallagher et al. (1972). Two males, separated by opaque partitions, were allowed to view a third fish (conspecific or different species) in a nearby chamber for several days or were kept isolated. When the opaque partition separating the two males was removed, isolates were much slower to approach the rival male than those not isolated, although once they began to fight both groups were equally aggressive.

C. Recovery from Habituation

Recovery of responsiveness following habituation has not been systematically investigated in studies of fish behavior. The few studies that have included recovery data seem to have added that operation as an afterthought. Russell (1967b) found that after habituation of Lebistes to a shadow stimulus repeated every 2 minutes, the response recovered to 66% of its initial value after a 2 hour recovery interval. Peeke and Peeke (1972) found that the habituated predatory response of biting a brine shrimp protected by a plastic barrier recovered more slowly in one species of fish (*Macropodis opercularis*) than in another (*Carassius auratus*) (see Fig. 1). The first species, *Macropodis*, recovered to only 4% of the peak responsivity after 5 days and to only 14% after 10 days. *Carassius*, on the other hand, recovered to 17% after 5 days and to 34% after 10 days. Clayton and Hinde (1968) found that chin display in their *Bettas* (which were habituated for 10 days to their own mirror image) recovered after 4 days rest to 65% of initial level. Figler (1970) demonstrated near complete recovery between days in a study also using *Bettas*, although such complete recovery between days suggests that Figler's habituation may have differed qualitatively from the other studies discussed since retention between days is frequently considered a criterion of habituation in similar studies. Finally, Peeke *et al.* (1971), studying habituation of conspecific aggressive behaviors in convict cichlids, found that the display (the response which habituated earliest and to the lowest level) recovered to 85% of the peak level of responsivity after a 21-day rest interval, whereas bites (which did not habituate as rapidly or completely) showed little recovery.

Such scattered evidence is not sufficient to make any confident statement regarding recovery from habituation in fish. The suggestion of a function that seems to be emerging, however, is that recovery is rapid and relatively more complete when the original habituation is accomplished by single session, short-term, constant stimulation (e.g., Figler 1970) or by massed, short, intertrial interval presentations of repeated stimulation (e.g., Russell, 1967a). More complete habituation brought about by multi-exposure, longer session methods (e.g., Clayton and Hinde, 1968; Peeke and Peeke, 1970; Peeke *et al.*, 1971) is more resistant to recovery. The preliminary conclusion appears to be that recovery rate is a negative function of relative completeness of habituation.

D. Covariant Behavioral Patterns during Habituation

When more than one measure of behavior is recorded simultaneously, one frequently finds that the various components differ in rate and degree of waning, if indeed waning occurs at all. [Increments rather than decrements in various components of behavior are reported often enough that many (e.g., Hinde, 1970; Groves and Thompson, 1970) suggest that response to repeated stimulation has both incremental and decremental aspects.] An example of such combined effects is the Clayton and Hinde (1968) study in which aggressive responses of *Bettas* to their mirror images were recorded. Two measures (frequency of gill cover erection and tail beats) waned over 10 days of continuous stimulation while two other measures (mean duration of gill cover erection and biting) showed a slight increment. Another example is a study by Russell (1967a) of the response by *Lebistes reticulatus* to a shadow stimulus. An initial jerk response (a "disorganized" flight) is followed by freezing. While the jerk response showed gradual waning, the freeze response showed an initial increase in duration followed by a slow diminution. Hinde (1970) suggested that the presence of simultaneous decremental and incremental effects indicates that multiple processes are responsible for a given level of behavior and that even during waning, incremental effects may be present although concealed (pp. 3–40). A similar position is held by Groves and Thompson (1970) and Thompson *et al.* (Chapter 7, this volume), who maintained that habituation and sensitization are independent processes which interact to produce the final behavioral outcome and that dishabituation is a case of sensitization of a previously habituated response.

When considering only the decremental aspects of a response, most often it seems to be the more vigorous components that wane first, followed to a less complete degree by the less vigorous components such as orientations. Thus, Rodgers *et al.* (1963) found that the tail-flip response to a "predatory" stimulus (tap on the tank) waned rapidly compared to the orientation response which only declined to 50% of initial level after the fifteenth day of stimulation. Peeke (1969), in a study of aggressive response of the stickleback toward a male stimulus, found that charges toward the stimulus waned first, followed by bites, and finally (to a much lesser extent), by orientations. While bites declined to about 15% of the initial level on day 10, orientations were still at 50% of the initial level. Peeke and Peeke (1970), using *Bettas*, found that bites directed at a male stimulus had declined to zero by day 7, whereas a low level of display was still present at day 20. However, in studies of aggression between two cichlids with adjacent territories (Peeke *et al.*, 1971; Gallagher *et al.*, 1972), the aggressive display waned first and biting first increased and then decreased (see Fig. 3). Biting reached its zenith only after the display began to wane, suggesting the hypothesis that display might serve as a remote warning by appearing first, and that biting follows only after the display fails to convince the antagonist to flee. Such differences in the rate with which various components wane might reflect species differences and/or differences in experimental methods.

There also are reports of incremental and decremental effects which cut across different motivational systems. For example, Peeke (1969) reported that as aggressive response toward the male stickleback declined with repeated stimulation, the sexual responses toward a female stimulus increased. A similar interaction is reported by van den Assem and van der Molen (1969) who studied rival sticklebacks with adjoining territories. These results have been interpreted as support for Sevenster's (1961) contention

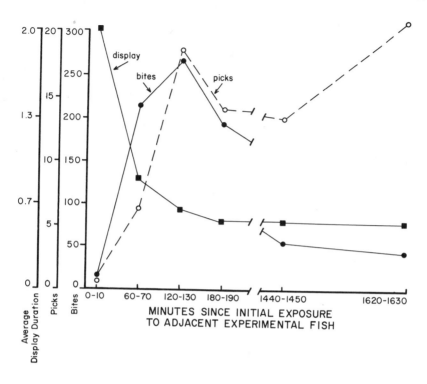

Fig. 3. Changes in rate of response for three behaviors of the cichlid *Cichlasoma nigro-fasciatum* during habituation of the aggressive responses directed at a conspecific territorial neighbor. Note differential rates of waning for bites and display and the increase in responses for picks (from Gallagher *et al.*, 1972).

that courtship and aggression act as antagonistic behavioral systems in the stickleback and that if aggressive stimuli become less effective as a result of waning, one of the main factors that make the occurrence of sexual responses improbable would be cancelled.

Another instance of the presence of antagonistic patterns of behavior is reported by Heiligenberg (1965) with the cichlid *Pelmatochromis sub-ocellatus kribensis*, where he found that sifting the substrate (an eating movement) was followed by a high frequency of attack bouts on a rival, whereas digging movements did not lead to increase in attack bouts. Heiligenberg suggested that digging is a substitute behavior for attacking and reduces the readiness to attack, whereas sifting does not. A similar finding was reported in another cichlid *C. nigrofasciatum* by Gallagher *et al.* (1972). As shown in Fig. 3, they found that as the two measures of aggression (biting and display) waned, "picks" at the substrate increased and remained high 24 hours later, after the aggressive responses had declined to a low level. Such picks might be analogous to the digging behavior reported by Heiligenberg and might be viewed as support for his interpretation.

It seems clear that changes in response to a constant or repeated stimulus lead to changes in many responses, decrements in some, increments in others. It is likely that more will be learned regarding the relationship between habituation and the complexities of behavior by observing and monitoring several responses rather than only one.

III. Habituation and Intraspecific Territorial Aggression

In this section, we will explore the hypothesis that habituation, as an adaptive modification of behavior, is the major process involved in the reduction of aggressive behavior between neighboring territorial conspecifics. Interest in studying the decremental process involved in the maintenance of lowered aggression stems from the observation that many territorial fish, during initial phases of pairing and territory establishment, appear to engage in frequent bouts of threatening and fighting directed at both sexes of the species. This fighting subsides within a short time until violent aggressive interactions are primarily restricted to attacks on an unfamiliar intruder when the territory is violated. Such an overview is reported by Baerends and Baerends-van Roon (1950) with cichlids and by van den Assem and van der Molen (1969) with the three-spined stickleback, and it has been substantiated in our laboratory with both sticklebacks and cichlids.

Processes other than habituation, such as flight and "surrender" (assuming an "attitude of inferiority"), which also result in a reduction in fighting in laboratory situations occur primarily in fights between intruder and resident of the territory. These latter processes are of less consequence in aggression between neighboring resident conspecifics since either flight (other than just back into one's own territory after an incursion) or surrender would probably result in the loss of territory. While this probably occurs to a limited extent, we are most concerned with the process that enables two antagonists to maintain neighboring territories without constant fighting while still being able to drive off intruders.

Lorenz (1964), addressing himself to the problem of how territorial pairs of cichlids were able to maintain a readiness to drive off intruding conspecifics while not attacking one another, hypothesized that habituation was the process evolved to aid in aggression reduction. Lorenz hypothesized two factors, both presumably inhibitory, to explain the "redirection" of aggression from mate to intruder. The first is concurrent sexual motivation and the second is habituation to the mate, a process requiring a faculty of individual recognition (p. 45). He later suggested that ". . . selective habituation to all stimuli emanating from individually known members of the species is probably the prerequisite for the origin of every personal bond . . ." (1966, p. 156). Similarly, Baerends and Baerends-van Roon (1950) reported that in partners that have been together for a long time, fighting is often inhibited and ". . . the fact that the mates often know each other personally . . . is responsible for the inhibition of the hostility in the male. . ." (p. 125).

Personal recognition, a factor of such importance for the inhibition of fighting in pairs, has also been hypothesized for neighboring territorial conspecifics. Baerends and Baerends-van Roon suggested that ". . . as a fish cannot keep all its neighbors constantly in sight, it has to recognize them either by their way of approach or by personal characteristics. . ." (1950, p. 89). Such personal recognition presumably would allow habituation to take place to the neighbor, thus reducing boundary fighting. The importance of habituation in diminution of fighting in territorial fish can be approached experimentally. One strategy used to test this hypothesis is that in which the probability of the correctness of the hypothesis is increased with each affirmative result. However, each instance of a negative result would eliminate or severely restrict the hypothesized role of habituation in the maintenance of lowered aggressive interactions.

Several questions are of particular importance in clarifying the role of habituation in aggressive interactions: (1) the representativeness (in species and situation) of habituation of aggressive behavior, (2) the stimulus specificity of habituation, (3) rate of recovery from habituation, (4) effect of stimulus strength on habituation, and (5) interactions between fluctuations in aggression and habituation.

A. Representativeness of Habituation

Restricted representativeness of habituation among species would raise questions as to the generality of the adaptive mechanism being studied. Finding that the mechanism exists in only a restricted class of fish would limit its usefulness as a mechanism to be postulated in a broader theory of aggressive behavior and territorial defense. In terms of species generality, the hypothesis appears viable. Habituation of intraspecific aggression has been demonstrated in members of three different families (Gasterosteus, Belontodea, and Cichlidae, see above). Situations in which habituation of aggression has been observed are also diverse and include habituation of fighting at artificially demarcated boundaries, habituation in free fight situations, habituation to a conspecific intruder in a transparent tube, models of conspecifics, and habituation to a mirror image stimulus.

B. Stimulus Specificity

Waning of aggressive tendencies toward an adjacently territorial rival would clearly provide an advantage for the species involved insofar as the territorial integrity could be maintained with less energy and time spent in border disputes enabling the fish to devote more time to behavior necessary to reproduction and species survival. However, such habituation must show some discrimination. If habituation to one rival were to generalize to all conspecifics, the territory would quickly be usurped by another fish, resulting in loss of eggs or young. Casual observation suggests that habituation of fighting is discriminable with some fish being attacked while others, often closer to the nest, are granted some immunity.

More formal observation of the specificity of habituation in territorial defense is provided by Kirchshofer (1953) who observed a mouth-breeding cichlid of North Africa. Members of this species build nests close to one another providing very small territories, just big enough for the pit containing the nest. Kirchshofer tagged each member of the population he was studying and was able to demonstrate that the males did not aggress against the near neighbors, but they could discriminate the strangers and would attack them.

If habituation does not generalize from one male conspecific to another the basis of the discrimination could be either individual cues (morphological or behavioral) or situation-geographic cues. The individual-cues hypothesis assumes that each individual fish looks and behaves in a characteristic manner [or perhaps, as Baerends and Baerends-van Roon suggested (1950, p. 89), all territorial fish behave in a characteristic way] and that habituation takes place to these characteristic stimuli. Wandering, nonterritorial fish elicit aggression because their behavior is unfamiliar or does not have the territorial characteristics. The situation-geographic hypothesis assumes that habituation is specific to the place (e.g., to any fish on the side near a clump of weeds) or to the situation (e.g., to any fish contained in a tube).

A laboratory test of the individual-cues hypothesis and situation-geographic hypothesis has been provided by Peeke and Veno (1973) (see Fig. 4) in a study of the ability of territorial three-spined sticklebacks to discriminate between antagonists to whom they had been previously habituated and those to whom they had not. Resident males were habituated for 30 minutes to a male "intruder" confined in a clear glass tube in a specific location in the tank (session 1). After a 15-minute interpolated rest period, session 2 was presented in which the tube was reintroduced into the tank in

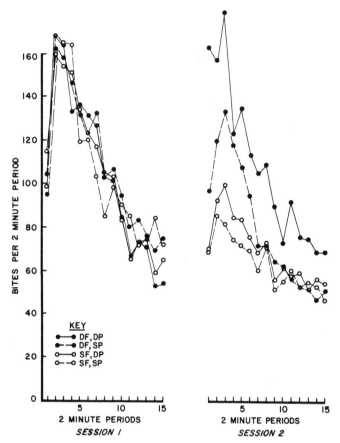

Fig. 4. Initial habituation (session 1) and rehabituation (session 2) of biting response by a male three-spined stickleback *Gasterosteus aculeatus* delivered to a live, male conspecific. Responsivity during session 2 is differentially affected depending upon familiarity, either through different place of presentation of the same stimulus fish as used in session 1 (SF, DP), presentation of a different fish at the same place (DF, SP), or whether both place and fish were altered (DF, DP). These groups may be compared to simple continuation of habituation to the same stimulus fish presented at the same place (SF, SP) (from Peeke and Veno, 1973).

either the same location or a different location and containing either the same stimulus fish or a different one.[2] Thus, four experimental conditions resulted in session 2; (1) different fish, different place (DF, DP); (2) different fish, same place (DF, SP); (3) same fish, different place (SF, DP) and; (4)

[2] When a different stimulus fish was presented, it was one which had been previously presented for 30 minutes to another territorial male in order to control for the effect of previous exposure on responsiveness of the stimulus fish; that is, the "same" and "different" stimulus fish had comparable experience prior to session 2.

same fish, same place (SF, SP). As illustrated in Fig. 4, the results indicate that varying either the location or the fish resulted in a resurgence of aggression (groups 2 and 3) with the greater effect resulting from a varied fish rather than a varied location. However, varying both the fish and the location (group 1) resulted in complete reinstatement of aggression with no savings in rate of habituation resulting from the first session's experience. On the other hand, presenting the same fish in the same location (group 4) caused no resurgence in aggression but rather continued habituation. These results indicate that habituation generalizes to some extent to the same fish in a new location and, to a lesser extent, to a different fish in the same location, and not at all to a different fish in a new location. Thus, individual recognition seems to have occurred in this study, at least to a limited degree.

A study by Gallagher *et al.* (1972) also suggests that habituation to one fish does not generalize significantly to another fish. In this study rival males were exposed constantly to another fish in a transparent chamber which was either a male conspecific or a fish of another species. The type of fish kept in the chamber had no effect on the amount of aggression directed at the rival male when the opaque partition between them was removed. Since more aggression would be elicited by a male conspecific in the chamber, it was assumed that more habituation of aggression would occur as well. However, no effect on responsiveness to the rival male was observed, suggesting that habituation of aggression to the chamber fish did not diminish aggression to the rival. But since observation of amount of response toward the chamber fish was not kept, the degree of habituation toward the conspecific in the chamber is not known.

However, a report by van den Assem and van der Molen (1969) can be interpreted as suggesting lack of discrimination between two male conspecifics by the resident male. They found that constant exposure to a rival male in a neighboring territory resulted in reduced responsiveness to a standard test male presented in a glass tube. Such reduction in response to the test male was not found in a control group which had been constantly exposed to a goldfish. The implication is that in the group with a conspecific as a neighbor, aggression habituated to the neighbor and then generalized to the test male. In the control group no aggression was elicited by the goldfish; consequently, no habituation took place and responding to the test male persisted. This interpretation is questionable, however, because observations were not made as to the response to the rival male, and consequently it is not known whether or not habituation took place to the rival. Similarity in geographical location of test male and rival male is also a factor since it is likely from the results of the Peeke and Veno study (referred to above) that habituation to a rival male would generalize to a test male more easily if the two appear in the same location in the tank.

In van den Assem and van der Molen's study the test male's tube was usually placed next to the glass partition separating the rivals, hence increasing the likelihood to generalization of habituation from rival to test male. The disparity of findings between these two studies might be explained by several differences. In one case (van den Assem and van der Molen) the habituation ostensibly took place to a resident of a territory and the generalization was to an intruder in a tube. In the other case (Gallagher *et al.*), the habituation ostensibly took place to a resident of a territory (the chamber fish) and the generalization test was also to a resident of a territory (the rival male). As Baerends and Baerends-van Roon (1950) pointed out, boundary fights in cichlids between neighboring residents take a different form than intraterritorial fights between a resident and an intruder. The same may be true for sticklebacks. The type of fighting used is determined by the behavior of the antagonist (Baerends and Baerends-van Roon, 1950, p. 80). It is likely that rate and degree of habituation would differ in the two types of fighting, and the amount of generalization of habituation from one type of aggressive encounter to the other would be likely to vary as well.

Experiments for testing the two hypotheses (individual and situation-geographic cues) are easily conceived; however, a positive result with one species cannot necessarily be generalized to another species since it is quite possible that various species use different mechanisms for making discriminations. In order to support the general notion that habituation is important in reducing intraspecies conflict, it is only necessary to show that discrimination occurs somehow in each species—it need not necessarily be the same mechanism in all species. If there is lack of discrimination, then the only way that habituation could still be involved in reducing intraspecies conflict is if recovery is very rapid.

C. Recovery from Habituation

In considering the hypothesis that habituation is an important process underlying the diminution of aggression between territorial conspecifics, the tendency for a male to show discrimination in his habituation to other males was considered of crucial importance unless the rate of recovery from habituation were rapid. Generalized habituation plus a slow rate of recovery would provide a rather unstable social structure where a male who had previously habituated his aggression to his neighbors would lose his territory to a more aggressive intruder, who in turn would habituate his aggression and lose the territory again. With even moderate population density, such a situation would make it impossible for the parents to hold the territory for the requisite number of days to rear their fry.

The evidence existing regarding recovery from habituation in fish indicates that habituation has relatively long-lasting effects with recovery being incomplete for a number of days. Clayton and Hinde (1968), using constant stimulation by a mirror image for 10 days, found that recovery was still incomplete after 48 hours. Peeke *et al.* (1971), in a study of boundary fighting in cichlids, failed to find complete recovery of biting after 21 days. It is possible, however, that these experiments produced a more profound decrement than might occur in nature. Figler (1970), as discussed in Section 11, found relatively complete recovery overnight after 40 minutes of stimulus exposure. These studies indicate that long rather than short time constants might prevail for recovery from habituation, and the question of stimulus specificity of habituation remains of crucial importance to the role of habituation.

D. Stimulus Strength

It has often been held that strong stimuli are more resistant to habituation and that some stimuli are strong enough to resist habituation altogether (Thompson and Spencer, 1966). However, of importance to the hypothesis under consideration is the fact that there is, so far, no example of a naturally occurring aggression-eliciting stimulus that fails to habituate. If such a stimulus existed, this theory would predict a species that spent all of its time fighting, defending, and enlarging territories with no time for courtship and rearing of young.

E. Fluctuations in Aggression and Habituation

While studies of aggressive interaction between territorial neighbors imply a gradual but steady diminution in aggression, in fact, such a description is only an abstraction from the real situation. Our observations of convict cichlid pairs in free fighting situations reveal the occurrence of frequent bouts of increased fighting and occasional changes in territorial boundaries punctuating an overall decrease in aggression. Such temporary resurgences of aggression can be interpreted as dishabituation or sensitization depending on whether or not habituation has previously taken place.[3] One study in progress in our laboratory indicates that resurgence in aggression toward a neighboring pair (previously habituated to) is correlated

---

[3] Groves and Thompson (1970) maintained that the terms dishabituation and sensitization actually refer to the same underlying process and that the only means for distinguishing between them is via their operational definitions where dishabituation refers to a resurgence in a previously habituated response and sensitization refers to an increase in response regardless of whether or not habituation has taken place. Whether or not the underlying process is the same in the two situations has not yet been unequivocally established.

with passing from the courtship stage to the egg laying stage. Another study (also in progress) suggests a sensitization process insofar as habituation had not previously taken place when an increase in aggression toward a stimulus fish was observed as the pair passed from courtship to egg laying and again when the larvae became free fry. This example is probably only one of a number of motivational or environmental changes which might dishabituate or sensitize aggressive responses.

F. Habituation of Intraspecific Territorial Aggression: Summary

The hypothesis that habituation is the process that enables territorial fish to diminish fighting with their neighbors while still maintaining a readiness to fight off intruders was explored by considering several aspects of habituation of aggression that are of crucial importance to the hypothesis. It was pointed out that habituation of intraspecific aggression is found in representatives of at least three families of teleosts and in a variety of experimental situations, suggesting that the findings are not restricted to a single species or method.

Of particular importance is the necessity for stimulus specificity of habituation, although the basis for the discrimination need not be personal recognition but may be based on behavioral, situational, or geographic cues. Lack of stimulus specificity could be tolerated if recovery from habituation of aggression were sufficiently rapid. However, available data indicate that recovery is slow and incomplete for long periods. Evidence with regard to stimulus specificity is somewhat in conflict at the present time, but it appears that a high degree of specificity is likely.

It is clear that habituation is not the only process involved in the modification of intraspecific aggression. Fish probably more often flee from aggressive overtures of other fish than perform any other response that would lead to habituation, and in confined situations such as the small laboratory tank various forms of surrender are also prevalent. With these reservations in mind, however, we conclude that habituation remains a viable candidate for the process involved in the reduction of fighting between territorial neighbors, thereby allowing other behavior such as mating and care of fry to be performed in the service of species survival.

References

Baenninger, R. (1966). Waning of aggressive motivation in *Betta splendens*. *Psychon. Sci.* **4**, 241–242.

Baerends, G. P. (1957). The ethological analysis of fish behavior. *In* "The Physiology of Fishes" (M. E. Brown, ed.), Vol. 2, pp. 229–270. Academic Press, New York.

Baerends, G. P., and Baerends-van Roon, J. M. (1950). An introduction to the study of the ethology of cichlid fishes. *Behaviour, Suppl.* **1**, 1–242.

Barlow, G. W. (1968). Dither: A way to reduce undesirable fright behavior in ethological studies. *Z. Tierpsychol.* **25**, 315–318.

Breder, C. M., and Halpern, F. (1946). Innate and acquired behaviour affecting the aggregation of fishes. *Physiol. Zool.* **19**, 154–190.

Clayton, F. L., and Hinde, R. A. (1968). Habituation and recovery of aggressive display in *Betta splendens. Behaviour* **30**, 96–106.

Davis, M., and Wagner, A. R. (1968). Startle responsiveness after habituation to different intensities of tone. *Psychon. Sci.* **12**, 337–338.

Davis, M., and Wagner, A. R. (1969). Habituation of startle response under incremental sequence of stimulus intensities. *J. comp. Physiol. Psychol.* **67**, 486–492.

Figler, M. H. (1970). The intensity, habituation, and retention of habituation of the threat display in male *Betta splendens* (Regan) as a function of eliciting stimuli. Unpublished Doctoral Dissertation, Michigan State University, East Lansing.

Gallagher, J. E., Herz, M. J., and Peeke, H. V. S. (1972). Habituation of aggression: The effects of visual social stimuli on behavior between adjacently territorial convict cichlids (*Cichlasoma nigrofasciatum*). *Behav. Biol.*, 359–368.

Groves, P. M., and Thompson, R. F. (1970). Habituation: A dual process theory. *Psychol. Rev.* **77**, 419–450.

Harris, J. D. (1943). Habituatory response decrement in the intact organism. *Psychol. Bull.* **40**, 385–422.

Heiligenberg, W. (1965). A quantitative analysis of digging movements and their relationship to aggressive behavior in cichlids. *Anim. Behav.* **13**, 163–170.

Herrick, C. J. (1924). "Neurological Foundations of Animal Behavior." Hafner, New York.

Hinde, R. A. (1970). Behavioral habituation. *In* "Short-term Changes in Neural Activity and Behavior" (G. Horn and R. A. Hinde, eds.), p. 3–40. Cambridge Univ. Press, London and New York.

Johnson, H. J., and Peeke, H. V. S. (1970). Unpublished observations.

Kirchshofer, R. (1953). Aktionssystem des Maulbruters Haplochromis desfontainesii. *Z. Tierpsychol.* **10**, 297–318.

Lorenz, K. Z. (1964). Ritualized fighting. *In* "The Natural History of Aggression" (J. D. Carthy and F. J. Ebling, eds.), pp. 39–50. Academic Press, New York.

Lorenz, K. Z. (1965). *In* "Evolution and Modification of Behavior." Univ. Chicago Press, Chicago.

Lorenz, K. Z. (1966). "On Aggression." Harcourt, New York.

Meral, J., and Barlow G. W., (1971). Personal communication.

Peeke, H. V. S. (1969). Habituation of conspecific aggression in the three-spined stickleback (*Gasterosteus aculeatus*). *Behavior* **35**, 137–156.

Peeke, H. V. S., and Peeke, S. C. (1970). Habituation of aggressive responses in the Siamese fighting fish (*Betta splendens*). *Behavior* **36**, 232–245.

Peeke, H. V. S., and Peeke, S. C. (1972). Habituation, reinforcement and recovery of predatory responses in two species of fish (*Carassius auratus* and *Macropodus opercularis*). *Anim. Behav.* **20**, 268–273.

Peeke, H. V. S., and Veno, A. (1973). Stimulus specificity of habituated aggression in three-spined sticklebacks (*Gasterosteus aculeatus*). *Behav. Biol.*, (In Press).

Peeke, H. V. S., Wyers, E. J., and Herz, M. J. (1969). Waning of the aggressive response to male models in the three-spined stickleback (*Gasterosteus aculeatus L.*). *Anim. Behav.* **17**, 224–228.

Peeke, H. V. S., Herz, M. J., and Gallagher, J. E. (1971). Changes in aggressive behavior in adjacently territorial convict cichlids (*Cichlasoma nigrofasciatum*): The role of habituation. *Behavior* **40**, 43–54.

Ratner, S. C. (1970). Habituation: Research and theory. *In* "Current Issues in Animal "Learning" (J. Reynierse, ed.), pp. 55–84. Univ. of Nebraska Press, Lincoln.

Rodgers, W. L., Melzack, R., and Segal, J. R. (1963). Tail-flip response in the goldfish. *J. Comp. Physiol. Psychol.* **56**, 917–923.

Russell, E. M. (1967a). Changes in behavior of *Lebistes reticulatus* upon a repeated shadow stimulus. *Anim. Behav.* **15**, 575–585.

Russell, E. M. (1967b). The effects of experience of surroundings on the response of *Lebistes reticulatus* to a strange object. *Anim. Behav.* **15**, 586–594.

Seligman, M. E. P. (1970). On the generality of the laws of learning. *Psychol. Rev.* **77**, 406–418.

Sevenster, P. (1961). A causal analysis of a displacement activity (fanning) in *Gasterosteus aculeatus*. *Behavior, Suppl.* **9** (Whole No.).

Simpson, M. J. A. (1968). The display of the Siamese fighting fish, *Betta splendens*. *Anim. Behav., Monogr.* **1** (Whole No.).

Thompson, R. F., and Spencer, W. A. (1966). Habituation: A model phenomenon for the study of neuronal substrates of behavior. *Psychol. Rev.* **173**, 16–43.

Thorpe, W. H. (1963). "Learning and Instinct in Animals." Harvard Univ. Press, Cambridge, Massachusetts.

Triplett, N. (1901). The educability of the Perch. *Amer. J. Psychol.* **12**, 354–360.

van den Assem, J., and van der Molen, J. (1969). Waning of the aggressive response in the three-spined stickleback upon constant exposure to a conspecific. 1. A preliminary analysis of the phenomenon. *Behavior* **34**, 286–324.

Welker, W. I., and Welker, J. (1958). Reaction of fish (*Eucinostomus gula*) to environmental changes. *Ecology*, **39**, 283–288.

Chapter 3

Habituation in "Lower" Tetrapod Vertebrates: Amphibia as Vertebrate Model Systems[1]

DAVID A. GOODMAN[2] AND NORMAN M. WEINBERGER

[1]Preparation of this chapter and mud puppy research reported herein was supported by PHS Research Grant No. MH 11250 from the National Institute of Mental Health to N.M.W. Our thanks to Sally D. Harris for outstanding secretarial assistance.

[2]Now at Newport Neuroscience Center, 9069 Washington Blvd., Culver City, California 90230.

I. Introduction

The purposes of this chapter are twofold: first, to present the state of the art in habituation research using "lower" tetrapod vertebrate subjects; second, to mildly proselytize the reader, to induce him to consider seriously the use of Amphibia in his laboratory for the study of vertebrate behavior. This chapter is divided into ten parts with short sections on habituation studies in Amphibia and some neural mechanisms which may underlie behavior. Also studies in Reptilia are discussed, but, as will be seen, systematic descriptive and analytic studies were yet to be reported as of May, 1971. Sections V and VI offer new data for the salamander *Necturus*. Section VII is a general discussion while the last sections review the present and look ahead to future research programs into amphibian habituation.

*   *   *

It is a curious fact that voices within psychology have been raised in support of the study of lower vertebrate behavior in general and that of the salamander in particular without, it would appear, much effect. Almost 25 years ago Hilgard wrote: "Possibly the first task is to find an organism appropriate for the purpose of studying [the neural basis of learning] as the fruit fly has been for genetics. The white rat is probably too complicated. Perhaps a simpler organism like ambystoma should be chosen in which the neural elements are few..." (Hilgard, 1948). More recently, we find the following: "It is quite possible that exhaustive psychological studies on lower animals might yield extraordinary insight into some of the problems at a higher level" (Breland and Breland, 1966). "... salamanders might provide valuable data on the role of the paleocortex in learning ... and be useful for studies on the nature of memory and the memory trace" (Ray, 1970). Other calls for behavioral work with salamanders have been sounded by Schneider (1968) and O'Leary and Bishop (1969) in the first "C. J. Herrick Memorial Essay."

Nevertheless, remarkably few systematic studies of amphibian and reptilian behavior, and even fewer concerned with habituation, can be found in the literature. In one sampling of all articles in *Animal Behavior* for 1970 there were 102 studies of which only one was concerned with Amphibia, and four with Reptilia. Few studies on habituation of lower tetrapod vertebrates appear in major texts on animal behavior (Thorpe, 1963; Marler and Hamilton, 1966; Hinde, 1966, 1970a) and reviews of habituation (Harris, 1943; Thompson and Spencer, 1966). This neglect seems particularly surprising in the light of the facts that Amphibia such as the frog *Rana*, toad *Bufo*, and salamander *Necturus* have been used for years in comparative anatomy courses as standard specimens of the "vertebrate body," and that a wealth of neuroanatomical information of this class has been available for some time (e.g., Herrick, 1948).

C. J. Herrick's professional life was devoted to the study of the amphibian brain, particularly that of the Caudata, salamanders. While "The Brain of the Tiger Salamander" (1948) is most widely known, Herrick published comprehensively on the mud puppy *Necturus* (Herrick, 1933) and to a lesser extent on the brains of frogs and toads. With respect to his devotion to the salamander brain, some of Herrick's own words may prove instructive.

> The internal texture of the brains of the generalized amphibians ... closely resembles that of the most primitive extant fishes; but the brain as a whole is organized on a higher plane, so that it can more readily be compared with those of reptiles, lower mammals, and man. For this reason the salamanders occupy a strategic position in the phylogenetic series (1948, p. 14).

With reference to the fact that the Amphibia lack phylogenetically recent systems such as the neocerebellum, neothalamus, and particularly neocortex, Herrick wrote: "In the absence of differentiated cerebral cortex, the intrinsic structure of the stem is revealed" (1948, p. 17). To the charge that amphibians constitute a "decadent class" (Hodos and Campbell, 1969) and are therefore suspect as choices for subjects yielding generalizable information, Herrick had himself raised the question and found it to be insufficient to disuade his research.

> It is probable that none of the existing Amphibia are primitive in the sense of survival of the original transitional forms and that the urodeles are not only aberrant but in some cases retrograde (Noble, '31; Evans, '44); yet the organization of their nervous systems is generalized along very primitive lines, and these brains seem to me to be more instructive as types ancestral to mammals than any others that might be chosen. They lack the highly divergent specializations seen in most of the fishes; and in both external form and internal architecture, comparison with the mammalian pattern can be made with more ease and security (1948, p. 16).

Herrick concluded, with reference to the salamander brain in general and that of *Ambystoma* in particular: "This brain may be used as a pattern or template, that is, as a standard of reference in the study of all other vertebrate brains, both lower and higher in the scale" (1948, p. 17). If the brain is the organ of behavior, and if Herrick was essentially correct, then the study of behavior in Amphibia, particularly in salamanders, might provide a "template" of vertebrate behavior. A logical beginning would seem to be with the study of "simple" behavior or responses to single stimuli. It is to this topic that we now turn.

II. Two Approaches to Behavioral Habituation

A. Habituation: Demonstration and Procedure

The standard habituation experiment generally has four components: (1) a subject, (2) a stimulus to be iterated and reiterated, (3) a response to be measured for each stimulus presentation or trial, and (4) a requirement by the investigator that the response exhibits habituatory decrement over trials. Such an experiment may be considered a demonstration of the process of habituation. Parametric studies using this paradigm are very valuable in elucidating the process of habituation including its temporal parameters, the degree of stimulus specificity involved, and the relationships between general organismic state and habituation.

The fourth component, that of the experimenter's own interest in studying habituatory response decrement, may result in a choice of stimuli, stimulus intensity, stimulus duration, and interstimulus intervals which are likely to result in a response decrement over trials. Recognition of this component of the experiment is not meant to imply that it is undesirable but rather permits the realization of a second possibility, the habituation procedure. For good or ill, the term habituation is used not only to refer to a particular type of response decrement but also to the procedure of iterated stimulation. It may be too late to initiate different terms for the process and procedure, thus, it is of particular importance that this distinction be understood by the reader.

The habituation procedure differs in no real operational sense from the demonstration type of experiment. In both, a particular stimulus, or stimulus complex, is simply presented and repeated at certain intervals. However, in the habituation procedure the experimenter does not attempt to set conditions that will reveal a habituatory response decrement. He may, in fact, wish to set conditions that will not yield a decrement, such as by employing very long interstimulus intervals. The data yielded from this procedure paradigm constitute part of a behavioral "mapping" wherein the type and intensity of the elicited behavior on sequential trials may be a function of the particular nature of the stimulus, or the state of the animal, rather than accruing experience with the stimulus. The distinction between the demonstration and procedure experiments may be elucidated when considered within the broader perspective of a general behavioral equation.

B. Behavioral Equation: $R = f(S, A, O)$

Behavior may be considered to be a function of three broad independent variables: stimuli, antecedent conditions (including experience), and general organismic state (Woodworth and Schlosberg, 1954). This may be summarized as $R = f(S, A, O)$, where R is the behavioral output, S the definable stimulus, A all antecedent variables (including learning), and O the organismic state (general arousal or excitability). Under strict laboratory conditions, two of these independent variables may be held relatively constant so that variations in behavior may be attributable to the third.

Each of the three basic paradigms generated by holding two variables constant has a special purpose. For example, $R = f(A)$, O and S assumed constant, says that the response to a constant stimulus depends on an antecedent variable (A) usually experience. This paradigm is used in the customary habituation demonstration. $R = f(S)$, O and A held constant, says that the form of the response depends mainly on the nature of the stimulus. Lastly, $R = f(O)$ with A and S constant holds that each response depends on the momentary state of the organism. For example, one could administer a constant stimulus so removed in time from any previous stimulus that the form, magnitude, and duration of the response depends only on spontaneous organismic state changes. Of the three types of experiments, $R = f(A)$ is common, $R = f(S)$ is less common, and $R = f(O)$ is seldom performed.

Within this context, the habituation demonstration is a case of $R = f(A)$, S and O held or assumed constant. The habituatory response decrement is considered to be a result of accruing experience with a constant stimulus. On the other hand, the habituation procedure is generally a case of $R = f(O)$, A and S constant. With this paradigm, behavior may be mapped against the states of an organism. Experiments which compare the effectiveness of a given stimulus during the sleeping and waking states fall into this class. Variations of state of arousal within wakefulness are widely recognized to exist, but little research has been reported (but see Hutt *et al.*, 1968). $R = f(S)$, A and O constant also constitutes in effect a behavioral mapping experiment to determine the specific responses elicited by particular stimuli. As such, it has found widescale usage in ethological approaches to stimulus control of behavior, particularly with reference to "releasers." However, this paradigm lies outside the scope of the present chapter because the essence of both habituation demonstrations and procedures is the repeated use of the same rather than a changing stimulus.

It should be understood that the difference between the habituation demonstration and procedure experiments may be very subtle, one blending into the other. For example, the use of short intertrial intervals (seconds) may result in a habituatory response decrement while use of the same stimulus with very long intervals (minutes and hours) may result in no response decrement. It seems likely that the response decrement with short intervals reflects accruing experience with an "insignificant" stimulus, while such accrued experience has a minimal effect with very long interstimulus intervals. However, behavior in the second situation will probably not be the same on every trial but actually reflect the state of the organism. Direct measurement of state, independent of the elicited behavior, would clarify relationships between the habituation demonstration and procedure. In any event, it is important to differentiate between the two, particularly when the experimenter may be performing essentially identical operations.

A concrete example might perhaps set the distinction between the habituation demonstration and the habituation procedure in the reader's mind. If the experimenter employs short interstimulus intervals and observes habituatory response decrement with repeated trials, that is a habituation demonstration. Alternately, if the experimenter uses long interstimulus intervals and observes no trend toward response decrement, then this is an exercise of the habituation procedure. The experimenter is mapping[3] responses with respect to state. This procedure emphasizes the form of the response or responses, not the magnitude of one response with respect to another.

In the present chapter there are reports on habituation demonstrations, the $R = f(A)$ paradigms, and some elaboration on the $R = f(O)$ procedure in Sections III–V and VI, respectively.

III. $R = f(A)$: Habituation in Reptilia

Habituation in Reptilia has been studied primarily in turtles and tortoises. Humphrey (1933) noted decrement of a withdrawal response in the musk turtle *Sternotherus odoratus* when its carapace was struck repeatedly with a mallet. Crampton and Schwam (1962), working with the box turtle *Terrapene c. carolina*, reported that its head turning response to angular acceleration showed little if any response decrement with repeated testing, a finding in contrast to habituation of nystagmus reported in cat and man.

Recently, Hayes *et al.* (1968) placed red-eared turtles *Pseudemys scripta* in rubber strap holders inside transluscent plastic cylinders which had vertical 1-in. black stripes separated by 1-in. intervals. Turtles were allowed 5–10 minutes to adapt to the testing situation which included an overhead 150-W incandescent lamp and direct observation by the investigators. After adaptation of the turtles to the testing environment, the cylinders were rotated around their major axis, eliciting head or eye movements, optokinetic responses. In Experiment I, magnitude of the optokinetic response (OKR) was observed during minutes 1, 60, 61, and 62. OKR was observed at other times only occasionally. No state measures were taken. Habituation to the continuously rotating stimulus was observed. They did not mention the possibility that de-arousal over time may be one source of the observed response decrement; rather, they defined habituation as the number of turning responses minute 60/minute 1. The habituated response

---

[3]The phrase behavior mapping has been selected with regard to terminology in genetics, genetic mapping. Just as each chromosome has a finite number of different loci, there are a finite number of different responses of an animal to a constant stimulus. When all responses to a stimulus can be described with the precision of genetic loci on a chromosome, then relationships of responses and the eliciting conditions for each response can be identified.

could be dishabituated in two ways: by a reversal of the direction of rotation and by stopping the cylinder for one minute then restarting it again.

In further experiments (Experiment II and III), Hayes *et al.* (1968) showed that habituation was faster on subsequent days than on the first day, was more rapid with an intense stimulus than with a moderate stimulus, and that the process did not require more than 16 minutes. The OKR response of turtles evidently demonstrates habituation.

Earlier Hayes and Saiff (1967) had studied habituation of withdrawal to the optical stimulus of looming. Turtles were restrained with rubber straps. Their noses were lined up with a translucent screen. Behind the screen at a distance was a point source of light. Between source and screen was a set of rails on which a wagon carried a pane of glass with an opaque spot. To produce the optical stimulus of looming, the wagon was propelled by a 0.10-hp motor along the tracks toward the turtle's snout. Head withdrawal was elicited by the looming shadow. Such a response could be habituated with repeated trials. This was surprisingly long-lasting (up to 10 days). Interestingly, the more "active" the turtle was on day 1, the slower was its habituation. The effects of interstimulus interval and dishabituation stimuli on rate of habituation were not studied.

The study of habituation in Reptilia appears to have been limited to turtles and responses to the head and eyes. Head withdrawal, to both tactile and visual stimulation, apparently habituates as do head and eye optokinetic responses. In contrast, head turning to vestibular stimulation does not habituate. Further studies are needed to determine whether or not this reluctance on the part of the vestibular system is apparent or real. Hopefully, the near future will also bring an extension of the ranges of Reptilia studied, and parameters of habituation employed.

IV. $R = f(A)$: Habituation in Toads and Frogs

Behavioral habituation has been studied more extensively in Amphibia than in Reptilia but even here present knowledge is still modest. The bulk of research with toads and frogs has been provided in an extensive set of experiments published only in German (Birukow, 1951; Eikmanns, 1955; Kuczka, 1956; Ewert, 1966, 1967a,b,c, 1968, 1969; Ewert and Rehn, 1969; Ewert and Härter, 1969). Several of these have been translated for purposes of this review, but the impact of these important studies will probably not be felt in the English-speaking world until full translations are available.

Habituation in toads and frogs is marked by three interesting characteristics: stimulus specificity, appreciable duration, and a definite periodicity to the habituation function.

With respect to stimulus specificity, Kimble and Ray (1965) have apparently resolved the anomalous finding of Franzisket (1963) who reported sensitization, not habituation, of the wiping reflex in spinal and intact frogs. Kimble and Ray noted that Franzisket had evoked the same reflex by repeated tactile stimulation of a general region of the skin. They repeated his experiment and also found reflex sensitization. Additionally, another group of animals received repeated stimulation in exactly the same tiny spot of skin, which resulted in habituation. Thus, habituation of the wiping reflex depended upon using essentially identical stimulation; stimulus generalization to stimulation of adjacent skin regions was not only absent but also caused the antagonistic process, sensitization. (Groves and Thompson, 1970).

Remarkable stimulus specificity also appears in the optokinetic sphere (Birukow, 1937, 1951; Butz-Kuenzer, 1957) and for the local visual sign (Eikmanns, 1955; Ewert, 1967a; Ewert and Härter, 1969; Ewert and Rehn, 1969). These include the optico-vestibular response to rotating stripes, the wiping reflex to tactile stimulation and a targeting to a moving prey dummy. This section emphasizes habituation of the toad targeting to a spot which is one taxic component of a behavioral chain beginning when the toad spies the presumed prey and ending when the toad has struck at the prey (Hinsche, 1935).

The studies of note are those by Eikmanns (1955) and Ewert (1967a) with emphasis on the latter. The taxic movement is "released" whenever a mealworm dummy intrudes into the toad's visual field. A toad finds itself inside a glass cylinder several centimeters above a disk with a series of holes around its perimeter. When the toad faces an empty hole, a moving meal worm dummy appears temporalward to its field of vision. To center the moving target, the toad turns toward the intruding stimulus. As soon as it has turned, the prey disappears to reappear beneath the next hole such that the new intruding stimulus subtends the same visual angle as the old one. The toad continues to turn toward the prey but never obtains it.

Eikmanns (1955) attempted to show the specificity of habituation with respect to the stimulus quality (local sign). He noted that a habituated response could be dishabituated by changing the location of the stimulus in the visual field. He presented a dummy to one location in the visual field and presented the dummy again until the toad no longer turned toward or actively turned away from the stimulus. After this criterion of habituation (*Ermüdung*) or extinction had been reached, the stimulus was again presented elsewhere in the visual field. Dishabituation indicated discrimination of a changed stimulus, a definition proposed by Sokolov (1960). Eikmanns (1955) also noted that the specificity of habituation extended to a certain angular velocity, duration, stimulus size, color, and brightness. There were savings when a smaller stimulus replaced a larger one, but none at all when a larger stimulus replaced the smaller, or when the smaller changed its direction of movement.

Ewert's (1967a) study touched on the duration of habituation and shows it to be "relatively permanent" (Fig. 1). Earlier Eikmanns (1955) had shown appreciable habituation with 60-minute interseries intervals. Generally speaking, when 1440 minutes (24 hours) elapses between series there is little or no savings in habituation learning (Fig. 1); hence, the term relatively permanent duration of habituation. Ewert (1967a) showed that recovery from habituation within a series is quite fast in the first 10 minutes, until it reaches 65–70% of the original value after 100 minutes. When the number of series was repeated until the response of turning toward was extinguished completely, then there was 50% recovery after 8 hours (Eikmanns, 1955). Thus, the greater the habituation, the more permanent the extent of the habituation, and the longer the time course to recovery.

With respect to the shape of the habituation curve, there is an exponential component (as others have shown) and also a periodic component (Eikmanns, 1955; Ewert, 1967a). Ewert (1968) has solved for the value of the exponential term (see Section VI). The periodic component to habituation is indicated by rhythmic oscillations of response magnitude during any one response series and periodicity in number of responses emitted in a daily

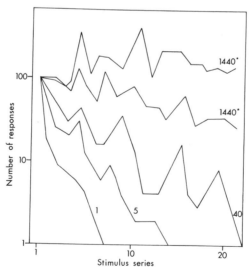

Fig. 1. Rate of habituation in toads as a function of interseries interval. Ordinate indicates number of turning toward responses per stimulus series. Family of curves describes effect of interseries interval: 1, 5, 40, and 1440 minutes. Top 1440 describes curve for non-habituators and second curve refers to habituating subjects given one series daily. Note rhythmicity in curves and that the ordinate is logarithmic. After Ewert (1967a).

response series. On plotting his data logarithmically, Ewert (1967a) noted both an exponential and a periodic component (Fig. 1). On the average, there was a secondary peak each 5 series ± 2 series. This rhythmicity could be eliminated by brain damage leaving the exponential term undisturbed (see Section VI). Figure 2, from Ewert (1967a), illustrated dramatically the periodicity of the habituation function and also the stimulus specificity of habituation. The toad notices the intruding prey dummy and turns toward it. Immediately the dummy disappears to reappear in the periphery of the same eye. When the response has habituated, the dummy is presented to the other eye without pause. The response then is extinguished (habitu-

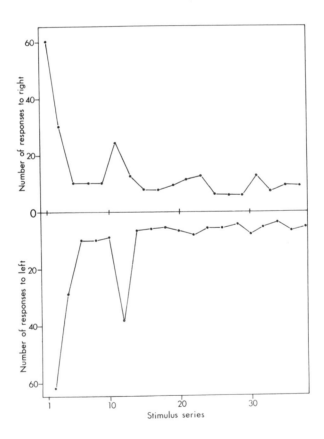

Fig. 2. Specificity of habituation in toads. In the first stimulus series the dummy is presented to one eye. When the toad no longer responds or turns away, the dummy is presented again to the other eye. When the toad ceases responding, the dummy reappears again at the original eye, etc. Interseries interval, 5 minutes. Note both an exponential decay and a rhythmic component. After Ewert (1967a).

ated) again whereby the stimulus is again presented to the original eye. This alternation continues 19 times (38 stimulus series). Note the mirror image habituation curves each with the same periodicities evident. (see also Eikmanns, 1955). In summary, toad and frog habituation curves with naturalistic stimuli of moderate intensity are quite stimulus specific, relatively permanent, and periodic in nature.

V. $R = f(A)$: Habituation in the Salamander

Systematic study of behavioral habituation in the salamander seems to have been limited to the recent studies of *Necturus* (Goodman, 1969). Early casual observations of the effect of an incidental stimulus upon the salamander had found the principal effect to be cessation of ongoing behavior (Gadow, 1890; Whitman, 1898). The effects of shadow and vibration stimulation upon heartbeat, gill beating, and tail waving in *Necturus* were studied more systematically by Goodman (1969). He also found interruption of ongoing behavior by such stimulation and further that the duration of heartbeat and gill beat cessation habituates. The general phenomenon of the interruption of these ongoing behaviors in hereafter referred to as pause. It has been claimed that pause constitutes the orienting reflex of *Necturus* (Goodman, 1969; Goodman and Weinberger, 1970). This claim will be examined below.

A. Methods of Studying Necturus Behavior

Because somewhat novel methods of study were employed, it is necessary to explain them briefly at this juncture. *Necturus* were tested individually in a small, shallow Plexiglas aquarium which was placed inside a larger plastic pan which served as a water jacket.[4] These were housed in a refrigerator maintained at 19°C. Direct observation of the animal could be accomplished through a small window in the door. Two types of exteroceptive stimulation could be presented, shadow and vibration. A moving shadow projected upon the surface of the testing aquarium was produced by sequential interruption of current to a parallel array of luminescent strips located 30 cm. above the aquarium, which also provided dim, heatless illumination (Weinberger and Goodman, 1969). Vibration was produced by a 6 in. speaker located beneath the aquarium which was driven by an oscillator at 60 Hz. Stimuli were controlled by solid state circuitry, to reduce noise, and the refrigerator was mounted on a shock absorber to attenuate external vibrations.

---

[4]The animals could escape from the testing aquarium into the water jacket or could hide under a small ledge within the testing aquarium. Those few animals that consistently escaped or hid, thus indicating their displeasure with the experiment, are not included in data presented in this chapter.

Electrodes were implanted in the walls and floor of the aquarium rather than in the animal in order to record physiological and behavioral variables. Heartbeat and electromyographic activity could be recorded by volume conduction to selected pairs of electrodes, while gill beating, tail movement, and gross body movements were revealed as specific voltage changes consequent to water waves or slight turbulence. Additional details and validation of this remote recording technique are presented elsewhere (Goodman and Weinberger, 1971a,b). Voltages picked up by selected pairs of electrodes were recorded on a Grass model 7 polygraph with standard low level ac coupled amplifiers. Selective filtering was employed as needed.

The salamander *Necturus* in its wired aquarium ready to behave upon receiving a shadow stimulus from above, or a vibrational stimulus from below, is presented in Fig. 3.

The degree to which remote sensing provides a complete behavioral picture of *Necturus* is shown in the next three figures. Figure 4 depicts behavioral records from a quiescent salamander in a wired aquarium. On

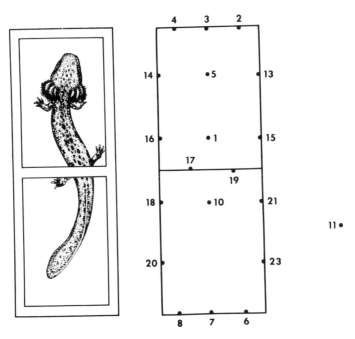

Fig. 3. Mud puppy in remote-sensing aquarium: (a) mud puppy showing external gills and willowy tail, and (b) the submerged electrodes number coded as in Goodman (1969). For the position of the animal illustrated, gill beat is recorded electrode 14–13; heartbeat 1–16 and tail movement 10–21.

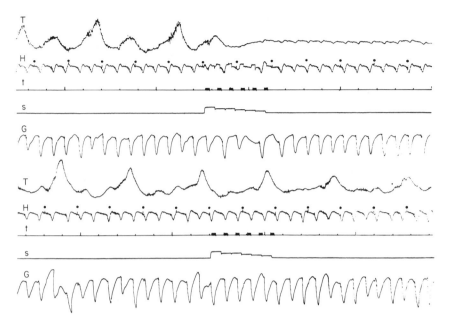

Fig. 4. Mud puppy responses to an overhead moving shadow (s), illustrating behavior of tail (T), heart (H), and gills (G). Top: an orienting reflex consisting of cessation of tail waving and slowed gill beating, without an effect on heartbeating. Note EMG on tail record and its disappearance during tail-wave cessation. Bottom: the absence of any effect of the same stimulus given after 10 intervening shadow trials. On time marker channel (t), calibrations are 1 second and 3 μV (solid bars during stimulus). S is the output of a photo cell on the aquarium, marking the passage of the shadow. In this figure, darkening is indicated by upward deflection, but in subsequent figures by downward deflection. (Dots have been placed over small EKG signal for emphasis.)

the three channels are tail waving, heartbeating, and gill beating from submerged electrode pairs across the tail, heart, and head, respectively.

Figure 5 depicts gill beat and heartbeat recorded from a quiescent salamander and one presented with a moving shadow.

With the remote sensing technique there is continuous recording of heartbeat, gill beat, tail waving and, at times, myographic activity except when the salamander moves vigorously, an infrequent event during the normal session. One aspect of behavioral analysis is shown in Fig. 6 which illustrates an orienting reflex elicited by a shadow. It is characterized by a minor disruption on ongoing activity. Stimulus onset elicits slowed gill beating and arrest of tail movement not accompanied by change in heart rate and no increase, perhaps a decrease, in somatic myographic activity. Gill beat

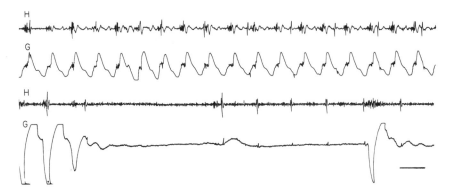

Fig. 5. General low level of heart signal overcome by filtering. Gill beat signals (G) include heartbeat signals (H). An active, high pass filter set at 12 Hz was used to filter gill activity, allowing visualization of EKG. Above; gills and heart beating continuously; below, interruption of gill beat and heartbeat by a stimulus not shown. Calibration, 1 second.

record is separated into three components: pre, the five prestimulus gill beats; the response (---), which in this case does not outlast the stimulus; and post, the five poststimulus gill beats. In this illustration the stimulus has very little effect: mean and variance of pre and post are almost identical. The gill beat response of this animal to the stimulus is not accomplished by an obvious poststimulus state change where state change is defined by a poststimulus change in gill beat mean and variance.

From Fig. 6, it is obvious that it would be possible to follow habituation

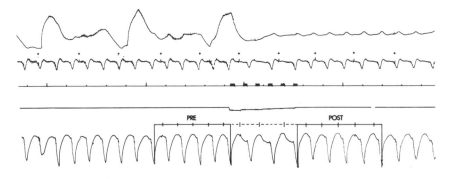

Fig. 6. Definition of state, response, and post-stimulus state change. Note prestimulus state defined here by mean and variance of 5 prestimulus gill beats (pre). Slowing (---) of gills is most pronounced during the stimulus while the tail wave cessation continues after the stimulus has passed. Poststimulus change (post) in gill beat is a slightly retarded rate compared to pre. Dots indicate low level EKG. Labels in figure as in Fig. 4.

in more than one system at the same time. For example, in this animal it was possible to measure diminution of the durations of gill beat, heartbeat, and tail movement interruption responses simultaneously. The course of habituation in all three systems is depicted in Fig. 7.

In summary, the remote recording technique eliminated handling of the subjects and possible stress consequent to affixing electrodes. It also eliminated the need to restrain the subject, permitting free movement within the aquarium. Thus, there was a serious attempt to approximate more naturalistic conditions than are often employed in laboratory studies of habituation. Additionally, this technique permitted continuous recording of different

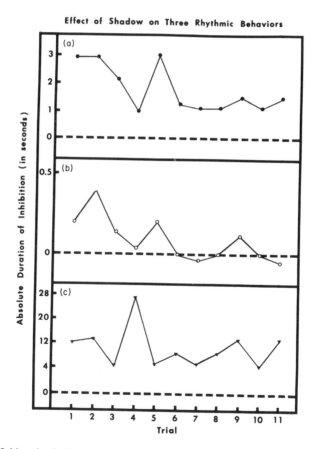

Fig. 7. Habituation in three systems studied simultaneously: (a) gill beat, (b) heartbeat, and (c) tail wave. Note general similarity of gill beat and heartbeat habituation curves and complete dissimilarity of tail wave "habituation", curve. Also note the differing ordinates for the gills, heart, and tail. After trial 11, the mud puppy stopped beating its gills.

behaviors or response systems; there was no preselection of data from among the recorded behaviors.

B. *Habituation of the* Necturus *Orienting Reflex*

The experimental paradigm used to study the elicitation and habituation of *Necturus'* behavior involved intensive investigation of each subject over a period of at least 3 consecutive days. The animal lived in the testing aquarium during this time without being handled or disturbed except by programmed stimulation. On day 1 only occasional shadow or vibrational stimuli were presented, this period serving mainly to allow the mud puppy to become acclimatized to its new environment. Two sessions, separated by 75–90 minutes were run on day 2, and a single standard habituation session was run on day 3. Each of these sessions consisted of 15 trials of shadow stimulation, followed by 10 trials of shadow interspersed with vibration or other stimulation. Details of the procedure are given in Fig. 8 and Table I. Data were obtained from basic groups of 10 mud puppies each, which were run with intertrial intervals of 30, 120, and 400 seconds, respectively.

The characteristic response of *Necturus* to the first presentation of an overhead moving shadow consisted of gill beat cessation or retardation, heartbeat interruption, and also tail-wave cessation if it was moving at stimulus onset. The effect upon gill beating was the single most reliable component of the response to the novel stimulus, occurring on 100% of the trials. Heartbeat interruption was seen on 85% of the trials. It should be emphasized that these effects are found unequivocally in healthy, quiescent salamanders. Shadow stimulation had little or no effect upon behavior if presented to *Necturus* during its vigorous exploration of the aquarium.

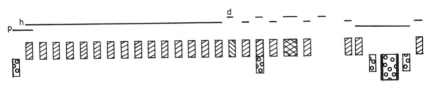

Fig. 8. Stimulus sequence during habituation run. Bar with small circles is a 4-second vibrational probe (P) followed in 4 minutes by a 4-second shadow probe (P) (striped bar). Fourteen shadows follow first at 30; 120; or 400-second intervals. This is habituation run (h). Then attempts are made to dishabituate (d) mud puppy. Four dishabituation stimuli alternating with original stimulus are a reversed shadow, a vibration paired with shadow, darkness for 8 seconds, and, lastly an omitted stimulus. Two shadow stimuli surrounding three vibrational stimuli (to the right) were used to probe animal excitability. This paradigm is completely described in Goodman (1969).

TABLE I

TESTING PROCEDURE

Procedure	Day 1	Day 2	Day 3
30 min pass with chamber constantly illuminated	+[a]	+	+
Vibrational stimulus; followed by 4-min interval and	+	+	+
Moving shadow (interruption of illumination)	+	+	+
14 more moving shadows[c]	0[b]	+	+
Alternation of dishabituation stimuli and moving shadows.	0	+	+
Vibrational probes	0	+	+
Last moving shadow	+[d]	+	+
(Wait 75–90 min. repeat entire procedure)	0	+	0

[a] +, present
[b] at 30-, 120-, or 400-second intervals
[c] 0, absent
[d] second shadow presented 60 minutes after first shadow.

Both gill beat suppression or slowing (GBS) and heartbeat interruption (HBI) exhibited habituatory response decrement with repeated stimulation. The rate of habituation was inversely related to interstimulus interval (Figs. 9A and 9B). Habituation of HBI was more rapid than that of GBS. Additionally, while HBI habituated in all three groups, habituation of the gill beat effect was less marked in the 400-second group than in both the 30- and 120-second groups.

As noted, habituation sessions 1 and 2 were given on day 2, separated by a 75–90-minute interval; session 3 was run about 24 hours after session 2 on day 3. Spontaneous recovery for GBS following habituation during session 1 was clearly in evidence on both sessions 2 and 3. Rate of habituation was faster for session 2 than 1, indicating potentiation of habituation (Fig. 9C). Heartbeat interruption, which habituated more rapidly than GBS, showed less spontaneous recovery (Fig. 9C).

No second daily run of habituation of HBI is shown for the 30-second group because the response had not recovered sufficiently for there to be a second habituation run for that response.[5] In an unexpected sense, this

[5]Some animals in Groups 30 and 400 showed such small HB1 responses on day 2 session 2 that meaningful comparison of these animals with Group 30 animals is difficult.

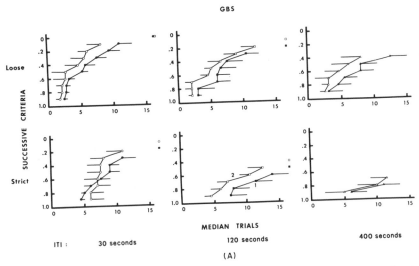

Fig. 9A. Gill beat suppression habituation curves *plotted as learning curves* showing median number of trials (abscissa) to reach proportion of response to first stimulus (ordinate). "Loose" refers to a single trial to criterion; "strict" to 3 consecutive trials to criterion. (■) first run on day 2; (□) second run on day 2. Horizontal rays are standard errors of the median.

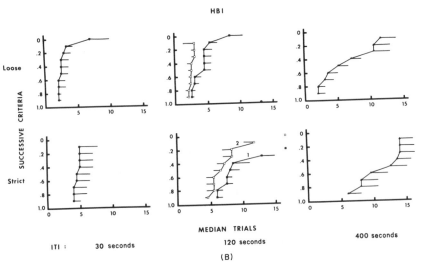

Fig. 9B. Habituation functions for heartbeat interruption. Note that only the 120-second group exhibited a sufficient heartbeat effect on session 2 to permit plotting of this data.

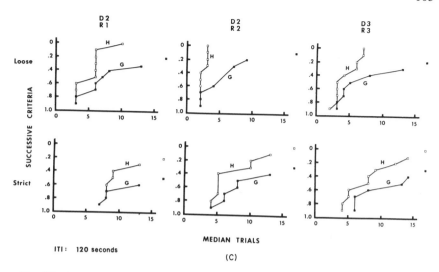

Fig. 9C. Habituation functions for the 120-second group for all three habituation runs, and both heart (h) and gills (G). Note more rapid habituation on day 2, run 2 than day 2, run 1 for gill and heart.

illustrates the concept of "habituation below zero" described by Thompson and Spencer (1966). If a group of animals is presented with an iterated stimulus and two responses are measured simultaneously, the response that habituates the faster and consequently is habituated below zero will be the slower response to recover. The data also show that in these two groups spontaneous recovery of GBS is inversely proportional to the speed of habituation. The animals that habituated the fastest (ITI Group 30) were the animals that showed the slowest spontaneous recovery.

On those few occasions during which tail waving was present on enough trials to plot a behavioral function, the interruption of tail waving was more resistant to habituation (e.g., Fig. 7). For most sessions, tail waving which was interrupted by the first stimulus did not resume during the subsequent trials. However, tail movements, such as abduction to one side or a single complete wave, were seen on many trials. This aspect of *Necturus* behavior is discussed more fully below.

Dishabituation of both the heart and gill effects was investigated using a shadow of reversed direction, vibration paired with the standard shadow, and a sudden darkening of the chamber (Fig. 8). The paired stimulation was most effective, consistently eliciting the previously habituated HBI and GBS effects. The application of the vibration—shadow stimulus also could elicit an increased response to the next programmed shadow stimulus, but the effects were not seen beyond that next trial.

In summary, mud puppy GBS and HBI illustrate the process of habituation to an overhead moving shadow. The HB effect habituates more rapidly than the GBS'. If the tail is waving throughout a session, tail-wave cessation elicited by the shadow is most resistant to habituation. When an animal has been habituated once, its rate of habituation when tested the second time on the same day is faster. The shorter the intertrial interval, the faster the habituation. Spontaneous recovery within a day is quite clear for the gill beat effect, less pronounced for heartbeat interruption. Finally, dishabituation is easily demonstrated by interposing vibration-shadow, which is more effective than a reversed shadow. It would seem that the pause syndrome in *Necturus*, or at least its respiratory and cardiac components, do habituate. The question of whether pause may constitute the mud puppy orienting reflex will be considered specifically in the subsequent discussion section.

How does the salamander compare with frogs and toads, particularly regarding three interesting characteristics of their behavioral habituation, stimulus specificity, duration of effect, and periodicity? First, there seems to be less stimulus specificity of habituation in *Necturus* than in *Bufo*, at least with respect to visual stimulation.[6] Subtle changes in the stimulus (e.g., direction of a moving shadow) are less potent dishabituators in *Necturus* than in the toad. This is not surprising considering their differing modes of life, but more extensive investigations must be carried out before generalizations are admissable. For example, *Necturus* might exhibit greater specificity or discriminability for lateral line stimulation. This conjecture seems reasonable because toads are surface dwellers while *Necturus* is a bottom dweller. In fact, *Necturus* have been found at depths of 75 ft (Reigle, 1967). Vision is undoubtedly more important on the surface than in the darker reaches which can be inhabited by *Necturus*. Conversely, the lateral line system would be very useful in the absence of adequate visual input. Second, it appears that habituation in *Necturus* does last up to 24 hours, as in the toad. Third, while periodicity seems to have been established in the Salientia, only preliminary statements can be made for *Necturus*. We have found some examples of periodicity revealed in the habituation function of gill beat suppression (Fig. 10). In fact, a salamander may appear to reproduce the shape of an earlier habituation curve on subsequent testing. More extensive considerations of periodicity would benefit from a knowledge of its causes. For example, if it is a function of a cycling in general organismic excitability, then the period of each cycle may be quite different (e.g., much longer) for

---

[6]Recent research indicates that *Necturus* eye might be more light sensitive than previously thought.

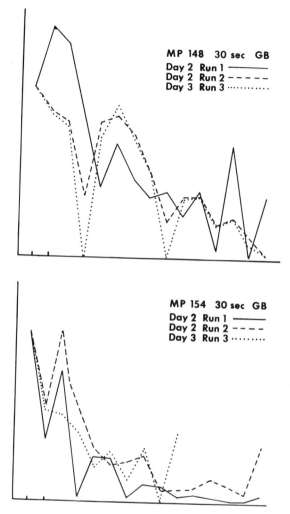

Fig. 10. Individual habituation functions of two mud puppies for gill beat suppression. Note the striking similarity of functions within each animal for three habituation runs, and the indication of periodicity in these functions.

some species. Thus for different genera or species the same periodicities might not be evident in their habituation curves.

C. Habituation Procedure for Behavioral Mapping

In Section II we discussed the possibility of using two methods to map behavior as a function of (O) state and (S) stimulus. The former involves the standard habituation procedure of presenting an iterated stimulus, particularly at interstimulus intervals so great response decrement was minimal, in order that changes in response could be attributed largely to the ambient state of organismic excitability. The second method consists of presenting differing stimuli and observing different elicited responses. While only the first method is within the purview of this chapter on habituation, strictly speaking, the second was also utilized in the study of *Necturus* behavior, and thus will be mentioned briefly below. The major point of this section, however, is that the habituation procedure can reveal interesting facets of behavior even if habituatory response decrement is not forthcoming for the stimulus and situational parameters used.

We begin with an example of a habituation experiment which had apparently gone awry. On trial 1 the mud puppy exhibited characteristic gill beat suppression; on trial 2 it not only stopped beating its gills but also crouched down closer to the aquarium floor; by trial 15 the animal was no longer beating its gills, and at the onset of the shadow it retreated rapidly (Fig. 11). This type of "sensitized" behavior, while unusual, could not be ignored and led us to consider the possibility that "spontaneous" changes in state or arousal level were responsible. This issue is considered specifically in Section VI. But what seems particularly intriguing in this example of "aberrant" behavior is that the same apparently innocuous shadow, which elicited only a minimal response on trial 1, should provoke such a wide variety of responses in one animal within one session. This led to a cataloging of all response patterns on all trials of the previously cited habituation experiments and to a subsequent behavioral taxonomy of brain reflexes of *Necturus*.

If the gill, heart, and tail response systems are each considered to comprise part of the total response of a mud puppy to stimulation, then an obvious question arises as to the relationships among these various systems. The "catalog" revealed an ordered relationship such that cessation of tail waving might appear with or without any effect upon gill or heart beating, but not the converse. Additionally, gill beating could be interrupted with or without any simultaneous effect upon heartbeating, but not the converse. Thus three response constellations were found to be evoked by stimulation, all characterized by interruption of ongoing behavior (pause), but varying in the degree of involvement of the tail, gill, and cardiac systems. The behavioral syndromes were referred to as orienting reflexes (OR's) and their characteristics are summarized in Table II. The three OR's are hereafter referred to as OR_0, OR_1, and OR_2, depending upon the extent of involvement of the tail, gill, and cardiac systems, respectively.

In addition to the orienting reflexes characterized as pause, many instances

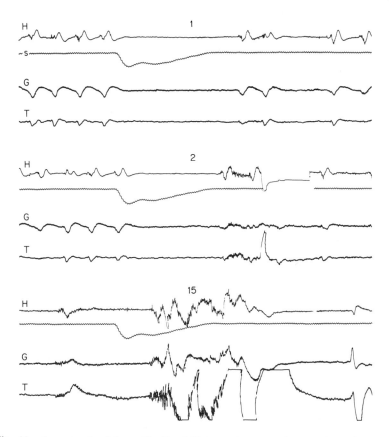

Fig. 11. An example of " sensitization." Note mud puppy orients to first stimulus (indicated by gill beat suppression). Response to the second stimulus is GBS followed by increase in somatic EMG and movement of the tail. By trial 15 the mud puppy is no longer beating its gills. To shadow 15 it retreats.

of overt or incipient movement were found to immediately follow the OR's. Incipient movement included swallowing or an increase in trunk EMG. The presence or absence of three variables characterized all instances of movement: (1) tail flexion,[7] (2) body movement downward toward the floor, and (3) actual body movement backward. As in the case of the behaviors characterized by pause, those of movement were also found to order themselves

---

[7]On many trials "swallow" rather than movement of the tail to the side of the body was seen. These two behaviors appear to have the same threshold and for present purposes may be considered interchangeable as components of defensive reflexes. Swallow is used here because this behavior appears identical to normal swallowing when a mud puppy has food in its craw.

TABLE II

ORIENTING REFLEXES OF *NECTURUS* TO VISUAL STIMULI

Terminology of Goodman (1969)	Common name	Suggested by: References	Operational definition		
			Tail stop	Gills stop	Heart stops
OR_0	Arrest of movement	Viala and Buser (1969); Dubignon and Campbell (1968); Hunter and Jasper (1949);	$+^a$	$\pm^b$	0^c
OR_1	Arrest of movement with apnoea	Kuroki; (1958); Fangel and Kaada (1960).	$+$	$+$	$\pm$
OR_2	Freeze	Krieckhaus and Chi (1966); Herrick (1934a)	$+$	$+$	$+$

^{a}+, present always.
^{b}±, present in most cases.
^{c}0, absent.

into few categories as follows: tail-aside with or without movement downward or movement backward, but not the converse; movement downward with or without movement backward, but not the converse. Thus three response constellations involving movement following an orienting reflex were found. These were termed defensive reflexes (DR's) and their characteristics are summarized in Table III. These three DR's are referred to as DR_0, DR_1, and DR_2, depending upon the type(s) of movement present.

To return to our aberrant mud puppy, its behavior on trials 1, 2, and 15 would be summarized as having been characterized by the elicitation of an OR_1, DR_1, and DR_2, respectively.

All six of the brain reflexes could be elicited by an overhead moving shadow but not with equal frequency. Strong stimuli, such as vibration, or vibration paired with the shadow were more likely to elicit a DR than simply an OR. In addition to stimulus intensity, a second variable affecting the type of reflex elicited was the time since first placement in the testing aquarium. For example, the greater the time, the smaller the proportion of DR's elicited (Table IV). These data also provide a rationale for allowing an animal to adapt to the testing situation before initiation of habituation, for the variability of responses to the first stimulus of each session is reduced thereby, and the probability of obtaining an orienting reflex is increased. (In fact, a mud puppy which is engaged in vigorous exploration will exhibit no unequivocal response to a novel shadow although there is good reason to believe that the stimulation reached its eyes.)

TABLE III

DEFENSIVE REFLEXES OF NECTURUS TO VISUAL STIMULI

Terminology Of Goodman (1969)	Common name	Suggested by: References	Operational definition			
			OR present	Movement present	Body moves downward	backward
DR_0	Swallow or tail-aside	Chase and McGinty (1970); Roman and Gar (1970)	$+^a$	+	0^b	0
DR_1	Crouch (cower)	Kaada (1951); Rodgers et al. (1963)	+	+	+	0
DR_2	Retreat (escape)	Hess (1954); Ursin and Kaada (1960)	+	+	+	+

[a] +, present always.
[b] 0, absent

TABLE IV
PERCENTAGE OF REFLEXES ELICITED BY SHADOW AS A FUNCTION OF TIME
IN TESTING AQUARIUM

| | Day 1 | | Day 2 | |
Reflex	+30 min	+90 min	Run 1 trial 1	Run 2 trial 1
Orient[a]	59	67	61	75
Freeze[b]	11	13	22	16
Protect[c]	8	8	14	9
Retreat[d]	8	9	3	0
Moving[e]	7	0	0	0
Hidden[f]	7	4	0	0

[a]Orient, $OR_0 + OR_1$.
[b]Freeze, OR_2.
[c]Protect, $DR_0 + DR_1$.
[d]Retreat, DR_2.
[e]Moving, subject's body moving, no response.
[f]Hidden, subject under ledge, not stimulated.

This reduction in DR's and variability of types of reflexes elicited as a function of time in the testing aquarium may be termed de-arousal. De-arousal refers specifically to a general decrease in responsivity over time in the testing situation. It may require as long as 10 days in fish (Rasa, 1971). De-arousal may be mistaken for habituation if the situation involves strong stimuli or if the animal begins "quieting down" at the same time that it is serving as a subject in a habituation experiment. The response decrement observed may not be stimulus-specific habituation, but could result from a generalized decrease in responsivity (Bûres, 1970). For example, Hutt et al. (1968) found apparent "habituation" in neonatal humans, response decrements being associated with a decrease in the level of arousal only; no habituation was seen within a constant state of arousal. Goodman (1969) reported that habituation in the salamander, using 120-second intertrial intervals, could not be attributed to a general state change; however, some potentiation of habituation across days might have resulted from de-arousal since the salamanders lived in the testing aquarium.

A major feature of the reflexes delineated here is the addition of response components from an OR_0 up to a DR_2, the latter consisting of all of the response components mentioned. It might seem therefore that some sort of continuum exists from the former to the latter, and indeed it may prove fruitful to hypothesize a continuum of arousal. On the other hand, the distinction made here between orienting and defensive reflexes also suggests a discontinuity. Indeed, such a discontinuity has been demonstrated by the "addition of physical energies" (Goodman, 1969). For example, an animal is presented with a shadow which evokes an OR. Ten minutes later, with no intervening stimulation, a vibratory stimulus is presented which also evokes an OR. After a second 10-minute quiet period the vibration and shadow are presented simultaneously. The result is not simply an orienting reflex equal in duration (of behavioral interruption) to the sum of the first and second OR's, but rather crouching or retreat; that is, defensive reflexes, DR's.

The addition of physical energies experiment constitutes one example of behavioral mapping as a function of a change in the nature of the stimulus. It is obvious that much more extensive parametric studies using this technique are needed to delineate stimulus–response relationships in *Necturus* and that the general technique could prove useful in more widespread approaches to animal behavior. By the same token, the brain reflexes delineated by the habituation procedure in *Necturus* suggest that further use of this other approach to mapping could serve as the basis for a more comprehensive catalog of behavior. There is certainly no reason to believe that all brain reflexes of *Necturus* have been described.

It would seem that behavioral mapping, whether by the habituation procedure or other means, has been barely exploited as of this time. While the reasons for this neglect are unclear, there seems to be no compelling rationale for continuing neglect of this approach in the future.

D. Discussion

1. THE OR

Is pause the orienting reflex of *Necturus*? Pause does fulfill the criteria for nonspecificity (Sokolov, 1960, 1963a,b) for it occurs in response to the presentation of a variety of stimuli of moderate intensity. Pause also appears to be a characteristic component of the OR in cats and humans, to cite two higher vertebrates. In the cat, Kaada and co-workers (Kaada, 1951; Ursin and Kaada, 1960; Ursin *et al.*, 1969) have carefully delineated the arrest or pause component of the OR (see also Buchwald *et al.*, 1961).

Instances of combined arrest of somatic activity, respiration, and bradycardia in cats and other higher vertebrates have been reviewed by Obrist *et al.* (1970a). Table V compares the *Necturus* pause reflex and the arrest bradycardia preceding movement reported in man and the OR in human infants.

Obrist *et al.* (1970a,b) have also reported pause as a preliminary to somatic

TABLE V

ORIENTING REFLEX OF MUD PUPPY AND MAN[a]

OR Components	Mud puppy	Man	References
1. EEG arousal	(?)[b]	+ +[c]	Sharpless and Jasper, (1956), Sokolov (1963a,b)
2. Arrest of movement	+ + +[d]	+ + +	Dodd and Lewis (1969), Lewis and Goldberg (1969), Obrist, et al. (1970a)
3. Bradycardia	+ +	+ +	Graham and Clifton (1966), Lacey (1967), Lewis and Spaudling Lewis, et al. (1967)
4. Apnoea	+ + +	+ +	Obrist et al. (1970), Steinschneider (1968)
5. Peripheral vasoconstriction	+[e]	+ + +	Sokolov (1963a,b)
6. Cephalic vasodilation	(?)	+ + +	Sokolov (1963a,b)
7. Decrease or no change in somatic myographic activity	+ +	+	Obrist et al. (1970a)
8. Galvanic skin response	(?)	+ + +	Sokolov (1963a,b), Crowell et al. (1965)
9. Potentiated by movement or state change	+ + +	+ + +	Sokolov (1963a,b), Koepke and Pribram (1968)
10. Habituates	+ + +	+ + +	Sokolov (1963a,b)

[a] Based on material of Goodman and Weinberger (1970) and Lewis (1971).
[b] (?) no data.
[c] + +, usually present.
[d] + + +, always present.
[e] +, reported but more data required.

activity in adult man. They found a dramatic cardiac–somatic relationship not previously described which sets the salamander work in a new perspective.

> In humans there is a marked concomitance between cardiac deceleration and cessation of ongoing somatic events during the preparatory interval of a simple RT [Reaction Time] task... under these conditions both cardiac and somatic events have similar latency and show their peak effects at the same time. The decrease in somatic effects appears quite extensive and is like a momentary state of *suspended animation* [italics authors']. All aspects of ongoing somatic activity evaluated thus far have shown these effects including respiratory frequency and amplitude, eye movements and blinks and spontaneous EMG bursts particularly from muscles in and around the chin.

If pause is the basic vertebrate orienting reflex, it may have been overlooked because investigators have emphasized turning or "targeting"

(Konorski, 1967) which is specific to the stimulus, a narrower range of stimuli than produce pause. The turning toward response of a toad to a mealworm (Hinsche, 1935) or a cat toward a mouse (Hernández-Peón et al., 1956) is a specific reaction.

At times we have dropped an earthworm in the mud puppy aquarium. The animal characteristically pauses prior to turning toward the food object, as previously reported by Coghill (O'Leary and Bishop, 1969). With cats, Weinberger and Lindsley (1965) have also reported two phases to orienting, a nonspecific reaction to change per se, and a subsequent specific response in which the subject directs its gaze toward the source of stimulation. With a nonlocalizable stimulus (such as direct electrical stimulation of the cat brain) the targeting component is absent and arrest or pause may comprise the total orienting reflex (Ursin et al., 1967).

We conclude that pause is nonspecific and common to most, if not all, vertebrates under a variety of conditions and that it constitutes the OR of Necturus.

2. HABITUATION OF THE OR

Data presented above indicate that habituation of the mud puppy OR resembles habituation in other vertebrate systems as proposed by Thompson and Spencer (1966). Humphrey (1933) and Thorpe (1963) have proposed additional criteria. Does habituation in Necturus fulfill these also?

Humphrey (1933) held that habituation is simple learning not to respond to stimuli which "tend to be without significance in the life of the animal." Habituation of the mud puppy OR as studied in the laboratory does seem to reflect (presumptive) habituation in the natural habitat to the types of stimuli identified by Humphrey. For example, gill beating is a characteristic behavior in the field which is interrupted by visual and vibratory stimulation (Eycleshymer, 1906). Harris (1959) has pointed out the adaptive significance of habituation in the sea anemone to drops of rain on the water; the same would be expected for Necturus, stimulated by the falling of rain or leaves on the water's surface as it feeds in a shallow stream. If each of these stimulations produced cessation of gill beating, the mud puppy's behavior would be inextricably tied to random perturbations in the environment; habituation of gill beat suppression is thus adaptive.

Thorpe (1963) defined habituation as a relatively permanent waning of a response, not attributable to receptor adaptation, effector fatigue, or trauma. The second part of the definition constitutes a warning against introducing new animals into the laboratory, the physiology of whose receptors and effectors is unknown, and which may have been submitted (inadvertently) to trauma. Can alternate explanations explain habituation in the mud puppy? Habituation of the salamander OR cannot be attributed to visual receptor adaptation because the eye of *Necturus* can process shadow stimulation at the low rates employed (Werblin and Dowling, 1969b). Habituation of the OR in *Necturus* cannot be attributed to effector fatigue although this is a valid explanation if frequent strong stimuli had been used. The salamander beats its gills to remove oxygen from the water. Gill beat suppression slows removal of oxygen. With a series of ten (or more) stimulus-elicited pauses in gill beating, it is possible that the mud puppy extinguishes the gill beat suppression response because it can no longer stop its gills. The inability of the gills to be stopped because of an oxygen debt (Lerfant and Johanson, 1967) is certainly a form of effector fatigue. It is unlikely that this is an explanation in the present case, owing to the mud puppy's low metabolic requirements, its alternate means of securing oxygen,[8] its very steep oxygen-hemoglobin association curves (Lerfant and Johanson, 1967), and its ability to survive in low pO_2 environments (Gordon, 1934).

With reference to trauma, we would caution the reader contemplating the study of unfamiliar animals, particularly lower tetrapods, that not all apparent habituation is genuine habituation. For example, if the animal is stressed by either the testing situation or a stimulus of great intensity, alternate explanations of response decrement can be formulated (see Section V,D,3). One way to avoid such stress, particularly with an animal whose sensitivity to various stimuli is unknown, would be to allow the animal to leave or escape from the testing situation. It was for this reason that we provided an outer basin into which the mud puppies could escape from the test aquarium. Therefore, our studies were limited to animals which did not repeatedly leave the testing aquarium and were consequently not stressed. However, habituation has been studied in animals which might have been stressed; and it is to this topic that we diverge briefly.

3. A Note on Stimulus Intensity

In the previous paragraph we stated that frequent application of strong stimuli can produce effector fatigue. In the extreme case, there actually can be tissue damage. While most habituatory response decrements are not attributable to effector fatigue or to tissue damage, those possibilities do exist. Davis and Wagner (1969) studied habituation to startle in the rat, using 750 tones of 120-dB intensity presented at 8-second intervals. Intense tones presented frequently for more than 100 minutes might damage the hair cells of the rat cochlea. *Bona fide* habituation in rats receiving intense stimulation

---

[8] For a discussion of mechanisms of respiration see Gans (1970).

would have been demonstrated by dishabituation using a less intense stimulus, a maneuver not employed.

The problems of effector fatigue and tissue damage as alternate explanations to "habituation" do not represent the major criticism against the use of strong stimuli to produce response decrement. Granted that the rats in the Davis and Wagner (1969) experiment habituate (Davis, 1970), we are still left with the fact that strong stimuli elicit "negative reactions" (Thorpe, 1944). These include defensive reactions such as escape. In an experiment where response decrement is demonstrated after repeated applications of strong stimuli, we must ask: "Would the animal have escaped from the stimulus if it could?" and "Were these escape attempts thwarted by the design of the testing situation?" The animal must cope with a possibly noxious stimulus from which no escape is possible in whatever way it can. In the startle experiment no escape from the sound is possible, hence the rat is helpless to terminate the stimulus. Its so-called habituation curve may be epiphenomenal to the rat's learned helplessness that the stimulus recurs regardless of its behavior. Habituation in this situation contrasts sharply with Humphrey's criterion that habituation refers to a response decrement to stimuli "without significance to the life of the animal." While habituation in a stressful situation may merit study, it should not be confused with habituation under more naturalistic conditions.

Finally, strong stimuli elicit movement. Movement itself may have many effects, direct and indirect, on response magnitude. Movement may have a disruptive effect on the fine organization of behavior and may be inimical to the ability to make fine discriminations which are so important in dishabituation based upon changes in stimulus quality.

Movements, often fixed action patterns (FAP's), elicited by stimuli are frequently studied in laboratory habituation experiments. Less frequently investigators emphasize habituation of pause, a halt in ongoing activity. The data presented in this chapter suggest that pause, a fixed *in*action pattern, (FIP), is a modifiable brain reflex appropriate for study by investigators of habituation.

4. Summary

The mud puppy OR not unexpectedly habituates. This can be readily demonstrated in subjects allowed at least 24 hours in their testing aquarium. Parametric characteristics of habituation (Thompson and Spencer, 1966) which have been clearly satisfied include the following: (1) decrement with repeated trials, (2) spontaneous recovery, (3) potentiation of habituation with repeated sessions, (4) faster habituation with more rapid stimulus presentation, (5) dishabituation, and (6) habituation below zero (for HBI). The exact operations used to demonstrate habituation are those required for a behavioral mapping procedure one in which according to experimental conditions the response is primarily a function of the animal state (O) prior to stimulus presentation.

This section emphasized $R = f(A)$; the next dwells on state (O) determinants of any one response in an habituation series.

VI. $R = f(O)$: State and Behavioral Dishabituation

In the preceding sections we considered habituation experiments of the general form $R = f(A)$, that is in which the behavior in question varied as a function of accrued antecedent experience with a given stimulus. In the present section, we consider situations in which behavior varies as a function of the organismic state of the subject, i.e., $R = f(O)$. This procedure requires that A be constant, that experiential factors do not determine R. This might be accomplished in two ways: (1) by permitting no prior experience with the selected stimulus (a procedure which would yield a highly restricted amount of data) and (2) by dissecting the effects of A from those resulting from O. The latter approach has been attempted in studies on relationships between animal state and responsiveness to iterated stimulation in *Necturus* (Goodman, 1969; Goodman and Weinberger, 1970).

A. States of Necturus

A definition of organismic state may be as arbitrary as the choice of response systems that are monitored during an habituation experiment. In studies on *Necturus* the authors have defined state by reference to the simultaneous measurement of heartbeat, respiration (gill beat), and tail waving during intertrial intervals. A relatively constant mean and variance of these measures within such an interval was considered to index a relatively constant organismic state. Spontaneous or stimulus-induced changes in these parameters were taken to indicate a change of state.

From analyses of *Necturus* behavior under conditions of an undisturbed environment at 19°C, three states have been delineated. These are the Q (quiet), P (pause), and M (move) states, respectively.

The salamander after a variable time in the testing aquarium can be described as residing in the Q state. The Q state represents the quiescent salamander with rhythmic heartbeat and gill beat, at times with rhythmic tail movement and a low level of somatic myographic activity. Operationally this state can be defined as that in which the variance of five consecutive gill beats, heartbeats, and tail beats approaches zero (is minimal), and the rate of the outputs depends on the temperature and other physical constants of the environment.[9] The Q state may be considered the "ground" state of *Necturus*.[10]

Significant deviations from the Q state may be considered to result in passage into either the P or M states, both of which may be referred to as "states of arousal." The P state, or pause arousal is operationally defined as a decrease in the rate of behavioral and physiological output with an increase in variance over that which characterizes the Q state. P arousal is gauged by slowed or stopped gill beat, heartbeat, and tail waving, diminished body myographic activity, and movement. On the other hand, the M state is defined as that extant under conditions of increased rate of output such as faster hearbeat and gill beat, the augmentation of myographic activity, and often overt bodily movement. Variance of these outputs is also greater than during the Q or ground state. Thus a change from the Q state is defined as a significant increase in variance of certain behavioral and physiological processes, particularly those which are highly rhythmic in nature, i.e., heart, gill, and tail beating. The nature of the state change, whether to the P or M states, is indicated by whether or not these physiological measures decrease or increase in value.

As the animal becomes more aroused or as the stimulus becomes more intense, the OR pause is followed immediately by movement, DR's. Since movement of some part of an animal's body is the response so frequently studied, it is the move component of the pause–move unit that has received much of the attention in behavioral studies. We believe that pause–move is the basic unit of behavior evoked by a stimulus of moderate intensity.

For the moment, it is assumed that general arousal or excitability level within the P and M states can vary, as evidenced by the degree of output retardation or acceleration. Extreme P arousal in *Necturus* may be analogous to "freezing" seen in more evolved vertebrates while extreme M arousal may be analogous to the "freedom reflex" (Pavlov, 1927). Use of these terms with reference to *Necturus* does not, of course, validate these analogies; nevertheless, they may serve as convenient descriptors for amphibian behavior, and hereafter are so used, without surplus meaning.

This review of pause–move and of P and M arousal precedes findings where state affects the shape of a salamander habituation curve or evidences dishabituation.

---

[9]The mean rate of behavioral outputs may be set for *Necturus* in a quiescent environment by varying water temperature; for example, Goodman (1969) found that heatbeat increased in an approximately linear fashion from 0.28 per second at 11.1°C to 0.56 per second at 22.8°C.

[10]Ingle (1968) notes that quiet frogs have been referred to as "stupid". Hobson *et al.* (1968) refer to this condition as torper.

B. State Affects the Rate of Habituation

An habituation curve may be reconstructed from an exponential decay function and a periodic function. One presentation of the two processes appears in Ewert (1967a) shown in Fig. 12. In the mud puppy, exponential habituation functions without the periodic component are generated by salamanders who responded to the first stimulus with exaggerated inhibition far outlasting the duration of the stimulus, in "pilot" mud puppies presented with frequent (once per 5 second) stimulation, and in animals which exhibited no movement. Exponential and rhythmic components in the habituation function were evident in salamanders that "spontaneously" moved during an intertrial interval.

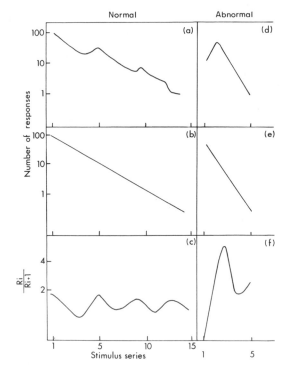

Fig. 12. Separation of toad habituation curve into its constituents: an exponential and a periodic component. Abscissa is number of stimulus series; ordinate is arbitrary units. Figure suggests two components to habituation curve which may be differentially affected by brain lesions (Abnormal), a is shape of the normal habituation curve decomposed into b, an exponential decay, and c, a rhythmic component. In the abnormal subject, the rhythmic component is absent. After Ewert (1967a).

An analysis of the relationship between movement and behavior was performed by listing all movements and comparing the duration of gill beat suppression on the trial following movement with that on the trial immediately preceding movement. The analysis included all animals in the habituation experiment discussed previously. A significant increase of GBS was found, indicating that movement in the midst of habituatory response decrement resulted in dishabituation on the following trial (Table VI).

The percentage of salamander movements that led to dishabituation on the next programmed stimulus was lowest in Group 400, receiving shadow stimulation each 400 seconds ——lower than in Group 120 and Group 30. This suggested a decay time for the movement-produced arousal. Analysis revealed that movements more than 120 seconds pretrial were not so effective as GBS dishabituation movements less than 120 seconds pretrial (Table VI).

The foregoing findings support the notion that M arousal, indexed by movement, has a dishabituatory effect and may cause "jags" in an habituation curve, and further that such arousal has a decay time such that its potential effects are dissipated within approximately 2 minutes.

Although changes in state toward increased activity (Arechiga and Wiersma, 1969; Koepke and Pribram, 1967) or toward somnolence (Sokolov, 1963a) can underlie dishabituation, a change in receptor orientation following movement as the source for dishabituation has also been suggested (see Kimble and Ray, 1965). However, if it is true that arousal *per se* antagonizes the process of habituation, then P arousal responses without movement should be just as effective sources for dishabituation as M arousal with movement. This was found to be the case. An analysis of the effects of infrequent application of a vibration which produced strong P arousal (i.e., no movement but rather a pronounced OR_1 or OR_2) also preceded response increment to a much greater extent than moderate P arousal (OR_0). This

TABLE VI

PROPORTION OF INCREASES IN GBS TO SHADOW FOLLOWING INTERSTIMULUS MOVEMENTS

Statistical Comparisons	Group (by duration of ITI in seconds)				
	30	120	400		
			Total	0–120	121+
Proportion of increases	9/11	29/39	47/73	20/26	27/47
p (sign test)	0.03	0.003	0.01	0.005	NS

strong vibrational stimulus was produced aperiodically by the onset of a refrigerator motor. An increase in GBS was found on 37 of 54 trials, across all groups (sign test $t = 2.6$, $p < 0.005$).

In summary, spontaneous arousal or state change superimposed jags toward response increment in the midst of a trend toward response decrement (Fig. 13). Changes to the M and P states are both effective. Thus, the habituation curve can be reconstructed from three components: an experience component leads to exponential response decrement (Thompson and Spencer, 1966; Ewert, 1969), an arousal component elicits temporary response increments (see Goodman, 1969), and a periodic component or components visible in studies of individual amphibian habituation curves described by Ewert, (1967a) Goodman (1969).

VII. General Discussion

The characteristics of habituation in lower tetrapod vertebrates are of interest for comparative purposes with other classes as well as in their own right. At the present time, however, there is insufficient data to permit any

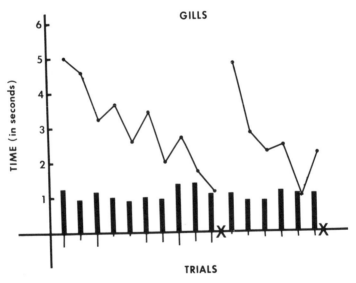

Fig. 13. Separation of mud puppy habituation curve into its constituents: an exponential factor, a periodic factor, and a third factor, a dishabituation factor. Solid bars are the means of the five prestimulus gill beats and the thin bars the standard deviations. Crosses indicate dishabituating movements of the salamander's body.

but premature comparisons with other vertebrates, particularly the Mammalia for which there exist copious data. Generally, the characteristics of habituation in the frog, toad, and salamander seem to be similar to those of other vertebrates. An interesting possible exception is the extreme sensitization of the wiping reflex in the frog consequent to slight variations in the locus of stimulation upon the skin (Kimble and Ray, 1965). With reference to the Reptilia, there is even a greater paucity of data. The turtle exhibits habituation of both head withdrawal and optokinetically induced head and eye movements. In contrast to Mammalia the turtle head turning response to vestibular stimulation fails to habituate (Crampton and Schwam, 1962). Further study is needed to determine whether this particular difference is more apparent than real. For example, parametric studies of stimulus intensity would be helpful.

With the understanding that not all criteria of habituation have been satisfied in all experiments on habituation, we may conclude that the Amphibia and Reptilia which have been studied do seem to have responses which may be evoked and habituated in much the same way as other vertebrates. But if this were all that such studies have revealed, we should expect the reader to be disappointed, and indeed would share this reaction with him. Fortunately, this is not the case for it seems that amphibian habituation has added interesting dimensions to the study of vertebrate behavioral plasticity: periodicity, delineation of brain reflexes, and organismic state.

A. Periodicity

In addition to the standard exponential decay, a periodic component has been found in habituation functions of Amphibia. Periodicities which have been noted in studies of the single animal are overlooked when averaged group data are presented. With respect to habituation, periodicity is evident in the individual functions presented by Ewert (1967a) and by Eikmanns (1955) and also Goodman (1969). The concept of periodicity in the amphibian learning curve was suggested by Haecker (1912) and emphasized by Trincker (1954a,b); see also Ewert (1971).

Whether or not this periodicity is characteristic of other vertebrates, particularly mammals, awaits painstaking and systematic study such as that devoted to the toad by Ewert. At any rate, the possibility that periodicity may characterize habituation should be given general recognition and hopefully expression in some future experimental endeavors.

B. Brain Reflexes

Basic elements of vertebrate behavior might be revealed in the Amphibia. In this chapter we have presented evidence for the existence of orienting and defensive reflexes in *Necturus*, specified their components, and noted that the

OR's (or pause reflexes) precede the DR's (or move reflexes) when the latter are evoked. Delineation of these two types of reflex, each consisting of three subvarieties, depended upon simultaneous recording of three response systems plus general body movement when the subjects were studied in a semi-naturalistic setting. We would emphasize that description of the OR's and DR's was fortuitous and *post hoc*, and possible only because a rather comprehensive record of *Necturus* behavior was available as ink-written records on several thousand feet of chart paper. Had any single response system, such as that of the gills, been preselected for study, a more fragmentary picture of *Necturus'* behavior would have emerged. At this point in time, we would emphasize the importance of the approach to the delineation of behavior patterns via the habituation procedure as much as the particular *Necturus* reflexes described above. Clearly, only a scratch has been made in the surface of the salamander "black-box" behavior machine.

Whether or not the surplus meaning which is inevitably attached to terms such as orienting and defensive survives future investigations, pause and move ought to have a secure place. Both the frog and salamander seem to be characterized by sequences of pause–move.

Although pause as "totalized inhibition" (Coghill, 1929; Herrick, 1948; O'Leary and Bishop, 1969) has been described in the salamander since at least 1915 (Herrick and Coghill, 1915) it has a history in Amphibia reaching far back into the nineteenth century (Diamond *et al*. 1963). In point of fact, Sechenov's *Reflexes of the Brain* concerns active inhibition of heartbeat and spinal reflexes by stimulation of the frog's midbrain (Sechenov, in 1865; see Sechenov, 1965). Wilson (1890) described an early example of pause arousal and its habituation, "It was noted that inhibition of heart beat [in the frog] occurred on stimulating the optic lobes: the stimulation appeared rapidly to cause fatigue as the effect passed off after repeated excitation."

From the toad and frog data there is evidence that alternating sequences of pause–move also characterize their behavior. For example, the response habituated by Eikmanns (1955) and Ewert (1967a) is the "turning toward" reflex, the taxic component in a *Handlungskette* or behavioral chain, beginning when the toad spies its presumed prey and ending when the toad has struck with its tongue and determined whether the prey has been taken into the mouth and swallowed (Hinsche, 1935). The entire chain reconstructed consists of the following segment: a pause when the prey enters the visual field, a turning toward movement, a pause followed by locomotion, usually a hopping toward the prey. The toad next fixates or regards the prey, then snaps it up. The sequence consists of pause, turn; pause, hop; pause, strike; etc. See Ingle (1968).

If the chain stops at pause too long, then continuous movement can result. The movement may not be appropriate. When one dummy is continuously presented, but the toad cannot strike at it, the toad assumes a "blank look" and remains immobile for 30–120 seconds then strikes almost continuously at empty space (Eikmanns, 1955, description of Hinsche's *T-Phänomenon*, 1935).

If a toad is presented with many moving mealworm larvae at the same time, it strikes at none of them, rather it releases an inappropriate movement as "yawning" or "washing" (see Ewert and Härter, 1969). These so-called displacement behaviors, then, seem to occur during excessive P arousal. Delius (1970) has postulated the same relationship between displacement behavior and high arousal from independent considerations.

If the investigator is interested in stimulus-elicited movement, as is often the case in behavioral experiments, then generalized pause arousal may interfere with elicitation of movement. For example, Ewert (1967b), who noted that toads turn toward a moving prey dummy in the visual field, presented a companion stimulus to another modality, either tactile or acoustic. The effect of the companion stimulus was a ready inhibition of the "turning toward" response. Similarly, if the toad's pond is disturbed just before it is going to turn toward the target, that response is inhibited.

Examples of pause as an elicited phenomenon to stimulation in Amphibia and other vertebrates are legion (e.g., Yerkes, 1904; Beritov, 1968). For example, pause can be observed in elasmobranchs (Lutz and Wyman, 1932), eels (McWilliam, 1885), teleost fish (Offutt, 1971; Shelton and Randall, 1962), turtles (Hough, 1895; Lumsden, 1923), caimans (Gault and Gans, 1969), and man (Ferrier, 1876; Obrist *et al.*, 1970a,b). Conjunct pause in both the somatic and cardiac spheres has been termed "cardiac-somatic integration" (Obrist *et al.*, 1970a) and "autonomic-somatic integration" (Gellhorn, 1967).

It would appear from amphibian data, particularly from studies of the frog and toad, that there is a delicate balance between pause and move. Ewert's reports (1969a,b) that brain damage upsets this balance and prevents habituation are of particular interest. Brain mechanisms underlying the two phenomena and their interrelationships should be at least as accessible in Amphibia as in Mammalia, if not more so; see Section VIII.

C. Organismic State

Habituation functions of individual animals are notoriously "rough"; while exponential functions can be fit to individual data, prominent deviations from a monotonic decrease in response magnitude are common. While Ewert (1969) has emphasized periodicity in the habituation function, we would add another process, "spontaneous" dishabituation.

Dishabituation may explain response increments in the midst of habituatory response decrement. These increments are short lasting and can be attributable to a change in the stimulus or to a change in state. With reference to the former, in a formal attempt to produce dishabituation the investigator often changes the stimulus. Nevertheless, there are small unintentional changes in the stimulus as in its location which lead to minor dishabituation. This is also important in the amphibian exposed to tactile stimuli (see Kimble and Ray, 1965). For this reason it is good laboratory procedure to work with a completely quiescent or "quieted down" preparation in which method of stimulus presentation is unvarying. (See Hinde, 1970b).

A change in organismic state can also produce dishabituation. As enumerated in Section VI, interstimulus episodes of strong pause or move precede response increment thereby producing a short-lived dishabituation. The time course of move arousal in *Necturus* was approximately 2 minutes; movements which preceded a trial within this interval were predictive of increased response magnitude (longer pause) during the next trial. (See Hinde, 1970b).

From the toad there is also evidence that a pause arousal residual tends to dissipate in the first 2 minutes. Ewert and Härter (1969) noted that a frog usually turns toward a moving prey dummy but if a second prey dummy is moving further out in the visual field, the frog pauses, its movement inhibited. This inhibition has a half-life of 1.7 minutes. If the original dummy is presented in that interval without its companion, the toad strikes less often and less intensely at the prey for some minutes thereafter.

The study of organismic state or arousal level may help not only to explain some deviations from an ideal exponential decay function during habituation but also could provide insights into the neural bases of behavioral excitability. For example, an arousal continuum is widely accepted to be adequate to describe vertebrate excitability. We now set forth a simple model, based upon studies of *Necturus*, which is at variance with this concept.

Previously, we have operationally defined three states in *Necturus*, the Q, M, and P states (see Section VI, A). Defensive reflexes, characterized by initiation of movement, and orienting reflexes, characterized by pause or interruption in behavior, were associated with the M and P states, respectively. Insofar as OR's preceded DR's, a single arousal continuum would seem to be appropriate; DR's would occur at higher levels of arousal than OR's. However, freezing, which seems to be an extreme pause reflex, would then have to be placed below the most mild defensive reflex on the arousal continuum. This paradox is derived from a common sense consideration of rabbit behavior. A more important finding is the fact that stimulation with shadow and vibration, each of which singly applied produce pause, an orienting reflex, do not elicit a greater OR when presented together. Rather, they produce a very brief pause, which immediately gives way to move, a defensive reflex. If the elicitation of a DR resulted from a greater level of arousal caused by a summation of stimulus energies, then an OR would not be elicited prior to DR onset.

Additionally, it was found that either a strong pause or strong move reflex could cause dishabituation on the subsequent trial. If dishabituation is a function of the amount of increase in arousal during an intertrial interval, then move reflexes should precede dishabituation to a greater extent than pause reflexes since move would reflect greater arousal than pause. However, this was not the case; both were quite effective (see Table VI).

We therefore postulate two arousal continua, a pause arousal during which OR's are elicited, and a move arousal during which DR's are elicited. This schema is summarized in Fig. 14. Both types of arousal diverge from the quiet or Q state. Within this framework, extreme P arousal would be revealed by "freezing" behavior and extreme M arousal by the "freedom reflex" or fleeing. It would follow that quantal or discrete qualitative "jumps" underlie the sudden transition from an OR to a DR (Fig. 14).

Further development or evaluation of this dual-arousal model must await further data.[11] We note in passing that it is consonant with McCleary's (1966) exposition that the brain of the rat contains two systems, one that facilitates immobility, to produce passive avoidance behavior, and a second that underlies active avoidance.

VIII. Machinery of Amphibian Habituation

At the present time very little is known about the machinery underlying habituation in Amphibia. A start toward elucidating the brain mechanisms underlying behavior and habituation has been attempted by Ewert (1966, 1967a,c; Ewert and Birukow, 1965). The full length paper (Ewert, 1967a) discusses effects of brain damage on the turning toward response. First, all toads were examined for their preoperative reactivity. Then animals were submitted to surgery and tested 24 hours after recovery. In general, the greater the forebrain extirpation, the fewer responses there are in a response series. Complete forebrain extirpation led to complete loss of the turning (Ewert, 1966) toward reaction. With longitudinal cuts in their dorso-medial thalamus medial to the optic lobes, some toads became completely dominated by jerky episodes of pause–move ["... gab es zu Beginn der Reizzerie

---

[11]Another type of dual-arousal model has been proposed by Routtenberg (1968). It is important to note that the model presented here is not concerned with goal-directed aspects of behavior nor does it consider the P state to represent a state of lower excitability than the M state. Thus, the P and M states are not respectively parallels of Hess' (1954) "trophotropic" and "ergotropic" states. The present formulation emphasizes the concept that nonmoving animals may be in a high state of arousal.

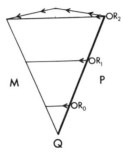

Fig. 14. Proposed dual-arousal schema linking the Q, P, and M states and brain reflexes for moving shadow or vibrational stimuli. The Q state is a steady state characterized by highly rhythmic behavioral outputs having minimal variance. If an impinging stimulus alters this state, the mud puppy will exhibit orienting reflexes (OR's) characterized by pause or retardation of behavioral outputs, which are hypothesized to occur in the P state of arousal. An OR may be quickly followed by a defensive reflex (DR) which is characterized by body movement and occurs in the hypothesized M state. Arrows from the P to M states indicate that state transitions may be from P to M but not the reverse. The distance along the P and M lines from Q indicates the degree of arousal within each of these states. The actual "distances" in amount of arousal between the various orienting reflexes (OR_0, OR_1, OR_2) within the P State are unknown.

eine Anlaufphase (warm up)]. Danach erscheinen die Richtbewegungen immer schneller, *von rhythmischen Pausen unterbrochen*" [italics ours]. When completely warmed up these toads permanently went around in circles snapping at their own toes (Ewert, 1969).

Continuous striking at moving targets without the intervening pauses is a pathological condition subsequent to damage of the midbrain (Ewert, 1967a, 1969. Frogs with midbrain damage do not habituate. This behavior contrasts sharply with animals having forebrain lesions, producing a condition characterized by a paucity of reaction to stimulation. Interestingly, some toads that ceased striking altogether would show complete ducking (crouching) or retreating reactions indicating that a spared system underlaid the defensive reflexes. This is illustrated by other studies of Ewert (1966, 1971).

With respect to the brain mechanism underlying the behavior of *Necturus*, little work has been done. Goodman and Weinberger (1969) were not able to isolate a definite change in brain activity during orienting although certain EEG changes were suggestive as rhythmic activity in the salamander paleocortex concomitant with movement.

The obvious direction of the salamander studies would be toward elaboration of mechanisms underlying modifiable brain reflexes as Ewert has done with the toads. With remote sensing of *Necturus* such complete records of behavior result that precise effects of brain damage might be identified.

To the investigator interested in activity of brain structures during habituation, the questions raised and as yet unanswered are many. Does the amphibian hypothalamic pre-optic area energize pause[12] and its posterior diencephalic area energize move such that pre-optic ablation leads to incessant activity and posterior extirpation produces absence of movement? Is it the interpeduncular nucleus in *Necturus* that metes endogenous and exogenous pause arousal (as suggested by Herrick, 1934b) and the midbrain "reticular formation" that forms the final common pathway for move-arousal stimuli? Does the primitive neuropil of the brain stem contain representations of recent stimulus events (Herrick, 1934b, Sokolov, 1960).

An alternate approach to amphibian brain function and the one stressed in this chapter treats the whole animals as a machine of unknown components. Responses must be measured so precisely that "function generators" and hook-ups from these generators can be hypothesized, then sought at that time when the state (O), experiential (A), and stimulus (S) determinants of the response have been delimited. Data reviewed in this chapter strongly suggest that amphibian behavior is particularly amenable to this approach.

IX. Study Programs

A guiding premise of this chapter reduces to a simple tautology: There have been few studies on habituations in Amphibia because there have been few studies in Amphibia. It is quite evident that at active and systematic experimentation in Amphibia is still at a very low level. For example, recent conferences on model systems for the study of simple behavioral plasticity have not seriously considered Amphibia (Bullock, 1966; Abraham, 1971). [On the other hand, the retina of *Necturus*, which permits intracellular recording from its elements, is being exploited with exciting results (e.g., Werblin 1970, 1971; Werblin and Dowling, 1968a,b).

In behavioral research as in other areas of human endeavor interest in a new process or technique may remain at a low level until a concerted effort by a few creates a snowball effect—rapid growth in a short time. Undoubtedly, the common laboratory preparations as the albino variant of *Rattus norvegicus* went through stages of disinterest, then development. Robinson (1965) placed the critical period of white rat acceptance in the first decade of the twentieth century. Similarly, the invertebrate *Aplysia californicus* or the sea hare owes its acceptance into the neurosciences to concerted efforts during the early 1960's.[13] Of course, the growth in interest depends critically upon the usefulness of the particular animal chosen. If it offers advantages for the study of delineated problems, and if in addition it can serve as a model from which reasonable

[12]See Bullock and Horridge (1965).

[13]Compare with "central lateral inhibition" described by Ewert *et al.*, (1970).

This section offers Amphibia, especially the salamanders, as model systems for the study of vertebrate behavioral plasticity. Toward that goal a number of study programs are presented. These may be pursued singularly or in combination as suits the experimenter. Study program I is the "habituation demonstration" with an option to tap in on the sensory side with recording electrodes. Study program II, already presented in the last section, includes the habituation demonstration plus stimulation and lesioning in the central nervous system. Study program III is the "habituation procedure" toward mapping the entire output of the selected amphibian. Study program IV emphasizes the habituation procedure in Amphibia as a means toward defining operationally their conceptual nervous system.

A. Study Program I

A toad, frog, salamander, or newt is selected. Stimulus parameters are adjusted so habituation with repeated trials is observed. Simultaneously there can be electrodes in an input system as the visual system. If the frog or toad is the subject, there is a long history of afferent system analysis from which one can select papers by Granit and Riddel (1934), Gaze (1958), Maturana *et al.*, (1960), Grüsser and Bullock (1964), and Ewert (1966). Study program I has been pursued by researchers interested in changes in afferent systems during behavioral habituation (cf. Horn, 1970).

B. Study Program II

Stimuli are presented to the amphibian at 1–30-second intervals with the expectation that the magnitude of a designated response will decrease with repeated trials. The candidate modifiable brain reflexes include the toad turning toward reflex (Eikmanns, 1955; Ewert, 1967a), toad "turning away from" response (Ewert and Rehn, 1969); toad "wiping" reflex (Kuczka, 1956), and the salamander orienting reflex. (Goodman and Weinberger, in preparation). To modify behavior, electricity of chemicals can be injected into the central nervous system or a surgeon's lesioning scalpel can intrude. Study program II has been pursued by Ewert (1967a, 1968).

C. Study Program III

This is the habituation procedure where it is assumed that any response $R = f$ (S, A, O) where S is the designated stimulus, A is accruing experience, and O is the organismic state. $R = f(A)$ experiments emphasize response decrement (or, at times, response increment, Hinde, 1970a) with repeated trials 1–30 seconds or 30–400 seconds apart. $R = f(O)$ experiments allow the subject to cycle endogenously, "running" with respect to its internal clock(s). The animal should by acclimatized to its aquarium and external stress should be minimal. Unobtrusive stimulus-administering and response-measuring techniques should be employed. $R = f(S)$ experiments should include infrequent presentation (400–1200 seconds or more apart) of these stimuli: a difficult-to-localize visual stimulus as a sudden moving shadow passing overhead (Russell, 1967; Hayes and Saiff, 1967; the *Luftfiend* of Ewert and Rehn, 1969), a vibrational stimulus applied to the substrate, and a reward stimulus—a mealworm larvae to a toad (Eikmanns, 1955) or a red wriggler earthworm to a mud puppy. The intensity of these stimuli should be increased and decreased systematically. Study program III is the basic habituation procedure referred to in this chapter.

D. Study Program IV

This is the study program attempted by Goodman (1969) with the salamander *Necturus maculosus*. He attempted to define organization of brain reflexes in *Necturus* by careful analysis of its output. Instrumental in the analysis was the observation that the classic habituation demonstration $R = f(A)$ for n trials can also be habituation procedure in which $R = f(O)$. $R = f(A)$ approaches $R = f(O)$ as the interstimulus interval reaches and exceeds 400 seconds. With this dissecting tool large amounts of information on psychobiological variables can be collected. The questions asked with study program IV were these: First, what are the optimal conditions for reproducing a behavioral finding? Second, what are the findings on the conceptual nervous system of *Necturus* (or other Amphibia) which should be investigated in greater detail? Third, what kind of brain machines might animate the salamander (Amphibia)?

Let us examine preliminary findings using study program IV. First, *Necturus* orienting or pause can be observed in all quiescent, acclimatized (to 19°C) subjects. Under what conditions can this study system become erratic? Paul Dye (1921) ran unacclimatized mud puppies at room temperature and noted that their response to a transient stimulus might be a decrease or an increase in gill beat rate. It appears that pause is not an invariant response to a transient stimulus when the subject is not acclimatized to the testing aquarium or has initiated excited activity just prior to stimulus onset. Similarly, when a strong stimulus precedes the stimulus that ordinarily would produce pause, the response is not observed. In pilot studies, mud puppies restrained in holders and those with electrodes in their skulls and beneath their skin or in the musculature responded to the shadow passing overhead with pause on only five of ten occasions. Strong stimuli applied proximally, not distally, especially strong vestibular and electric shock stimuli generalizations may be forthcoming, then all that remains is its exploitation in experiments. We believe that Amphibia qualify as highly acceptable candidates on the basis of data and other considerations presented in the preceding sections. may not produce an obvious pause episode. Lastly, when the moderate stimulus normally eliciting pause is not the first stimulus in a series and when there is reason to believe the mud puppy is temporally conditioned, not pause but acceleration can be the response. The worst possible attempt to reproduce the findings reported in this report would utilize unacclimatized, recently handled mud puppies at room temperature with electrodes in their gills and presented with a strong tactile stimulus which has been preceded by other strong stimuli. If the study program IV prerequisites are followed, pause as the salamander orienting reflex occurs 100% of the time.

Data collected using this study program suggest a basic pattern of operation to the amphibian central nervous system, a reciprocity between a system that produces the arrest of ongoing activity and a system that initiates and maintains that activity. It would be of appreciable interest to demonstrate physiologically that reciprocal inhibition exists in the arousal system just as it exists in the sensory and motor systems. In the present report, we have suggested that pause and move might be reciprocal, an idea that derives from concepts of Gellhorn (1943, 1957, 1967) on functional properties of a two-arousal system. The strongest evidence for such an arousal system derives from the almost universal finding that exaggerated activity greatly accentuates the intensity of responses marked by a cessation of activity (see, e.g., Samaan, 1935; Babskii and Ul'Yaninskii, 1964). The more intense the movement, the greater the subsequent induced pause. This appears constantly in the diving reflex literature (see Goodman and Weinberger, 1970). As to the dramatic immobility response called animal hypnosis, Prestrude and Crawford (1970) wrote ". . . tonic immobility . . . may be conceptualized as a longer state of unresponsiveness followed and induced by an initial transitory, albeit intense experience." A great number of instances of pause linked reciprocally to move were reported on by Gellhorn (1943, 1957). Investigation of Gellhorn's ideas (See Gellhorn, 1968) led to the rather surprising conclusion that the present amphibian study program (IV) might have been initiated in 1950 when Karl S. Lashley (Lashley, 1950) called for new approaches to the study of brain and behavior. Amphibian research reported here derives from a rather eclectic tradition including Herrick's (1948) *Brain of the Tiger Salamander*, Wiener's (1948) *Cybernetics*, supplemented by speculations on arousal by Gellhorn (1957) and on rhythmicities in behavior observed by von Holst (1934, 1936, 1938).

Conjunct use of Study Programs I–IV will encourage careful investigation of output for clues to organization of the function generators and hook-ups in the brain. The first step suggested can be identification of the brain structure(s), which on mild direct stimulation produce(s) the OR's and on stronger

Ursin and Kaada, 1960). Also, lesions of the type performed by Ewert (1967a, stimulation produce(s) defensive reflexes (the amygdala region perhaps, 1968) and chemical stimulation will follow naturally. Yet to stop at this point would delimit the scope of the study program prematurely. At all levels of analysis new approaches to the study of brain function thrust themselves into view. Does it appear that reciprocal inhibition is widespread in the salamander brain? Then Swigert (1967) suggested that this is one requisite condition for neural "holography." Does it appear that the quiescent salamander can be described in terms of loosely coupled oscillators? Goodman and Richards (1971) suggested search for periodically active "ciliated" or pacemaker neurons active with a constant phase angle between them. Do small transients "release" complicated action patterns? Perhaps the neural mechanism is the holophone of Longuet-Higgins (1968) or the phased ensembles of John (1967) demonstrating coherent wave activity.

E. Advice in Parting

The study of novel animals, such as lower tetrapods involves a few precautions without which the experimenter may find his subjects unyielding in divulging meaningful and reliable behavioral information.

A naturalistic testing situation may prove beneficial, but in any event the organism should be allowed to equilibrate with its new environment. Procedures which inadvertently cause continual "freezing" thereby obscuring other normal behavior should be avoided or at least minimized parts. Animals should be tested under low stress conditions with adequate time for full acclimatization. There should be a behavioral means of proving that the testing situation is low stress. If the quiescent state is a normal state of low arousal, the animal should be tested when it is in that state.

When feasible, remote sensing or special forms of biomedical telemetry (Mackay, 1968) may be beneficial or even necessary. Remote sensing has been used in ecology (Odum and Kendeigh 1940). Kleerekoper and Sibakin (1956) recorded fish respiration remotely while Barham et al., (1969) sensed fish EMG underwater remotely. Quite exciting is the report of Gulyaen et al., (1968) of sensing of muscle, nerve, and heart activity with remote probes and high impedance amplifiers. The most recent report on remote sensing (Tremor and Rogallo, 1970) uses ballistocardiography. If direct sensing of behavior and physiological processes is suspected of interfering with the organism's normal adaptation to the experimental situation, then remote sensing would seem to be in order. Because of Necturus' extreme sensitivity to shadows, vibration, and even the slight restraint imposed by implanted wires, we found remote sensing to be more than merely a luxury. Alternately, the experimenter may be willing and even eager to study a disturbed animal; in any event, he should be aware.

X. Concluding Remarks

The foregoing review of habituation in lower tetrapods has revealed three salient points. (1) There has been a paucity of research. (2) These organisms exhibit habituation which is similar in form to habituation in mammalians. (3) The study of amphibia in semi-naturalistic settings has revealed the possibility of understanding the relationships between organismic state and behavioral response to an iterated stimulus. Let us consider these briefly, in turn.

A. Use of Lower Tetrapods

Most scientific disciplines have a favorite preparation which serves as a convenient standardized model for the general problem area of interest. As biochemistry has chosen *Escherichia coli*, and genetics *Drosophila melanogaster*, so psychology has *Rattus novegicus* and its close relatives. The widespread use of the rat has had benefits, not the least of which is ready comparison of results from different laboratories. Yet one may question whether the rat is the optimal model for all vertebrate behavior, in the present case, habituation. This process of behavioral plasticity is so widespread throughout the vertebrates that lower forms might be more suitable for revealing the basic aspects of habituatory response decrement. Hodos and Campbell (1969) have pointed out that rat-cat-monkey-man does not form a direct evolutionary sequence; thus, the choice of these animals cannot be made only on the basis of evolutionary proximity to man. Some lower tetrapods, such as the salamander, predate the forerunners of mammals and have been relatively unchanged for 50 million years. Thus, basic mechanisms of basic vertebrate behavior might profitably be sought in such organisms. In order to do so, scientists will have to overcome their great inertia to use only mammals as models for all vertebrate behavior.

B. Habituation in Lower Tetrapods

We have seen that lower tetrapods exhibit habituation, but Hernández-Peón (1969) has argued that attention first evolved in Aves and is not a property of reptilian (and by implication amphibian and fish) behavior. Without entering the arena of semantics to do battle with the various meanings of "attention" (cf. Weinberger, 1971), let us grant that Hernández-Peón (1969) had in mind selective attention including the exclusion of "irrelevant" stimuli from behavioral control. But what else is *bona fide* behavioral habituation if not a definitive demonstration that an animal can selectively attend to stimuli and selectively "exclude" them as their novelty or importance declines? One may surely ask about the discriminative limits of an organism during habituation, and it may be that birds are superior to lower tetrapods on this dimension. But we think it is inappropriate to argue about the existence of attention on absolute grounds and far more important to provide behavioral data which must form the bases for such decisions. It is certainly worse than merely inappropriate to follow Hernández-Peón in drawing conclusions about the behavioral capabilities of organisms from purely nonbehavioral, neurophysiological data. In closing, let us reiterate that if the presence of an orienting reflex and its habituation be admitted as criteria for attention, then attention is clearly present in Amphibia (and we strongly suspect all vertebrates). If one must discriminate against their use, other grounds must be sought.

C. Organismic State and Habituation

A behavioral equation must include a term representing the state of the organism at the time it is presented with a stimulus. State, experience, and stimulus properties must surely interact to determine the behavioral response. We have seen that "states" can be defined for salamanders, and that changes in state may predict spontaneous dishabituation.

If one is interested in the general organization of vertebrate behavior, lower tetrapods might prove useful because their behavioral repertoire is less extensive than that of higher vertebrates. In the present case, stereotyped orienting and defensive reflexes have been delineated for *Necturus*. In order to solve behavioral equations with stereotyped behavior as the dependent variable, knowledge of state is essential. With regard to salamanders, which exhibit rhythmic behavior of the cardiac, gill, and tail systems, let us assume that they are finite state automata whose brain mechanisms cycle endlessly. If one could measure state changes for a sufficiently long time, certain behavioral fragments would repeat. By the method of overlapping fragments, it should be possible to expose the fine structure of this state machine. Knowledge of the cycling of the animal would facilitate solution of behavioral equations because the state component could be specified rather precisely.

In closing, we cannot but help mentioning that the study of habituation in lower tetrapods is particularly exciting because of the present paucity of knowledge about the behavior of these organisms. We believe it is possible to view behavior from a fresh perspective when investigating a little-known animal. Yet this kind of excitement should give way to that consequent to solid progress in understanding amphibian and reptilian behavior which will come only with extensive research. This progress would be demonstrated by rendering the present review obsolete in the near future, a prospect which we welcome and encourage.

Note Added in Proof

There have been recent developments related to research described in this chapter which are worthy of note. Work from J. P. Ewert's laboratory continues to show extraordinarily high standards. North American workers are fortunate that Ewert's work is now occasionally available in English as well as in German. With Ingle (Ewert and Ingle, 1971), Ewert has demonstrated that a toad who no longer responds to a stimulus presented repetitively to one retinal locus can be "hyperreactive" to the same stimulus presented to a new locus. In a second recent paper, Ewert and Kleinlogel (1971) analyze the toad's wiping reflex and show not only that it demonstrates decrement with repeated elicitation, but that the response shows a distinct seasonal variation.

In another recent development, Spoor and his coworkers (Spoor et al., 1971) developed independently a technique for indirect recording of behavior, in fish. Their preliminary findings indicate that arousal in fish is quite similar to arousal in *Necturus*. Pause includes arrest of opercular (gill) activity and loss of altitude in the aquarium.

Lastly, comment should be made on further research toward identifying two stages in the arousal response of higher vertebrates. As Weinberger and Lindsley (1965) noted, it appears to consist of two separate sequential processes, an initial arrest of ongoing activity on stimulus presentation followed by a targeting of the receptors toward the stimulus. Discrete systems located in such structures as the hippocampus could underlie activation of this two-stage arousal system. (see Anchel and Lindsley, 1972).

References

Abraham, F. D. (1971). Neurobiology of learning. *BIS Conf. Rep*, No. 10.

Anchel, H., and Lindsley, B. (1972). Differentiation of two reticulohypothalamic systems regulating hippacompal activity. *Electroencephalogr. Clin. Neurophysiol.* **32**, 209–226.

Arechiga, H., and Wiersma, C. A. G. (1969). The effect of motor activity on the reactivity of single visual units in the crayfish, *J. Neurobiol.* **1**, 53–69.

Babskii, E., and Ul'Yaninskii, D. D. (1964). Effects of the heart rate on the duration of ventricular arrest during vagus nerve stimulation. *Dokl. Biol. Sci.* **159**, 868–870.

Barham, E. G., Huckabay, W. B., Gowdy, R., and Burns, B. (1969). Microvolt electric signals from fishes and the environment. *Science* **164**, 965–968.

Beritov, I. S. (1968). Central inhibition according to I. M. Sechenov's experiments and concepts and its modern interpretation. *Prog. Brain Res.* **22**, p. 21–26.

Birukow, G. (1939). Untersuchungen über den optischen Drehnystagmus und über die Sehschärfe des Grasfrosches (*Rana temporaria L.*) *Z. Vergl. Physiol.* **25**, 92–142.

Birukow, G. (1951). Ermüdung und Umstimmung bei Gleichgewichtsreaktionen der Amphibien. *Verh. Deut. Zoo. Ges.* 144–150.

Breland, K., and Breland, B. (1966). "Animal Behavior." Saunders, Philadelphia, Pennsylvania.

Buchwald, N. A., Wyers, E. J., Lauprecht, C. N., and Heuser, G. (1961). The "caudate-spindle." IV. A behavioral index of caudate-induced inhibition. *Electroencephalogr. Clin. Neurophysiol.* **13**, 531–537.

Bullock, T. H. (1966). Simple systems for the study of learning mechanisms. *NRP Bull* **4**.

Bullock, T. H., and Horridge, G. A. (1965). "Structure and Function in the Nervous Systems of Invertebrates." Freeman, San Francisco, California.

Bûres, J. (1970). Comments on Gabriel Horn's paper. In "The Neural Control of Behavior" (R. E. Whalen et al., eds.) pp. 128–129. Academic Press, New York.

Butz-Kuenzer, E. (1957). Optische und labyrinthäre Auslösung der Lagerreaktionen beim Amphibien. Z. Tierpsychol. 14, 429–447.

Chase, M. H., and McGinty, D. J. (1970). Modulation of spontaneous and reflex activity of the jaw musculature by orbital cortical stimulation in the freely moving cat. Brain Res. 19, 117–126.

Coghill, C. E. (1929). "Anatomy and the Problem of Behavior." Macmillan, New York.

Crampton, G. H., and Schwam, W. S. (1962). Turtle vestibular responses to angular acceleration with comparative data from cat and man. J. Comp. Physiol. Psychol. 55, 315–321.

Crowell, D. H., Davis, C. M., Chun, G. J., and Spellacy, F. J. (1965). Galvanic skin response in newborn humans. Science 148, 1108–1111.

Davis, M. (1970). Effects of interstimulus interval length and variability on startle-response habituation in the rat. J. Comp. Physiol. Psychol. 72, 177–192.

Davis, M., and Wagner, A. R. (1969). Habituation of startle response under incremental sequence of stimulus intensities. J. Comp. Physiol. Psychol. 67, 486–492.

Delius, J. D. (1970). Irrelevant behavior, information processing and arousal homeostasis. Psychol. Forsch. 30, 165–188.

Diamond, S., Balvin, R. S., and Diamond, F. N. (1963). "Inhibition and Choice." Harper, New York.

Dodd, C., and Lewis, M. (1969). The magnitude of the orienting response in children as a function of changes in color and contour. J. Exp. Child Psychol. 8, 296–305.

Dubignon, J., and Campbell, D. (1968). Sucking in the newborn in three conditions, non-nutritive, nutritive and a feed. J. Exp. Child Psychol. 6, 335–350.

Eikmanns, K. H. (1955). Verhaltensphysiologische Untersuchungen über den Beutefang und das Bewegungssehen der Erdkröte (Bufo bufo L.). Z. Tierpsychol. 12, 229–253.

Ewert, J–P. (1966). Auslösung des Beute- und Flacht-verhaltens durch elektrische Mittelhirn-Reizung bei der Erdkröte (Bufo bufo L.) Naturwiss 53, 539.

Ewert, J–P. (1967a). Untersuchungen über die Anteile zentralnervöser Aktionen an der taxisspezifischen Ermüdung beim Beutefang der Erdkröte (Bufo bufo L.). Z. Vergl. Physiol. 37, 263–298.

Ewert, J–P (1967b) Aktivierung der Verhaltensfolge beim Beutefang der Erdkröte (Bufo bufo L.) durch electrische Mittelhirnreizung. Z. Vergl. Physiol. 54, 455–481.

Ewert, J–P. (1967c). Der Einfluss von Störreizen auf die Antwortbereitschaft beim der Richtbewegung der Erdkröte (Bufo bufo L.). Z. Tierpsychol. 24, 298–321.

Ewert, J–P. (1968). Der Einfluss von Zwischenhirndefekten auf die Visuomotorik un Beute- und Fluchtverhalten der Erdkröte (Bufo bufo L.) Z. Vergl. Physiol. 61, 41–70.

Ewert, J–P. (1969). Das Beuteverhalten Zwischenhirn-defekter Erdkroten (Bufo bufo L.) gegenuber bewegten und ruhenden visuellen Mustern. Pfluegers Arch. 306, 210–218.

Ewert, J–P. (1971). Neural mechanisms of prey-catching and avoidance behavior in the toad. Brain Behav. Evol. 3, 36–56.

Ewert, J–P., and Birukow, G. (1965). Über den Einfluss des Centralnervensystems auf die Ermüdbarkeit der Richtbewegung im Beuteschema der Erdkröte (Bufo bufo L.). Naturwissenschaften 52, 68–69.

Ewert, J–P., and Härter, H–A. (1969). Der hemmende Einfluss gleichzeitig bewegter Beuteattrappen auf das Beutefangverhalten der Erdkröte (Bufo bufo L.). Z. Vergl. Physiol. 64, 135– 153.

Ewert, J–P., and Ingle, D. (1971). Excitatory effects following habituation of prey-catching activity in frogs and toads. J. Comp. Physiol. Psych. 77, 369–374.

Ewert, J.-P. and Kleinlogel, H. (1971). Jahreszeitliche Änderung der Wisch-Aktivitat bei der Erdkröte. (*Bufo bufo L.*). *Z. Tierpsychol.* **28**, 479–486.

Ewert, J-P., and Rehn, B. (1969). Quantitative Analyse der Reiz-Reaktion Ä beziehungen bei visuellem Auslösen des Fluchtvehaltens der Wechselkröte (*Bufo viridis Laur*). *Behaviour*, **35**, 212–234.

Ewert, J-P., Speckhardt, I., and Amelang, W. (1970). Visuelle Inhibition und Exzitation im Beutefangverhalten der Erdkröte (*Bufo bufo L.*). *Z. Vergl. Physiol.*, **68**, 84–110.

Eycleshymer, A. C. (1906). The habits of *Necturus maculosus*. *Amer. Natur.* **40**, 123–136.

Fangel, C., and Kaada, B. R. (1960). Behavior "attention" and fear induced by cortical stimulation in the cat. *Electroencephalogr. Clin. Neurophysiol.* **12**, 575–588.

Ferrier, D. (1876). "The Functions of the Brain." Smith Elder, London.

Franzisket, L. (1963). Characteristics of instinctive behavior and learning in reflex activity of the frog. *Anim. Behav.*, **11**, 318–324.

Gadow, H. (1890). "Amphibia and Reptiles" Cambridge Univ. Press, London and New York.

Gans, C. (1970). Strategy and sequence in the evolution of the external gas exchanges of ectothermal vertebrates. *Forma Functio* **3**, 61–104.

Gault, A., and Gans. C. (1969). Diving bradycardia and withdrawal bradycardia in Caimam crocodiles. *Nature (London)* **223**, 207–208.

Gaze, R. M. (1958). The representation of the retina on the optic lobe of the frog. *Quart J. Exp. Physiol.* **43**, 475–486.

Gellhorn, E. (1943). "Automatic Regulations." Interscience, New York.

Gellhorn, E. (1957). "Autonomic Unbalance and the Hypothalamus." Univ. of Minnesota Press, Minneapolis.

Gellhorn, E. (1967). "Principles of Autonomic-Somatic Integration." Univ. of Minnesota Press, Minneapolis.

Gellhorn, E. (1968). Central nervous system tuning and its implications for neuropsychiatry. *J. Nerv. Ment. Dis.* **147**, 148–162.

Goodman, D. A. (1969). Some brain reflexes of *Necturus maculosus*, the mud puppy. Unpublished Doctoral Dissertation, University of California, Irvine.

Goodman, D. A., and Richards, C. (1971). Are cilia in neurons functional? *Proc. 1st Annu. Meet. Soci. Neurosci.*

Goodman, D. A., and Weinberger, N. M. (1969). An electroencephalographic study of *Necturus maculosus* (mud puppy). *Physiol. Zool.* **42**, 348–410.

Goodman, D. A., and Weinberger, N. M. (1970). Possible relationships between orienting and diving reflexes. *Nature (London)* **225**, 1153–1154.

Goodman, D. A., Weinberger N. M. (1971a). Remote sensing of behavior in aquatic amphibia especially in *Necturus maculosus, Commun. Behav. Biol.* **6**, 67–70.

Goodman, D. A., and Weinberger, N. M. (1971b). Submerged electrodes in an aquarium: Validation of a technique for remote sensing. *Beh. Res. Methods. Instrus.* **3**, 281–286.

Goodman, D. A., and Weinberger, N. M. The orienting reflex of *Necturus. maculosis* I. Habituation. In preparation.

Gordon, A. S. (1934). Effect of low pressure on the blood pressure of *Necturus maculosus*. *Proc. Soc. Exp. Biol. Med.* **32**, 820–822.

Graham, F. K., and Clifton, R. K. (1966). Heart rate change as a component of the OR. *Psychol. Rev.* **65**, 305–320.

Granit, R., and Riddel, H. A. (1934). The electrical responses of light and dark adapted frog's eyes to rhythmic and continuous stimuli. *J. Physiol. (London)* **81**, 1–28.

Groves, P. M., and Thompson, R. F. (1970). Habituation: A dual process theory, *Psychol. Rev.* **77**, 419–450.

Grüsser, O–J., and Bullock, T. H. (1964). Functional organization of receptive fields of movement detecting neurons in the frog's retina. *Pfluegers Arch.* **279**, 88–93.

Gulyaev, P. I., Zabotin, V. I., and Shippenbakh, N. (1968). The electroauragram of the frog's nerve, muscle, and heart and of the human heart and the musculature. *Dokl. Biol. Sci.* **180**, 359–361.

Haecker, V. (1912). Über Lernversuche bei Axolotln. *Arch. Psychol.* **25**, 1–12.

Harris, J. D. (1943). Habituatory response decrement in the intact organism. *Psychol. Bul.* **40**, 385–422.

Harris, J. P., Jr. (1959). The natural history of *Necturus*. I. Habitats and habits. *Field Lab.* **27**, 11–20.

Hayes, W. N., and Saiff, E. I. (1967). Visual alarm reactions in turtles. *Anim. Behav.* **15**, 102–106.

Hayes, W. N., Hertzler, D., and Hogberg, D. (1968). Visual responsiveness and habituation in the turtle, *J. Comp. Physiol. Psychol.* **65**, 331–335.

Hernández-Peón, R. (1969). "A neurophysiological and evolutionary model of attention." *In* "Attention in Neurophysiology" (C. R. Evans and T. B. Mulholland, eds.), pp. 417–432. Appleton, New York.

Hernández-Peón, R., Scherrer, H., and Jouvet, M. (1956). Modification of electrical activity in cochlear nucleus during "attention" in unanesthetized cats. *Science* **123**, 331–332.

Herrick, C. J. (1933). The amphibian forebrain. VI. *Necturus. J. Comp. Neurol.* **58**, 1–289.

Herrick, C. J. (1934a). The amphibian forebrain. X. Localized functions and integrating functions, *J. Comp. Neurol.* **59**, 239–266.

Herrick, C. J. (1934b). The interpeduncular nucleus of the brain of *Necturus. J. Comp. Neurol.* **60**, 111–135.

Herrick, C. J., (1948) "The Brain of the Tiger Salamander (*Ambystoma tigrinum*)." Univ of Chicago Press, Chicago, Illinois.

Herrick, C. J., and Coghill, G. E. (1915). The development of reflex mechanisms in *Ambystoma. J. Comp. Neurol.* **25**, 65–86.

Hess, W. R. (1954). "Das Zwischenhirn. Schwabe, Basel.

Hilgard, E. R. (1948). "Theories of Learning." Appleton, New York.

Hinde, R. A. (1966). "Animal Behavior. McGraw-Hill; New York.

Hinde, R. A. (1970a). "Animal Behavior: A Synthesis of Ethology and Comparative Psychology. McGraw-Hill, New York.

Hinde, R. A. (1970b). Behavioral habituation. *In* "Short-term Changes in Neural Activity and Behavior" (G. Horn and R. A. Hinde, eds.), pp. 3–40. Cambridge Univ. Press. Cambridge, London and New York.

Hinsche, G. (1935). Ein Shnappreflex nach "Nichts" bei Anuren. *Zool. Anz.* **111**, 113–122.

Hobson, J. A., Goin, O., and Goin, C. J. (1968). Electrographic correlates of behavior in tree frogs. *Nature (London)* **220**, 386–387.

Hodos, W., and Campbell, C. B. G. (1969). Scala Naturae: Why there is no theory in comparative psychology. *Psychol. Rev.* **76**, 337–350.

Hough, T. (1895). On the escape of the heart from vagus inhibition. *J. Physiol. (London)* **18**, 161–200.

Humphrey, G. (1933). "The Nature of Learning in its Relation to the Living. System." Harcourt, New York.

Hunter, J., and Jasper, H. (1949). Effects of thalamic stimulation in unanesthetized animals. *Electroencephalogr. Clin. Neurophysiol.* **1**, 305–324.

Hutt, C., von Bernuth, H., Lenard, K., Hutt, S. J., and Prechtl, H. (1968). Habituation in relation to state in the human neonate. *Nature (London)* **220**, 618–620.

Ingle, D. (1968). Releasers of prey-catching behavior in frogs and toads. *Brain Behav. Evol.* **1**, 500–518.

John, E. R. (1967). "Mechanisms of Memory." Academic Press, New York.

Kaada, B. R. (1951). Somato-motor, autonomic and electrocorticographic responses to electrical stimulation of 'rhinencephalic' and other structures. *Acta Physiol. Scand.* **24**, Suppl. 3.

Kimble, D. P., and Ray, R. S. (1965). Reflex habituation and potentiation in *Rana pipiens*. *Anim. Behav.* **13**. 530–533.

Kleerekoper, H., and Sibakin, K. (1956). An investigation of the electrical "spike" potentials produced by the sea lamprey (*Petromyzon marinus*) in the water surrounding the head region, *J. Fish. Res. Bd. Can.* **13**, 325–383.

Koepke, J. E., and Pribram, K. H. (1967). Habituation of the vasoconstriction response as a function of stimulus duration and anxiety. *J. Comp. Physiol. Psychol.*, **64**, 502–504.

Konorski, J. (1967). "Integrative Activity of the Brain." Univ. of Chicago Press, Chicago, Illinois.

Krieckhaus, E., and Chi, C. (1966). Role of freezing and fear in avoidance decrements following mammillothalomic tractotomy in cat. I. Two-way avoidance behavior. *Psychon. Sci.* **4**, 263–264.

Kuczka, H. (1956). Verhaltenphysiologische Untersuchungen über die Wischhandlung der Erdkröte (*Bufo bufo L.*). *Z. Tierpsychol.* **13**, 185–207.

Kuroki, T. (1958). Arrest reaction elicited from the brain stem. *Folia Psychiat. Neurol. Jap.* **12**, 317–340.

Lacey, J. I. (1967). Somatic response patterning and stress: Some revisions of activation theory. *In* "Psychological Stress: Issues in Research" (M. H. Appley and R. Trunbull, eds.), pp. 14–42. Appleton, New York.

Lashley, K. S. (1950). In search of the engram. *Symp. Soc. Exp. Biol.* **4**, 454–482.

Lerfant, C., and Johanson, K. (1967). Respiratory adaptations in selected amphibians. *Resp. Physiol.* **2**, 247–260.

Lewis, M. (1971). Individual differences in the measurement of early cognitive growth. *In* "Exceptional Infant" (J. Hellmuth, Vol. II, Brunner, Mazel, Bainbridge Island, Washington.

Lewis, M., and Goldberg, S. (1969). The acquisition and violation of expectancy: An experimental paradigm. *J. Exp. Child Psychol.* **7**, 70–80.

Lewis, M., and Spaulding, S. (1967). Differential cardiac response to visual and auditory stimulation in the young child. *Psychophysiology* **3**, 229–237.

Lewis, M., Kagan, J., and Kalafat, J. (1967). Patterns of fixation in infants. *In* "The Child: A Book of Readings" (J. M. Seidman, ed.). Holt, Rinehart, and Winston, New York.

Longuet-Higgins, H. S. (1968). The non-local storage of temporal information. *Proc. Roy. Soc. Ser., B* **171**, 327–334.

Lumsden, T. (1923). Chelonian respiration (Tortoise). *J. Physiol. (London)* **58**, 259–266.

Lutz, B., and Wyman, L. (1932). Reflex cardiac inhibition of branchiovascular origin in *Squalus acanthias* and *Necturus maculosus*. *Amer. J. Physiol.* **101**, 69.

McCleary, R. A. (1966). Response-modulating functions of the limbic system: Initiation and suppression. *Progr. Physiol. Psychol.* **1**, 210–272.

Mackay, R. S. (1968). "Bio-medical Telemetry," 2nd ed. Wiley, New York.

McWilliam, J. A. (1895). On the structure and rhythm of the heart in fishes with especial reference to the heart of the eel. *J. Physiol. (London)* **6**, 192–244.

Marler, P., & Hamilton, W. J. (1966) III. "Mechanisms of Animal Behavior." Wiley, New York.

Maturana, H. L., Letvin, J. Y., McCulloch, W. S., and Pitts, W. H. (1960). Anatomy and physiology of vision in the frog (*Rana pipiens*). *J. Gen Physiol.* **43**, 129–175.

Obrist, P. A., Webb, R. A., Sutterer, J. R., and Howard, J. L. (1970a). The cardiac-somatic relationship: Some reformulations. *Psychophysiology* **6**, 569–587.

Obrist, P. A., Webb, R. A., Sutterer, J. A., and Howard, J. L. (1970b). Cardiac deceleration and reaction time: An evaluation of two hypotheses. *Psychophysiology* **6**, 695–706.

Odum, P., and Kendeigh, S. C. (1940). The cardio-vibrometer: A new instrument for measuring the heart rate and other body activities of animals. *Ecology* **21**, 105–106.

Offutt, G. C. (1971). Response of the Tautog (Tautoga onitis, Teleost) to acoustic stimuli measured by classically conditioning the heart rate. *Cond. Refl.* **6**, 205–214.

O'Leary, J. L., and Bishop, G. H. (1969). C. J. Herrick, scholar and humanist: A memorial essay written for his centenary. *Perspect. Biol. Med.* **12**, 492–513.

Paul Dye, W. J. (1921). The relation of the lateral line organs of *Necturus* to hearing. *J. Comp. Psychol.* **1**, 419–471.

Pavlov, I. P. (1927). "Conditioned Reflexes." Oxford Univ. Press, London and New York.

Prestrude, A., and Crawford, F. (1970). Tonic immobility in the lizard *Iguana iguana. Anim. Behav.* **18**, 391–395.

Rasa, O., Anne Ie. The causal factors and the functions of young in Microspathodon Chrysurus (Pisces: Comacritridae) *Behavior* **39**, 39–57.

Ray, A. J., Jr. (1970). Instrumental avoidance learning by the tiger salamander *Ambystoma tigrinuri. Anim. Behav.* **18**, 73–77.

Reigle, N. J. Jr. (1967). The occurrence of *Necturus* in the deeper waters of Green Bay *Herpetol* **23**, 232–233.

Robinson, R. (1965). "Genetics of the Norway Rat." Pergamon, Oxford.

Rodgers, W. L., Melzack, R., and Segal, J. R. (1963). Tail flip response in gold fish. *J. Comp. Physiol. Psychol.* **56**, 917–923.

Roman, C., and Gar, A. (1970). Déglutitiones et contractions oesophagrennes reflexes obtenues par la stimulation des nerfs vagal et larynge supérieur. *Exp. Brain Res.* **11**, 48–74.

Routtenberg, A. (1968). The two-arousal hypothesis: Reticular formation and limbic system. *Psychol. Rev.* **75**, 57–80.

Russell, E. M. (1967). Changes in the behavior of *Lebistes reticulatus* upon a repeated shadow stimulus. *Anim. Behav.* **15**, 574–585.

Samaan, A. (1935). The antagonistic cardiac nerves and heart rate. *J. Psychol.* **83**, 332–340.

Schneider C. L. (1968). Avoidance learning and response tendencies of the salamander *Amblystoma punctatum* to photic stimulation. *Anim. Behav.* **16**, 492–495.

Sechenov, I. M. (1965). "Reflexes of the Brain." MIT Press, Cambridge, Massachusetts (English translation).

Sharpless, S. K., and Jasper, H. (1956). Habituation of the arousal reaction. *Brain* **79**, 655–679.

Shelton, G., and Randall, D. (1962). The relationship between heart beat and respiration in teleost fish. *Comp. Biochem. Physiol.* **7**, 237–250.

Sokolov, E. N. (1960). Neuronal models and the orienting reflex. *In* "The Central Nervous System and Behavior" (M. A. B. Brazier, ed.), pp. 187–276. Josiah Macy, Jr., Founda., New York.

Sokolov, E. N. (1963a). "Perception and the Conditioned Reflex." Pergamon, Oxford.

Sokolov, E. N. (1963b). Higher nervous functions: The orienting reflex. *Annu. Rev. Physiol.* **25**, 545–580.

Spoor, W. A., Neiheisel, T. W., and Drummond, R. A. (1971). An electrode chamber for recording respiration and other movements of free-swimming animals. *Trans. Amer. Fisheries Soc.* **100**, 22–28.

Steinschneider, A. (1968). Sound intensity and respiratory responses in the neonate: Comparison with cardiac rate responsiveness. *Psychosom. Med.* **30**, 534–541.

Swigert, C. (1967). Computational properties of a nerve and nerve model. University of California, Berkeley.

Thompson, R. F., and Spencer, W. A. (1966). Habituation: A model phenomenon for the study of neuronal substiates of behavior. *Psychol. Rev.* **173**, 16–43.

Thorpe, W. H. (1944). Some problems in animal learning. *Proc. Linn. Soc. Lond.* **156**, 70–83.

Thorpe, W. H. (1963). "Learning and Instinct in Animals." Methuen, London.

Tremor, J. W., and Rogallo, V. L. (1970). A small animal acto-ballistocardiograph: Description and illustration of its use. *Physiol. & Behav.* **9**, 247–257.

Trincker, D. (1954a). Zur Dynamik der Selbststeuerung bei Anpassungsvorgangen. I. Mitteilung. Periodisch ablaufende Lernvorgange bei *Amblystoma*. *Z. Verg. Physiol.* **36**, 115–134.

Trincker, D. (1954b). Zur Dynamik der Selbststeuerung bei Anpassungsvorgangen. II. Mitteilung. Periodischer Ablauf der Anpassung bei einer Lichtreaktion von *Carassius*. *Z. Vergl. Physiol.* **36**, 135–146.

Ursin, H., and Kaada, B. R. (1960). Functional localization within the amygdaloid complex in the cat. *Electroencephalogr. Clin. Neurophysiol.* **12**, 1–20.

Ursin, H., Wester, K., and Ursin, R. (1967). Habituation to electrical stimulation of the brain in unanesthetized cats. *Electroencephalogr. Clin. Neurophysiol.*, **23**, 41–49.

Ursin, H., Sundberg, H., and Menaker, S. (1969). Habituation of the orienting response elicited by stimulation of the caudate nucleus in the cat. *Neuropsychologia* **7**, 313–318.

Viala, G., and Buser, P. (1969). Inhibition, par la stimulation lumineuse intermittente, des activités locomotrues rhythmiques chez le lapin sous narcose légère. *Physiol. Behav.* **4**, 415–420.

von Holst, E. (1934). Studien über Reflexe und Rhythmenen beim Goldfisch (*Carassius auratus*). *Z. Vergl. Physiol.* **120**, 584–597.

von Holst, E. (1936). Die relative Koordination als Rahmen und als Methode zentralnervoser Funktion–analyse. *Ergeb. Physiol.* **42**, 228–306.

von Holst, E. (1938). Neu Versuche zur Deutung der relativen Koordination. *Pfleugers Arch.* **240**, 1–43.

Weinberger, N. M. (1971). Attentive processes. *In* "Psychobiology" (J. L. McGaugh, ed.), pp. 129–198. Academic Press, New York.

Weinberger, N. M., and Goodman, D. A. (1969). A solid-state device for presenting moving shadows. *Behav. Res. Methods Instrum.* **1**, 192–193.

Weinberger, N. M., and Lindsley, D. B. (1965). Behavioral and electroencephalographic arousal to contrasting novel stimulation. *Science* **144**, 1355–1357.

Werblin, F. S. (1970). Response of retinal cells to moving spots: Intracellular recording in *Necturus maculosus*. *J. Neurophysiol.* **32**, 342–350.

Werblin, F. S. (1971). Adaptation in a vertebrate retina: Intracellular recording in *Necturus. J. Neurophysiol.* **34**, 228–241.

Werblin, F. S., and Dowling, J. E. (1969a). Organization of retina of the mud puppy, *Necturus maculosus*. I. Synaptic structure, *J. Neurophysiol.* **32**, 315–338.

Werblin, F. S., and Dowling, J. E. (1969b). Organization of retina of the mud puppy, *Necturus maculosus*. II. Intracellular recording, *J. Neurophysiol.* **32**, 330–355.

Whitman, C. O. (1898). "Animal Behavior," 16th Lecture on Animal Behavior from Biological Lecture Series (1898) of Marine Biological Laboratory at Woods Hole, Massachusetts. Ginn, Boston, Massachusetts.

Wiener, N. (1948). "Cybernetics." MIT Press, Cambridge, Massachusetts.

Wilson, W. (1890). Note on the time relations of stimulation of the optic lobes of the frog. *J. Physiol. (London)* **11**, 504–506.

Woodworth, R. S., and Schlosberg, H. (1954). "Experimental Psychology." Holt, New York.

Yerkes, R. M. (1904). Inhibition and reinforcement of reaction in the frog. *Rana clamitans. J. Comp. Neurol. Psychol.* **14**, 124–138.

Chapter 4
A Species-Meaningful Analysis of Habituation[1]

LEWIS PETRINOVICH

I. Introduction

While midway in the preparation of this chapter, the volume of papers entitled *Short-term Changes in Neural Activity and Behaviour* (Horn and Hinde, 1970) appeared, containing an excellent chapter by Hinde (1970) who discusses behavioral habituation in view of the aspects which have been accepted at a molecular level of analysis (e.g., Horn, 1967; Thompson and Spencer, 1966). The original intent of this chapter was quite similar to the effort of Hinde and the present author has, therefore, decided to write more generally than originally intended, emphasizing some of the points touched on by Hinde, surveying some pertinent literature, and stressing the adoption of a molar functional view if one is to understand behavioral habituation.

This discussion of habituation begins by dealing with a terminological problem. Specifically, what is the difference, if any, between the processes of learning and extinction and those of habituation? The most generally accepted definitions of learning run something along the lines of the following: "A change in behavior as a function of experience and not due to maturation, fatigue, or other short-term effects" (cf. Hilgard and Bower, 1966).

Habituation has been defined as follows: "The relatively permanent waning of a response as a result of repeated stimulation which is not followed

[1]The preparation of this manuscript was supported in part by Research Grant HD-04343 from The National Institute of Child Health and Human Development and an intramural research grant from the University of California.

by any kind of reinforcement. It is specific to the stimulation and relatively enduring" (Thorpe, 1963, p. 61).

There is a great deal of overlap between the two definitions: both stress the role of stimulation (experience), both stress the occurrence of a behavioral change, and both imply a relatively stable change in behavior. The major difference between habituation and learning is that the former always involves a decrease in response strength, whereas the latter can involve either increases or decreases in response strength.

Let us examine some of the more common characteristics of learning, then examine those of habituation, and in this way determine the similarities and differences in characteristics for the two processes. Obviously, as Kling and Stevenson (1970) have indicated, such an analysis is difficult because of differences in such things as experimental procedures, species of animals, and parameters of stimulation. However, if any striking similarities do appear in the face of such analytic problems they should indicate rather strong communalities.

II. Characteristics of Learning

1. Spontaneous Recovery. If a learned response is extinguished by either withholding reward or by punishing the response until it no longer appears, the response will reappear at some strength (usually less than the pre-extinction value) as a function of elapsed time. An example of this can be found in Pavlov's studies of classical conditioning of the salivary response in dogs (Pavlov, 1927). He paired the sound of a bell (CS) with the presentation of food powder (US) and obtained a stable conditioned response (CR). At the end of the conditioning procedure the dogs were releasing an average of 10 drops of saliva with an initial latency of 3 seconds upon the presentation of the CS. He then gave 7 extinction trials by presenting the CS but not following it with the US. The number of drops of saliva dropped from 10 to 3 and the latency of the first drop increased from 3 to 13 seconds. Twenty-three minutes later the animals spontaneously recovered to a level of 6 drops with a latency of 5 seconds.

Spontaneous recovery is also seen when instrumental conditioning procedures are used. If a hungry rat is taught to press a bar to obtain food reward until it is responding at a high level and after this level has been reached it is no longer rewarded until it stops responding, the number of bar presses following an interval of time will be a function of the length of that time interval.

It has also been found that repeated presentations of a CS after the extinction criterion has been reached decreases the amount of spontaneous recovery which will occur as a function of time.

2. Stimulus Generalization. If a response is conditioned to a stimulus of a specific value, the response will generalize to other stimuli along the same qualitative or quantitative dimension. It has been found that the response gradient narrows with more frequent presentation of the stimulus.

3. Stimulus Discrimination. If only one stimulus value is rewarded and all others are not rewarded then the animal will cease to respond to any stimulus value other than the rewarded one. This cessation of responding is a function of the number of presentations of the to-be-discriminated stimulus.

4. Acquisition Parameters. The rate of acquisition of a response will vary as a function of the spacing of the training trials. Learning occurs in fewer trials with distributed practice than with massed practice. Extinction occurs more quickly under massed practice in classical conditioning.

The above characterizations are quite general and exceptions can be found in the literature to many of them. They do, however, represent a generally accepted set of statements, and we will now inquire whether or not the same characterizations are true of habituation.

III. Characteristics of Habituation

Thorpe (1963) believed that habituation implies a tendency to drop out responses, not to incorporate new ones or to complicate those already present. He characterized habituation as being the simplest kind of learning and believed that something like it is universal in animals.

In order to compare habituation to learning it might be useful to examine the nine characteristics of habituation as outlined by Thompson and Spencer (1966) and to add a tenth suggested by Hinde (1961).

1. If a stimulus elicits a response, repeated application of the stimulus results in a decreased response strength. This decrease is a negative exponential function of the number of stimulus presentations. Based on this characterization it looks as though habituation is a specific type of learning which has the same acquisition characteristics as other types of learning. It has also been found, by Hinde (1961), that an increase in the length of time of the initial presentation of a stimulus results in a decrease in the response strength when the stimulus is presented a second time.

2. If a stimulus is withheld, the response tends to recover over time. This is such a universal finding in habituation that the amount of spontaneous recovery occurring following different time intervals is often taken as an index of the strength of habituation. As noted above, this is one of the general characteristics of learning as well.

3. If a series of habituation sessions occur, habituation becomes more

and more rapid. This, too, tends to characterize a series of learning sessions when the task involves either novel problems or relearning after extinction.

4. The more rapid the frequency of stimulation, the more rapid and strong is the resulting habituation. This tends to be true for learning when the time required to reach a learning criterion is considered, but not to be true when the total number of presentations required to reach a learning criterion is considered.

5. The weaker the stimulus, the more rapid and strong is the habituation. This, of course, is not true for learning. If anything, learning takes place more quickly with a strong stimulus (certainly, performance is stronger) than with a weak stimulus. This difference is probably because habituation always involves a weakening of an existing response. There is, however, some behavioral evidence that this is not always the case (cf. Curio, 1969).

6. The effects of habituation may proceed beyond zero. This tends to be true for the acquisition of both positive and negative learned responses as well. It may, with learned responses, be a qualitative change that takes place in terms of such things as the cues the subject selects to attend.

7. Habituation of a response to a stimulus exhibits stimulus generalization. As noted above, this is a ubiquitous finding in learning situations as well.

8. A novel stimulus dishabituates a previously habituated response. This result was noted quite early in Pavlov's laboratory and has been noted by many investigators in situations ranging from maze learning to operant conditioning.

9. A dishabituating stimulus will itself habituate in time. Again, this is true in general learning situations.

10. Hinde (1954b) found that habituation of the chaffinch mobbing response to owls proceeds more rapidly with spaced trials than with massed trials. He reported that two, three, four, of five 3-minute presentations of an owl model on successive days results in more habituation than does one presentation of 20 minutes on each day. This same effect has been observed with the spacing of learning trials.

It is clear that in many respects learning and habituation display some of the same regularities and that they are probably closely related processes. It seems fair to conclude, with Thorpe, that habituation is probably a basic form of learning and that some aspects of it are probably universal in animals. The latter portion of this conclusion received even stronger support in view of the elegant demonstrations of habituation in *Aplysia* by Kandel and his associates (e.g., Castellucci *et al.*, 1970; Kandel and Spencer, 1968).

It is also clear that habituation does not result merely from sensory adaptation; if it did, one would not be able to dishabituate with a novel stimulus. Similarly, habituation does not result merely from motor fatigue; if it did, there is no reason for a weak stimulus to be more effective or for there being cumulative effects upon repeated presentation of a stimulus after the response has habituated completely. If habituation merely resulted from motor fatigue one should not obtain either stimulus generalization or dishabituation.

IV. Orienting Response

Sharpless and Jasper (1956) found that electroencephalographic (EEG) arousal exhibits all nine of the characteristics of habituation as outlined by Thompson and Spencer. They reported that although a tone initially evokes widespread EEG activation its effect becomes gradually more restricted until the activation is seen only in the auditory cortex. Gradually, the activation becomes of shorter duration and finally disappears.

Sokolov (1960) has studied the orienting response (OR) utilizing several response measures (among them EEG, galvanic skin response, eye movements, respiration, and heart rate). He found the same effects as those outlined above. If a stimulus is without significance, the OR wanes with the repetition of the stimulus, and this waning is not the result of sensory adaptation. One such demonstration of this point was accomplished by selecting a visual stimulus which was just above threshold as a habituation stimulus. When the response ceased and the intensity of the light was reduced a bit, the response reappeared. Clearly, this would not occur if the habituation resulted from sensory adaptation.

Sokolov suggested that the OR appears whenever sensory input does not seem to coincide with a "neuronal model" previously established in the brain. If the stimulus does not coincide with the parameters of the neuronal model, the OR occurs, and the organism's power for obtaining information about unusual properties of the stimulating environment is increased.

The most compelling evidence for this type of model has been presented by Sokolov (1960) in studies in which a sound of a certain duration is presented until habituation occurs. When a sound of a shorter duration is presented, the OR appears at its termination. When a sound of a longer duration is presented, the OR appears when the sound should have terminated. He took this to mean that when the parameters of the incoming stimulus do not coincide with those of the neuronal model the OR occurs.

No good purpose will be served by presenting the Sokolov neuronal model in detail here. A few words of caution might be in order, however. This is a post hoc model which has been generated to coincide with obtained results. In conception, then, it is nonphysiological and terms such as neuronal model involve a transfer from a level of discourse based on behavioral reality to another level of discourse based on physiological reality. This type of translation must be made with extreme caution in view of the considerable difficulties involved in establishing analogous relationships based on different data bases. Sokolov indicated where some of the analogous units might be located. For example, he located the amplifying system in the reticular formation and the modeling system in the cerebral cortex. He suggested that if impulses from the cortex match the neuronal model which has been established previously, then impulses from the cortex prevent the sensory input from affecting the reticular formation. This involves an active gating process which is controlled by the output of a matching system. In order for this system to function there must be some comparator mechanism whose nature and location remain a mystery.

One problem with this neurological analogy is that habituation can be obtained in species which have none of the neural structures specified in the model, and, also, can be obtained in spinal preparations. Because habituation can be obtained in the absence of the cortex does not mean, of course, that the cortex is not involved in the normal state for those organisms which have a functional cortex, but it does raise some doubts regarding the universality of the proposed mechanism.

Thompson and Spencer (1966) have obtained all aspects of behavioral habituation in the decerebrate spinal cat. On the basis of their work they concluded that the acute spinal cat exhibits habituation that is as genuine as that for any response of an intact animal. The time relationships they reported are well within the range of those found with an intact animal. In a more recent article, Groves and Thompson (1970) proposed a dual-process theory of habituation drawing on both neurophysiological and behavioral evidence. They argued that "An adequate theory of habituation may well provide a basis for increased understanding of learning and other more complex forms of plasticity" (p. 419), and to this end proceeded to relate their molecular-synaptic hypotheses of habituation to more molar theories of behavioral response habituation.

It is safe to conclude that habituation exists at a variety of levels, both in terms of species and in terms of physiological and behavioral systems. Thompson and his co-workers have provided a good operational definition of habituation, and it looks as though habituation can be accepted to be a special type of learning—probably a basic, primitive type of organismic response. It might even be possible that one could consider learning to be a special type of habituation which begins with the same mechanism (the OR) and then is molded with the addition of positive and negative reinforcement contingencies.

V. Naturalistic Studies of Habituation

Granted that we now have a great deal of evidence regarding the course of habituation in both neurophysiological preparations and in laboratory-based behavioral preparations, can it then be concluded that we are close to an understanding of the general phenomenon of habituation? It seems that we are not since we have little information concerning the distribution of the response in the natural environment. We can understand how such a mechanism as habituation might be adaptive, but doubt can be raised concerning whether or not it is a process with as little inherent flexibility as the laboratory findings would suggest.

If we are interested in establishing the limits of generality and in inquiring into the behavioral significance of habituation, it would be wise to heed Seligman's recent advice (Seligman, 1970) regarding the establishment of general laws of learning. He stressed the necessity of considering what he referred to as prepared responses. A prepared response is one whose associability has been enhanced by natural selection during the process of evolution. "I suggest that when CSs or responses are followed by such biologically important events as need reducers, drive reducers, or consummatory responses, learning should take place readily because natural selection has prepared organisms for such relationships" (p. 412). Usually, the learning psychologist works with unprepared responses—those which are not normally high in the organism's behavioral hierarchy. The ethologist, on the other hand, tends to work with mainly prepared responses. If we are interested in understanding the adaptive significance of a response system, it is essential that we examine the response systems in the context of the natural environment of the species. Otherwise, we have only an understanding of behaviorally neutral events in the animal's laboratory world.

To develop this point a few studies will be surveyed on avoidance responses and their habituation in birds. The results of these studies suggest that we must consider the environmental significance of a given stimulus to the animal if we are to predict its fear evoking power and its subsequent rate of habituation.

The classic naturalistic study of habituation was done by Lorenz and Tinbergen (Lorenz, 1939). Models of different shapes were flown over each of several species of birds. If the model had wings, a short neck, and a long tail (a hawlike shape) then escape behavior was evoked. If the model was moved in the reverse direction (a gooselike shape) then no escape or fear responses were observed. They also reported that the birds habituate to the model but still display a strong response to a live hawk following the habituation.

Schleidt (1961) studied the same behavior and found it to be more complicated than did Lorenz and Tinbergen. A series of models was flown over young turkeys and the presence or absence of escape responses was noted. The stimuli used included a circle, a long rectangle, a hawklike model, a gooselike model, and a realistic hawk model. The birds habituated easily to both the circle and the rectangle. If they were occasionally exposed to the realistic hawk model they habituated to it, yet would respond strongly to the circle. There was a general unresponsiveness to objects of a certain apparent size and rate of movement. Schleidt's explanation of the results imples a high degree of stimulus specificity since he concluded that in the natural environment birds habituate to other types of birds. Since hawks are relatively rare there is no habituation to them, and the birds are thus continually responsive to this natural predator.

Melzack (1961) inquired into how it is that the chaffinch and duck manage to survive if they habituate rapidly to visual patterns that characterize predators. He also made a more fine-grained analysis of the response to the models than is done usually. Three-day-old ducks were raised in isolation cages and different models were flown over them from days 4–21. The experimental manipulations after day 21 were quite varied and complex but essentially involved the use of different models presented at different speeds and at different distances. On days 4–21 one group was exposed to 120 presentations of the hawk each day and another group was exposed to 120 presentations of the goose each day. Two control groups were included which had no early experience with either hawk or goose models. Both orienting responses and fear responses were recorded. The former were of three types: (a) looked up at the model; (b) looked up at the model and followed it with neck and head movements; and (c) looked up at the model and moved in the same direction, keeping it in the field of vision. In order to qualify as an orienting response no fear could be present. A fear response was scored when the bird crouched and issued fright calls. On the first test, made on day 25, the controls which received no models on days 4–21 showed both orienting and fear responses when either of the models were presented. The experimental animals (which had had 2000 presentations at this point) showed only orienting responses and few fear responses. As the testing series progressed the fear responses disappeared completely but the orienting responses were always present.

In the context of this experiment it can be concluded that if an object is strange a fear response appears; if it is familiar, there is still an orientation toward it. Thus, repeated experience with predators would be expected to produce a loss of the fear response—a situation which would not often occur in the natural environment.

Hinde has published three classic studies of the habituation of mobbing responses in chaffinch *Fringilla coelebs* (Hinde, 1954a,b, 1961). He exposed both wild caught and hand-reared birds to owl models and noted the occurrence of mobbing behavior. This behavior is characterized by the emission of a vocalization (a fright "chink"), the crest is usually raised, the legs slightly flexed, and the wings slightly raised from the supporting feathers. When a stuffed owl is introduced into the bird's cage, the response gradually increases in intensity, ranging from examination at a distance to finally mobbing the model. Hinde reported great variability in the number of calls issued. With a live little owl in a cage with single chaffinches for 20 minutes the number of calls issued during the period for different birds ranged from 87 to 1238. He stated that ". . . although any strange bird may evoke some response from a chaffinch . . . owls are particularly effective in doing so" (Hinde, 1954a, p. 321).

With hand-reared birds he found no response to owl models prior to one month of age and noted moderate fleeing after that age. A brown box which was dropped in front of the young bird and allowed to swing caused a stronger response than did an owl. These two findings argue, first, that maturation is necessary for the response to occur and, second, that the lack of response to the owl is not because of a lack of motor ability.

In the second paper of the series, Hinde (1954b) studied the waning of the mobbing response of a wild caught chaffinch to a stuffed owl which was presented for 30 minutes. He noted the number of calls emitted during the first 6 minutes of the period. Following the 30-minute period, the owl was removed for a time varying from $\frac{1}{2}$ minute to 24 hours and was then presented for another 6 minute period. There was rapid recovery of the response as a function of time. The response level had recovered to about 40% of its initial with a 15-minute interval, 50% at 30 minutes and 56% at 24 hours.

Hinde found less stimulus specificity than the Schleidt and the Melzack studies would lead us to expect. He exposed chaffinch to the following series: (1) live snake for 3 minutes, (2) 24–48 hours later a stuffed owl for 20–30 minutes, (3) live snake for 3 minutes, (4) undisturbed for 24 hours and (5) live snake for 3 minutes. During (1) the mean number of calls was 59, during (3) the mean was 6, and during (5) the mean was 62. Thus, when the response to the owl had waned the response to the snake was less as well. He also reported little difference in the rate of habituation to live owls and to models. He concluded that the more characteristics two models have in common the more habituation transfers from the first to the second model.

In the final paper of this series (Hinde, 1961) two stimuli were used and the number of calls in the first 6 minutes of a 30-minute period were noted. One stimulus was a stuffed tawny owl (O) and the other was a toy dog (D). The response level was higher to O than to D as indicated by more calls, shorter latency to the first call, peak minute of calling occurring sooner, and a slower waning of the response. The two stimuli were presented in different combinations twice for 12, 24, and 48 minutes and for 24 hours. Following a rest interval of 24 hours the number of calls for a 6-minute presentation was noted. In all cases the number of calls was less than for birds which had had no exposure to either model. If the arrangement of the two presentations was D-D or O-O, an increase in the length of the initial presentation caused a decrease in the response level on the second presentation.

This was also the case when the order was D-O, although not as much so. When the order was O-D, the response level was higher on the second presentation than on the first. It would appear that habituation persists if the same stimulus is presented on the second occasion, that it is still in evidence if the weak stimulus (D) is followed by the strong one (O), but that there is a sensitization of the response if the strong stimulus (O) is followed by the weak one (D).

Milligan and Verner (1971) did a field study of the responses of white-crowned sparrows to playbacks of native and of alien dialects. They found that territorial males responded to both types of playback and that the response to the native dialect was stronger. They reported that if the native dialect is followed by the alien dialect 5 minutes later there is a sensitization effect, while if the alien dialect is followed by the native dialect there is a lessened responsiveness to the latter. This result appears to be similar to that reported by Hinde, and it may be that species vary in this characteristic.

What can be concluded from this brief lieterature survey regarding an innate bias to show fear (or orientation) and slower habituation to certain classes of stimulation than to others? Melzack (1961) found such a tendency when he noted a higher response level to a hawk flown overhead than to a goose. Lorenz and Tinbergen (Lorenz, 1939) also reported a stronger effect with the hawklike than with the gooselike model. Schleidt's (1961) findings force us to qualify this conclusion since he found novelty to be the more important factor. However, it is possible that he evoked a competing response system in his study and thus evoked another prepared response system. Hinde suggested that such a system might be invoked by the sudden change in retinal stimulations as a result of a dark object moving overhead and that this overrides the qualitative characteristics of shape.

Hinde (1954a) found that, with chaffinch, owls are particularly effective in evoking the mobbing response, although any strange bird might evoke it at some strength. He also reported a stronger response to an owl than to a red brick and to an owl model than to a toy dog (Hinde, 1961).

Thus, there is some evidence suggesting a differential response to certain classes of meaningful stimuli. This suggestion is strengthened by several other reports. Nice and ter Pelkwijk (1941) hand-reared young song sparrows. They reported that the birds showed alarm to a model of an owl but not to cats, snakes, dogs, or rats. They also found that the reactions were stronger to moving than to stationary objects. In general, the better the model the stronger the reaction. The response did tend to habituate, but it returned to the original intensity a day or two later.

Rand (1941a,b) hand-reared curved billed thrashers and then introduced animals into the living cage. He found the birds exhibited shyness of unfamiliar, slowly moving objects and fled when approached rapidly.

Rouse (1905) reported that when pigeons are exposed either to what he classified as "significant" sounds or to "meaningless" sounds they remain senstitive to the significant ones and habituate to the meaningless ones.

Orr (1945) found that the Galapagos finches which have been isolated for centuries with no predatory land mammals or hawks in the environment still exhibit an alarm reaction to hawks.

Curio (1969) has reported an extremely interesting field study of habituation in Darwin's finches *Goespizinae*. He selected four islands for study: birds on two of the islands suffered selection pressure by the Galapagos hawk; birds on the other two islands suffered no predation. Curio found, as did Melzack (1961) and Schleidt (1961), that every new bird evokes fear. Later, the finches habituated to harmless species which were encountered frequently. Thus, the stimulus value of the rarer predator (hawk or owl) becomes relatively more effective. This finding supports the view that there is a good deal of stimulus specificity in habituation. He also found that experience with predators was not required for recognition since fear reactions were observed on the islands that suffered from no predators. The Galapagos mockingbird, which is fierce predator, released only weak fear. This led Curio to conclude that recognition of resting avian predators must have evolved under selection pressure from such predators since they do not avoid mammalian predators without experience (there are no mammalian predators present on the islands). He also reported that finches exposed to the strongest pressure show more fear to those predators than do finches from a predator-free environment.

One additional point of interest is that the finches habituate to repetitive stimulation more if they responded to it more strongly on the first occasion. This might mean that the bird is "prepared" to give a strong initial response, and if the stimulus is repeated the response shows a rapid decrement to the "nonpredator" stimulus. This finding suggests that for this species there is a mode of adaptation to the environment which is different from those we have previously encountered. In previous instances a stimulus which evokes a stronger response has taken longer to habituate: here, the reverse seems to be the case. This suggests the possibility of even more inherent flexibility in complex organismic response processes such as habituation than would be suspected on the basis of laboratory preparations alone.

Vowles and Prewitt (1971) studied stimulus specificity of habituation to models as a function of the state of the internal hormones in the ring dove. They found that when doves had been habituated to the model of a spider and then were injected either with progesterone plus estrogen or with pro-lactin that the habituated response did not appear to the spider but did to a novel model of a human skeleton. They concluded that "...it seems that during habituation to the spider the doves learn to classify it as a non-dangerous stimulus; so that it is recognized as not constituting a threat when the birds are subsequently made broody by progesterone or prolactin" (p. 86).

Habituation has been found to be slower to species-significant stimuli in other species as well. For example, Peeke and Zeiner (1970) reported that habituation proceeds more slowly in rats when the habituation stimulus is a rat distress cry than when it is a tone. In mice it has been found by Zippelius and Schleidt (1956) that the retrieving response triggered by the high frequency squeal of mouse pups is practically nonhabituable.

There are also several indications that habituation is involved in the response of birds to song stimulation. Thompson (1969) has reported that male buntings *Passerina* show differential response in the field to playback of their own species song as compared to that of two other species of bunting. He also reported that the birds respond to the conspecific song played backward but not to the extent when it is played forward. Stuffed dummies were also employed in this study, and it was found that the birds were generally unresponsive to a dummy, often directing attention to the loudspeaker rather than the dummy. This is evidence for a selective responsiveness to species-meaningful stimuli, and, in this instance, an indication that auditory stimuli predominate over visual ones with this species.

It has been reported that white-crowned sparrows *Zonotrichia leucophrys* rapidly habituate in the field to playbacks of the conspecific song (Verner and Milligan, 197!). These investigators do not report the length of time elapsing between their three brief habituation trials, however. Since habituation is a time dependent phenomenon this omission makes it impossible to assess the meaning of their results. Further, it is possible that they have confounded effects resulting from habituation with those resulting from changes in reproductive cycle. This seems likely in view of their statement that "... some of the subjects included here were used only every two weeks or every month" (p. 59). In addition, they found that there are seasonal changes in the basic response level. It was also found that there was a greater responsiveness to the native dialect than to nonnative dialects, although there was some response to both (Milligan and Verner, 1971). A high degree of stimulus specificity is suggested since the birds were not responsive at all to a song sparrow *Melospiza melodia* song. They did not investigate habituation in the latter study, but it would be expected, on the basis of the survey presented here, that the rate of habituation should be different for the different dialects.

Petrinovich and Peeke (1973) have studied the aggressive responses of territorial male white crowned sparrows to the playback of a song of the local dialect, the subsequent habituation of that response, and its recovery after a standard time interval. All animals were color banded and all either had nestlings or newly fledged young. The speaker was located inside the territorial boundary of the pair and an 8-trial habituation series was run. Each trial consisted of 10 presentations of the local dialect with an 11-second inter song interval (ISI), a 1-minute pause, another 10 presentations, and a 5-minute silent period. This series was followed by a 70-minute silent period in turn followed by 3 more trials.

The following measures were taken: number of songs in each period, number of flights in each period, and the ISI of all songs in a bout of singing. The mean number of flights per minute is shown in Fig. 1a for the seven birds over the 8 habituation trials and the 3 recovery trials for both the playback and silent periods. Inspection of Fig. 1a indicates that there is a rapid increase in the number of flights during the first 3 trials, followed by a gradual waning of the response. The number of flights and songs during the first series is spuriously low since the birds initially were not in the vicinity of the speaker and hence do not respond at once to the playback. Therefore, this point was not included in the analyses of the data. A 2 × 7 repeated measures analysis of variance supported the conclusion that the mean number of flights per minute is significantly lower during the 5-minute silent period than during playback, and that the response is decreasing over trials. The interaction was not significant.

The mean number of songs per minute is shown in Fig. 1b. Again, the response level is significantly lower during the 5-minute silent period than during the playback and the response decreases over trials. The interaction is not significant.

The results for the mean of the median ISI are shown in Fig. 1c. The mean ISI is not different during playback than during the 5-minute silent period but does change over trials.

These results indicate that for flights per minute there is an initial sensitization effect, followed by a gradual habituation, and that for songs and mean ISI there is a gradual habituation. The birds are more active during playback than during silence on both response rate measures, as might be expected.

Following the 70-minute recovery period there was recovery of the response on all measures as indicated by a test of the regression equations describing the regression lines before and after the 70-minute period. From inspection of the figures it is evident that the regression line describing the trend prior to the 70-minute period cannot be extrapolated to describe the

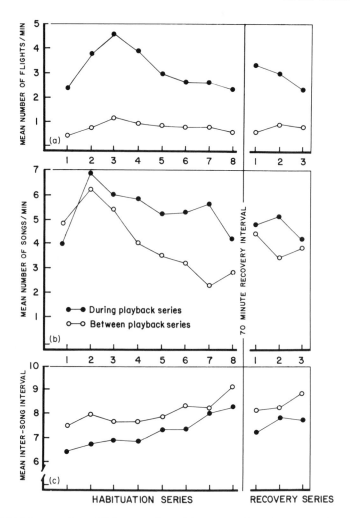

Fig. 1.(a) Mean number of flights per minute (b), mean number of songs per minute, and (c) the mean of the median inter-song interval for seven territorial white-crowned sparrows *Zonotrichia leucophrys*. (●) During playback and (○) between playback series. Note initial sensitization, gradual habituation and recovery after a 70-minute rest interval. From Petrinovich and Peeke (1973).

trend after the 70-minute period. Immediately following the 3-trial rehabituation series three of the birds received one dishabituation trial consisting of a playback of a song from a different dialect area. All three birds showed an increase in response level which, if substantiated in further tests, would provide support for stimulus specificity.

The procedure of playing songs to territorial birds in the field will un-doubtedly gain wide acceptance since the input has great salience for the animals and permits an investigator to study a well-defined response system with a minimal amount of interference with the natural environment. The data obtained with this method to date suggest that it will be possible to maintain a precise level of quantitative control of stimulus parameters while still retaining the species-meaningfulness of the stimuli relevant to the or-ganism-environment context.

If seems safe to accept Thorpe's (1963) conclusion that there is an innate tendency to take avoiding or self-protective action to a wide range of stimuli likely to be signals for danger, especially (1) any moving object, (2) any strong stimulus, (3) any sudden stimulus, or (4) unusually high intensity stimuli. Further, it seems that the rate of habituation is usually slower to stimuli of these four classes. In addition, it is likely that there are innate biases to respond more strongly and to habituate more slowly to certain species-meaningful stimulus configurations than to meaningless ones, that certain stimulus configurations evoke a prepared response in Seligman's terms, and that these prepared responses habituate slowly. [The results of Curio (1969) suggest that this might not be a universal conclusion, however.] Lorenz (1965) has suggested the interesting possibility that there will be an abnormally fast habituation if the stimulus situation involved displays of great uniformity from trial to trial (as would be the case with the usual experimental procedures). In wild life, however, no response is ever elicited "even twice under exactly identical conditions."

Curio (1969) reported that a stimulus situation which is visually more complex evokes more variable responses than does a simpler one. Both of these views suggest that the organism is involved in an active sampling of the environment and, if there is a complex of cues, habituation pro-ceeds more slowly. These considerations offer yet another stumbling block to our efforts to generalize from the laboratory to the field: The very advantages of stimulus control which the laboratory afford us make it quite different from the natural environment which is characterized by both variable cue systems and vicarious response systems.

It can be concluded that habituation is important in adaptation. Objects and situations which fail to give any satisfaction or to cause any damage are neglected. Those stimuli which have some "significance" are then responded to in the manner we would expect on the basis of principles of associative learning. This latter point is illustrated by Schaller and Emlen (1961) who studied yet another bird, the common grackle *Quiscalus versicolor*. At first the young grackle gaped to everything (probably in response to tactile stimu-lation). After pattern vision was well developed it could distinguish the rewarding parent stimulus from that of strange objects. The reaction to these strange stimuli was, at first, negative until either the positive or negative nature was established through experience. After experience with the objects they were then responded to in a manner appropriate to their consequences.

VI. Evolution and Probabilistic Functionalism

Since habituation is a behavioral process which has evolved in response to environmental pressures, it is necessary to consider the environmental demands to which the organism is responding to gain a thorough understanding of the functional significance of habituation. Effort should be made to establish a systematic base of naturalistic observation in order to classify stimuli along a dimension of species-meaningfulness.

It will be useful for those of us interested in studying behavioral habituation in a molar, environmental context to take to heart the methodological contributions of Egon Brunswik. "Brunswik's psychology is Darwinian; it is a form of functionalism because its main focus is on the adaptive interrelation of the organism with the environment" (Hammond, 1966, p. 16). Brunswik has demonstrated, using research in human perception as a prototype, that one must deal with the nature of the environment as carefully as one deals with the nature of the organism. Brunswik focused on the functional achievements of organisms and directed concern to the relationship between the organism and the environement. This point of view has been developed within a more general context elsewhere (Petrinovich, 1973), and only the high points of the argument will be outlined here. The preceding reference should be consulted to understand the historical context and to appreciate the significance of the argument for contemporary behavioral science.

Brunswik called his system "probabilistic functionalism" because of the "intrinsic undependability of the intra-environmental object—cue and means—end relationships that must be utilized by the organism ..." (Brunswik, 1952, p. 23). The organism is dealing with cues of limited trustworthiness in a semi-chaotic environment. We must, when dealing with molar functional attainments such as habituation, regard behavior in terms of biological adjustment rather than in terms of physiological mediation. This leads us to a statistically based science which will deal with behavior in terms of conditional probabilities. It should be understood, as Brunswik has stated, that this "probabilistic character of behavioral laws is not primarily due to limitations in the researcher and his means of approach but rather to inperfection inherent in the potentialities of adjustments on the part of the behaving organism living in a semi-chaotic environment medium" (Brunswik, 1952, p. 28). In dealing with organism—environment interactions we must accept the fact that there are a multitude of stimuli to which the organism is exposed and that each of these stimuli has a differential significance depending on such things as the state of the organism, the context within which the stimulus is embedded, and the preceding experience of the organism. In turn, the response of the organism cannot be absolutely predicted when we deal with the natural environment since it depends on a host of factors such as the behavioral supports for action available in the environment and the immediately preceding action patterns. This vicariousness of cues and of actions makes it necessary to establish statistical links between behavior and the environment. The resulting lack of absolute predictability is not a sign of weakness in the science but is, rather, required by the complexity of the behavioral systems involved.

This line of reasoning leads to the conclusion that we cannot seek our salvation in the lawful and predictable realm of molecular neurophysiology to understand the behavioral phenomenon of habituation. Molar behavioral phenomena are macrostatistical just as are molar neurophysiological phenomena, in contrast to the microstatistical nature of physics. Physics tends to become probabilistic at the most molecular levels of inquiry while both neurophysiology and behavior tend to become probabilistic at the most molar levels of inquiry. Becasue of this probabilism we can never attain the complete nomothetic ideal and must recognize that systematically based parametric studies of the mediators of habituation can never answer the molar functional questions regarding habituation.

Most behavioral research has employed what Brunswik (1956) calls systematic design, in which a relatively small number of variables is chosen for study and these variables are then systematically manipulated. The ideal of this design is to hold all variables constant but one, then to control that one, and to allow another to vary, and so forth. This manner of proceeding is regarded by most scientists as representing an optimal strategy.

Brunswik objected to the use of systematic designs in the study of behavior on the grounds that these designs almost inevitably involve the use of atypical backgrounds for the behaviors in question and embed the behavior in atypical contexts.

Brunswik has discussed the limitations inherent in such systematic designs at some length. One such limitation involes the artificial tying of variables. His example of this, from the field of perception, involves the judgments of the lengths of lines presented at the same distance from the observer. When this is done the physical lengths of the lines and the size of the projected retinal image (the distal and the proximal cue, respectively) are ". . .inseparably tied by arrangement of the experimenter. . . . The two variables then vary in perfect unison, their correlation is artificially made to be 1" (Brunswik, 1956, p. 97).

One can artificially untie variables by eliminating whatever natural covariation there is between two variables. For example, if one is interested in rating the personality of students as "social objects" it would be possible to eliminate differences between students in such things as clothing and general muscle tonus. In this way ". . . correlations between clothing habits, or general muscle tonus on the one hand, and personality on the other, which very likely would be found to exist outside the confines of the experiment [would be] destroyed in the experiment" (Brunswik, 1956, p. 9).

"The main function both of art and of systematic experimentation, then, is to shape and mold us by exaggeration and extreme correlation or absence of correlation. But exaggeration is distortion, and this distortion must in science eventually be resolved by allowing the more palatable systematic design to mature into, and to be superseded by, the more truthful representative design" (Brunswik, 1955, p. 215).

On the positive side Brunswik has outlined the advantages of using a representative design and has outlined some of the technical requirements of such an approach. In representative design the probabilistic nature of environmental circumstances is exhibited. This is attained by the representative sampling of situations from the organism's ecology—the natural cultural habitat of the organism. Thus, variables remain correlated as they are in the environment. Any control that is exerted is a passive control and the experimenter proceeds by actuarial registration of the values of the relevant variables. This design implies that the choice of the variables themselves should be based on their biological relevance.

This demands that an experimenter will have to devote as much attention to studying the structure of the environment and to take as much trouble to obtain representative samples from that environment as he usually does to the problem of obtaining a representative sampling of subjects.

Brunswik argued that "No matter how much the results of systematic experiments may anticipate those of a representative survey, in a technical sense only representative design can answer functional problems definitely" (Brunswik, 1956, p. 70). In fact, Brunswik makes the interesting point that systematic design is useful to demonstrate *possibility* whereas representative design is adequate to the task of investigating *probability*.

Quite often the demonstration of mere possibility . . . is all that is necessary and desired of a piece of research, and may be fully sufficient to establish tentatively a principle for purposes of further verification and thus to stimulate further research; in all cases of this kind the systematic experiment is in place and may save the burdens that would go with a proof of ecological generality. In other cases, a systematic experiment may serve to exclude certain trivial factors from the explanation of a phenomenon.

On the other hand, the most striking shortcomings in the generalizability of results of systematically rather than representatively conducted experiments are given when it comes to a quantitative estimate of the relative contribution of competing factors in functional adjustment to the environment (Brunswik, 1956, p. 55).

This same point has been emphasized by Tinbergen who wrote: "... it might be useful to approach learning phenomena from a more naturalistic standpoint than is usually done and to ask, not what can an animal learn, but what does it actually learn under natural conditions?" (Tinbergen, 1951, p. 142).

This brings us to two basic concepts in representative design: ecological validity and functional validity. Ecological validity is defined as the correlation between a proximal cue and a distal object. Functional validity is defined as the correlation between the distal object and the distal response. It is the study of the cues *as used* by the organism to make the response. In a perceptually well-adjusted organism, the rank order of utilization of environmental cues (functional validity) should be the same as the order of their environmental significance (ecological validity).

Brunswik's statement of probabilistic functionalism is a sophisticated methodological development. It focuses on the functional adaptation of organisms to their environment and outlines the research strategies adequate to the task of understanding these adaptations. In addition, Brunswik demonstrated the necessity of studying the ecology itself and of insuring that a representative sample is obtained from the ecology in order to derive conclusions with ecological generality.

There is, undoubtedly, a place for both systematic and representative design. Clearly, we need systematic research in order to identify the possible mechanisms related to an outcome so that they might be sampled and allow us to proceed to the study of such things as ecological validity and functional validity.

The utilization of what Brunswik (1956) refers to as representative designs will result in molar generalizations of more naturalistic and general significance than it is possible to obtain with strict reliance on results from the experimental laboratory. We must, if we are to achieve a more complete understanding of habituation, allow the environment to enter into our "predictive equations" and we must also be satisfied with less than absolute predictability. Since complex behavioral processes are organized with a great deal of flexibility regarding means–end relationships, it will be profitable to view behavior from the standpoint of probabilistic functionalism. As outlined above, this approach stresses the probabilistic texture of environmental events and inquires into the relationships between the stimulating environment and behavior at a molar functional level. We will not be able to make predictions of specific molar behaviors with a very high degree of certainty but must rest content with issuing a series of statements of conditional probabilities. Hinde (1970) reflected this same point of view in his recent article. He wrote: "It can be taken as axiomatic that changes in the behavior of intact organisms rarely, if ever, depend on unitary changes in underlying mechanisms" (pp. 35–36).

Ghiselin (1969) has developed this same point in relation to the strength of the Darwinian method in general and argued convincingly that this recognition of the conditional probabilities inherent in environment–organism interaction made it possible for Darwin to understand the processes of organic evolution. Complex organisms have evolved with an inherent potential for flexibility in the face of environmental demands. Therefore, we should attempt to understand the normal interplay of variables and to develop a series of "If . . . if . . . then" statements in terms of distal stimulus and distal response variables, in Brunswik's terminology (Brunswik, 1952). In this way we should be better able to reach the goal of establishing a theory of habituation which is adequate at both the molar and the molecular levels of analysis.

In order to understand behavioral habituation we are going to have to abandon research strategies which give us a spurious air of precision. These strategies are appropriate to study transformation between stimulus and response and the mediation mechanisms involved in these transformations. Certainly, to establish the identity of such mediating mechanisms and to specify the operating characteristics of these mediating mechanisms is a challenging and exciting task for science. However, the task of understanding behavioral habituation must be undertaken at a different level of complexity and with a different set of more naturalistic and representative research tools. In this way, and this way only, will we be able to work our way through the tangled thicket of organism–environment interactions.

References

Brunswik, E. (1952). "The Conceptual Framework of Psychology." Univ. of Chicago Press, Chicago, Illinois.

Brunswik, E. (1955). Representative design and probabilistic theory in a functional psychology. *Psychol. Rev.* **62**, 193–217.

Brunswik, E. (1956). "Perception and the Representative Design of Psychological Experiments," 2nd ed. Univ. of California Press, Berkeley.

Castellucci, V., Pinsker, H., Kupferman, I., and Kandel, E. R. (1970). Neuronal mechanisms of habituation and dishabituation of the gill withdrawal reflex in Aplysia. *Science* **167**, 1745–1748.

Curio, V. E. (1969). Funktionsweise und Stammesgeschichte des Flugfeinderkennens einiger Darwinfinken (*Goespizinae*). *Z. Tierpsychol.* **20**, 394–487.

Ghiselin, M. T. (1969). "The Triumph of the Darwinian Method." Univ. of California Press, Berkeley.

Groves, P. M., and Thompson, R. F. (1970). Habituation: A dual-process theory. *Psychol. Rev.* **77**, 419–450.

Hammond, K. R. (1966). Probabilistic functionalism: Brunswik's integration of the history, theory, and method of psychology. *In* "The Psychology of Egon Brunswik" (K. R. Hammond, ed.), p. 15–80. Holt, New York.

Hilgard, E. R., and Bower, G. H. (1966). "Theories of Learning." Appleton, New York.

Hinde, R. A. (1954a). Factors governing the changes in strength of a partially inborn response, as shown by the mobbing behavior of the chaffinch (*Fringilla coelebs*). I. The nature of the response, and an examination of its course. *Proc. Roy. Soc. Ser. B* **142**, 306–331.

Hinde, R. A. (1954b). Factors governing the changes in strength of a partially inborn response, as shown by the mobbing behaviour of the chaffinch (*Fringilla coelebs*). II. The waning of the response. *Proc. Roy. Soc, Ser. B* **142**, 331–358.

Hinde, R. A. (1961). Factors governing the changes in strength of a partially inborn response, as shown by the mobbing behaviour of the chaffinch (*Fringilla coelebs*). III. The interaction of short-term and long-term incremental and decremental effects. *Proc. Roy. Soc. Ser. B* **153**, 398–420.

Hinde, R. A. (1970). Behavioural habituation. *In* "Short-term Changes in Neural Activity and Behaviour" (G. Horn and R. A. Hinde, eds.) pp. 3–40. Cambridge Univ. Press, London and New York

Horn. G. (1967). Neuronal mechanisms of habituation. *Nature* (*London*) **215**, 707–711.

Horn, G., and Hinde, R. A., eds. (1970). "Short-term Changes in Neural Activity and Behaviour." Cambridge, Univ. Press, London and New York.

Kandel, E. R., and Spencer, W. A. (1968). Cellular neurophysiological approaches in the study of learning. *Physiol. Rev.* **48**, 65–134.

Kling, J. W., and Stevenson, J. G. (1970). Habituation and extinction. *In* "Short-term Changes in Neural Activity and Behaviour" pp. 41–61. Cambridge Univ. Press, London and New York.

Lorenz, K. Z. (1939). Vergleichende Verhaltensforschung. *Zool. Anz., Suppl.* **1** , 69–102.

Lorenz, K. Z. (1965). "Evolution and Modification of Behavior." Univ. of Chicago Press, Chicago, Illinois.

Melzack, R. (1961). On the survival of mallard ducks after "habituation" to the hawk-shaped figure. *Behaviour* **17**, 9–16.

Milligan, M. M., and Verner, J. (1971). Inter-populational song dialect discrimination in the white-crowned sparrow. *Condor* **73**, 208–213.

Nice, M. M., and ter Pelkwijk, J. J. (1941). Enemy recognition by the song sparrow. *Auk* **58**, 195–214.

Orr, R. T. (1945). A study of captive Galapagos finches of the genus *Geospiza. Condor* **47**, 177–201.

Pavlov, I. P. (1927). "Conditioned Reflexes." Oxford Univ. Press, London, and New York.

Peeke, H. V. S., and Zeiner, A. R. (1970). Habituation to environmental and specific auditory stimuli in the rat. *Commun. Behav. Biol.* **5**, 23–29.

Petrinovich, L. (1973). Darwin and the representative expression of reality. *In* "Darwin and Facial Expression: A Century of Research in Review. (P. Ekman, ed.) Academic Press, New York (in press).

Petrinovich, L., and Peeke, H. V. S. (1972). Habituation to territorial song in the White-crowned sparrow (*Zonotrichia leucophrys*) *Behav. Biol.* In Press.

Rand, A. (1941a). Results of Archbold Expeditions. No. 33. Development and enemy recognition of curve-billed thrasher. *Bull. Amer. Mus. Natur. Hist.* **78**, 213–242.

Rand, A. (1941b). Results of Archbold Expeditions. No. 34. Development and enemy recognition of curve-billed thrasher. *Bull. Amer. Mus. Natur. Hist.* **79**, 517–524.

Rouse, J. E. (1905). Respiration and emotion in pigeons. *J. Comp. Neurol.* **15**, 404–513.

Schaller, G. B., and Emlen, J. T. (1961). The development of visual discrimination patterns in the crouching reactions of nestling grackles. *Auk* **78**, 125–137.

Schleidt, W. M. (1961). Reaktionen von Truthühnern auf fliegende Raubvögel und Versuche zur Analyse ihrer AAM's. *Z. Tierpsychol.* **18**, 534–560.

Seligman, M. E. P. (1970). On the generality of the laws of learning. *Psychol. Rev.* **77**, 406–418.

Sharpless, S. K., and Jasper, H. (1956). Habituation of the arousal reaction. *Brain* **79**, 655–680.

Sokolov, E. N. (1960). Neuronal models and the orienting reflex. *In* "The Central Nervous System and Behavior" (M. A. B. Brazier, p. 187–276) Josiah Macy, Jr. Found., New York.

Thompson, R. F., and Spencer, W. A. (1966). Habituation: A model phenomenon for the study of neuronal substrates of behavior. *Psychol. Rev.* **73**, 16–43.

Thompson. W. L. (1969). Song recognition by territorial male buntings (*Passerina*). *Anim. Behav.* **17**, 658–663.

Thorpe, W. H. (1963). "Learning and Instinct in Animals." Methuen, London.

Tinbergen, N. (1951). "The Study of Instinct." Oxford Univ. Press, London and New York.

Verner, J., and Milligan, M. M. (1971). Responses of male white-crowned sparrows to playback of recorded songs. *Condor* **73**, 56–64.

Vowles, D. M., and Prewitt, E. (1971). Stimulus and response specificity in the habituation of anti-predator behaviour in the ring dove (*Streptopelia risoria*). *Anim. Behav.* **19**, 80–86.

Zippelius, H. M., and Schleidt, W. M. (1956). Ultraschallaute bei jungen Mausen. *Naturwissenschaften* **21**, 502.

Chapter 5
Habituation and Dishabituation of Responses[1]
Innervated by the Autonomic Nervous System

FRANCES K. GRAHAM

I. Introduction

Traditionally, the autonomic nervous system (ANS) has been viewed either as a single system determining the general level of arousal or activation of the organism or as two antagonistic systems, the sympathetic and parasympathetic, which have arousal and modulating functions, respectively. A specificity view has also had its adherents and is perhaps the most

[1]Preparation of this paper was supported by grants HD01490 from the National Institutes of Health and K5-21762 from the National Institute of Mental Health. The author is indebted to Mary Beth Boland for help in searching and abstracting the literature and to Kathleen M. Berg, W. Keith Berg, Jan C. Jackson, and Lois E. Putnam for many stimulating discussions as well as for a critical review of the manuscript.

common approach of modern psychophysiologists. This view treats ANS activities, or more precisely, the activities of effectors innervated by the ANS, as specific responses whose complex interrelations with other ANS and striate muscle activities must be individually traced. This spectrum of views on the nature of ANS function may also be found in recent theories of habituation. Thompson and collaborators (Groves and Thompson, 1970; Thompson and Spencer, 1966), in proposing a "dual-process" theory of habituation, accord a central role to generalized arousal. Sokolov's theory (1963b) of habituation of the orienting reflex (OR) distinguishes between two generalized arousal systems, the OR and the defensive reflex (DR), although it also makes a place for specific responses through the concept of adaptive reflexes. While ANS activities are not explicitly considered in a theory of habituation proposed by Ratner (1970), they would presumably be treated like any other measured activity; i.e., they should interact with competing responses to yield either facilitation or decrement depending upon stimulation conditions and response topography.

The present paper reviews the rapidly growing literature on ANS response habituation in the light of the theories of Thompson and of Sokolov. These two approaches are chosen, not only because of their important influence on the field but also because Thompson's relatively traditional view of the ANS and of learning principles can be contrasted with Sokolov's "systems" view of the ANS and his "cognitive," information-processing view of learning. The validity of a specificity theory is not denied but, at the present time, there do not seem to be any lively issues with regard to specificity in ANS habituation research. Out of respect for space limitations, the review will be largely restricted to English-language studies using waking, adult human and, in a few instances, animal subjects. Although a sizable and interesting literature exists in the developmental field, the problems are more complex and require extensive treatment in their own right.

The province of the paper is the review of effects on electrodermal and cardiovascular ANS response of repeated presentations of the same non-signal stimulus and of subsequent change in the stimulus. Attention is devoted, primarily, to the question of how habituation varies as a function of intensive and temporal characteristics of stimuli since these variables can easily be manipulated parametrically and have considerable theoretical interest. A number of other problems in the general area of ANS habituation not only have important implications for understanding habituation phenomena but also are being actively investigated. Interesting problems include habituation during sleep, habituation of the response to stimulus offset, the effects of stimulus modality, complexity, and predictability on habituation, the effects of making a stimulus a signal, the relation between habituation of ANS and non-ANS responses, and individual and group differences in habituation functions. Regretfully, discussion of these functions has been omitted entirely rather than treat them in a too superficial fashion.

A. Contrasts between the Theories of Thompson and Sokolov

Thompson and Spencer (1966), in their excellent review of habituation, proposed that the hindlimb flexion reflex of the acute spinal cat could be used as a model system for analysis of the neuronal mechanisms involved in response habituation and dishabituation. On the basis of studies of this preparation, they suggested that two processes are involved. One, a decremental process, could be shown to take place during transmission through interneurons. A second process, called sensitization, was also hypothesized to explain the fact that when a stimulus change was introduced, the habituated response temporarily increased in strength. They argued that a second, independent process was required to explain the fact that a habituated response might increase above control level and that subsequent decline to the habituated level could occur even without further stimulation. In a later article, Groves and Thompson (1970, p. 421) suggested that the habituation process occurs in S-R pathways, i.e., in "the most direct route through the central nervous system," while sensitization occurs in the "state" system, "the collection of pathways, systems, and regions that determines the general level of responsiveness of the organism." The authors further elaborated the description of state as "the general level of excitation, arousal, activation, tendency to respond, etc., of the organism. State need not be a unitary entity or construct, but merely a shorthand summary of the many factors that influence the general excitability or tendency to make responses of the organism, . . ." (Groves and Thompson, p. 440f).

Sokolov's theory is discussed in a number of English-language publications of which the most comprehensive is the 1963 translation of his book *Perception and the Conditioned Reflex* (Sokolov, 1963b); other valuable sources include Sokolov (1960, 1963a, 1969). The theory states that "the extrapolating properties of the nervous system," especially the cerebral cortex, produce a model of the properties of external stimulation which includes not only simple qualitative, intensive, and temporal characteristics but also more complex relationships such as the sequence or pattern of stimuli, the meaning of words, and the probability of occurrence (Sokolov, 1963b, p. 286–289). Subsequent stimulation is compared with the model which is not a static imprint but "constantly undergoes revisions in order to account for the characteristics of the stimulus which is operating at a given moment" (Sokolov, 1969, p. 677). The comparison produces signals of match or mismatch that serve either to dampen or to amplify the activity in nonspecific pathways. Signals of mismatch lead to elicitation of the orienting reflex, a generalized system of responses which includes central, motor, and ANS components that enhance stimulus reception. Signals of match block stimulus-produced impulses arriving over nonspecific paths and thus lead to habituation of the OR. Since activity in specific pathways is not affected, adaptive reflexes appropriate to the particular characteristics of a stimulus continue to be elicited. Presumably, adaptive reflexes may also undergo decrement with long-repeated stimulation, but, if so, the mechanism would be different from that producing OR habituation. A third type of reflex also exists, the defensive reflex, for which the mechanisms are less clearly described. The DR, like the OR, is a nonspecific reflex and has many components in common with the OR. However, it is evoked not by stimulus change but by intense stimulation, and it habituates only slowly or may even be intensified by repetitive stimulation.

The theories of Sokolov and Thompson thus differ in many respects. While Thompson seeks to develop a general theory of response habituation, his model is derived from a spinal reflex. Sokolov's theory embraces a wider variety of responses but, insofar as habituation is concerned, deals in detail only with a habituation process that depends primarily on a stimulus analyzing mechanism in cerebral cortex and affects a particular response system, the OR. Both theories involve response incrementing and response decrementing processes, but Thompson's incrementing process, sensitization, is described as first rising and then showing subsequent decay even in the face of continued stimulation. Both theories also distinguish between activities in direct and indirect pathways, if specific can be equated with direct and nonspecific with the state system. However, Sokolov distinguishes between the eliciting conditions, function, response components, and rates of response habituation of two generalized reflex systems generated in the indirect pathways. Thompson, while noting that a unitary construct of state is unnecessary for dual-process theory, does not distinguish more than a single state system nor assign different properties to different parts of the system.

B. Arousal System(s)

The concept of a unitary dimension of arousal or activation has had a long history in psychology, and it took on added importance with the discovery in 1949 (Moruzzi and Magoun, 1949) of the activating properties of the reticular system. However, unidimensionality has been vigorously challenged by recent work. Lacey (1967) reviewed the most critical findings which include low intercorrelations among ANS measures of arousal, dissociation of central, behavioral, and ANS arousal, and specificity of ANS responses as a function of eliciting conditions. A consideration of ANS physiology also makes it clear that while excitation can spread more diffusely than in the peripheral somatic nervous system, a single preganglionic axon serving as many as 20 ganglionic cells (Koelle, 1970), there is not only provision for, but many demonstrations of, independent activity even within a single system such as the cardiovascular. Folkow (1960) stated, for example, that vasomotor fiber control "is hardly inferior to the somatomotor innervation as concerns specialized differentiation." The most important evidence that the ANS does not respond as a unit is probably the recent success of Neal Miller (e.g., 1969) and colleagues in demonstrating the instrumental learning of a wide variety of ANS responses. Finally, even the central arousal system no longer appears to be completely undifferentiated. There are important differences between regions such as the brain stem and thalamic reticular formation and inhibitory as well as facilitatory connections both to and from the cortex (Magoun, 1963).

Malmo, who had been one of the principal proponents of activation theory (e.g., Malmo, 1959), has recently revised his position to accommodate the criticisms offered by Lacey (1967). In a paper by Malmo and Bélanger (1967), it was argued that the theory may still be valuable as a general description but the importance of specific stimuli in determining the nature of response was recognized. The authors stated that "there is no conflict between revised activation theory and the principles of physiological response specificity" (Malmo and Bélanger, p. 306).

The concept of two generalized arousal systems is perhaps a more recent one than unidimensional theory, but it is not without historical precedent as Schneirla (1959) has pointed out. Routtenberg (1968), reviewing neurophysiological findings, argued that many inconsistencies could be resolved by postulating two mutually inhibiting systems. He associated the classic reticular activating system of Moruzzi and Magoun (1949) with a functional system responsive to high intensities of stimulation and serving to energize reaction while a second system, involving limbic structures, responds to low or moderate stimuli and, by prolonging the effects of stimulation, serves to facilitate memory and learning processes. Graham and Jackson (1970) noted that Routtenberg's hypothesis has many features in common with Sokolov's DR and OR systems.

While a two-arousal system approach may better accommodate the empirical data than does a unidimensional approach, it also is susceptible to specificity arguments since different components of the same system do not always behave concordantly, especially with regard to habituation of ANS components (e.g., Stern and Plapp, 1969, p. 210f). Lack of concordance may, of course, result from measurement problems. Direct comparison of different responses requires not only nominally comparable units such as percentages or standard scores but also underlying scales of equal sensitivity in measuring different responses, free of distortion by ceiling effects, and having the same relation to base level. Measurement techniques in ANS work have not generally achieved this level of sophistication. However, even if measurement were improved, specificity could probably be demonstrated at some level. The question is not whether there is some variability among responses, stimuli, subjects, or whatever are assumed to be replicates, but whether one conceptualization can account for more of the variability than another. A specificity theory does not improve predictions unless it goes beyond the statement that some other theory does not account for *all* of the variability.

For present purposes, the relevant question is how well Thompson's and Sokolov's theories predict the effects of stimulation on habituation and dishabituation of ANS responses. Although Groves and Thompson (1970) did not directly suggest an appropriate measure of state or sensitization, their description of the concept, and the literature cited by them, indicates that changes in cardiovascular and electrodermal activities should be appropriate. State is usually treated as a relatively slow change in level of activity, but it is the rapidly changing characteristics that are important to Thompson's theory; that is, the theory's use of sensitization refers to a process, initiated by a stimulus, which can exhibit change within less than a second and which decays, in the absence of further stimulation, within a minute (e.g., Groves and Thompson, 1970, Figs. 2 and 3). While Thompson's theory does not make any distinction among ANS activities Sokolov's does, of course, distinguish between activities which are components of the OR and DR. A number of components participate in both reflexes but direction of cephalic vasomotor changes, of heart rate (HR) change (Graham and Clifton, 1966), and, perhaps, of skin potential change (Raskin *et al.*, 1969a) presumably vary depending on whether an OR or DR is elicited. Slow as well as rapid changes are encompassed by the theory.

II. Effects of Repeated Stimulation as a Function of Response

This section briefly surveys studies of electrodermal and cardiovascular activity that have employed the habituation paradigm. Although some other ANS systems have been investigated there is relatively little work available, and the methodology offers special problems beyond the reviewer's area of competence. Since an ANS response is not an all-or-none effect but some change in a steady state, the problem of characterizing a "response" is more complex than is true of many "behavioral" responses. It is common to distinguish between the steady state or level of the activity and two types of transient change, "phasic" and "tonic." These are not precisely defined terms but refer to relatively rapid and brief or relatively slow and longer lasting changes, respectively. The identification problem is further complicated by the fact that ANS activities may show rapid changes in direction which are obscured by averaging. In addition, the amount and direction of change is usually dependent upon the existing level of activity. In short, both the problems of detecting changes in ANS activity and of mensuration are formidable. Two recent textbooks (Brown, 1967; Venables and Martin, 1967) deal with instrumentation questions, but there is no comprehensive discussion of measurement problems. Papers by Lacey (1956) and Benjamin (1963, 1967) discuss initial level effects; the present writer has discussed a number of the measurement questions arising in connection with HR responses (Graham and Jackson, 1970, pp. 69–78).

The review of findings, in this section, summarizes the extensive work on GSR and HR briefly and generally without citation since specific studies are considered under later sections dealing with the effects of variation in stimulus parameters. There has been only scattered work on other responses, sufficient to determine whether or not response habituation and sensitization have been demonstrated but not to draw conclusions about particular stimulus effects. These studies are cited and discussed in more detail since they receive little subsequent attention.

The phasic, exosomatic electrodermal response, expressed as *skin resistance or skin conductance* change or log change (GSR), has been the most widely investigated ANS response. It has generally been measured from palmar surfaces and may not show the same characteristics if measured from other areas (Edelberg, 1967; Sokolov, 1963b, p. 56). Habituation has usually been very rapid with the greatest decrement occurring between trials 1 and 2 and with an asymptotic level reached in from 3 to approximately 20 trials. However, with very high stimulus intensities, there may be little decrement. No studies were located in which the phasic GSR, measured as a difference from prestimulus level, showed increased sensitization on the second trial. In contrast, most of the studies that reported absolute levels showed tonic increases in conductance or decreases in resistance, lasting, in some cases, for several trials or, with high intensity stimulation, persisting throughout the experimental session (Bernstein, 1969; Coombs, 1938; Germana, 1968; Hare, 1968; Lader, 1964; Raskin *et al.*, 1969a; Scholander, 1961; Zimny and Kienstra, 1967). Sokolov (1963b, e.g., p. 117) has also described a change in skin resistance which may persist for several stimulations as a "tonic orientation reaction." This usually gives way to increased skin resistance as the phasic response habituates.

The endosomatic or *skin potential* response has been measured less frequently, and habituation rate depends upon whether the negative or positive potential wave is considered. In some instances, a change in either direction has been scored as a response (e.g., Gaviria, 1967; Uno and Grings, 1965), but this probably reflects primarily the contribution of the larger positive component. There is agreement that this positive component shows relatively rapid habituation, reaching asymptote in 4–10 trials, while the negative component may fail to show habituation, especially to intense stimuli (Forbes and Bolles, 1936; Raskin et al., 1969a; Thetford et al., 1968). The two components appear to involve different effectors and may reflect different psychological processes, but a precise delineation of the psychological differences cannot yet be made (Wilcott, 1967).

Various cardiovascular responses have also been investigated, particularly changes in *heart rate*. Early work tended to study changes in maximum HR increase, while more recent studies have recognized that a multiphasic response is commonly obtained and have investigated both accelerative and decelerative components or the difference between them (Lang and Hnatiow, 1962). In general, any decelerative component has been found to habituate rapidly while accelerative components show greater variability dependent on stimulus conditions. In situations eliciting startle, a large short latency acceleration may show marked decrement in 1 or 2 trials while a longer latency accelerative component is frequently found to increase across trials. The pattern of relatively gradual increase in phasic acceleration and its persistence is not the pattern of sensitization and decay described by Groves and Thompson (1970). Tonic changes in HR have received little attention. Raskin et al. (1969a) reported that, when 120 dB white noise was given at 15-second intervals, HR level increased for 2–3 trials and then declined. The pattern was not observed in groups receiving 100 dB or less intense stimuli or with interstimulus intervals (ISI) of 45 seconds.

Other measures of cardiovascular activity have included changes in *systolic or diastolic blood pressure*, in skin temperature, and in pulse volume or blood volume in a restricted area such as a digit. Since blood pressure is difficult to measure continuously, it has been used mainly for studies of long-term habituation. Dykman et al. (1965) found that systolic pressure in dogs declined across 8 days of repetitive tone stimulation. The exact conditions under which blood pressure was recorded were not given, and these results may indicate a tonic rather than a phasic change. Several British physiologists have also measured blood pressure in studying the effects of repeated immersions of the hand in water at high (47°C) or low (4°C) temperatures (Glaser, 1966). Both systolic and diastolic pressure showed large increases initially and, in one experiment, greater increases on the second immersion (Glaser and Whittow, 1957). However, habituation occurred within the 6 trials of a session and across the several experimental days. In another study (Glaser et al. 1959), habituation was shown to be specific to the repeatedly stimulated hand. When the nonstimulated control hand was immersed at the end of training, responses were as large as those on the initial trials of the first day.

The Glaser *et al.* (1959) study also reported one response which did *not* show habituation in the course of repeated immersions. The *skin temperature* of the immersed hand always approximated the water temperature and did not vary systematically across trials or sessions. Similar temperature findings were reported in an earlier study with human subjects (Glaser and Whittow, 1957) and in a later study of tail immersions in rats (Glaser and Griffin, 1962). These findings, considered in conjunction with absence of any histological evidence of tissue damage to the tails or of changed response following iontophoresis with an antihistamine substance, suggested that habituation was not the result of localized changes.

However, skin temperature change has been shown to habituate rapidly, in 2–3 trials, with repetition of 75 dB tones (Hord *et al.*, 1965). In short, a decrease in skin temperature, which reflects vasoconstrictive changes in blood vessels of the skin, shows habituation to nonthermal stimuli as rapidly as do other cardiovascular responses, but temperature changes do not habituate to a locally applied thermal stimulus. These observations are in line with Sokolov's distinction (1963b) between the rapidly habituating orienting response and the nonhabituating "adaptive reflexes," i.e., reflexes such as the pupillary response to light which are specialized for adapting to a particular quality and intensity of stimulation. Had skin temperature been measured during the first few seconds of immersion at high temperatures, a brief decrease in skin temperature might have been observed, on initial trials, to precede the adaptive rise.

The least consistent findings have been obtained with the so-called "vasomotor" responses. These responses are measured by transducers which are primarily sensitive to variation in the amounts of blood in some local body region. Plethysmographic transducers measure changes in the volume of the whole area, whether due to increased blood or to fluid in the interstitial spaces while photocells, depending on their spectral response, may be sensitive in varying degrees to blood oxygenation. Further differences arise, depending upon whether the system is direct or resistor-capacitor coupled. When slow changes are filtered out, the response may be referred to as the pulse volume since the record shows only the transitory phasic changes in blood volume accompanying each pulse wave. With direct coupling or a low pass filter with a very long time-constant, the record more closely reflects the total blood volume in the part. Since a blood vessel resists stretch more strongly the more it is already distended, pulse and volume measures may show changes in opposite directions.

The major work in this area has been done by Soviet investigators who have reported that, under conditions appropriate for eliciting orienting, rapidly habituating vasodilation is obtained in the head and vasoconstriction in the finger. Although Davis *et al.* (1955) and Davis and Buchwald (1957) obtained findings in agreement with this distinction, Western investigators have generally had difficulty in replicating the report of *cephalic vasomotor* changes. This may result from measurement problems since the several studies have not succeeded in identifying any consistent response pattern. Raskin *et al.* (1969b) obtained either a solely constrictive change in blood pulse volume or brief dilation followed by constriction, while Cohen and Johnson (1971) and Keefe and Johnson (1970) obtained a response of initial constriction followed by dilation. With blood volume rather than pulse volume as the measure, dilation only (Cohen and Johnson, 1971; Raskin *et al.*, 1969b), dilation followed by constriction (Raskin *et al.*, 1969b), constriction followed by dilation (K. M. Berg, 1970), and triphasic responses (W. K. Berg, 1968) have been reported. In view of the variety of response patterns, it is not surprising that consistent effects of repeated stimulation or of stimulus intensity have not been found. There is some suggestion that dilation components, if they have a relatively long latency of several seconds, habituate rapidly (Berg, 1968; Brotsky, 1969; Cohen and Johnson, 1971; Raskin *et al.*, 1969a,b), which would agree with Sokolov's formulation. However, the relation to stimulus intensity does not. Raskin *et al.* (1969b) and Berg (1970) reported that intense stimuli, which should evoke a defensive rather than an orienting reflex, elicited relatively large dilations. It is possible, as Berg pointed out, that this can be attributed to stimulus-induced respiratory changes. She suggested that photometric methods, which were used in the above studies, may be more sensitive to rapid changes in blood distribution (Hocherman and Palti, 1967) and less sensitive to baseline shifts (Royer, 1966) than the volumetric transducers employed by Sokolov. Another difference between western and Soviet studies is implicated by a recent report (Cook, 1972) that cephalic vasomotor changes, replicating Sokolov, can be obtained if a temporal artery site is monitored.

In contrast to the uncertain nature of the cephalic change, *peripheral vasoconstriction* of the finger has been found in response to a wide range of stimulus conditions. The extent to which the constrictive response habituates is disputed, however. Furedy (1971a) suggested that instances of apparent habituation may result from either a short intertrial interval producing sensory adaptation or from change in motivational factors due to associating neutral with aversive stimuli. The intertrial-interval argument is weakened by the fact that several investigators have obtained significant habituation using mean intervals as long as or longer than the 45 seconds at which Furedy (1968b, 1969a) did *not* obtain habituation. Studies obtaining habituation include K. M. Berg (1970), W. K. Berg (1968), Davidoff and McDonald (1964), Davis *et al.* (1955), Lidberg *et al.* (1969), McDonald *et al.* (1964), and

Uno and Grings (1965). Significant habituation was also found by Cohen and Johnson (1971) with a mean interval of 40 seconds (range 20–60), by Gaviria (1967) with 24–44 second intervals, and by Koepke and Pribram (1967) when subjects received 20-second stimuli at offset-to-onset intervals of 10–40 seconds or 5-second stimuli at offset-to-onset intervals of either 10–40 or 30–60 seconds. Other studies reporting habituation include Bernstein *et al.* (1971), Burch (1961), Gabriel and Ball (1970), and Unger (1964), but they either used relatively short intertrial intervals or did not subject their habituation findings to statistical test. Since all of the cited studies employed nonsignal stimuli, there was no opportunity for association with aversive stimulation.

Although the majority of studies have reported habituation of the vaso-constrictive response, Furedy (1968b, 1969a) is not alone in his failure to obtain habituation. Hare (1968) found that the response was highly variable and showed no consistent trends; Gross and Stern (1967), while noting that response amplitude probably habituated as judged from inspection of polygraph records, did not obtain any significant decrease in the percentage of subjects responding. Lader (1965) also failed to find significant habituation although the mean response decreased with stimulus repetitions.

It is not clear whether Hare (1968) and Gross and Stern (1967) recorded pulse volume or area volume, but both Furedy (1968b, 1969a) and Lader (1965) measured pulse volume. As noted previously, pulse and area volume may not vary concomitantly and it is the area measure which was used by Sokolov. Uno and Grings (1965), who recorded both measures, found that area volume, but not pulse volume, habituated. However, Davis *et al.* (1955) found that the reverse was true although they also pointed out that the pulse measure was more variable than the area measure. It thus appears that pulse volume may be a less consistent measure of vasomotor response as well as less appropriate for replicating Sokolov. In any case, interpretation would be simplified if investigators established that changes labeled response are, in fact, significantly greater than the operant level, that is, than activity during a nonstimulus control period which is selected according to the same criteria used to determine when a stimulus is administered. Although periods selected just prior to a stimulus or in the middle of an ISI obviously do *not* meet the same criteria as stimulus periods and may reflect, for example, systematic changes resulting from a preceding response, even this kind of control is rarely employed. Furedy and Gagnon (1969) did attempt to show that their vasomotor measures could detect differences between activity before and after a stimulus. They did not report GSR and vasomotor detections separately in making a statistical test, but a later paper (Furedy, 1969a) indicated that vasomotor activity, considered alone, did change significantly.

To summarize the general findings with regard to effects of repeated stimulation as a function of the type of ANS response, there are several points of interest. First, increased sensitization over the first few trials does occur quite frequently when absolute levels are measured. The level changes may or may not show subsequent decay. Second, some phasic responses show very rapid habituation, reaching asymptote within 2–20 trials, while others have shown little or no habituation over an experimental session. Rapidly habituating responses include HR deceleration, the GSR unless stimulus intensity is high, and skin temperature when a nonthermal stimulus is used. Except for skin temperature, it has been suggested that these responses are components of an OR. Rapid habituation which may be associated with startle has also been reported for a short latency HR acceleration and for positive skin potentials. Longer latency HR acceleration is difficult to habituate and may even increase across trials. Negative skin potentials, GSR with high stimulus intensity, and skin temperature change in response to thermal stimuli are also slow to habituate. Finger vasoconstriction has shown rapid habituation in some situations and slow habituation in others, but it is not clear that a response has always been distinguished from background.

III. Effects of Stimulus Intensity on Habituation

A. Habituation Measures

Section II briefly surveyed the general findings with regard to sensitization and habituation of electrodermal and cardiovascular response. The present section will consider in more detail the evidence for differential change as a function of intensive characteristics of stimulation. How response habituation is measured becomes a critical factor in interpreting conclusions about intensity effects since the literature does not use a consistent terminology. Although habituation is usually described as a decrement in response and decrement implies change, a change measure is not always employed. Frequently, the measure is either the final level of response or the number of trials to reach a fixed criterion of no-responding. However, of two responses reaching the same final level in the same number of trials, one may have begun at a higher level and consequently exhibited more change and a faster rate of change. Interpretation of such findings has varied. Thus, Koepke and Pribram (1966) concluded that there was no difference in response habituation as a function of stimulus duration since responses reached a no-response criterion in the same number of trials, although the amount of change was greater with the longer stimulus and thus, also the rate of decline. On the other hand, Ratner (1970) concluded that response habituation was greater with high stimulus intensity because there was more difference between initial and final level of responding, despite the fact that the final level was higher with the intense than with a less intense stimulus.

Change may also be measured as a percentage of the initial response or of some control level of responding. Thompson and colleagues (e.g., Groves and Thompson, 1970; Thompson and Spencer, 1966) have used a control level which is the amplitude of response to a stimulus delivered at rates slow enough to maintain a nonhabituating response. This method would not be applicable to human ANS responses since such a rate would be difficult to determine except for high intensity stimuli. In any case, a percentage measure equates differences in "control" or initial response amplitude and means that a response which was initially small might be judged to show greater habituation than a response which was initially large and had undergone a greater reduction in response amplitude. For example, if a low intensity stimulus elicited a control or initial response of 4 units and the response declined to 2 units, the 50% decrement would be said to indicate greater habituation than that elicited by a high intensity stimulus with a control amplitude of 10 units and a decline to 6 units.

B. The Intensity–Habituation Function

Thompson and Spencer (1966), in listing parametric characteristics of habituation, stated that response habituation is an inverse function of stimulus intensity: "The weaker the stimulus, the more rapid and/or more pronounced is habituation. Strong stimuli may yield no significant habituation" (p. 19). Sokolov (1963b) suggested a more complex relationship between stimulus intensity and repetition effects. Weak stimuli near threshold elicit an OR which is larger and more resistant to habituation than OR's elicited by somewhat stronger stimuli. As stimulus intensity increases further, the OR also increases and is slower to habituate. With very strong stimuli, a DR is elicited which shows little or no habituation and may even intensify with stimulus repetitions. This implies that stimulus intensity and the amount of decrement are related by a nonmonotonic function with two points of inflection, one slightly above sensory threshold and one slightly below pain threshold. For sound stimuli, Sokolov's data suggest that these points may lie at 20 and 75 dB re sensation level (1963b, pp. 180–181). Sokolov's position also implies that final response level should be a no-response, operant level for stimuli below the pre-pain range (65–85 dB re sensation level), but for stimuli within or above the range final response level of DR components should increase with stimulus intensity.

Evaluating the effects of intensity on habituation, as measured by change, is complicated by the fact that many stimuli, particularly acoustic stimuli, have sudden onsets. Fleshler (1965) has shown that rise time interacts with intensity such that a sufficiently high intensity reached within a sufficiently short time evokes startle. Certain short latency components of startle decrement in a few trials and include, in addition to gross and electromyographic muscle activity (Davis, 1948), HR acceleration (Hatton *et al.*, 1970), positive skin potential (Forbes and Bolles, 1936), and, if a sharp inspiration occurs, perhaps an accompanying cephalic vasodilation (K. M. Berg, 1970). Since these ANS changes also participate in an OR or in a DR, it is difficult to distinguish the rapid habituation that should be ascribed to sudden onset from the changes that should be ascribed to an OR or DR. Startle can be eliminated by using gradual onsets, but very few studies have included this control.

Startle should also be eliminated when intensities are near threshold. There is, however, little data on the effects of threshold stimuli. Although translation of a study by Asafov (1965) supplements the evidence reported by Sokolov (1963b, pp. 63, 175–181, 196) that threshold stimuli produce relatively large responses, neither of these accounts is presented in sufficient detail to permit adequate evaluation of the procedure and, especially, to determine whether intensity and order could have been confounded. Leavy and Geer (1967) were unable to replicate the effect with the GSR, but they may have used stimulus intensities that were too high since their lowest value was 20 dB, presumably referenced either to 0.0002 μbar or to the American Standard for Audiometers.[2] As Graham and Clifton (1966, p. 311) pointed out, this is probably equivalent to 30 dB using Sokolov's individually determined reference, and thus Leavy and Geer's stimuli would all lie within the range where Sokolov predicted a monotonic relation. Rousey and Reitz (1967), using tones from 50 dB to -15 dB referenced to the American Standard, found the greatest respiratory slowing within 10 dB of the individually determined threshold and Jackson (1972), using tones from 0–40 dB re. 0.0002 microbars, found the largest HR decelerations at 0 dB. However, Jackson did not find a threshold effect with GSR.

When stimuli 20 dB or stronger are considered, intensity has generally had a significant effect on habituation, the direction of the effect varying depending on how habituation is measured and what response is involved. In the case of GSR, a response common to both the OR and DR, only two reports were located that failed to find an intensity-habituation effect (Badia and Harley, 1970; Leavy and Geer, 1967). Leavy and Geer used a narrow range of intensities, from 20 to 50 dB, and did not find any effect on GSR amplitude or on the number of trials eliciting a GSR except when adjustment was made for spontaneous GSR frequency.

A number of other GSR studies agreed, although not always by statistical test, that weaker stimuli elicited smaller initial responses which reached a no-response criterion or asymptotic level in fewer trials. Except for one

[2]Z24.3–1951: American Standards Association, 10 East 40th Street, New York, New York.

study varying the concentration of sapid stimuli (Fisher and Fisher, 1969), tones or white noise have been used, ranging from 40–70 dB at the low end of the range to 90–120 dB at the high end (Davis *et al.*, 1955; Germana, 1968; Harper, 1968; Hart, 1970; Katkin and McCubbin, 1969; Raskin *et al.*, 1969a; Uno and Grings, 1965). Although the number of stimulus repetitions ranged only between 4 and 30, responses to stimuli up to about 80 dB with white noise and 100 dB with tones appeared to be habituating to a common final level. Consequently, within this range, the amount of change was greater for the stronger than for the weaker stimuli, indicating a direct relationship between intensity and response habituation. The difference between tones and white noise may result from greater startling and/or aversive properties of noise (Arezzo, 1969), but the larger initial responses to strong stimuli could not have resulted solely from startle since rise time was controlled in both the Hart and Harper experiments. As Fig. 1 shows, the same relationship with intensity was observed. For white noise stimuli above 80 dB, responses remained at a high level (Raskin *et al.*, 1969a; Uno and Grings, 1965).

A few studies have examined the effect of intensity on habituation of

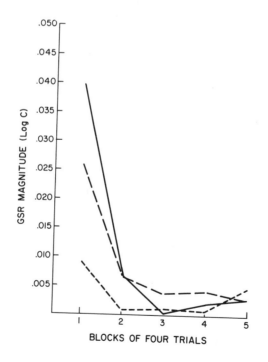

Fig. 1. Galvanic skin response to repetition of 2-second, 1000-Hz tones of (- - -) 40, (— —) 70, or (———) 100 dB. From Harper (1968) with permission of the author.

finger vasoconstriction, also a response common to both the OR and DR. Cohen and Johnson (1971) and Davis *et al.* (1955) found that stimuli of 90–120 dB elicited large vasoconstrictions which showed little change or some intensification with repeated stimulation. Less intense tones of 60–70 dB elicited smaller constrictions which did diminish with stimulus repetition. Uno and Grings (1965) also found large responses and no decrement with a 100-dB white noise stimulus and smaller initial responses with weaker stimuli. The amount-of-change measure paralleled the results obtained for GSR, with a relatively large decrement at 80 dB and smaller decrements at 60 and 70 as well as 90 and 100 dB. Figure 2 shows similar results obtained by K. M. Berg (1970) with slowly rising, 10-second tones of 50, 75, and 90 dB; the reduced habituation at 90 dB was not apparent with a 2-second tone, however. It should be noted that both Berg and Uno and Grings, as well as

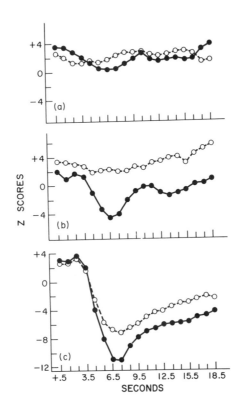

Fig. 2. Peripheral vasomotor response to 10-second stimuli of varying intensity: (●) average of trials 1 and 2; (○) average of trials 3, 4, and 5; (a) 50, (b) 75, and (c) 90 dB. From K. M. Berg (1970) with permission of the author.

Davis *et al.* (1955) and Germana (1968), used within-subject designs. Such a design may not only result in slower habituation but may produce sensitization effects (Weisbard and Graham, 1971) as well as adaptation level and criterion effects (Grice, 1968).

As indicated above, negative and positive skin potential responses, cephalic vasodilation and vasoconstriction, and HR deceleration and acceleration may distinguish between an OR and a DR. Except for HR, there is relatively little data available on habituation of these responses as a function of stimulus intensity. Although Raskin *et al.* (1969a) studied all three response systems, it is difficult to draw any conclusions about the relationship between amount of change and intensity because of the complicating startle reflex. These investigators attributed to startle the decreases in magnitude of HR acceleration and of positive skin potentials which occurred within three stimulations of 100 and 120 dB white noise. Effects may also have occurred at lesser intensities. Hatton *et al.* (1970) found an initial HR acceleration at 90 dB with a fast, but not with a slow, rise time and Arezzo (1969) found very marked differences, presumed to result from startle, between the initial effects of 85 dB tones and white noise. Figure 3 shows response on the first two presentations of the tone and white noise stimuli and the large decrease in response to white noise on the following two.

While the presence of rapidly habituating components of startle complicates interpretation, response on later trials may be unaffected. Raskin *et al.* (1969a) did find consistent differences in final response level as a function of intensity. Components of the DR showed a direct relationship between intensity and final response amplitude with both cephalic vasoconstriction and HR acceleration showing some tendency to increase across trials. In contrast, the OR components of HR deceleration and cephalic vasodilation did *not* show any relationship between intensity and final response level. After the first two trials to low intensity stimuli, HR deceleration, as measured, was no longer present. Cephalic vasodilation responses, while still present after 30 trials, had "converged to a common level" which may represent the operant level since the method of scoring maximum change would not be expected to reveal reductions to zero responding (Graham and Clifton, 1966). Negative skin potential was the only component, implicated as an OR, which reflected an intensity difference on final trials. Cohen and Johnson (1971) and K. M. Berg (1970) also studied effects of intensity on habituation of cephalic vasodilation, but as noted in Section II they obtained inconsistent findings.

Other HR data are in general agreement with Raskin *et al.* (1969a) in finding that HR deceleration is a rapidly habituating response elicited by low intensity stimuli and HR acceleration is a slowly incrementing or unchanging response elicited by moderate to high intensity stimuli. Two studies

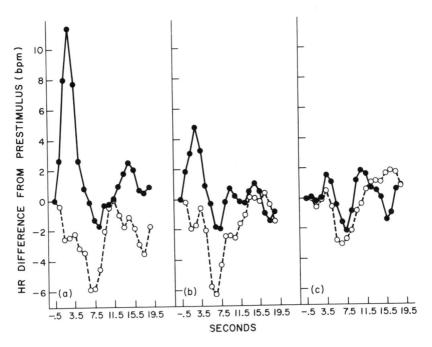

Fig. 3. Heart rate response to 5-second white noise and tone stimuli on the first three trial blocks of two trials each (a) Trial block 1, (b) trial block 2, and (c) trial block 3. (●) 85 dB white noise and (○) 85 db tone. From Arezzo (1969) with permission of the author.

directly compared intensity effects on habituation and also controlled rise time. One was a doctoral thesis by Hart (1970), under the direction of P. J. Lang, and the other a master's thesis (K. M. Berg, 1970), carried out in the writer's laboratory (Fig. 4). Both found a solely decelerative response to 50 dB tones, although with a plateau or hump of relative acceleration at 4–5 seconds. The response was reduced but not eliminated by 5–10 stimulus presentations interspersed with presentations of two higher intensity tones. The most intense tones, 90 or 100 dB, elicited a triphasic response of small deceleration, larger acceleration, and subsequent deceleration. The accelerative component accentuated with stimulus repetitions. Response to the 75 dB stimulus differed in the two studies, being more like the 50 dB response in Berg's study and more like the 100-dB response in Hart's study. Despite the relatively few trials and the intermixing of stimulus intensities, both studies found significant change with repetitions. Berg obtained a significant change in quadratic trend across seconds in two experiments, one with 2-second and one with 10-second tones. Hart found significant habituation

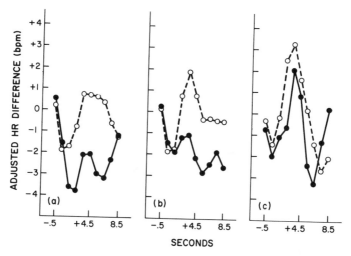

Fig. 4. Heart rate response to 10-second stimuli of varying intensity: (●) average of trials 1 and 2; (○) average of trials 3, 4, and 5. (a) 50, (b) 75, and (c) 90 dB. From K. M. Berg (1970) with permission of the author.

of the decelerative component to 50 and 75 dB tones and significant increase in the accelerative component. However, intensity did not produce differential amounts of change in either study. A more recent study by Jackson (1972) did find differential habituation to tones of 0 dB compared to tones ranging from 20 to 60 dB. As predicted from Sokolov's theory, habituation was slower with the near-threshold tones.

Since low intensity stimuli, at least below 65 dB, should not elicit startle (Hatton *et al.*, 1970), the findings of Hart (1970) and of K. M. Berg (1970) can be meaningfully compared with other studies. In addition to the study by Raskin *et al.* (1969a) and the earlier studies reviewed by Graham and Clifton (1966), other recent work supports the generalization. Uno and Grings (1965) found a solely decelerative response, with relative acceleration on beats 4 and 5, to their 60 dB white noise stimuli. They reported that the response "generally decreased" with 5 repetitions interspersed among 20 other stimuli presentations. Porges and Raskin (1969) also found a decelerative response to light that habituated in 5–6 trials. Chase and Graham (1967) obtained sustained decleration on initial presentations of 18-second tones, ranging from 11 dB below to 16 dB above a 71 dB white noise background, with a shift to acceleration by trials 7–10. Other studies from our laboratory agree on the shape of the initial response to low intensity (50 dB) tones although habituation has not been examined. W. K. Berg and Graham (1970) summarized six then-unpublished studies which included K. M. Berg (1970) and Hatton *et al.* (1970). All six studies showed immediate deceleration with a hump or plateau at 4–5 seconds and a return to baseline that varied with stimulus duration. In some cases, the return to baseline was followed by an insignificant acceleration. Gatchel, in unpublished work from P. J. Lang's laboratory, has found a similar response to 65 dB tones with controlled rise time.

Two other laboratories have reported that low intensity stimuli elicit deceleration in the first few beats, but they also found later phases of acceleration. With 40 dB tones of 1- or 15-second duration, Smith and Strawbridge (1968) obtained initial HR decrease followed by substantial HR increase above prestimulus at beats 4–5. The 15-second stimulus elicited a further, prolonged decelerative phase lasting for approximately 15 beats. Both decelerative components were markedly reduced by trials 5–6. The accelerative component could have been ascribed to instructions to count stimuli, but in a later study when this instruction was omitted, Smith and Strawbridge (1969) again obtained an acceleratory phase following initial deceleration to 54 dB tones. Although the initial deceleration was absent by trials 9–10, a statistically significant habituation was not obtained. Low intensity light, in contrast, elicited a primarily decelerative response on initial trials with a significant shift to acceleration on later trials. The authors suggested that the rapidly habituating decelerative phase meets Sokolov's criteria of an OR and that the acceleratory phase, which is resistant to habituation, is secondary to respiratory changes. Since it is not clear what stimulus characteristics elicit the respiratory change or why the acceleratory component has not been found on initial trials in other studies of low intensity stimuli, this is not a wholly satisfying explanation.

Germana and Klein (1968) also reported an acceleratory component which occurred later (8–15 beats) and which they believed met the criteria for an OR. Since their response curves, based on six Ss, were highly variable in appearance and the short, 10-second ISI would not only make carry-over effects probable but might mean that the last portion of response to one stimulus included the beginning of response to a succeeding stimulus, it is doubtful that late phases indicate a reliable response. As Graham (1971) pointed out, the statistical analysis is uninterpretable. Their curves do indicate that the first presentation of a 50-dB tone was followed by deceleration which was no longer present by trial 3.

Another study, by Roessler *et al.* (1969), did not find initial deceleration to a 40-dB stimulus when response was averaged over 5 trials interspersed among 20 trials with stimuli ranging from 94 to 120 dB. The investigators conjectured that their experimental conditions were such as to induce a defensive "stance," and Weisbard (1970) suggested that the results may indicate a sensitization or "dominant focus" effect. No habituation of the response, a biphasic acceleration–deceleration, was obtained over or within 4 monthly sessions, but average peak acceleration was greater with greater intensity.

Studies of ANS response habituation thus indicate that stimulus intensity is important in determining the effects of stimulus repetition, but it does not appear to have the simple inverse relationship with response habituation proposed by Thompson (Thompson and Spencer, 1966; Groves and Thompson, 1970). The intensity–habituation relationship appears to vary depending both on how habituation is measured and on the response system elicited. If low response levels are taken to indicate pronounced response habituation, the inverse relationship holds for DR components such as HR acceleration and perhaps cephalic vasoconstriction. However, OR components appear to habituate to a common no-response or operant level while components participating in both OR and DR systems habituate to a common no-response level over a wide range of low-to-moderate intensities and show higher final levels only with intense stimuli.

If response habituation is measured by the amount of change or decrement, the intensity–habituation relationship is more complex. For DR components, the relationship is direct in the sense that responses to high intensity show a small decrement while responses to lower intensities may increment. This assumes that the effects of sudden onset are not confounded with intensity effects. For OR components, the relationship is also direct for stimuli clearly beyond threshold and up to pre-pain intensity. Since the initial OR response is greater with greater stimulus intensity and responses decrement to the same no-response level, response to high stimulus intensity undergoes a greater amount of decrement. The intensity–change relationship may be reversed for intensities above and below this range.

IV. Effects of Temporal Characteristics on Habituation

A. Stimulus Duration

An effect of stimulus duration on habituation is not included among the parametric characteristics described by Thompson and Spencer (1966). However, it is discussed by Sokolov (1963b, p. 119) who described a U-shaped relation such that "a sound of very short duration either gives rise to no reaction, or the reaction produced is quickly extinguished. The effects of a stimulus of longer duration are more difficult to suppress, but if the duration is very long, the difficulty is less and the rate of extinction is even greater." These complex effects of stimulus duration arise because stimuli have two components—stimulus onset, a transient component which signals the presence of a stimulus, and stimulus prolongation, a steady state component which signals the specific characteristics of the stimulus (Sokolov, 1963b, p. 68). While onset of a stimulus activates the generalized orienting or protective reflexes, prolongation evokes either specific adaptive reflexes or an unconditioned inhibitory or habituation process. With repetition of the stimulus, onset becomes a conditioned stimulus which elicits the inhibitory process (Sokolov, 1960, p. 212). Presumably, with more prolonged stimuli, more inhibition would develop and habituation would take place more rapidly.

An effect of stimulus duration on habituation has not been easy to demonstrate, but when significant results have been found they have been in the direction of more rapid habituation with longer stimulus durations. Badia and Defran (1970), Koepke and Pribram (1966), and Wolfensberger and O'Connor (1967) found no difference in the number of trials required for habituation of GSR responses when stimulus durations were 0.5 and 5 seconds, 2 and 20 seconds, or 2, 3, and 15 seconds, respectively. However, Koepke and Pribram did report longer duration, larger responses with the longer stimulus, suggesting that a greater change was required to reach criterion in the same number of trials required by the shorter stimulus. Differential habituation also failed to occur with any of the response measures used by Raskin et al. (1969a) or in a study of HR in rats (Fitzgerald and Teyler, 1970). Other studies of HR, using dogs (Lynch, 1967), human adults (K. M. Berg, 1970), and human newborns (Clifton et al. 1968) have obtained a slight duration effect. Lynch's stimuli were unusually prolonged (11 and 42 seconds), but Berg found a difference between 2- and 10-second tones and Clifton et al., between 2- and 6-second or longer tones. Both of the latter studies measured the degree of change across repeated stimulations rather than the number of trials to reach a criterion, and this difference in the method of measuring habituation could account for the difference in findings. In these studies, as in a study by Smith and Strawbridge (1968), the initial response to the longer stimuli was a larger, longer lasting response.

While the evidence is not strong, it does appear that increasing stimulus duration tends to increase the duration and magnitude of the initial response and that this larger response may decline to asymptotic level in the same number of trials and thus at a more rapid rate than does response to a shorter stimulus. The range of durations that has been investigated is not wide and does not include very brief durations, less than 0.5 second.

B. Interstimulus Interval

Time between stimulations also defines the frequency of stimulation and Groves and Thompson (1970) have suggested that the effects of stimulus frequency differ for state and S-R systems. While increased frequency should lead to increased habituation in S-R paths, in state systems, it should lead to increased sensitization, provided the stimulus is sufficiently intense. Unfortunately, there is little data available on tonic changes in autonomic activity as a function of stimulus frequency. Coombs (1938) did report lower skin resistance levels with 15- than with 30-second intervals. However, several studies of phasic GSR change agree in finding that a shorter ISI, that is, greater frequency of stimulation, leads to more rapid habituation of the GSR within the range of 5 to 240 seconds (Coombs, 1938; Geer, 1966, Germana, 1969; Schaub, 1965; Winokur, et al., 1962). This was revealed both by differences in response amplitude at or near asymptote and by the steepness of decline. The function appears to be exponential (Germana, 1969).

Findings with respect to HR change are less clear-cut although little work has been carried out. Both Raskin et al. (1969a) and Bloch (1970) found that intervals as short as 10 to 15 seconds were too brief to permit completion of one response before a succeeding stimulus was presented. While the GSR is a less complex response than HR, it also may suffer interference from a preceding response when stimuli are given too close together. Grings and Schell (1969) showed that the magnitude of response to a second stimulus, occurring at offset of a first stimulus, was a function of the duration of the first stimulus. With a 6-second first stimulus, magnitude of response to the second stimulus was only about 50% of its magnitude with an 8-second first stimulus. However, magnitude was no greater with a 10- than with an 8-second first stimulus.

Some of the response decrement occurring at short ISI may thus result from response interference but, presumably, beyond about 8 seconds for GSR and longer for HR, decrement results from some other process. It is this process which is usually called habituation and which is assumed to be a central process. The central process may not be unitary, however, but may itself include both a short-term process which shows spontaneous recovery and a long-term process which is more permanent. There is some evidence that the greater decrement found with shorter intervals may result from less complete spontaneous recovery during the shorter time since stimulation and not from the more rapid accumulation of an inhibitory process.

The study by Winokur et al. (1962) indicates that at least a sizable portion of the ISI effect must be so explained. They found that even with habituation near asymptotic level, after a number of stimulus presentations at variable intervals of 30, 60, or 90 seconds, response amplitude following a 60-second interval was greater than on the preceding trial with a 30-second interval and less than on the preceding trial with a 90-second interval. Coombs (1938) also found that when subjects habituated for 5 trials with a 15-second ISI were shifted to a 30-second ISI, response amplitude immediately increased to the level of subjects who had been stimulated with a 30-second ISI from the beginning and that the habituation curves for the originally different groups were virtually superimposed over the remaining 10 trials. Although the Coombs study did not control, by shifting some subjects from a longer to a shorter ISI, for occurrence of an orienting response to stimulus change, such control was provided by the Winokur *et al.* study. The data thus suggest that short ISI's do not produce greater habituation because of any cumulative inhibitory process, greater than that developing with longer ISI's, but rather, they imply a transitory function such as a refractory period, i.e., a performance-like rather than a learning effect.

Davis (1970) has recently made this point explicit in a study of startle in rats. More important, he found that if the interval used during training was not confounded with the interval used in testing for spontaneous recovery, training on short intervals produced *less* habituation than training on longer intervals. Animals trained with a 2-second interval and tested after 1 minute or 24 hours on a 2-, 4-, 8-, and 16-second interval showed less response decrement than animals trained with a 16-second interval and tested according to the same schedule. Since there was some decrement, relative to pre-training tests, even when testing was delayed for 24 hours, it was clear that some "habituation" was relatively long-lasting. What is particularly interesting about these data is the finding that short-range habituation, associated with intervals up to about 1 minute, is inversely related to ISI while long-range habituation is directly related to ISI. Two different inhibitory processes must, therefore, be active—one, a refractory process which decays relatively quickly and the other, a process which accumulates and/or consolidates with time, analogous to a learning process.

Long-term retention of habituation has also been demonstrated for autonomic responses, including GSR, HR, and blood pressure. With a 24-hour interval, studies have consistently reported some retention whether the organisms are dogs (Dykman *et al.*, 1965; Soltysik *et al.*, 1961), cats (Wickens *et al.*, 1966), rats (Glaser and Griffin, 1962), or adult human subjects (Bishop and Kimmel, 1969; Davis, 1934; Duffy and Lacey, 1946; Farmer and Chambers, 1925; Greenwood and Lewis, 1959; Griffin, 1963; Montagu, 1963). Retention has occurred even with as few as 6 presentations of a relatively intense stimulus (cold or hot water) or 10 presentations of a moderately intense tone. A number of studies have tested after still longer intervals, up to 6 months, and these too have generally found a savings in trials to criterion or a reduction in response amplitude at least over a 1-week interval (Bishop and Kimmel, 1969; Davis, 1934; Frankenhaeuser *et al.*, 1967; Galbrecht *et al.*, 1965; Glaser and Griffin, 1962; Harding and Rundle, 1969;

Kimmel and Goldstein, 1967; Montagu, 1963; Porter, 1938; Roessler *et al.*, 1969; Stern *et al.*, 1965). With repeated testings, there is usually less spontaneous recovery at each test with the decrease approximating a negatively accelerated curve. However, it may be more difficult to produce habituation of HR acceleration than of either GSR or blood pressure, at least in human subjects (Galbrecht *et al.*, 1965; Griffin, 1963; Greenwood and Lewis, 1959; Roessler *et al.*, 1969).

While the autonomic studies indicate that habituation may be retained over long enough periods of time to suggest a learning process, there is no data on autonomic responses comparable to that of Davis (1970) which tests for the differential effects of massed (short ISI) and spaced (long ISI) trials on short- and long-range retention. One study by Bishop and Kimmel (1969) did compare the retention of habituation with the retention of a classically conditioned GSR. They found that, over the same intervals that showed varying degrees of loss of habituation, there was almost complete retention of the conditioned response.

The existence of a long-range, cumulative, decremental process in state systems would, like decrements below control levels, appear to require a habituation process and not simply decay of sensitization. That is, if phasic responses continue to show decrement even after the ANS level has reached an asymptote, whether within or across sessions, the decrement cannot result solely from a sensitization process which spontaneously returns (decays) to its original level or, if unidentified factors intervene, to some new steady state. However, Groves and Thompson (1970, p. 441) allow for the possibility of below-control-level habituation on the grounds that it "may be due to interaction with elements within the S-R pathway or may be a property of state systems."

C. Constant and Variable Interstimulus Intervals

On the basis of Sokolov's position (1963b), it might be expected that orienting responses should habituate more slowly with variable interstimulus intervals since the ISI is encoded as part of the neuronal model of the stimulus and more samples would be required to form a model of a variable than of a constant interval. However, presenting an unconditioned stimulus at fixed intervals is the basic paradigm for producing temporal conditioning, and if temporal conditioning occurs with simple sensory stimuli this would imply increased responding, in short, the opposite of habituation. Further, Groves and Thompson (1970) suggested that temporal conditioning is seen primarily with state variables and they believed that the concept could explain the increased responding or dishabituation produced by a missing stimulus.

Unfortunately, temporal conditioning is so loosely defined that it is not clear what conditions are necessary even to demonstrate its occurrence. According to Pavlov (1927), presenting a stimulus at fixed intervals leads to increased responding near the point of unconditioned stimulus (UCS) occurrence and reduction of responding during the intertrial interval. However, "near the point of" is somewhat ambiguous. If a response occurs *before* the UCS, i.e., is anticipatory, it should be detectable during ordinary acquisition trials. If the temporally conditioned response occurs at the point of the UCS or shortly thereafter, as in the example given by Pavlov, it could only be detected by omitting the UCS. The evidence is equivocal that either of these changes occurs as a result of a conditioning process.

In 1966, Lockhart was able to locate only one American study, by Rouse (reported in Hull, 1934, 1943), which had used the basic temporal conditioning procedure. Other studies of temporal conditioning had altered the procedure so that a CS–UCS combination rather than UCS alone was presented at fixed intervals. The Rouse experiment presented shock stimuli every 38.5 seconds and found no evidence of GSR habituation after 30 trials. On the following 3 trials, shock was omitted and a response occurred shortly *after* the end of each of the 38.5-second intervals. The amplitude of these temporally conditioned responses was less than the amplitude on preceding trials and diminished over the three periods without shock. Lockhart pointed out that the Rouse study lacked controls for spontaneous responding, time estimation, sensitization, and reactive inhibition but believed that his own study controlled for these effects and did demonstrate temporal conditioning although he, admittedly, did not see how the pattern of findings could be accommodated within traditional conditioning theory.

Lockhart defined response on omitted stimulus trials in three ways: (1) any GSR response occurring within 5 seconds before the end of the elapsed interval, (2) any GSR occurring within 5 seconds after the elapsed interval, and (3) the maximal GSR occurring within either 5 seconds before or 5 seconds after the interval. Responses of individual subjects were corrected for spontaneous responding during an adaptation period before shock was introduced, a procedure which would reduce variability but, unfortunately, in the present instance also capitalized on adaptation-period differences between the temporal conditioning (fixed ISI) and control (variable ISI) groups. The corrected responses did differ significantly in the two groups, but this was true only for the anticipatory and for the maximum responses. There was no significant difference in the response occurring at the time of the unconditioned response (UCR). It was also noted that the anticipatory response tended to increase over the 10 test trials, interspersed among 50 shock trials, while response at the UCR latency tended to diminish over trials. These facts would suggest that what was conditioned was an anticipatory response, but, if so, an anticipatory response should also have occurred on the regular UCS trials. These data were not reported, but an analysis of responses during the second half of the 40-second ISI did not show any increase over trials.

A curious feature of Lockhart's data was the persistence, undiminished, of the temporally conditioned response through 10 successive extinction trials. Lockhart noted that earlier results found extinction occurring in one or two trials and concluded with the observation that his results posed a theoretical puzzle which appeared insoluble using the traditional concepts of stimulus trace or response-produced stimulus trace.

Subsequent studies by Kirk (1969) and by Badia and Harley (1970) also investigated temporal conditioning by measuring responses occurring before a regularly spaced shock stimulus. Unlike Lockhart (1966), Badia and Harley found no change in GSR anticipatory responses across trials and Kirk found that the anticipatory response decreased with trials in both variable and fixed ISI groups. These studies present evidence that is difficult to reconcile with the idea that a response is gradually conditioned to a temporal period. Even in Lockhart's study where the response increased over trials, it apparently did so only on test trials and it failed to extinguish even when the presumed CS, the stimulus trace of a prior UCS, was no longer present.

With regard to habituation of response to the shock itself, Lockhart (1966) did not provide data, but Kirk (1969) found that the response diminished at a relatively slow rate which was nearly identical in the variable and fixed ISI conditions. Badia and Harley (1970) also found diminution of the response to shock with a fixed ISI; they did not employ a variable ISI condition. When less intense stimuli have been used, no clear pattern emerges. Less habituation was obtained with fixed than with variable intervals by Pendergrass and Kimmel (1968) using GSR and by Katkin and Nelson (1966) using HR. More habituation was obtained with fixed than with variable intervals by Zeiner (1970) and by Schaub (1965), using GSR. Making the stimulus a signal for judging its intensity reversed the results of Pendergrass and Kimmel. The available data thus afford little basis for testing theories that depend on concepts of temporal conditioning or of uncertainty as these are reflected by differences in autonomic response to stimuli presented at constant or variable intervals.

V. Effects of Stimulus change

The experimental manipulation of introducing a stimulus change after repeated stimulation may be used either to study stimulus discrimination or the generalization of habituation. In the first case, a comparison is made between responses to two different stimuli, to the habituating stimulus S_1 on the final habituation trial and to the changed stimulus S_2 on the subsequent trial. In the second case, the comparison is between responses to the same stimulus S_2, presented before and after habituation to S_1. Both models have been used in autonomic research although the former has been more frequent and has sometimes been described as dishabituation. This is confusing since dishabituation or disinhibition, as Pavlov and many other investigators have used the term, refers to the recovery of response to the *original* habituating stimulus following the presentation of a different stimulus, i.e., a comparison of responses to S_1 before and after presentation of S_2. The change in usage has apparently arisen because, as with the traditional dishabituation paradigm, recurrence of the habituated response can be used to argue that habituation was not the result of effector fatigue.

A. Response Recovery to a Test Stimulus

In general, studies comparing the responses to different stimuli have either been directed toward problems such as the discriminative capacities of infants, retardates, or other special groups, problems which are not directly related to the understanding of habituation, or they have served to test Sokolov's theory of the neuronal model (1963b).

Without considering the degree of change, a number of studies have verified the simple fact that intermodal change (Forbes and Bolles, 1936; Furedy, 1968b, 1969a; Hammond, 1967; Houck and Mefferd, 1969; Zimny and Kienstra, 1967; Zimny and Miller, 1966) or within modality change along qualitative dimensions such as pitch (Bagshaw and Benzies, 1968; Bagshaw et al., 1965; Hare, 1968; Korn and Moyer, 1968; Weisbard and Graham, 1971) leads to increased amplitude of habituated autonomic responses. Responses studied have included HR and vasomotor changes as well as GSR. Where the changed stimulus has itself been repeated, rehabituation has been obtained, usually more rapidly than with the original stimulus. However, Fried et al. (1966a,b) failed to obtain any change in skin resistance level when a light of different hue was interspersed among presentations of four other colored lights. It is not clear whether this is the result of their response measure, as Furedy (1968a, 1969b) has suggested, or of embedding a relatively unobtrusive change in a continuously present stimulus.

Recovery of a habituated response has also been found with other types of stimulus change such as the complex differences in the sounds generated by a tuning fork, clapper, and buzzer (Coombs, 1938), change in rate of modulating a tone (Weisbard and Graham, 1971), presentation of a stimulus after a shorter than usual ISI (Kirk, 1969), presentation of a longer or shorter than usual stimulus (Koepke and Pribram, 1966, 1967), reversal of the sequence of components in a 2-tone stimulus (Meyers and Gullickson, 1967), change in complex visual patterns (Berlyne *et al.*, 1963), rearrangement of the 10 digits comprising a visual stimulus (Germana, 1969), and a digit out of ordinal sequence (Unger, 1964). Repetition of a light stimulus previously given in alternation with another stimulus produced recovery in a study by Berlyne (1961) but not in a similar experiment by Furedy (1968b).

In addition to these studies showing an effect of what may be called changes in the relationship among stimuli, Allen *et al.* (1963) and Badia and Defran (1970) have confirmed the "missing stimulus" effect by presenting stimulus components after habituating response to a stimulus compound. Both studies used a compound consisting of tone and light components presented successively and both manipulated duration of the first compon- ent. Badia and Defran found that, when either the first or second of their two components was subsequently presented alone, GSR magnitude in- creased. Allen *et al.* used three components and found that omitting either the first or second element not only restored the habituated response but that the magnitude of response was a complex function of the temporal relations among components. They interpreted this as reflecting the greater salience of elements whose onsets were separated by intervals favorable for sensory conditioning. Two other studies failed to demonstrate a missing stimulus effect. Zimny and Kienstra (1967) obtained smaller responses to tone alone than to the preceding trials with tone plus shock, and Fried *et al.* (1967) did not find any effect on skin resistance level when they introduced a gap in their otherwise continuous presentation of colored lights. As noted earlier, this technique also failed to show any effect of hue change.

Other studies have not only demonstrated response recovery with stimulus change but also have shown that the degree of recovery is a direct function of the amount of change. Sokolov and colleagues have reported several experiments in which test stimuli, administered after the OR had been habituated to one stimulus, elicited OR's which were larger and included more components, the greater the difference between the test and the habitu- ating stimulus. One experiment reported a symmetrical gradient of response to frequencies, scaled in multiples of 2.0, above and below the 1000-Hz tone which served as the habituating stimulus. The response measure was the duration in seconds, presumably of the alpha blocking response (Soko- lov, 1960, p. 209), although in the English translation of the original report (Sokolov and Paramonova, 1961) the same data are ascribed to the galvanic skin reaction. Gradients in the GSR and alpha blocking response also occur- red with shift in the spatial location of a light on the retina (Sokolov, 1960, p. 201; Voronin and Sokolov, 1960) or in the location of a tactile stimulus applied to the wrist (Sokolov, 1963b, p. 124f). The most important finding, from the point of view of theory, was that response recovered with a shift to a stimulus that was less intense than the habituating stimulus (Sokolov and Paramonova, 1961). Unfortunately, these studies are reported only briefly in the available translations and it is not clear how well the results, illustrated by data of single, experienced subjects, would characterize the behavior of groups of unselected subjects. However, successful replications of some of the findings have been reported.

Variations in the amount of change in tone frequency have produced a gradient for GSR response in several studies. Williams (1963) obtained a linear gradient over the range from 380 Hz, the habituating frequency, to 1850 Hz with four test stimuli at 250 mel intervals (Stevens and Volkmann, 1940). Corman (1967), using stimuli at 250 mel intervals in the range from 670 to 1850 Hz, showed that Williams' findings could also be obtained with a between-subjects design, with a longer, variable ISI, and with a decrease as well as an increase in frequency. However, he did not report whether there was any difference in the gradients as a function of the direction of change. Geer's data (1969) showed a gradient with change from 1000 Hz to 1010, 1100, or 2000 Hz although response amplitude to the 1010-Hz tone was less than on the preceding trial with 1000 Hz. A significant effect of dissimilarity was not demonstrated for the absolute amplitude of response to test stimuli, but the significance of changes in response amplitude or of the monotonic ordering of stimulus dissimilarity and response amplitude was not tested. These studies all employed the GSR response. Cicirelli, working in the writer's laboratory, has unpublished data (1970) showing that a gradient, determined by pitch change of 125, 250, or 1000 mels in the range 380–1850 Hz, can be demonstrated for the HR decelerative response as well as for the GSR.

Two studies failed to obtain differential GSR recovery as a function of the amount of frequency change, but in one case frequency and intensity change were confounded so that a large frequency change and a small intensity change was compared to a small frequency change and a large intensity change (Zimny and Schwabe, 1966). In the other case (O'Gorman et al., 1970), there was no significant effect of frequency change when a frequency increase from 1000 to 1350 Hz (250 mels) or decreases from 1000 to 650 Hz (250 mels) and 1000 to 380 Hz (500 mels) were employed. These are relatively small pitch changes to be detected with an N of only 5 subjects per group.

Recently, Gabriel and Ball (1970) also showed the effects of change in spatial location. After applying tactile stimuli to thumb, middle, ring, or little finger, test stimuli were applied to a different finger either alone or simultaneously with application of a stimulus to the locus of the habituating stimulus. Proximity of test to habituating locus interacted with an effect resulting, presumably, from the distinctiveness of the extreme loci, i.e., thumb and little finger. Finger pulse constriction was measured as well as the GSR.

The effects of variation in intensity change are more difficult to determine since dynamogenic effects of both the habituating and test stimuli must be controlled. Bernstein (1968, 1969) reported response recovery with a change in brightness and with a change in tone intensity and, in both cases, found a higher percentage of response when the change was an increase rather than a decrease in intensity. Although the experiments on brightness change did not control for difference in the intensity of the test stimuli, this control was introduced in the tone intensity experiments. Half of the subjects received 15 habituation trials with a 60-dB and half with a 90-dB tone, and both groups were tested with a tone of 75 dB. Unfortunately, this design does not control for differences in the amount of habituation that may be produced by differences in the intensity of the habituating tone. If the results of Davis and Wagner (1968), using the startle response, are applicable to the GSR, greater habituation should be produced by the high intensity stimulus and thus the lesser recovery following a decrease to 75 dB could result, not from the fact that the intensity change was a decrease, but from the fact that subjects were already more completely habituated and thus showed greater transfer of nonresponding.

A study by James and Hughes (1968) used a similar design but tested two degrees of increase and decrease. Subjects were habituated to either a 67- or 76-dB tone and presented with either 70 or 73 dB test stimuli. Although the increase in GSR amplitude was greater with the 6-dB increase than with the 3-dB increase, a greater response with a 6-dB change would be expected because of the greater absolute intensity of the 73-dB stimulus. Similarly, the relatively smaller GSR to the 6-dB decrease than to the 3-dB decrease is also confounded with a difference in absolute intensity. A study by O'Gorman *et al.* (1970) suffers from similar difficulties.

In brief, while Bernstein (1968, 1969) reported GSR recovery following intensity increase and lesser recovery following intensity decrease and two other laboratories (James and Hughes, 1969; O'Gorman *et al.*, 1970) reported recovery with intensity increase but not with decrease, none of the studies has separated or controlled for both the differences in habituation produced by stimuli of different intensity and for the differences in the response-evoking properties of test stimuli that vary in intensity. Bernstein's results confirm Sokolov and Paramonova's report (1961) that some response recovery occurs to stimuli less intense than the stimulus to which response was habituated, but it is uncertain whether a given decrease in intensity does or does not have less effect than the same increase if other factors are controlled. A study by Jackson (1972) which did include the necessary controls also obtained evidence for response recovery to less intense stimuli but was completed too recently to be fully reviewed in the present paper.

In addition to evidence that varying the amount of change along simple stimulus dimensions is related to response recovery, the degree of discrepancy in more complex characteristics may also by systematically related to recovery. Yaremko *et al.* (1970) presented the numbers 10–19 in serial order and then introduced a number which was either 1 or 11 steps out of sequence. The GSR was larger when the stimulus was displaced ±11 steps than when it was ±1 step out of place. Zimny *et al.* (1969) achieved differences in stimulus probability by presenting the same test stimulus after varying kinds of prior stimulation. The GSR of three groups of subjects was habituated by presenting either the number 21 for 40 trials, the numbers 21 through 60 in serial order, or the numbers 21 through 60 in random order. With all groups, the same test stimulus, the number 600, was interpolated following trials 8, 14, 24, 32, and 38. Response recovered on the first test presentation in the group given unvaried stimulation, did not recover until after 24 trials of serially ordered stimulation, and never recovered following randomly ordered stimuli.

B. *Generalization of Habituation to a Test Stimulus*

Although most of the studies cited above were concerned with recovery of an orienting response and not with the generalization of habituation, i.e., with a difference in response to S_2 before and after habituating to S_1, some data relevant to generalization are available. Sokolov (1963b) regularly established the prehabituation strength of responses to the stimuli which would later serve as test stimuli. As noted above, his findings have not ordinarily been presented in detail or for groups of subjects so that many questions remain unanswered, including the method of controlling for presentation order. It appears, however, that habituation effects usually generalized and that the recovered orienting response to test stimuli was smaller and included fewer response components than the response evoked by the same stimuli prior to habituation. This also appears to be true for some but not all of the Western studies that have been reviewed.

Geer (1969) used responses on the initial trials with a 1000-Hz habituating stimulus to estimate the prehabituation response to test stimuli of 1010, 1100, and 2000 Hz since Corman (1966) had shown that GSR amplitude did not differ for tones of 670 and 1850 Hz. It should be noted that Corman's statistical test was based on data from 10 trials; thus, if a difference did exist on initial trials and not on later trials, the initial trial difference might not have been detected by the overall test. There appears to be little data on the effects of frequency difference although studies of infants indicate that some responses may differ for frequencies below 500 or above 2000 (Eisenberg, 1965; Hutt *et al.*, 1968). In any case, if it is assumed that within the middle range, frequency does not affect GSR amplitude, Geer's data indicate that response to all test stimuli was significantly smaller following habituation and that the greatest generalization occurred to stimuli closest in frequency to the habituating stimulus. Although not tested statistically, generalization of habituation can also be observed from graphed responses to a frequency change from 600–1200 Hz (Houck and Mefferd, 1969) or 380–1850 Hz (Cicirelli, 1970), to an intensity change of 3 or 6 dB (James and Hughes, 1969), and to a change in the numerical value of verbal stimuli (Zimny *et al.*, 1969).

In contrast to the findings of smaller response following than preceding habituation to a different stimulus, three studies suggest that responses may sometimes be increased by repeated presentations of a different stimulus. Houck and Mefferd's data (1969, Fig. 1) showed that GSR responses were larger when subjects were given a tone after 14 light presentations than when tone was given on the first trial. Significance of the difference was not tested, however, and the authors' statement that 10 of the 12 subjects showed larger responses on the shift trial is not relevant to the present question which requires a comparison between the 6 subjects receiving tone on trial 1 and the 6 subjects receiving tone after light. Figure 1 of Furedy (1969a) and a comparison of Figs. 1 and 2 of Furedy (1968b) also suggest that responses to a tone or light shift after 15 habituation trials were larger than responses on the first trial. The phenomenon occurred with both GSR and peripheral vasomotor responses, but again a statistical test was not made.[3] Jackson's recent study (1972) provides further evidence for such an effect with GSR.

If these findings are reliable, they are important on theoretical grounds since a stimulus-model-comparator theory seems better able to predict such an increase than does the overlapping elements approach exemplified by dual-process theory. Presumably, a greater response following habituation could result if repetitive stimulation produces a model—or defines a set of to-be-expected stimuli—which is relatively restricted compared to the set defined before the first trial when the only information is provided by background stimuli, instructions, and past experience with laboratory situations. Before the first stimulus is presented, any of a number of stimuli would have some appreciable if low probability of occurring, but as the habituating stimulus is presented repeatedly, with variations too small to be identified by the experimenter as a different stimulus, the probability of a narrow set of stimuli should increase and, consequently, the probability of stimuli outside that set must decrease. If magnitude of an orienting response is a direct function of the degree of discrepancy or, stated in probability terms, an

---

[3]Although the data plotted in Fig. 2 of Furedy (1968b) are based on trial blocks, the author is indebted to Furedy (1971b) for supplying trial 1 data. These show the same pattern: for GSR response, trial 1 = 1.54, trial 16 = 2.42; for peripheral VM response, trial 1 = 22.3 and trial 16 = 39.2.

inverse function of the probability of a stimulus, response magnitudes should be greater whenever the test-training stimuli difference in probability is greater than the training-background stimuli difference in probability.

If it is assumed that greater response magnitude on test than on initial trials could be predicted from stimulus-model-comparator theory, the phenomenon would obviously be more likely to occur when test-training stimulus differences are large. Consequently, it is not unexpected that the phenomenon should be easier to obtain with an intermodal than with an intramodal change. However, if it can occur with an intramodal shift, it should be more likely with a large than a small intramodal difference or after a long habituation series which established a more restricted stimulus set than after a short habituation series. It is interesting, therefore, that the only two intramodal studies with any suggestion of greater response on change trials were the Williams (1963) study which used frequency changes ranging from 380 to 1850 Hz and the Bagshaw et al. (1965) study in which more than 50 trials were given before a shift was introduced.

This review has given more emphasis than the data warrant to the possibility of greater response on change than initial trials. However, the question merits more explicit attention in habituation research, especially with autonomic measures which may reflect an orienting response. Although, in many respects, autonomic responses appear to mirror the findings obtained with other responses, those measures which are components of an orienting reflex should, from Sokolov's theory, be more susceptible to variations in the degree of stimulus unexpectedness.

It was suggested above that a longer habituation series should define a more restricted stimulus set, or a more precise stimulus model, but this is not easily tested directly since changes in unexpectedness or novelty are confounded with changes in generalization of habituation gradients. Corman (1967) argued against an "expectancy" hypothesis on the grounds that generalization of habituation along a frequency dimension showed an "overlearning" effect; that is, the GSR on test trials decreased as the number of "no responses" immediately prior to the stimulus change increased. The argument was that according to expectancy theory, a subject ceases to respond to the habituating stimulus because he expects its occurrence and, therefore, the more no response trials, "the greater should be his expectancy and the greater his surprise when a different stimulus occurs." However, hypothesizing an increase in expectancy, i.e., a change in the set of to-be-expected stimuli, as a function of habituation trials does not obviate the fact that the amount of habituation is also related to the number of repetitions of the habituating stimulus. That habituation does increase with the number of trials has virtually the status of a definition although the relationship of generalization or transfer of habituation to the number of habituation trials is no better understood than is the relationship of conditioned response generalization to the number of acquisition trials. If such scale-dependent properties as the concavity or convexity of generalization gradients is not considered, the problem of whether gradients are broader and flatter early in training and narrower and steeper late in training still remains.

As Fig. 5a illustrates, an increasingly narrow and steep generalization of habituation gradient would, taken alone, predict greater response to extreme stimuli as a function of trials. Response to the large stimulus change will show decrement early in habituation training (point L) but not late in

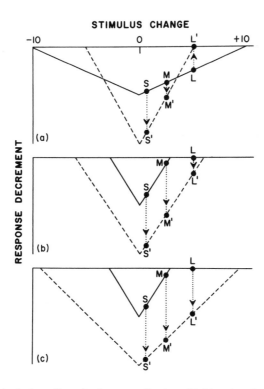

Fig. 5. Hypothetical gradients in the generalization of habituation showing equal decrement in response to the habituating stimulus (0 stimulus change) but differences in slope and, consequently, in the range of stimuli to which habituation is generalized. (——) early and (---) late. Points L, M, and S represent response to large, moderate, and small stimulus changes early in training and L', M', and S' represent response to the same stimulus changes late in training. (a) A flat gradient and broad generalization early in training with a steeper gradient and narrower generalization as habituation increases. (b) A steep gradient and narrow generalization early in training with no change in gradient slope but broader generalization as habituation increases. (c) Same as (b) early in training but slope flattens producing relatively broader generalization late in training.

training (point L'). As noted earlier, response to a stimulus would not, of course, exceed its value before any habituation training was introduced if habituation were the only factor operating. In contrast to a steepening gradient, a gradient which was broader and flatter or did not change slope as a function of trials would predict reduced response to extreme stimuli late in training (Figs. 5b and 5c). In the absence of knowledge about the slope of generalization gradients, it is difficult to see how any outcome of tests relating number of habituation trials to response evoked by differing degrees of stimulus change could affect the status of an expectancy, novelty, or perceptual disparity hypothesis.

While it is frequently assumed that Sokolov's neuronal model theory requires increasing response to change with increasing numbers of habituation trials, the theory is not explicit on this point. As noted above, Sokolov (1963b) spoke of, and obtained evidence for, the generalization of habituation, and Voronin and Sokolov (1960, p. 338) assumed that "the degree of extinction generalization increases with the repetition of presentations of various stimuli." The term extinction is here synonymous with the present use of habituation. They illustrated the principle with empirical data, showing percent of response plotted against the spatial separation of stimulation points on the retina. Response percentages decreased with more habituation trials, but while the text described a concomitant extension in the range of stimuli to which habituation was generalized, the graph (Voronin and Sokolov, 1960, Fig. 3) showed a constant range. The authors did not discuss how changes in the generalization gradient compared with changes resulting from development of the neuronal model, but they clearly indicated that both processes were involved. Generalization of extinction was treated in a traditional manner as spreading to adjacent points determined by the organization of the afferent projections. In addition to the excitability remaining in the afferent system due to points not overlapping those which had been extinguished, impulses occur "as a result of the non-coincidence" of the test stimulus and the neuronal model formed by previous stimulation (Voronin and Sokolov, 1960, p. 340).

Although it appears impossible to predict the magnitude of response that should result from two processes whose variation as a function of repetitive stimulation can be stated only in qualitative terms, it is possible to determine whether or not a single process, either one of increasing habituation and its generalization or of increasing unexpectedness, could account for empirical findings. As noted above, the occurrence of a response to one stimulus which is *larger* following than preceding habituation to a different stimulus could not be easily explained by a single process of habituation. Thompson and Spencer (1966, p. 27) argued in a similar vein that since "a strong dishabituating stimulus was seen to increase the response well above the control level," an additional process which they called sensitization must be invoked. However, they referred to an increase in response to the habituating stimulus following interposition of a different or test stimulus and not to change in response to the test stimulus. By the same logic, occurrence of a test stimulus response which is *smaller* following than preceding habituation training would be difficult to explain by a single process of excitation such as that attributed to unexpectedness. It could occur, of course, if unexpectedness of the test stimulus did not increase monotonically with habituation trials.

Despite the problem of drawing conclusions about the characteristics of two underlying processes assumed to vary with repetitions, some possibilities could be eliminated by empirical findings. If, with more trials, response to a small stimulus difference showed *relatively* more decrement than response to a large stimulus difference, the results could not be accounted for solely by a generalization of habituation gradient which did not change shape or whose slope flattened with increasing repetitions. As Figs. 5b and 5c illustrate, any stimulus change which shows some response decrement early in training, i.e., is not beyond the generalization range, will produce more decrement late in training, and the increasing decrement to the larger stimulus change (MM') will be greater than or equal to the increasing decrement produced by the smaller stimulus change (SS'). If the larger stimulus change (MM') produced *relatively* less decrement than the smaller stimulus change (SS'), this would require either a generalization gradient whose slope steepened (Fig. 5a) or an expectancy gradient in addition to a generalization gradient.

Geer (1969) provided data relevant to this point. After repeating a 1000-Hz tone on 5, 10, 15, or 20 trials, he presented independent groups with either a 1010-, 1100-, or 2000-Hz test stimulus. Electrodermal responses to the first two test stimuli did not differ significantly as a function of either trials or stimulus difference. However, if compared to response at the end of habituation, it can be seen from Fig. 6a that while there was an increasing gradient with stimulus difference following 15–20 habituation trials, the gradient was flat following 5–10 habituation trials. The reference response to 1000 Hz is, of course, somewhat higher than it should be since, in the absence of a control group who continued to receive the habituating tone on test trials, it was estimated by the published data for average response on the last 4 habituation trials.

A similar study, using a wider frequency range and a within-subjects design, was conducted in our laboratory by Cicirelli (1970). After 5 or 18 habituation trials with a 380-Hz tone, each subject received 8 generalization test trials that included 5 repetitions of the habituating stimulus and interspersed presentations of a 516-, 670-, and 1850-Hz tone. Presentation order

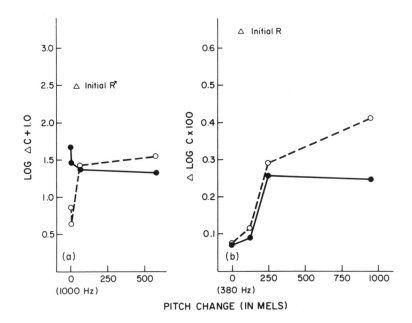

Fig. 6. Galvanic skin response gradients of generalization over the pitch dimension (mels) after 5–10 trials (early) or 15–20 trials (late) of habituation training: (———) early and (- - -) late. (a) Data from Geer (1969), with permission of the publisher, the American Psychological Association. (b) Data from Cicirelli (1970).

was balanced across subjects. Again there was a difference between the gradients as a function of the length of the habituation series (Fig. 6b). With a longer habituation series, there was relatively greater recovery of response to distant than to near stimuli.

For the reasons discussed earlier, these findings imply either a generalization of habituation gradient whose slope steepens with trials or an expectancy gradient in addition to a habituation gradient. While this conclusion, taken alone, represents little progress in eliminating alternatives, it at least focuses attention on the fact that hypotheses specifying two processes acting in opposite directions can account for a wide variety of findings. If the law of parsimony is followed, the hypothesis of a single habituation gradient with steepening slope would be favored over the two-process alternative. This would accord well with other data on generalization of excitatory gradients where the responses studied do not directly measure orienting (Shepard, 1965), although responses to novelty might interfere with the generalized conditioned responses (Bindra, 1959). It requires other operations, such as studies of test compared to initial response magnitude, to determine whether an expectancy gradient is also required.

C. Dishabituation of Response to the Habituating Stimulus

Relatively few autonomic studies have investigated the effect of inter-polating a stimulus on response to the habituating stimulus although Sokolov (1963b, p. 87) demonstrated that the OR did show recovery after such an in-terpolation. As noted earlier, this is the original meaning of the term dis-habituation. It was usually applied in situations where the response being habituated was not the same as the response elicited by the dishabituating stimulus while, in autonomic studies of the OR, both the habituating and interpolated stimuli elicit the response being studied. Interest has con-sequently tended to focus on the reappearance of response to the novel or dishabituating stimulus rather than on response to a subsequent presenta-tion of the habituating stimulus. However, Zimny and colleagues, in several studies, have shown convincingly that response to the original stimulus also recovers. Their procedure has been to present, without interruption, three to five series in each of which there are six to eight successive presentations of a standard stimulus followed by a test stimulus. Variations in the standard or test stimuli are accomplished with a between-subjects design.

In the first of the studies, Zimny and Schwabe (1966) argued that not only should the interpolated stimulus produce an OR but also it should lead to recovery of orienting to the habituating stimulus since the habituating stimulus would no longer match the neuronal model which incorporated the test stimulus. From this, it followed that the greater the difference between test and habituating stimuli, the greater the recovery should be. Unfor-tunately, test stimuli were employed that differed from the standard tone on two dimensions so that it is difficult, *a priori*, to know which was the more discrepant. A 3500-Hz increase in frequency combined with an approxi-mately 10-sone decrease in loudness elicited significant GSR recovery follow-ing each of four presentations. Response also increased, but not significantly, following three of four presentations of a 500-Hz increase combined with an approximately 25-sone decrease.

More clear-cut results were obtained by Zimny and Kienstra (1967) when an 86-dB test tone was interpolated in either a shock habituation series or a shock-plus-tone habituation series. Dishabituation occurred with the greater difference between dishabituating and habituating stimuli (tone after shock) but not when the dishabituating and habituating stimuli were more similar (tone after shock-plus-tone). A third study (Zimny *et al.*, 1969) did not directly test for recovery of response to the habituating stimulus, but recovery can be observed on a graphic illustration of the data (Zimny *et al.*, 1969, Fig. 1). Zimny and Miller (1966) also showed recovery of the peripheral vasomotor constriction response, a component of the OR, to either a hot or a cold stimulus following an interpolated sound stimulus. Although recovery was statistically significant only after the first presentation of the test stimulus, some increased constriction could be observed even after the third interpolated stimulus. Similar findings were obtained in Cicirelli's unpublished study of heart rate and GSR response.

Hammond (1967) has also reported dishabituation effects in a recent study of pseudo-conditioning of the GSR. A light and a 400-Hz tone, at 80 dB over 68 dB white noise, were habituated for 30 intermixed trials each. An automobile horn of 110 dB was then presented six times during an additional 50 trials of tone and light. Throughout this latter period, basal skin resistance was lower and GSR higher than during the approximately 40-trial period of habituated responding that preceded it. Hammond argued that the dishabituation could not be a function of similarity of habituating and disinhibiting stimuli since there was no difference between dishabituated responses to tone and to light, and he assumed that tone was more like horn than light was like horn. However, any effect of the quality difference might well have been masked by the large difference in intensity between both tone and light and the horn stimulus. Hammond also questioned whether sensitization could account for the increased GSR response since the correlation between GSR response frequency and basal skin changes following horn stimulation was only -0.58 which was no greater than the correlation of -0.52 which existed between basal skin resistance and response frequency during the first 10 habituation trials. The logic of this argument would seem to require that sensitization refer not only to an increase in tonic and phasic responsiveness but to an increase in the degree of their covariation.

Several studies have failed to obtain any dishabituation of response to the habituating stimulus. Although Houck and Mefferd (1969) found that a change from tone to light or vice versa produced a large GSR response after 15 habituation trials, there was no GSR on the immediately following presentation of the original stimulus. This could have resulted from peripheral response interference since there was only a 5-second ISI between the 5-second stimuli. Williams (1963) also used a short ISI of 7 seconds between 2-second stimuli and failed to obtain recovery of GSR response to the habituating stimulus following responses to four successive frequency changes. However, peripheral effects could not account for the absence of dishabituation after introduction of an out-of-sequence number (Yaremko et al., 1970) or following a shock sufficiently strong to itself produce GSR's larger than even the initial response to a tone–light compound (Wickens et al., 1966). The failure of shock to dishabituate the GSR is surprising and might be ascribed either to a species difference, the subjects being cats, or to the unusual length of the habituating series. The animals had been habituated for 10 days before the shock stimulus was presented.

Despite these failures to obtain dishabituation, the bulk of the evidence indicates not only that dishabituation of an autonomic response can be demonstrated but also that the dishabituating stimulus does not need to be intense. In both the Zimny and Schwabe (1966) and Cicirelli's unpublished study (1970) the habituating and test tones were equal in loudness while Zimny *et al.* (1969) used a change in the value of a number to produce dishabituation.

VI. Discussion and Summary

The present paper has reviewed ANS habituation literature in the context of theories proposed by Thompson (Thompson and Spencer, 1966; Groves and Thompson, 1970) and by Sokolov (1963b). Both theories postulate response incrementing and decrementing processes and both accord an important role to ANS activity. Thompson identifies an incrementing process, sensitization, which is an increase in "arousal" while Sokolov identifies "orienting" and "defensive" systems which may be viewed as increments in two types of arousal.

With regard to the incrementing process, the literature suggests that two types of arousal can be distinguished and that they are elicited by different stimulus conditions, change versus high intensity. Change elicits an OR system which includes some components that are the same as those elicited by high intensity and some components which are different or directionally opposite. Sokolov has also cited evidence that the two arousal systems have different effects on other processes, in particular, that thresholds for response to other stimuli will be decreased in the presence of an OR and increased in the presence of a DR. There has been substantial further work testing these implications of Sokolov's theory, but such material is not reviewed in the present paper. Thompson's theory does not distinguish between sensitization elicited by change as opposed to high intensity, and it would presumably follow that stimulus change and high intensity should have similar effects not only in eliciting the same ANS responses but on non-ANS responses as well. Presumably also, a theory hypothesizing a general arousal or sensitization would not predict that a stimulus should elicit greater sensitization after than before habituation to a different stimulus. Further studies of the situations in which this phenomenon occurs, if it does occur reliably, are needed.

Although Thompson's theory allows for the effectiveness of stimulus change as an elicitor of an incrementing process, it is questionable whether a spinal reflex model will prove adequate to explain occurrence and recovery of the OR to complex types of stimulus change. Recovery of the OR has been demonstrated with such variations as rearrangement of a stimulus sequence, change in the duration of a stimulus, decrease in intensity, and presentation of one component of a compound stimulus. Thompson's theory explains these as instances of "incomplete stimulus generalization of habituation" resulting from stimuli "having somewhat different central connections" (Thompson and Spencer, 1966, p. 34). However, as an example of how reduced stimulus intensity could lead to recovery, work was cited demonstrating the existence of neurons in inferior colliculus and auditory cortex which fire to weak but not to strong tones. Other types of "comparator" neurons have also been identified, of course, but the question is how much capability for complex distinctions exists in cord internuncials. In any case, this aspect of Thompson's theory would seem to be a restatement of Sokolov's stimulus-model-comparator theory. It appears that Groves and Thompson (1970, p. 438) agree since they stated that "the difference between a stimulus model being formed in the brain and our inferred process of habituation may be primarily semantic." However, Thompson's theory has the disadvantage that predictions must be made on the basis of knowledge of the central pathways employed by stimulus traces. In contrast, predictions from Sokolov's theory are based on stimulus characteristics viewed as information which is extracted by the nervous system.

There is an additional problem in trying to account for ANS changes in terms of the sensitization process described by Thompson. While sensitization theoretically grows and then decays in the face of repetitive stimulation (Groves and Thompson, 1970, p. 441), ANS measures which show an increase with stimulation may sometimes maintain that increase throughout a habituation training session. Although the number of stimulations in the typical ANS study is relatively small, the finding does raise the question of whether it is useful to postulate an incrementing process that under the same stimulation can also decrement. The postulate would be necessary to explain decrement in ANS responses if the state system were affected only by sensitization and could not interact with the habituation process occurring in direct S-R pathways. However, since interaction is postulated (Groves and Thompson, 1970, p. 441), a second decrementing process adds nothing to the predictive power of the theory, and it does have the disadvantage that sustained excitation is not explained.

If sensitization did *not* interact with the S-R pathway, then ANS activity might directly measure the amount of sensitization although, as noted in Section III,B, it would be difficult to explain decrement below control levels. Or, if sensitization interacted with the S-R pathway but did *not* decay, the sensitization produced by a particular stimulus might be measured by the ANS activity occurring on the initial stimulus presentation before any cumulative habituation developed. However, with both interaction and decay postulated, sensitization cannot be measured by any response output.

Since central habituation also cannot be measured directly, a response output which is determined by the joint action of sensitization and central habituation can not provide an empirical basis for assuming particular relationships between changes in either process and changes in stimulus parameters such as frequency and intensity. Sensitization and habituation might, of course, be independently measurable at the neuronal level, but to date such work has not resulted in quantitative functions from which deductions could be tested at the response level.

Given that the observable response habituation is jointly determined by two central processes, it is not clear why Thompson's dual-process theory postulates an inverse relationship between intensity and habituation. Groves and Thompson (1970) did not state on what grounds this postulate was adopted, but they cited empirical data obtained from measuring the contraction of a hindlimb flexor muscle (Groves *et al.*, 1969). However, the empirical data can equally well support other assumptions about the intensity–central habituation function, including the assumption that habituation varies directly with intensity. This is illustrated in Fig. 7 which reproduces, approximately, the response outputs (solid line) and the central habituation and sensitization functions (dashed lines) shown in Groves and Thompson (1970, Fig. 1) but, in addition, represents central habituation as varying directly instead of inversely with intensity (dotted line). The figure also

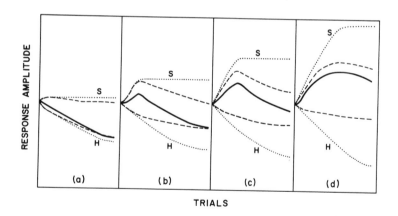

Fig. 7. Responses are the combination of hypothetical processes of sensitization (S) and habituation (H): (——) responses; (—) hypothetical S and H processes approximating functions graphed by Groves and Thompson (1970, Fig. 1, with permission of the publisher, the American Psychological Association). As stimulus intensity increases from (a) to (d), sensitization increases and habituation decreases to produce a decrease of response habituation. (. . .) S and H processes in which both sensitization and habituation increase with intensity, but their combination produces the same decrease of response habituation.

shows sensitization as a nondecaying function of repeated stimulation (dotted line) although the same output could be obtained by combining a direct intensity–habituation function with a decaying sensitization function.

Since either a direct or an inverse intensity–habituation function could account, in conjunction with a direct intensity–sensitization function, for the response output, such data provide no basis for choosing between the alternative assumptions. However, there are other findings, by Davis and Wagner (1968) using the startle response and by Jackson (1972) using GSR, which are more easily accounted for by assuming a direct rather than an inverse intensity–habituation function. As Davis and Wagner pointed out, the usual test of habituation measures the effect of repeated stimulations on response to the habituating stimulus and thus confounds the intensity of training and test stimuli. When they gave habituation training with an intense stimulus and tested with other stimuli, they found greater decrement than following habituation training with a weaker stimulus. If Groves and Thompson's graphed values (dashed lines, Fig. 7) are used and if it is assumed that the amounts of habituation developed to the weak stimulus (Fig. 7a) and to the strong stimulus (Fig. 7d) generalize completely, or with equal loss, to the moderate stimuli (Figs. 7b and 7c), then the response outputs at Figs. 7b and 7c will be smaller following habituation training with the weak than with the strong stimulus—the opposite of Davis and Wagner's finding. However, if the values assumed in the present paper are used (dotted lines, Fig. 7) and the same generalization assumptions are made, response outputs at Figs. 7b and 7c will be larger following habituation to the weak stimulus and thus in agreement with the empirical data.

Instead of accounting for Davis and Wagner's results by postulating a direct intensity–central habituation function, Groves and Thompson (1970, p. 425) introduced the terms relative and absolute habituation to refer to the conditions under which different relations to stimulus intensity should occur. Thus, they "adopt the view that relative habituation (habituation measured under constant stimulus intensity conditions) is inversely related to the habituation stimulus intensity, but that absolute degree of habituation (determined by varying the test stimulus relative to the habituation stimulus) is directly related to the habituation stimulus intensity."

Since relative and absolute habituation refer to the conditions under which a response is measured, it is not clear what relationship they imply between stimulus intensity and central habituation. If they refer only to response habituation, the problem remains of showing how an inverse intensity–central habituation function could predict absolute response habituation. If the terms refer to two central processes, this would not be a parsimonious assumption when a single process having a direct relationship with intensity could predict both types of response habituation.

It should be noted that, no matter what assumptions are made about the relation of intensity and central habituation, the empirical results imply an inverse relationship between intensity and relative habituation only if habituation is measured by response level. This is shown in Fig. 8, a diagrammatic representation of Davis and Wagner's findings (1968, Fig. 1). The linear relationship between control levels and test stimulus intensity is an approximation of the prehabituation findings in the left-hand panel of Davis and Wagner's figure. The results of testing at various intensities, after habituating to a 108-dB tone (the weaker stimulus) and to a 120-dB tone (the stronger stimulus), are shown as linear functions parallel with the control function and are a simplified representation of the findings in the center panel of Davis and Wagner's figure.[4] The amount and the percentage decrement from control levels is clearly greater and the response amplitude lower for all test stimuli, following habituation to the 120-dB tone. Thus, absolute habituation is a direct function of intensity by any habituation measure. However, if response to the 108-dB tone, after habituating to 108-dB, is compared with response to the 120 dB tone after habituating to 120 dB, this relative habituation (dashed line) is a direct function of intensity when measured by amount and percentage change from control levels but an inverse function of intensity when measured by response amplitude since lower response amplitude would indicate more habituation to the weaker stimulus.[5]

Sokolov's discussion of the intensity—habituation relationship refers to response rather than to central habituation, and it is not self-evident that the theory implies any independent effect of intensity on a central habituation process. The changes in response habituation as a function of intensity might be ascribed entirely to differences in the magnitude and kind of arousal system elicited; i.e., OR's, in general, should decrement more rapidly than DR's, and larger OR's could take longer than smaller OR's to reach a common level whether the rate of decrement were faster, equal, or slower. However, if it is assumed that initial response measures a non-decaying sensitization process, the rate of change from initial to asymptotic response level should provide a measure of the central habituation process. If a direct intensity—habituation function holds, as suggested by the above discussion, not only the amount of change but also the rate of change should be greater with the more intense of two OR-eliciting stimuli. While experimental data have not been analyzed in this manner, and there could be

[4]Davis and Wagner's empirical functions showed a curvature as response amplitude approached zero, but this is not relevant to the present argument.

[5]The author expresses appreciation to J. C. Jackson for pointing out these relationships.

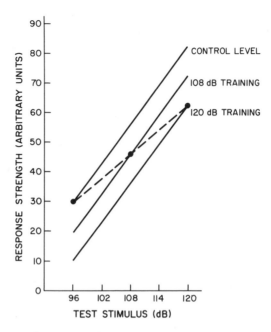

Fig. 8. Diagrammatic representation by Jackson (1971) of data from Davis and Wagner (1968, Fig. 1) showing that habituation training with more intense stimulus yields less response strength when test intensity is constant (greater absolute habituation) but more response strength for intense stimulus when test is made only with training stimuli (lesser relative habituation shown by dashed line). Habituation measured by decrement from control level is greater after training at 120 dB under either test condition.

problems of interpretation if the response changes from an OR to a DR, some data are in accord with a direct intensity–*central* habituation function as well as a direct intensity–*response* habituation function (e.g., Fig. 1).

Sokolov's theory does, of course, postulate that different central mechanisms are involved in habituation of an OR and a DR. One mechanism, presumably applying to both OR and DR habituation, is similar to Thompson's in that an inhibitory process develops in the direct pathways and its generalization depends on how the projection systems are organized, i.e., on the extent of overlap in pathways. However, an additional mechanism exists for the more rapid habituation of the OR, namely, the signals of match arising from the neuronal model-comparator process. These signals are a function of the information in the stimulus and the discriminating-extrapolating capabilities of the nervous system. Both of these attributes can be investigated independently of an effect on habituation.

Groves and Thompson (1970) believed that Sokolov's theory was not consistent with the effects of stimulus intensity. "It would seem that a strong stimulus should provide a 'clearer' substrate for the formation of a model and hence more habituation than a weak stimulus, when in fact a strong stimulus often produces increased rather than decreased response" (Groves and Thompson, 1970, p. 438). Apparently, Groves and Thompson felt that Sokolov's theory implied a direct intensity–OR habituation function and that such a function is contradicted by the data. As pointed out in Section III,B, however, the ANS data suggest that for components which participate only in the OR the amount of decrement, and, at least in some cases, the rate of decrement is greater with a strong than a weak stimulus. For intensities sufficient to evoke a DR, the model-comparator mechanism would not determine habituation rate. In any case, it is possible to have a direct intensity–central habituation function and still obtain an inverse response habituation function (e.g. Fig. 7).

Another difficulty for Sokolov's theory, according to Groves and Thompson (1970, p. 437), is the "incremental stimulus intensity effect." This effect refers to the relatively low level of final responding which is obtained when stimulus intensity is increased to a high intensity very gradually over trials in contrast to the relatively high level of final responding when the high intensity stimulus is repeated on all trials or when the high intensity stimulus is given after habituating to a medium intensity stimulus or to the gradual series presented in a random order (Fig. 9). Davis and

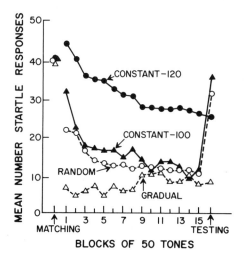

Fig. 9. Number of startle responses per 50 tone exposures under four conditions (see text) and during matching and testing with single blocks of 50 120-dB tones. From Davis and Wagner (1969) with permission of the publisher.

Wagner (1969) demonstrated the effect on startle responses in the intact rat, and Groves and Thompson replicated it in acute spinal cat. Both sets of investigators felt that Sokolov's theory was embarrassed by their findings since repetition of the same stimulus should, according to Sokolov, produce signals of a match to prior stimulation and thus lead to faster habituation than when the model of prior stimulation had to include a gradually changing stimulus.

There are two problems with this analysis. First, Sokolov's signals of a match lead to habituation of an *orienting* response and an OR was not measured in either of these studies. Startle and a spinal flexion reflex represent defensive or adaptive reflexes, and a stimulus may continue to evoke these reflexes for a long period of time after an OR has habituated. Second, the differences in habituation, considered as decrement, and in response to stimulus change are not difficult to account for by any theory that allows for generalization of habituation. When differences between the level of responding to the stimuli with which the habituating series began are compared with the final level of responding, the constant 120 series shows some decrement and the gradual series a small increment. The constant 100 and the random series also showed habituation from trial block 1 to 14 but showed a large increment to the large stimulus change introduced on trial block 15. Viewed in terms of the effect of stimulus change, therefore, the results indicate a large response increment with large stimulus change (constant 100 or random series), a small increment with small change (gradual series), and a small decrement with no change (constant 120 series).

What is difficult to account for is the differences in the absolute level of responding, and it is not clear that any theory has been successful in this. Sokolov's theory is not addressed to the question. Groves and Thompson (1970, p. 442) felt that the difference could be predicted from dual-process theory, but their explanation requires many assumptions about the relative amounts of generalization of relative and absolute habituation, of sensitization, and of decay of sensitization, for none of which are quantitative functions available. Davis and Wagner (1969, p. 491) proposed that sensitization, or arousal, was less with the gradual series because "each intensity had been rendered less arousing, or disruptive, by virtue of the prior habituation to less intense values." However, the constant 120 stimuli should also have been rendered less arousing by prior habituation and, from Davis and Wagner (1968), prior habituation should have been greater in amount following the constant 120 series. Subsequent statements by Davis and Wagner (1969, p. 492) suggest that with a low level of response there may be more opportunity "to engage in antagonistic or non-facilitatory behavior."

One additional point deserves comment. The habituation literature has taken relatively little cognizance of the distinction between short- and long-term habituation. Thompson and Spencer's handling (1966, p. 37) is perhaps typical. They stated that since short-term and long-term habituation "exhibit the same parametric features," except for time course, "some identity of underlying processes may be implied." However, Davis's results (1970) indicate that the two processes do *not* bear the same relation to ISI and that the difference is consistent with a distinction between a refractory period effect and a learning process. Hull (1943, 1952) made a similar, although not directly analogous, distinction between inhibitory potential (I_R) and conditioned inhibition ($_SI_R$). Sokolov (1963b, 1969) also made allowance for the occurrence of conditioned inhibition and Stein (1966) has developed a conditioned inhibition theory of habituation. Groves and Thompson (1970, p. 438f) criticized Stein's theory both on the grounds that it would seem to require a direct intensity–central inhibition function and that it was in conflict with findings of increased habituation following massed presentations. Clearly, if long-term habituation is facilitated by spaced presentations and if a direct intensity–central inhibition function is required by Davis and Wagner's results (1968), Stein's theory would be quite viable. While the ANS literature has given little attention to the theoretical importance of a distinction between short-term and long-term habituation, there is evidence of a refractory period effect up to at least 90 seconds (Section IV,B) as well as evidence for retention of habituation over intervals of at least a week.

In conclusion, it appears that while dual processes may be necessary to account for the phenomena of habituation, response recovery, and dishabituation, hypothesizing an incrementing (sensitization) process that does not decay under continued stimulation and a decrementing (habituation) process that is a direct function of stimulus intensity may better account for the empirical phenomena than the functions proposed by Thompson. A more fundamental question is whether any model of spinal reflex behavior will prove adequate to account for behavior in the adult human. Thompson's theory does not predict differences in the rate of habituating ANS responses either as a function of the type of response involved or as a function of stimulus characteristics other than frequency and intensity. In contrast, Sokolov's stimulus-model-comparator theory is primarily concerned with the problem of specifying stimulus conditions which elicit and lead to habituation of a particular type of response, the orienting reflex. These conditions require a nervous system capable of responding to the amount of information provided by very complex stimulus variations. As indicated in the introductory section (Section I,A), Sokolov's theory is not so much a general theory of response habituation as a general theory of perception and conditioning. Since the present paper reviewed only those studies dealing with habituation and dishabituation of ANS response to nonsignal stimuli, it has not considered the other types of data which would be important in evaluating Sokolov's general theory.

References

Allen, C. K., Hill, F. A., and Wickens, D. D. (1963). The orienting reflex as a function of the interstimulus interval of compound stimuli. *J. Exp. Psychol.* **65**, 309–316.

Arezzo, D. A. (1969). Cardiac response to repeated non-signal tone or white noise stimuli. Unpublished M. A. Thesis, University of Wisconsin, Madison.

Asafov, B. D. (1965). Change in the dynamics of autonomic components of the orienting reflex with employment of sound stimuli of progressively increasing intensity. *In* "Orienting Reflex and Exploratory Behavior" (L. G. Voronin *et al.*, eds.), pp. 155–162. Amer. Inst. Biol. Sci., Washington, D.C.

Badia, P., and Defran, R. H. (1970). Orienting responses and GSR conditioning: A dilemma. *Psychol. Rev.* **77**, 171–181.

Badia, P., and Harley, J. P. (1970). Habituation and temporal conditioning as related to shock intensity and its judgment. *J. Exp. Psychol.* **84**, 534–536.

Bagshaw, M. H., and Benzies, S. (1968). Multiple measures of the orienting reaction and their dissociation after amygdalectomy in monkeys. *Exp. Neurol.* **20**, 175–187.

Bagshaw, M. H., Kimble, D. P., and Pribram, K. H. (1965). The GSR of monkeys during orienting and habituation and after ablation of the amygdala, hippocampus and inferotemporal cortex. *Neuropsychologia* **3**, 111–119.

Benjamin, L. S. (1963). Statistical treatment of the law of initial values (LIV) in autonomic research: A review and recommendation. *Psychosom. Med.* **25**, 556–566.

Benjamin, L. S. (1967). Facts and artifacts in using analysis of covariance to "undo" the law of initial values. *Psychophysiology* **4**, 187–206.

Berg, K. M. (1970). Heart rate and vasomotor responses as a function of stimulus duration and intensity. Unpublished M. A. Thesis, University of Wisconsin, Madison.

Berg, W. K. (1968). Vasomotor and HR responses to non-signal auditory stimuli. Unpublished M. A. Thesis, University of Wisconsin, Madison.

Berg, W. K., and Graham, F. K. (1970). Reproducible effects of stimulus intensity on heart rate response curves. *Psychophysiology* **6**, 653–654.

Berlyne, D. E. (1961). Conflict and the orientation reaction. *J. Exp. Psychol.* **62**, 476–483.

Berlyne, D. E., Craw, M. A., Salapatek, P. H., and Lewis, J. L. (1963). Novelty, complexity, incongruity, extrinsic motivation and the GSR. *J. Exp. Psychol.* **66**, 560–567.

Bernstein, A. S. (1968). The orienting response and direction of stimulus change. *Psychon. Sci.* **12**, 127–128.

Bernstein, A. S. (1969). To what does the orienting response respond? *Psychophysiology* **6**, 338–350.

Bernstein, A. S., Taylor, K., Austen, B. G., Nathanson, M., and Scarpelli, A. (1971). Orienting response and apparent movement toward or away from the observer. *J. Exp. Psychol.* **87**, 37–45.

Bindra, D. (1959). Stimulus change, reactions to novelty, and response decrement. *Psychol. Rev.* **66**, 96–103.

Bishop, P. D., and Kimmel, H. D. (1969). Retention of habituation and conditioning. *J. Exp. Psychol.* **81**, 317–321.

Bloch, R. M. (1970). The influence of long inter-stimulus intervals on the cortical evoked potential and heart rate response. Unpublished M. S. Thesis, University of Wisconsin, Madison.

Brotsky, S. (1969). Cephalic vasomotor responses as indices of the orienting reflex, the defensive reflex, and semantic conditioning and generalization: A failure to replicate Soviet research. *Psychon. Sci.* **17**, 228–229.

Brown, C. C., ed. (1967). "Methods in Psychophysiology." Williams & Wilkins, Baltimore, Maryland.

Burch, G. E. (1961). Digital rheoplethysmographic study of the orienting reflex in man. *Psychosom. Med.* **23**, 403–412.

Chase, W. G., and Graham, F. K. (1967). Heart rate response to non-signal tones. *Psychon. Sci.* **9**, 181–182.

Cicirelli, J. S. (1970). Unpublished data.

Clifton, R. K., Graham, F. K., and Hatton, H. M. (1968). Newborn heart-rate response and response habituation as a function of stimulus duration. *J. Exp. Child Psychol.* **6**, 265–278.

Cohen, M. J., and Johnson, H. J. (1971). Effects of intensity and the signal value of stimuli on the orienting and defensive responses. *J. Exp. Psychol.* **88**, 286–288.

Cook, M. R. (1972). The cephalic vasomotor response. *Psychophysiol.* **9**, 273–274.

Coombs, C. H. (1938). Adaptation of the galvanic response to auditory stimuli. *J. Exp. Psychol.* **22**, 244–268.

Corman, C. D. (1967). Stimulus generalization of habituation of the galvanic skin response. *J. Exp. Psychol.* **74**, 236–240.

Davidoff, R. A., and McDonald, D. G. (1964). Alpha blocking and autonomic responses in neurological patients. *Archives of Neurol.* **10**, 283–292.

Davis, M. (1970). Effects of interstimulus interval length and variability on startle-response habituation in the rat. *J. Comp. Physiol. Psychol.* **72**, 177–192.

Davis, M., and Wagner, A. R. (1968). Startle responsiveness after habituation to different intensities of tone. *Psychon. Sci.* **12**, 337–338.

Davis, M., and Wagner, A. R. (1969). Habituation of startle response under incremental sequence of stimulus intensities. *J. Comp. Physiol. Psychol.* **67**, 486–492.

Davis, R. C. (1934). Modification of the galvanic reflex by daily repetition of a stimulus. *J. Exp. Psychol.* **17**, 504–535.

Davis, R. C. (1948). Motor effects of strong auditory stimuli. *J. Exp. Psychol.* **38**, 257–275.

Davis, R. C., and Buchwald, A. M. (1957). An exploration of somatic response patterns: Stimulus and sex differences. *J. Comp. Physiol. Psychol.* **50**, 44–52.

Davis, R. C., Buchwald, A. M., and Frankmann, R. W. (1955). Autonomic and muscular responses, and their relation to simple stimuli. *Psychol. Monogr.* **69**, 1–71.

Duffy, E., and Lacey, O. L. (1946). Adaptation in energy mobilization: Changes in general level of palmar skin conductance. *J. Exp. Psychol.* **36**, 437–352.

Dykman, R. A., Mack, R. L., and Ackerman, P. T. (1965). The evaluation of autonomic and motor components of the nonavoidance conditioned response in the dog. *Psychophysiology* **1**, 209–230.

Edelberg, R. (1967). Electrical properties of the skin. *In* "Methods in Psychophysiology" (C. C. Brown, ed.), pp. 1–53. Williams & Wilkins, Baltimore, Maryland.

Eisenberg, R. B. (1965). Auditory behavior in the human neonate. I. Methodologic problems and the logical design of research procedures. *J. Audit. Res.* **5**, 159–177.

Farmer, E., and Chambers, E. G. (1925). Concerning the use of the psychogalvanic reflex in psychological experiments. *Brit. J. Psychol.* **15**, 237–254.

Fisher, G. L., and Fisher, B. E. (1969). Differential rates of GSR habituation to pleasant and unpleasant sapid stimuli. *J. Exp. Psychol.* **82**, 339–342.

Fitzgerald, R. D., and Teyler, T. J. (1970). Trace and delayed heart-rate conditioning in rats as a function of US intensity. *J. Comp. Physiol. Psychol.* **70**, 242–253.

Fleshler, M. (1965). Adequate acoustic stimulus for startle reaction in the rat. *J. Comp. Physiol. Psychol.* **60**, 200–207.

Folkow, B. (1960). Range of control of the cardiovascular system by the central nervous system. *Physiol. Rev.* **40**, Suppl. 4, 93–99.

Forbes, T. W., and Bolles, M. M. (1936). Correlation of the response potentials of the skin with "exciting" and non-"exciting" stimuli. *J. Psychol.* **2**, 273–285.

Frankenhaeuser, M., Fröberg, J., Hagdahl, R., Rissler, A., Björkvall, C., and Wolff, B. (1967). Physiological, behavioral, and subjective indices of habituation to psychological stress. *Physiol. Behav.* **2**, 229–237.

Fried, R., Korn, S. J., and Welch, L. (1966a). Effect of change in sequential visual stimuli on GSR adaptation. *J. Exp. Psychol.* **72**, 325–327.

Fried, R., Welch, L., and Friedman, M. (1966b). Stimulus novelty and intraseries primacy in GSR adaptation. *Percept. & Psychophys.* **1**, 345–346.

Fried, R., Welch, L., Friedman, M., and Gluck, S. (1967). Is no-stimulus a stimulus? *J. Exp. Psychol.* **73**, 145–146.

Furedy, J. J. (1968a). Novelty and the measurement of the GSR. *J. Exp. Psychol.* **76**, 501–503.

Furedy, J. J. (1968b). Human orienting reaction as a function of electrodermal versus plethysmographic response modes and single versus alternating stimulus series. *J. Exp. Psychol.* **77**, 70–78.

Furedy. J. J. (1969a). Electrodermal and plethysmographic OR components: Repetition of and change from UCS-CS trials with surrogate UCS. *Can. J. Psychol.* **23**, 127–135.

Furedy, J. J. (1969b). Some uses and abuses of electrodermal measures. *Psychon. Sci.* **15**, 98–99.

Furedy, J. J. (1971a). The nonhabituating vasomotor component of the human orienting reaction: Misbehaving skeleton in OR theory's closet. *Psychophysiology* **8**, 278.

Furedy, J. J. (1971b). Personal communication.

Furedy, J. J., and Gagnon, Y. (1969). Relationships between and sensitivities of the galvanic skin reflex and two indices of peripheral vasoconstriction in man. *J. Neurol., Neurosurg. Psychiat.* **32**, 197–201.

Gabriel, M., and Ball, T. S. (1970). Plethysmographic and GSR responses to single versus double-simultaneous novel tactile stimuli. *J. Exp. Psychol.* **85**, 368–373.

Galbrecht, C. R., Dykman, R. A., Reese, W. G., and Suzuki, T. (1965). Intrasession adaptation and intersession extinction of the components of the orienting response. *J. Exp. Psychol.* **70**, 585–597.

Gaviria, B. (1967). Autonomic reaction magnitude and habituation to different voices. *Psychosom. Med.* **29**, 598–605.

Geer, J. H. (1966). Effect of interstimulus intervals and rest-period length upon habituation of the orienting response. *J. Exp. Psychol.* **72**, 617–619.

Geer, J. H. (1969). Generalization of inhibition in the orienting response. *Psychophysiology* **6**, 197–201.

Germana, J. (1968). Rate of habituation and the law of initial values. *Psychophysiology* **5**, 31–36.

Germana, J. (1969). Differential effects of interstimulus interval on habituation and recall scores. *Psychon. Sci.* **17**, 73–74.

Germana, J., and Klein, S. B. (1968). The cardiac component of the orienting response. *Psychophysiology* **4**, 324–328.

Glaser, E. M. (1966). "The Physiological Basis of Habituation." Oxford Univ. Press, London and New York.

Glaser, E. M., and Griffin, J. P. (1962). Influence of the cerebral cortex on habituation. *J. Physiol. (London)* **160**, 429–445.

Glaser, E. M., and Whittow, G. C. (1957). Retention in a warm environment of adaptation to localized cooling. *J. Physiol. (London)* **136**, 98–111.

Glaser, E. M., Hall, M. S., and Whittow, G. C. (1959). Habituation to heating and cooling of the same hand. *J. Physiol. (London)* **146**, 152–164.

Graham, F. K. (1971). Analysis of heart rate response curves: A comment on pooled interaction error terms. *Psychophysiology* **7**, 485–489.

Graham, F. K., and Clifton, R. K. (1966). Heart-rate change as a component of the orienting response. *Psychol. Bull.* **65**, 305–320.

Graham, F. K., and Jackson, J. C. (1970). Arousal systems and infant heart rate responses. *Advan. Child Develop. Behav.* **5**, 59–117.

Greenwood, R. M., and Lewis, P. D. (1959). Factors affecting habituation to localized heating and cooling. *J. Physiol.* **146**, 10–11.

Grice, G. R. (1968). Stimulus intensity and response evocation. *Psychol. Rev.* **75**, 359–373.

Griffin, J. P. (1963). The role of the frontal areas of the cortex upon habituation in man. *Clin. Sci.* **24**, 127–134.

Grings, W. W., and Schell, A. M. (1969). Magnitude of electrodermal response to a standard stimulus as a function of intensity and proximity of a prior stimulus. *J. Comp. Physiol. Psychol.* **67**, 77–82.

Gross, K., and Stern, J. A. (1967). Habituation of orienting responses as a function of "instructional set." *Conditional Reflex* **2**, 23–36.

Groves, P. M., and Thompson, R. F. (1970). Habituation: A dual-process theory. *Psychol. Rev.* **77**, 419–450.

Groves, P. M., Lee, D., and Thompson, R. F. (1969). Effects of stimulus frequency and intensity on habituation and sensitization in acute spinal cat. *Physiol. Behav.* **4**, 383–388.

Hammond, L. J. (1967). Human GSR pseudoconditioning as a function of change in basal skin resistance and CS-US similarity. *J. Exp. Psychol.* **73**, 125–129.

Harding, G. B., and Rundle, G. R. (1969). Long-term retention of modality- and non-modality-specific habituation of the GSR. *J. Exp. Psychol.* **82**, 390–392.

Hare, R. D. (1968). Psychopathy, autonomic functioning, and the orienting response. *J. Abnormal Psychol. Monogr. Suppl.* **73**, 1–24.

Harper, M. M. (1968). The effects of signal property and stimulus intensity on the skin resistance response to repetition of auditory stimuli. Unpublished M. A. Thesis, University of Wisconsin, Madison.

Hart, J. D. (1970). Physiological responses of anxiety neurotics and normal controls to simple signal and non-signal stimuli. Unpublished Doctoral Dissertation, University of Wisconsin, Madison.

Hatton, H. M., Berg, W. K., and Graham, F. K. (1970). Effects of acoustic rise time on heart rate response. *Psychon. Sci.* **19**, 101–103.

Hocherman, S., and Palti, Y. (1967). Correlation between blood volume and opacity changes in the finger. *J. Appl. Physiol.* **23**, 157–162.

Hord, D. J., Johnson, L. C., and Rumbaugh, D. M. (1965). Physiological response patterns in cardiac patients. *U.S. Navy Med. Neuropsychiat. Res. Unit, Rep.* No. 64–10.

Houck, R. L., and Mefferd, R. B., Jr. (1969). Generalization of GSR habituation to mild intramodal stimuli. *Psychophysiology* **6**, 202–206.

Hull, C. L. (1934). Learning. II. The factor of the conditional reflex. *In* "Handbook of General Experimental Psychology" (C. Murchison, ed.), pp. 382–455. Clark Univ. Press, Worcester, Massachusetts.

Hull, C. L. (1943). "Principles of Behavior." Appleton, New York.

Hull, C. L. (1952). "A Behavior System." Yale Univ. Press, New Haven, Connecticut.

Hutt, S. J., Hutt, C., Lenard, H. G., von Bernuth, H., and Muntjewerff, W. J. (1968). Auditory responsivity in the human neonate. *Nature (London)* **218**, 888–890.

Jackson, J. C. (1971). Personal communication.

Jackson, J. C. (1972). Elicitation and habituation of the orienting reflex at differing levels of stimulus intensity. Unpublished Ph.D. Thesis, University of Wisconsin, Madison.

James, J. P., and Hughes, G. R. (1969). Generalization of habituation of the GSR to white noise of varying intensities. *Psychon. Sci.* **14**, 163–164.

Katkin, E. S., and McCubbin, R. J. (1969). Habituation of the orienting response as a function of individual differences in anxiety and autonomic lability. *J. Abnormal Psychol.* **74**, 54–60.

Katkin, E. S., and Nelson, J. S. (1966). Temporal conditioning of cardiac components of the orienting reflex. Paper presented at the Meeting of the Society for Psychophysiological Research, Denver, Colorado.

Keefe, F. B., and Johnson, L. C. (1970). Cardiovascular responses to auditory stimuli. *Psychon. Sci.* **19**, 335–337.

Kimmel, H. D., and Goldstein, A. J. (1967). Retention of habituation of the GSR to visual and auditory stimulation. *J. Exp. Psychol.* **73**, 401–404.

Kirk, W. E. (1969). UCR diminution in temporal conditioning and habituation. Paper presented at the Mid-Western Psychological Association, Chicago, Illinois.

Koelle, G. B. (1970). Neurohumoral transmission and the autonomic nervous system. *In* "The Pharmacological Basis of Therapeutics" (L. S. Goodman and A. Gilman, eds.), 4th ed., pp. 402–441. Macmillan, New York.

Koepke, J. E., and Pribram, K. H. (1966). Habituation of GSR as a function of stimulus duration and spontaneous activity. *J. Comp. Physiol. Psychol.* **61**, 442–448.

Koepke, J. E., and Pribram, K. H. (1967). Habituation of the vasoconstriction response as a function of stimulus duration and anxiety. *J. Comp. Physiol. Psychol.* **64**, 502–504.

Korn, J. H., and Moyer, K. E. (1968). Effects of set and sex on the electrodermal orienting response. *Psychophysiology* **4**, 453–459.

Lacey, J. I. (1956). The evaluation of autonomic responses: Toward a general solution. *Ann. N.Y. Acad. Sci.* **67**, 123–164.

Lacey, J. I. (1967). Somatic response patterning and stress: Some revisions of activation theory. *In* "Psychological Stress: Issues in Research" (M. H. Appley and R. Trumbull, eds.), pp. 14–37. Appleton, New York.

Lader, M. H. (1964). The effects of cyclobarbitone on the habituation of the psychogalvanic reflex. *Brain*, **87**, 321–340.

Lader, M. H. (1965). The effects of cyclobarbitone on the pulse volume, pulse rate, and electromyogram. *J. Psychosom. Res.* **8**, 385–398.

Lang, P. J., and Hnatiow, M. (1962). Stimulus repetition and the heart rate response. *J. Comp. Physiol. Psychol.* **55**, 781–785.

Leavy, A., and Geer, J. H. (1967). The effect of low levels of stimulus intensity upon the orienting response. *Psychon. Sci.* **9**, 105–106.

Lidberg, L., Schalling, D., and Levander, S. E. (1969). Some characteristics of digital vasomotor activity. *Lab. Clin. Stress Res.* **7**, 1–22.

Lockhart, R. A. (1966). Temporal conditioning of GSR. *J. Exp. Psychol.* **71**, 438–446.

Lynch, J. J. (1967). The cardiac orienting response and its relationship to the cardiac conditional response in dogs. *Conditional Reflex* **2**, 138–152.

McDonald, D. G., Johnson, L. C., and Hord, D. J. (1964). Habituation of the orienting response in alert and drowsy subjects. *Psychophysiology* **1**, 163–173.

Magoun, H. W. (1963). "The Waking Brain," 2nd ed. Thomas, Springfield, Illinois.

Malmo, R. B. (1959). Activation: A neuropsychological dimension. *Psychol. Rev.* **66**, 367–386.

Malmo, R. B., and Bélanger, D. (1967). Related physiological and behavioral changes: What are their determinants? *Res. Publ., Ass. Res. Nerv. Ment. Dis.* **45**, 288–318.

Meyers, W. J., and Gullickson, G. R. (1967). The evoked heart rate response: The influence of auditory stimulus repetition, pattern reversal, and autonomic arousal level. *Psychophysiology* **4**, 56–66.

Miller, N. E. (1969). Learning of visceral and glandular responses. *Science* **163**, 434–445.

Montagu, J. D. (1963). Habituation of the psycho-galvanic reflex during serial tests. *J. Psychosom. Res.* **7**, 199–214.

Moruzzi, G., and Magoun, H. W. (1949). Brain stem reticular formation and activation of the EEG. *Electroencephalogr. Clin. Neurophysiol.* **1**, 455–473.

O'Gorman, J. G., Mangan, G. L., and Gowen, J. A. (1970). Selective habituation of galvanic skin response component of the orientation reaction to an auditory stimulus. *Psychophysiology* **6**, 716–721.

Pavlov, I. P. (1927). "Conditioned Reflexes: An Investigation of the Physiological Activity of the Cerebral Cortex." Oxford Univ. Press, London and New York.

Pendergrass, V. E., and Kimmel, H. D. (1968). UCR diminution in temporal conditioning and habituation. *J. Exp. Psychol.* **77**, 1–6.

Porges, S. W., and Raskin, D. C. (1969). Respiratory and heart rate components of attention. *J. Exp. Psychol.* **81**, 497–503.

Porter, J. M., Jr. (1938). Adaptation of the galvanic skin response. *J. Exp. Psychol.* **23**, 553–557.

Raskin, D. C., Kotses, H., and Bever, J. (1969a). Autonomic indicators of orienting and defensive reflexes. *J. Exp. Psychol.* **80**, 423–433.

Raskin, D. C., Kotses, H., and Bever, J. (1969b). Cephalic vasomotor and heart rate measures of orienting and defensive reflexes. *Psychophysiology* **6**, 149–159.

Ratner, S. C. (1970). Habituation: Research and theory. *In* "Current Issues in Animal Learning" (J. Reynierse, ed.), Chapter 3, pp. 55–84. Univ. of Nebraska Press, Lincoln.

Roessler, R., Collins, F., and Burch, N. R. (1969). Heart rate response to sound and light. *Psychophysiology* **5**, 359–369.

Rousey, C. L., and Reitz, W. E. (1967). Respiratory changes at auditory and visual thresholds. *Psychophysiology* **3**, 258–261.

Routtenberg, A. (1968). The two-arousal hypothesis: Reticular formation and limbic system. *Psychol. Rev.* **75**, 51–80.

Royer, F. L. (1966). The "respiratory vasomotor reflex" in the forehead and finger. *Psychophysiology* **2**, 241–248.

Schaub, R. E. (1965). The effect of interstimulus interval on GSR adaptation. *Psychon. Sci.* **2**, 361–362.

Schneirla, T. C. (1959). An evolutionary and developmental theory of biphasic processes underlying approach and withdrawal. *In* "Current Theory and Research on Motivation" (M. R. Jones, ed.), Vol. 7, pp. 1–42. Univ. of Nebraska Press, Lincoln.

Scholander, T. (1961). The effects of moderate sleep deprivation on the habituation of autonomic response elements. *Acta Physiol. Scand.* **51**, 325–342.

Shepard, R. N. (1965). Approximation to uniform gradients of generalization by monotone transformations of scale. *In* "Stimulus Generalization" (D.I. Mostofsky, ed.), pp. 94–110. Stanford Univ. Press, Stanford, California.

Smith, D. B. D., and Strawbridge, P. J. (1968). Stimulus duration and the human heart rate response. *Psychon. Sci.* **10**, 71–72.

Smith, D. B. D., and Strawbridge, P. J. (1969). The heart rate response to a brief auditory and visual stimulus. *Psychophysiology* **6**, 317–329.

Sokolov, E. N. (1960). Neuronal models and the orienting reflex. *In* "The Central Nervous System and Behavior" (M. A. B. Brazier, ed.), pp. 187–276. Josiah Macy, Jr. Found., New York.

Sokolov, E. N. (1963a). Higher nervous functions: The orienting reflex. *Annu. Rev. Physiol.* **25**, 545–580.

Sokolov, E. N. (1963b). "Perception and the Conditioned Reflex." Macmillan, New York.

Sokolov, E. N. (1969). The modeling properties of the nervous system. *In* "A handbook of Contemporary Soviet Psychology" (M. Cole and I. Maltzman, eds.), pp. 671–704. Basic Books, New York.

Sokolov, E. N., and Paramonova, N. P. (1961). Extinction of the orienting reaction. *Pavlov J. Higher Nerv. Activ.* **11**, 1–11.

Soltysik, S., Jaworska, K., Kowalska, M., and Radom, S. (1961). Cardiac responses to simple acoustic stimuli in dogs. *Acta Biol. Exp. (Warsaw)* **21**, 235–252.

Stein, L. (1969). Habituation and stimulus novelty: A model based on classical conditioning. *Psychol. Rev.* **73**, 352–356.

Stern, J. A., and Plapp, J. M. (1969). Psychophysiology and clinical psychology. *Curr. Top. Clin. & Community Psychol.* **1**, 197–254.

Stern, J. A., Surphlis, W., and Koff, E. (1965). Electrodermal responsiveness as related to psychiatric diagnosis and prognosis. *Psychophysiology* **2**, 51–61.

Stevens, S. S., and Volkmann, J. (1940). The relation of pitch to frequency. *Amer. J. Psychol.* **53**, 329–353.

Thetford, P. E., Klemme, M. E., and Spohn, H. E. (1968). Skin potential, heart rate, and the span of immediate memory. *Psychophysiology* **5**, 166–177.

Thompson, R. F., and Spencer, W. A. (1966). Habituation: A model phenomenon for the study of neuronal substrates of behavior. *Psychol. Rev.* **73**, 16–43.

Unger, S. M. (1964). Habituation of the vasoconstrictive orienting reaction. *J. Exp. Psychol.* **67**, 11–18.

Uno, T., and Grings, W. W. (1965). Autonomic components of orienting behavior. *Psychophysiology* **1**, 311–321.

Venables, P. H., and Martin, I., eds. (1967). "A Manual of Psychophysiological Methods." Wiley, New York.

Voronin, L. G., and Sokolov, E. N. (1960). Cortical mechanisms of the orienting reflex and its relation to the conditioned reflex. *Electroencephalogr. Clin. Neurophysiol. Suppl.* **13**, 335–344.

Weisbard, C. (1970). Heart rate change in monkeys to tones varying in intensity and novelty. Unpublished M. A. Thesis, University of Wisconsin, Madison.

Weisbard, C., and Graham, F. K. (1971). Heart-rate change as a component of the orienting response in monkeys. *J. Comp. Physiol. Psychol.* **76**, 74–83.

Wickens, D. D., Nield, A. F., and Wickens, C. D. (1966). Habituation of the GSR and of breathing disturbances in the cat. *Psychon. Sci.* **6**, 325–326.

Wilcott, R. C. (1967). Arousal sweating and electrodermal phenomena. *Psychol. Bull.* **67**, 58–72.

Williams, J. A. (1963). Novelty, GSR, and stimulus generalization. *Can. J. Psychol.* **17**, 52–61.

Winokur, G., Stewart, M. A., Stern, J. A., and Pfeifer, E. (1962). A dynamic equilibrium in GSR habituation: The effect of interstimulus interval. *J. Psychosom. Res.* **6**, 117–122.

Wolfensberger, W., and O'Connor, N. (1967). Relative effectiveness of galvanic skin response latency, amplitude and duration scores as measures of arousal and habituation in normal and retarded adults. *Psychophysiology* **3**, 345–350.

Yaremko, R. M., Blair, M. W., and Leckart, R. T. (1970). The orienting reflex to changes in a conceptual stimulus dimension. *Psychon. Sci.* **2**, 115–116.

Zeiner, A. R. (1970). Orienting response and discrimination conditioning. *Physiol. & Behav.* **5**, 641–646.

Zimny, G. H., and Kienstra, R. A. (1967). Orienting and defensive responses to electric shock. *Psychophysiology* **3**, 351–362.

Zimny, G. H., and Miller, F. L. (1966). Orienting and adaptive cardiovascular responses to heat and cold. *Psychophysiology* **3**, 81–92.

Zimny, G. H., and Schwabe, L. W. (1966). Stimulus change and habituation of the orienting response. *Psychophysiology* **2**, 103–115.

Zimny, G. H., Pawlick, G. F., and Saur, D. P. (1969). Effects of stimulus order and novelty on orienting responses. *Psychophysiology* **6**, 166–173.

Chapter 6
Habituation, Habituability, and Conditioning[1]

H. D. KIMMEL

I. Introduction and Background

There are two different logical approaches which may be taken in studying the relationship between habituation and conditioning. Starting with the assumption that habituation and conditioning both refer ultimately to similar central nervous system (CNS) processes, as well as identifying somewhat similar objective behavioral phenomena, we might wish to consider the logical possibility that one is merely a variety of the other. In other words, habituation may simply be a special kind of conditioning or conditioning may be a special kind of habituation. A somewhat different logical approach could consider the possibility that, although habituation and conditioning may be conceptually independent CNS processes and objectively different behavioral phenomena, nevertheless one may significantly influence the other. The latter approach, for example, might provide a basis for studying the effect of prior habituation upon subsequent conditioning or vice versa.

The purpose of this chapter is to consider both of these approaches in terms of some of the evidence and theories presently available. In advance

[1]Done under NIMH grant No. 5 RO1 MH16839–03. The author expresses his thanks to Dr. Frank Terrant for his various helpful suggestions during the preparation of this manuscript and to Messrs. Frank Gurucharri, Michael McCauley, and John Welch for their assistance.

of this consideration it would be appropriate to "telegraph" the author's present bias since the evidence and arguments to be presented may best be understood and assessed in the light of their ultimate applicability to the major propositions to be asserted. It will be argued that habituation is at once a simple and phylogenetically primitive variety of conditioning, although not identical with it by any means, and that the degree to which a particular S-R correlation displays habituation, a property hereafter referred to as habituability, significantly influences the manner in which conditioning may be accomplished and also influences the consequences of the conditioning procedure for the particular S-R. The suggestion will be made that the traditional distinction between "classical" and "instrumental" conditioning may be understood in a new and entirely different way when the habituability of the S-R in question is considered.

Since these two logical approaches to studying the relationship between habituation and conditioning are relatively independent of one another, the plan of this chapter will be to consider them sequentially. First, the possibility that habituation is a simple and more primitive manifestation of conditioning will be evaluated. Second, the role of S-R habituability in conditioning will be considered.

II. Habituation as a Simpler Variety of Conditioning

Psychologists tend to define conditioning rather broadly to include any relatively permanent change in behavior potential which results from previous behavioral practice. Explicitly excluded from the category of conditioning are changes in behavior potential which result from maturation or disease or other trauma, even though these too may be more or less permanent. The term relatively permanent is intended to exclude changes of short duration such as those resulting from effector fatigue, sensory adaption, and, allegedly, habituation. Among these three types of relatively temporary changes in behavior potential resulting from prior behavior, habituation has admittedly been the least understood. Although it is commonly agreed that habituation is a CNS rather than a peripheral phenomenon, and, at least in this respect, is somewhat like conditioning, recovery from habituation following nonstimulation has been a persuasive basis for distinguishing between it and conditioning (Rosvold, 1959) since conditioning is most frequently thought of as a durable change.

Even those subspecies of conditioning which are procedurally highly similar to habituation, for example, extinction, are thought to be more complex (Razran, 1971), although it does not seem illogical on procedural grounds to refer to extinction as habituation of conditioned responses, or to refer to habituation as extinction of unconditioned responses. As will be noted below, Razran's assertion that extinction and habituation differ in

that the former but not the latter may be affected by proprioceptive feed-back and cognition (Razran, 1971, p. 30) may be questionable empirically.*
Furthermore, the similarities and differences between the procedures and outcomes of habituation and *temporal* conditioning provide yet another unplumbed area of possibly significant study.

A. Retention of Habituation

During the past 5 years, the author and his students have been investiga-ting the question of whether habituation may be differentiated from con-ditioning solely on the grounds of its dissipation over time in the absence of continued response elicitation. This research effort stems from the common sense notion and frequent observation that the tendency to become non-reactive to certain stimulus events as a result of their repeated occurrence does not totally vanish with rest and also from the theoretical proposition that repeated elicitation of either conditioned responses (CR's) or uncon-ditioned responses (UCR's) should have effects that differ only to the extent that their S-R strengths differ. Even a traditional UCR such as salivation to the presentation of food in the mouth may be construed as an "evolutionary" CR, especially since it extinguishes (or should we say habituates?) with repeated elicitation in an esophagostomized dog. Accordingly, "temporary" connections such as those which result from Pavlovian conditioning should simply extinguish more readily than "permanent" connections habituate, but not necessarily by means of different neural processes.

Our first formal experimental investigation of this problem began with a simple empirical question: If a UCR is weakened by repeated presentation of the stimulus in relatively massed trials, and if an interval of one week without further exposure to the experimental setting or stimulus transpires, would a second habituation session require as many trials to achieve the same criterion of habituation as had been required in the first session? This study was conducted by Dr. Alan Goldstein (Kimmel and Goldstein, 1967) using the galvanic skin response (GSR) of human subjects (Ss) and both visual and auditory stimuli of brief duration and moderately weak intensity. The college student Ss received repeated presentations of either a white light or a pure tone until two successive presentations without measurable response (or 50 trials) had been given. At the conclusion of this procedure the S was dismissed from the laboratory and instructed to return exactly one week later at the same hour. The second session was exactly the same as the first, with the same criterion of habituation being employed. At the con-

---

*In personal communication, Razran states that he by no means meant to imply that habituation, unlike extinction, is unaffected by cognition and proprioceptive feedback, but only that the basic mechanism of habituation, unlike that of extinction, cannot be attri-buted to them. [cf. Razran (1971) p. 30. footnote].

clusion of the second session, the *S* was again asked to return to the laboratory one week later for a third habituation session. The third session was run to the same criterion of habituation as had been employed previously.

Figure 1 presents the data of principal interest, the average number of trials needed to attain the habituation criterion on each session, separately plotted for the light and the tone stimuli. The data shown in Fig. 1 indicate quite clearly that the number of trials needed to reach the habituation criterion declined from one habituation session to the next. Analysis of variance of these data established that the decline was highly significant statistically and that it did not interact significantly with the type of stimulus employed. Our interpretation of these results was that habituation, at least as it was defined in this study, is *not* an entirely temporary state of affairs which dissipates completely when the stimulus is withheld. Rather, since there were clear-cut savings in the trials data from one habituation session to the next, one week later, it was argued that retention of habituation (i.e., learning) was demonstrated by this study.

Another aspect of the results of the Kimmel and Goldstein experiment which deserves attention is the fact that while the magnitude of the GSR on the first trial of each successive session did not decline significantly (in fact, it increased from the first week to the second week) the magnitude of the GSR on the second trial of each successive session declined significantly.

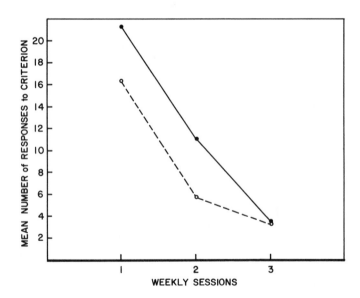

Fig. 1. Mean number of trials to habituation criterion on successive weekly sessions for light and tone: (●) light and (○) tone. From Kimmel and Goldstein (1967).

This finding conflicts with Razran's assertation that proprioception plays no significant role in habituation (but does in conditioning) since the most reasonable interpretation of the decline in second-trial but not first-trial GSR magnitudes is that proprioceptive stimuli resulting from the response on the first trial acquired inhibitory properties quite apart from whatever inhibition accrued to the habituation stimulus itself.

A study done by Dr. Paul Bishop (Bishop and Kimmel, 1969) followed Goldstein's work and investigated the shape of the habituation retention function over time without stimulation. Essentially the same habituation procedure was employed in this study as in the previous one, except that only pure tones were used. In the first session a criterion of two successive nonresponses was again employed.

Figure 2 shows Bishop's habituation data. The second habituation session was administered to different groups of Ss either immediately, 20 minutes later, 24 hours later, 1 week later, 4 weeks later, or 6 months later. Substantial savings (over 40%) in number of trials needed to reach the habituation criterion were found in the two shortest interval groups, and veritably no savings were found in the two longest interval groups. In general, the retention function resembled Ebbinghous' classic verbal retention curve in that about half of what is "learned" is "forgotten" within 24 hours and the remainder is relatively stable thereafter.

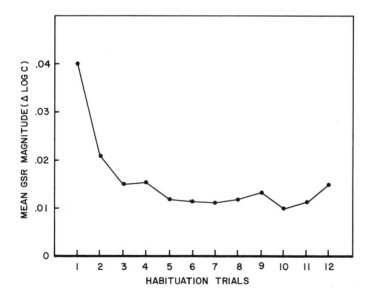

Fig. 2. Mean magnitude of first-session GSR to tone in combined habituation groups. From Bishop and Kimmel (1969).

Bishop's experiment also included groups of Ss who were run in a typical GSR conditioning procedure, up to their peak acquisition GSR magnitudes, and then extinguished at different time intervals thereafter. Electric shock was used as the unconditioned stimulus (UCS). The same time intervals between the two sessions were used for the conditioning groups as had been used for the habituation groups. While the retention of habituation found in the habituation groups appeared to lend itself to the interpretation that habituation *is* a variety of learning (by virtue of not being totally temporary), the conditioning retention data were so completely different from what had been found in the habituation groups as to rule out the possibility that the two are simply minor variations of the same basic phenomenon. Both in terms of GSR magnitude on the first extinction trial and number of trials needed to attain an extinction criterion of two successive nonresponses, no differences were found among the various interval conditions in the conditioning groups. In fact, the GSR on the first extinction trial did not differ in magnitude from that on the last acquisition trial, no matter how long the interval between acquisition and extinction. Thus, 100% retention of CR magnitude was shown on the first extinction trial even as long as 6 months after acquisition. Furthermore, apparently because of the novel acquisition procedure of giving paired trials only up to two trials beyond the peak magnitude, resistance to extinction, averaging near 40 trials, was astonishingly higher than that which is typically obtained in GSR conditioning.

B. Habituation and Temporal Conditioning

Another approach which we have taken to the problem of comparing habituation and conditioning is to employ a temporal conditioning procedure since the temporal conditioning procedure avoids the complexities of double stimulation in classical conditioning (as well as controlling the number and type of stimuli employed in the two procedures to be compared). It should be noted that temporal conditioning and habituation differ procedurally only with respect to whether the temporal spacing of the sequence of stimuli during "acquisition" is regular or irregular.

In order to provide as direct a comparison between the habituation and conditioning procedures as possible, the magnitude of the UCR during acquisition was the measure of principal interest. Several studies have established that diminution of the UCR is a normal concomitant of classical eyelid (Kimble and Ost, 1961), heart rate (Fitzgerald, 1966), and GSR (Kimmel, 1966) conditioning. The question we wished to answer was whether diminution of the UCR in temporal (classical) conditioning is in any significant way different from diminution of responding in habituation. The first study on this question was done by Dr. Virginia Pendergrass (Pendergrass and Kimmel, 1968), employing a 90-dB, 1000-Hz tone and the human GSR. Because prior work in our laboratory suggested that diminution of the UCR in classical conditioning is accelerated by having the S judge the intensity of the UCS (E. Kimmel, 1967), a factorial experiment involving stimulus regularity–irregularity and judgment–nonjudgment was conducted. Each S received 40 presentations of the pure tone. The temporal conditioning groups received the tones spaced exactly 40 seconds apart throughout, while the habituation groups received them unsystematically at intervals varying from 20 to 60 seconds with a mean of 40 seconds. Half of the Ss in each of these conditions were required to judge the intensity of each tone after it was terminated by rotating a plastic lever through a rotary distance which was proportional to the perceived intensity. The other half simply listened to the tones.

The results of this experiment were somewhat surprising. Figures 3 and 4 show the average magnitude of the UCR in blocks of two trials for the nonjudgment and judgment groups, respectively.

The simplest contrast between the effects of temporal conditioning and habituation on diminution of the UCR was seen in the two groups which did not judge the intensity of the stimulus on each trial (Fig. 3). Here it was found that substantially greater reduction in the GSR elicited by the tone occurred in the habituation group, which had received a variable temporal interval between successive tones, than in the temporal conditioning group, which had received the tones at fixed 40-second intervals. On the basis of this comparison, it may be possible that yet another important difference between habituation and conditioning in human Ss exists. However, it must be pointed out that no conventional evidence for the acquisition of temporal conditioning, in the form of GSR's which anticipated the regularly occurring tone, was found in the nonjudgment groups. Our interpretation of the difference in the course of UCR magnitudes in the two nonjudgment groups was that the fixed temporal interval between the tones somehow interferes with habituation, the latter being shown in the variable interval group. This may result from attentional consequences of the fixed time intervals. When the S was required to judge the intensity of the tones, a condition in which evidence for temporal conditioning was shown in the anticipatory GSR data, the judgment task interfered with habituation in the variable interval condition, while the temporal conditioning group's UCR's showed somewhat more diminution of the UCR. Interference with habituation resulting from the judgment task (Fig. 4) may be the same attentional phenomenon as has been reported by Garcia-Ausst et al. (1964), who found that habituation of cortical evoked potentials elicited by repetitive visual stimuli was disrupted when the S was required to attend to and count the number of stimuli presented. It may be that the critical similarity between the two

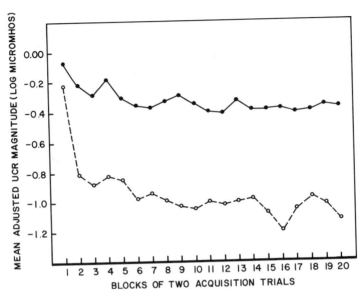

Fig. 3. Mean adjusted UCR magnitudes during acquisition in blocks of two trials for the nonjudgment groups: (●) fixed and (○) variable. From Pendergrass and Kimmel (1968).

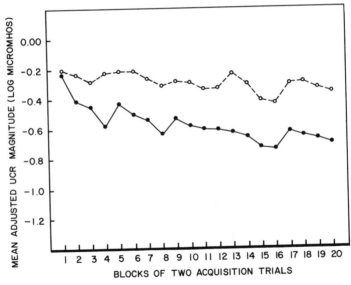

Fig. 4. Mean adjusted UCR magnitude during acquisition in blocks of two trials for the judgment groups: (●) fixed and (○) variable. From Pendergrass and Kimmel (1968).

tasks is that they both require that the S maintain careful attention to the stimuli, or it may be that a motivational effect resulting from the task requirement (i.e., elevated drive) was responsible.

In addition to identifying additional possible differences between habituation and conditioning, Pendergrass and Kimmel's (1968) results clearly conflict with Razran's assertion that cognition plays no role in habituation since the introduction of a cognitive (judgment) task definitely influenced the habituation phenomenon. Perhaps a more parsimonious version of Razran's proposition would be that cognition influences habituation to a lesser degree than it does conditioing or any other more complex processes, rather than not influencing it at all.

Further possibly important differences between habituation and temporal conditioning have been identified in a study by Kirk (1970). In this study the basic comparison between temporally regular and variable presentations of stimuli, which was employed by Pendergrass and Kimmel (1968), was followed by a probing phase in which the stimulus was delivered at some time earlier than the time used in the regularly spaced condition. The stimulus employed was an electric shock to the volar surface of the forearm. Each subject received 40 shocks during the first phase of the experiment. The subjects in the regularly spaced condition (temporal conditioning) received the shocks every 40 seconds. The subjects in the variable interval condition (habituation) received them at intervals ranging from 8 to 72 seconds with an average of 40 seconds. Figure 5 shows the course of UCR magnitude for the two groups during the first phase in 4 trial blocks. As is clear in the figure, the groups did not differ markedly in the manner in which their UCR's declined under the two conditions, although the quadratic component of the difference between their trends was significant. This quadratic trend effect reflected the slight tendency for the variable interval condition (habituation) to reach asymptote more rapidly, a result which is not unlike the Pendergrass and Kimmel (1968) data.

Following the first 40 presentations of the shock, each of the major experimental groups was divided randomly into five subgroups to receive the forty-first shock either 8, 16, 24, 32, or 40 seconds after the fortieth shock. Figure 6 shows the UCR magnitudes (as difference scores between trials 41 and 40) adjusted to account for the relative refractoriness affecting the response when only 8 seconds intervened between stimuli.

Since the Ss in the variable interval condition had experienced their first 40 shocks at varying temporal intervals, the size of the GSR on the forty-first trial did not depend upon the time at which it occurred, as is shown in the figure. However, the Ss in the regularly spaced condition, having had their first 40 shocks regularly spaced at 40-second intervals showed a definite downward trend in UCR magnitude as the interval between trials 40 and

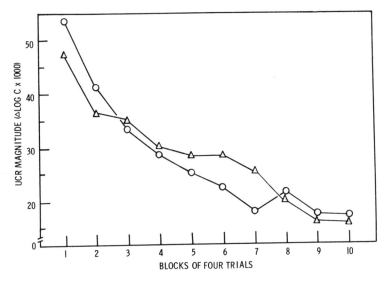

Fig. 5. Unconditioned response magnitude to repeated presentations of shock, in (○) habituation and (△) temporal conditioning, averaged in 4 trial blocks.

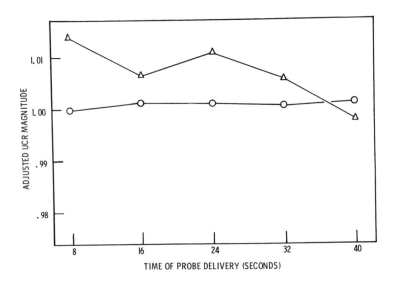

Fig. 6. Difference in UCR magnitudes between last habituation or temporal conditioning trial and probe trial, for (○) habituation and (△) temporal conditioning groups, as a function of time between last habituation or temporal conditioning trial and probe trial.

41 approached 40 seconds, the last temporal point being the only one at which the two groups made UCR's of approximately equal size. This more or less regular decline in the size of the UCR, as the time between trials 40 and 41 increased to 40 seconds, may have been the result of either a perceptual disparity effect (dishabituated orienting reflex), resulting from receiving the stimulus at an unexpected time, or a gradually increasing conditioned inhibitory process, as the internal proprioceptive stimuli between trials became more and more similar to those previously associated with the occurrence of the UCS, somewhat analogous to inhibition of delay in double-stimulation classical conditioning (cf. Kimmel and Greene, 1964). In either case, it is clear that the temporal conditioning situation produces results which differ from those of habituation, whether or not the latter is a "kind" of learning.

The present evidence from our laboratory on the question of whether habituation is a variety of conditioning may be summarized as follows. Retention of habituation over relatively long periods without elicitation of the response has been demonstrated with sufficient reliability to establish that habituation cannot be differentiated from conditioning simply on the grounds of its temporariness. However, relatively permanent as it may be, habituation is nevertheless not nearly as permanent as classical conditioning (Bishop and Kimmel, 1969). Furthermore, habituation, although procedurally very similar to temporal conditioning, is different from it in a number of important respects, particularly regarding the manner in which cognitive task variables influence the course of response diminution in it and conditioning. A conservative summary statement would be one that notes that habituation *is* somewhat like conditioning in being relatively permanent, but not as permanent. Perhaps its apparent temporariness results from the conjoint influence of sensitization as has been suggested by Groves and Thompson (1970). Furthermore, it is somewhat like conditioning in that proprioception and cognitive factors influence it, but not to the extent to which these factors influence conditioning. Perhaps habituation is a more primitive form of conditioning which is neither temporary nor noncognitive, but it is also not as dependent upon those higher nervous structures and processes which are typically assumed to influence conditioning. Exactly what the major differentia are remain to be determined empirically.

III. Habituability and Conditioning

Although the term conditioning has been used to mean Pavlovian conditioning up to the present point in this discussion, it will be used more broadly hereafter. In this section the term conditioning will refer both to what is traditionally referred to as classical or Pavlovian conditioning and to what is usually separately treated under the label instrumental or Thorndikian conditioning. The reason for this deviation from orthodox nomenclature will become clear in the presentation which follows. Conditioning hereafter will mean *any* change in behavior potential which results from prior behavioral practice. Whether it takes the forms known as Pavlovian or Thorndikian conditioning will be related to whether the modified S-R is or is not readily habituable.

A. Positive and Negative Feedback Reflexes

Although the relative habituability of an S-R may be thought of as a continuously variable property of the S-R, it will be of value to consider that all reflexes, or S-R correlations, may be reliably dichotomized into those which are positive feedback reflexes and those which are negative feedback reflexes (Kozak and Westerman, 1966).

Positive feedback reflexes are those whose motor acts tend to increase the afferent input to the CNS. Orienting and searching reflexes direct the sense organs toward the source of a stimulus as well as potentiating the primary sensory areas of the cerebral cortex for enhanced reception of these sensory inputs. Cleaning reactions direct the claws and limbs, the tongue and teeth, toward irritated parts of the skin. Scratching, licking, and biting all increase the stimulation of the skin in the irritated region. Sexual stimulation also sometimes results in reactions which mainly increase sexual stimulation. Negative feedback reflexes are those whose motor acts tend to reduce the afferent input to the CNS. The postural reflexes (e.g., righting in response to removal of support of a limb) reduce the afferentiation from both the muscles and the labyrinthian receptors. Protective or nociceptive reflexes tend to reduce nociceptive stimulation by withdrawal and escape as well as by reduction in sensory intake (closing of mouth, flaring of nostrils, etc.). Food intake reduces afferentiation both from the buccal and visceral cavities (the latter after some dalay), as well as from the chemoreceptors in the circulatory system. In addition to differing with regard to whether their motor acts tend to reduce or increase sensory stimulation, it is also true that these two types of reflexes differ with respect to whether they habituate easily or at all, and whether they function homeostatically as reinforcers, whether in Pavlovian or Thorndikian conditioning. Negative feedback reflexes are generally nonhabituable and reinforcing, while positive feedback reflexes tend to be plastic and habituable as well as usually being nonreinforcing.

Positive feedback reflexes, such as the orienting reflex, tend to be plastic reflexes in the sense that their relative strength appears to fluctuate according to the conditions of their elicitation. It is probably not adaptively accidental that all these positive feedback reflexes are eminently habituable since habituation prevents positive feedback reflexes from excessive increase as a result of self-excitation. Anyone who has scratched an irritating insect bite has learned of the self-perpetuating vicious circle of stimulus–response–stimulus which often occurs. In fact, in chronic thoracic spinal cats, whose neural feedback circuitry has been interrupted surgically, an exaggerated scratch reflex may get out of control and be easily converted into a generalized mass reaction of all muscles of the hind part of the body in the form of spinal fits (Kozak and Westerman, 1966).

Negative feedback reflexes, on the other hand, do not habituate in the long run. On the contrary, they show a tendency to increase with use (Shurager and Dykman, 1951) and they are difficult to extinguish (Soltysik, 1963). Monosynaptic reflex responses from muscle nerves normally do not habituate (Thompson and Spencer, 1966). Strong nociceptive stimuli, which do not habituate and show a progressive sensitization instead (Hogbarth and Kugelberg, 1958) are widely used as good reinforcers. And food reflexes, above all, are clearly nonhabituable, except following surgical intervention such as esophagostomy.

The easiest way of establishing a conditioned response of the Pavlovian type is to pair any member of the plastic, positive feedback reflexes with any member of the nonhabituating, negative feedback reflexes. By "repetition" of such pairing the plastic habituable reflex gives way to the nonhabituable one. As Kozak and Westerman have aptly suggested, "the homeostatic reflexes employ the plastic ones to attain the necessary feedback more efficiently and quickly" (1966, p. 537). It must be emphasized that the foregoing proposition holds only for Pavlovian conditioning.

In the case of free-operant Thorndikian conditioning, as has been pointed out previously (Kimmel, 1972), the stimulus antecedents of the modified response tend to be unidentified and are probably highly variable from occasion to occasion. It is important to note that variability of S-R elicitation is an established basis for either eliminating or greatly attentuating habituability of the S-R (Kimble and Ray, 1965). In the Kimble and Ray experiment, variable locations of tactile stimulation of one limb were compared with fixed repetitive stimulation of the other limb. In the case of fixed location, habituation was the result. But variable stimulation resulted in nonhabituation.

The general notion thus appears feasible that the principal factor determining whether the result of close temporal pairing of one reflex with another (with the second reflex being of the negative feedback, homeostatic type relative to the first) could be whether the first reflex is easily habituable or not. If the first reflex is easily habituable, its response will soon disappear and be replaced by some semblance of the second reflex (i.e., it will be "used" to attain feedback by the homeostatic reflex). If the first reflex is nonhabituable, or not easily habituable, it may gain in strength (sensitization?) and frequency, in the fashion of instrumental conditioning (i.e., it will use the reinforcement of a subsequent homeostatic reflex to enhance its own strength).

The basis of the nonhabituability of the first reflex may range from experimentally controlled factors (e.g., variability of stimulation and task factors requiring attention) to "natural" factors (negative neural feedback functioning in homeostasis). A proposition of this type, interesting as it may be at first glance, will obviously require a systematic research program, probably involving more than one research laboratory, for adequate empirical evaluation.

B. Empirical Approaches to Evaluation

The systematic empirical program currently underway in our laboratory involves two major lines of attack. Our first effort is concerned with unlearned, nonexperimentally established differences in reflex habituability, some of which have been observed informally previously in our conditioning work. To be specific, we have found that the unelicited base rates of GSR and vasomotor (VMR) behavior appear to differ under conditions of nonexperimental manipulation. We have found, further, that these two reflexes appear to differ in ease of instrumental (as well as classical) conditionability. Almost twice as many unelicited GSR's were observed than unelicited VMR's in the absence of experimental stimulation of manipulation by Kimmel and Kimmel (1967). When an instrumental reinforcement contingency (light presented to subject in dark room) was introduced in relation to either the GSR or the VMR for different subjects, we found that reinforcing the VMR had an instrumental conditioning effect (relative to a noncontingent control group) on both the VMR and the GSR responses. However, reinforcing the GSR had an instrumental conditioning effect (relative to noncontingent controls) only in the GSR data but had the opposite effect in the VMR data. To follow up on these highly complex and somewhat confusing findings, we decided to study simple habituation of the GSR and the VMR, simultaneously in the same subjects, using either very mild electric shock or brief cool air stimuli, and introducing the experimental variable of whether or not the S was required to judge the intensity of the stimulus following its presentation. The judgment task was introduced on the assumption that it would be likely to influence habituability of these reflexes, and, in further study, that their habituability might be related to whether or not and to what extent they could be modified instrumentally. This unpublished study was done by Mr. John Welch. Figures 7 and 8 show

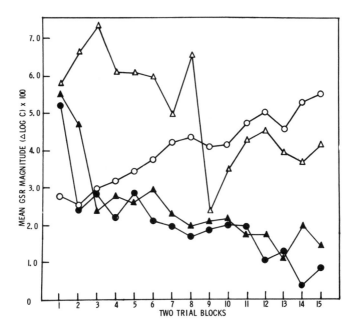

Fig. 7. Habituation of GSR to repeated presentations of S or A in J or NJ groups: (△) S-NJ, (○) S-J, (▲) A-NJ, and (●) A-J.

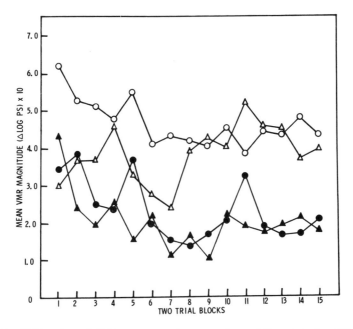

Fig. 8. Habituation of VMR to repeated presentations of S or A in J or NJ groups. Key same as in Fig. 7 legend.

the manner in which the size of the GSR and VMR habituated under shock and air stimulation, with Ss either judging or not judging the intensity of the stimulus in question.

Figure 7 shows the GSR magnitude data under conditions of either shock (S) or air (A) as stimulus and judgment (J) or nonjudgment (NJ) experimental conditions. It is quite clear in this figure that the GSR to cool air as a stimulus habituates quite readily, both under judgment and nonjudgment conditions. On the other hand, the size of the GSR to shock as a stimulus increased when the intensity of the shock had to be judged by the S, while it tended to show habituation under nonjudgment conditions. These results are somewhat like those found by Pendergrass and Kimmel (1968) insofar as the judgment task in that study also had a decidedly interfering effect on habituation of the GSR. In general, it could be said that the judgment variable had no influence on habituation of the GSR (or the VMR) when air was the stimulus used, but it definitely had an influence when shock was the stimulus to be judged. Judging the intensity of a shock is apparently a rather different psychological task situation from judging the intensity of air as a stimulus. Since we have previously found certain similarities in the effect of the judgment task when very loud pure tones or weak shocks were used as stimuli (Pendergrass and Kimmel, 1968; Kirk, 1970), it would appear to be profitable to extend investigation of the judgment effect with factorial variation of either tone or shock intensity.

As the data in Fig. 8 show, the VMR response was influenced by the requirement that stimulus intensity be judged in a rather different way from what was shown by the GSR. To be sure, when air was the stimulus to be judged, both the judgment and nonjudgment groups showed similar decremental effects characteristic of habituation. But judging the intensity of the shock seemed to have the effect of potentiating VMR habituation as compared with VMR habituation when shock intensity was *not* judged. Thus, the effect of the judgment task on habituation was in the opposite direction in the two response systems. What psychophysiological significance these differences may have remain to be studied and comprehended before this aspect of our research on the relationship between habituability and conditioning may be pursued, at least by means of the judgment variable as a device intended to influence habituability.

Another line of investigation is currently being pursued by Dr. Frank Terrant and the author. Again, the basic aim is to investigate an independent variable which may be shown to influence reflex habituability so that variations in habituability itself may then be studied in relation to conditioning. The first study in this current series is one in which Ss will be habituated to either a single stimulus which is repeatedly presented, to two which appear in an unsystematic alternating sequence, or to three unsystematically alternating stimuli. Each stimulus will always be presented singly on individual trials, but some Ss will experience only one stimulus, some will experience two, and some will experience three.

The basic response measure again is the GSR, although VMR responses are also being recorded for additional analysis. The stimuli being used are a light, a pure tone, and a very mild electric shock. Some Ss receive repeated presentations of only the light, some receive repeated presentations of only the tone, while some receive repeated presentations of only the weak shock. The foregoing Ss are all in the experimental condition in which only a single repeated stimulus is used for habituation. Another group of Ss receive two of the stimuli, presented separately on individual trials, either the light and the tone, the light and the shock, or the tone and the shock. Subjects in the third experimental group receive all three of the stimuli, presented separately on individual trials and in an unsystematic balanced order. The principal experimental hypothesis is that rate of habituation of the response will vary inversely with the number of different stimuli employed to elicit the habituating response, even though each single trial never involves more than a single stimulus. The most rapid habituation is expected when only a single stimulus is used; the least rapid is expected when three stimuli are used. This prediction is based in part upon the finding of Kimble and Ray (1965) that variable spatial locations of tactual stimulation attenuated habituation as compared with fixed spatial locations of stimulation.

Varying the number of different stimuli to be employed in habituation of a response is intended to bring under manipulative experimental control what the author believes is a major difference between the experimental conditions of classical and instrumental conditioning. In classical conditioning, normally, only a single conditioned stimulus is used, while in instrumental conditioning, the number of different stimuli which may antedate and elicit the conditioned response (e.g., in a Skinner box) is undoubtedly quite high. It has already been found that multiplicity of CS's in classical conditioning (delivered on separate trials) attenuates the conditioning obtained (Kimmel et al., 1962), as does multiplicity of either CS's. UCS's, or both (again, delivered on separate trials) (Kimmel and Reynolds, 1972). But while increasing the number of stimuli involved in the positive feedback reflex used as the first reflex in classical conditioning tends to interfere with the acquisition of classical conditioning, probably by interfering with its habituation, so that the negative feedback, homeostatic reflex which follows it may begin to "use" it, this manipulation should have exactly the opposite effect in fostering instrumental conditioning; that is, the greater the number of stimuli used to elicit the first reflex, the less it will habituate, and the greater the probability that an instrumental increase in responding will result.

C. Advantages and Disadvantages

It is both an advantage and a disadvantage that the preceding theoretical analysis must be evaluated using response systems as labile as the GSR or VMR are known to be. At the time that this author and his students first established that an autonomically mediated response *could* be modified by means of instrumental conditioning methods (Kimmel and Hill, 1960), the results were in direct conflict with a tradition of misbelief which had lasted over 30 years and had been promulgated (Miller and Konorski, 1928), defended (Kimble, 1961; Skinner, 1953), or acquiesced to (Dollard and Miller, 1950) by most major figures in psychology and psychophysiology on both sides of the Atlantic. It can be seen in retrospect that Skinner and Delabarre's (Skinner, 1938) futile attempt to condition the VMR instrumentally and Mowrer's equally ineffective effort with the GSR (Skinner, 1938) each involved easily habituable responses which were being elicited with single stimuli, an experimental condition which was most likely to result in habituation and failure to obtain instrumental effects. The first successful results (Kimmel and Hill, 1960) employed the unelicited GSR, thus dealing with a lower likelihood of habituation and a greater chance of obtaining instrumental effects. The later successful work done in Miller's laboratory (Miller, 1969), following the earlier breakthroughs in our laboratory, were done under circumstances which tended to increase non-habituability (e.g., spontaneous salivation and spontaneous intestinal contraction). The disadvantage referred to above stems from the fact that the GSR and VMR are very easily habituable reflexes and thus very, very, unlikely candidates for augmentation by instrumental conditioning, especially if elicited with few stimuli. The advantage, on the other hand, is that these reflexes are eminently classically conditionable because they are so easily habituable; yet their habituability may be controlled sufficiently so they can be studied "both" ways. Only by using reflexes of this type can the false dichotomies of operant and respondent behavior and classical and instrumental conditioning finally be purged altogether from our conceptual system. Thus, the overall goal of our earlier and current work on habituation and habituability is decidedly more ambitious and therefore requires closer scrutiny and more thorough empirical analysis than at first might be assumed.

References

Bishop, P. D., and Kimmel, H. D. (1969). Retention of habituation and conditioning. *J. Exp. Psychol.* **81**, 317–321.
Dollard, J., and Miller, N. E. (1950). "Personality and Psychotherapy." McGraw-Hill, New York.

Fitzgerald, R. D. (1966). Some effects of partial reinforcement with shock on classical conditioned heart rate in dogs. *Amer. J. Psychol.* **79**, 242–249.

Garcia-Ausst, E., Bagacz, J., and Vangulli, A. (1964). Effects of attention and inattention upon visual evoked responses. *Electroencephalogr. Clin. Neurophysiol.* **17**, 136–143.

Groves, P. M., and Thompson, R. F. (1970). Habituation: A dual-process theory. *Psychol. Rev.* **77**, 419–450.

Hogbarth, K. E., and Kugelberg, E. (1958). Plasticity of the human abdominal skin reflex. *Brain* **81**, 305–318.

Kimble, G. A. (1961). "Hilgard and Marquis' Conditioning and Learning." Appleton, New York.

Kimble, G. A., and Ost, J. W. P. (1961). A conditioned inhibitory process in eyelid conditioning. *J. Exp. Psychol.* **61**, 150–156.

Kimble, D. P., and Ray, R. S. (1965). Reflex habituation and potentiation in *Rana pipiens. Anim. Behav.* **13**, 530–533.

Kimmel, E. (1967). Judgments of UCS intensity and diminution of the UCR in classical GSR conditioning. *J. Exp. Psychol.* **73**, 532–543.

Kimmel, H. D. (1966). Inhibition of the unconditioned response in classical conditioning. *Psychol. Rev.* **73**, 232–240.

Kimmel, H. D. (1972). Conditioning at the crossroads. *In* "Behavior Therapy at the Crossroads: Problems and Prospects" (D. F. Jacobs and M. R. Denny, eds.). Case-Western Reserve Univ. Press, Cleveland, Ohio (in press).

Kimmel, H. D., and Goldstein, A. J. (1967). Retention of habituation of the GSR to visual and auditory stimulation. *J. Exp. Psychol.* **73**, 401–404.

Kimmel, H. D., and Greene, W. A. (1964). Disinhibition in GSR conditioning as a function of the number of CS-UCS trials and temporal location of the vowel stimulus. *J. Exp. Psychol.* **68**, 567–572.

Kimmel, H. D., and Hill, F. A. (1960). Operant conditioning of the GSR. *Psychol. Rep.* **7**, 555–562.

Kimmel, H. D., and Kimmel, E. (1967). Inter-effector influences in operant autonomic conditioning. *Psychon. Sci.* **9**, 191–192.

Kimmel, H. D., and Reynolds, T. W. (1972). On the locus of extinctive inhibition. *Acta Neurobiol. Exp.* **31**, 1971, 227–236.

Kimmel, H. D., Hill, F. A., and Fowler, R. L. (1962). Inter-sensory generalization in compound classical conditioning. *Psychol. Rep.* **11**, 631–636.

Kirk, W. E. (1970). Unconditioned response magnitude of the galvanic skin response in temporal conditioning and in habituation. Unpublished Doctoral Dissertation, Ohio University, Athens.

Kozak, W., and Westerman, R. A. (1966). Basic patterns of plastic change in the mammalian nervous system. *Symp. Soci. Exp. Biol.* **20**, 509–544.

Miller, N. E. (1969). Learning of visceral and glandular responses. *Science* **163**, 434–445.

Miller, S., and Konorski, J. (1928). Sur une forme particuliere des reflexes conditionels. *C.R. Soc. Biol.* **99**, 1155–1157.

Pendergrass, V. E., and Kimmel, H. D. (1968). UCR diminution in temporal conditioning and habituation. *J. Exp. Psychol.* **77**, 1–6.

Razran, G. (1971). "Mind in Evolution." Houghton, Boston, Massachusetts.

Rosvold, H. E. (1959). Physiological psychology. *Annu. Rev. Psychol.* **10**, 415–454.

Shurager, P. S., and Dykman, R. A. (1951). Walking spinal carnivores. *J. Comp. Physiol. Psychol.* **44**, 252–262.

Skinner, B. F. (1938). "The Behavior of Organisms." Appleton, New York.

Skinner, B. F. (1953). "Science and Human Behavior." Macmillan, New York.

Soltysik, S. (1963). Inhibitory feedback in avoidance conditioning. *Bol. Inst. Estud. Med. Biol. [Univ. Nac. Auton. Mex.]* **21**, 433–449.

Thompson, R. F., and Spencer, W. A. (1966). Habituation: A model phenomenon for the study of neuronal substrates of behavior. *Psychol. Rev.* **73**, 16–43.

Chapter 7
A Dual-Process Theory of Habituation: Theory and Behavior[1]

RICHARD F. THOMPSON, PHILIP M. GROVES[2], TIMOTHY J. TEYLER, AND RICHARD A. ROEMER

I. Introduction

Response to environmental change is the most fundamental behavioral property of organisms. If the stimulus does not have strong consequences for the organism, repetition results in decrement or habituation of the response. If the consequences are stronger, the response may increase or sensitize with repetition. These two phenomena, habituation and sensitization, are perhaps the most elementary forms of behavioral plasticity. If a strong extra stimulus is given following habituation of a response, to

[1]This work was supported by Research Scientist Award MH 06650 from the National Institute of Mental Health, research grant NS 07661 from the National Institutes of Health, research grant MH 19314 from the National Institute of Mental Health, and grant GB 14665 from the National Science Foundation (RFT), postdoctoral fellowship MH 35534 (TJT) from the National Institute of Mental Health, predoctoral fellowship MH 42399 (PMG) from National Institute of Mental Health, predoctoral fellowship MH 48912 (RAR) from National Institute of Mental Health, and Research Training Biological Sciences Grant MH 11095 from the National Institute of Mental Health.

[2]Present address: Department of Psychology, University of Colorado, Boulder, Colorado 80302.

some other stimulus, the response typically increases or "dishabituates." Thompson and Spencer (1966) first presented evidence that dishabituation is in fact a superimposed sensitization rather than a specific disruption only of the habituated response, and they suggested that the amplitude of response to repeated stimulation depends on the balance existing between these two processes. Groves and Thompson (1970) recently developed this idea into a dual-process theory of habituation in which the strength of behavioral response elicited by repeated stimulation is assumed to be the net outcome of two inferred independent processes of habituation and sensitization.

In abbreviated form the basic assumptions are as follows:

1. Every stimulus that evokes a behavioral response has two properties: It elicits a response and influences the "state" of the organism. The S-R pathway is the most direct route through the central nervous system from stimulus to discrete motor response, however circuitous, redundant, and variable that pathway may be and regardless of whether the response is learned or unlearned. State is the general level of excitation, arousal, activation, tendency to respond, etc., of the organism.

2. Repetition of an effective stimulus results in an inferred decremental process in the S-R pathway which may be termed habituation.

(a) During habituation training, habituation develops exponentially and reaches an asymptotic level.

(b) The rate of development and degree of relative habituation are directly related to stimulus frequency and inversely related to stimulus intensity. Frequency has strong effect and intensity a weak effect on habituation.

(c) Upon cessation of the habituating stimulus, habituation decays spontaneously (spontaneous recovery).

(d) Repeated series of habituation training and spontaneous recovery result in progressively more habituation.

(e) Response habituation will exhibit generalization to a test stimulus to the extent that the habituating and test stimuli activate common "habituation" elements.

3. Presentation of an effective stimulus results in an inferred incremental process in a state of excitation or tendency to respond of the organism which may be termed sensitization.

(a) The process of sensitization occurs in state system(s) but not in S-R pathways.

(b) During habituation training, sensitization first grows and then decays.

(c) The amount and duration of sensitization are directly related to stimulus intensity. At higher intensities, sensitization is directly related to stimulus frequency. At low intensities there may be little or no sensitization.

(d) Upon cessation of a stimulus that has produced sensitization, sensitization decays spontaneously.

(e) Repeated presentations of a sensitizing stimulus result in progressively less sensitization, that is, sensitization decreases or habituates.

(f) Response sensitization will exhibit generalization to a test stimulus to the extent that the sensitizing and test stimuli activate common sensitization elements.

(g) Dishabituation, the increase in a habituated response following presentation of a stimulus other than the habituation stimulus, is simply an instance of sensitization.

(h) Under certain circumstances (strong stimulus presented regularly at relatively slow rate) temporal conditioning of sensitization of state may occur.

4. The two processes of habituation and sensitization occur and develop independently of one another but interact to yield the final response output function. Habituation may be primarily "phasic" in its action on response output, while sensitization may be primarily "tonic."

The basic idea is illustrated in Fig. 1. The solid line is an example of behavioral response to repeated stimulation. The two dashed lines represent hypothetical processes of habituation (H) and sensitization (S) which sum to give the net behavioral outcome, here a brief period of response sensitization followed by pronounced response habituation. As we indicated (Groves and Thompson, 1970), this general form of behavioral response, increment followed by decrement, has been obtained in a wide variety of habituation experiments ranging from human galvanic skin response (GSR)

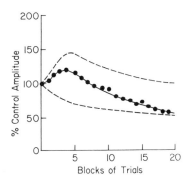

Fig. 1. Inferred processes of sensitization (upper dashed line) and habituation (lower dashed line) hypothesized to develop with repeated stimulation and add together to yield characteristic behavioral outcome (filled circles and solid line) of initial increase and subsequent decrease in response amplitude to a repeated stimulus. Actual data points (filled circles) are hindlimb flexion reflex of acute spinal cat.

to acoustic startle in intact rat to hindlimb flexion reflex in acute spinal cat.

The theory was presented both at a molar level, as above, and at a molecular-neural level by assuming the existence of two subpopulations of "plastic" interneurons, one in the S-R pathways that code habituation (type H neurons) and another reflecting state (type S neurons). Extensive behavioral and neural evidence supporting the theory was reviewed at length (Groves and Thompson, 1970). Possible neural mechanisms are considered further in the companion chapter in Volume II of this treatise (Groves and Thompson, 1972). These discussions will not be reduplicated here. Instead, we will recast certain of the assumptions more precisely, deduce a number of specific predictions that can be tested from the literature, and present new supporting evidence.

There are at least two major conceptual problems concerning the definition of habituation. One has to do with the definition of behavioral response habituation and the other relates to level of definition. "Given that a response is elicited by a stimulus, response habituation is a decrement in response as a result of repetition of the stimulus." This operational definition of response habituation was established some years ago (Harris, 1943; Humphrey, 1933; Prosser and Hunter, 1936) and has attained widespread acceptance (Thompson and Spencer, 1966). Perhaps because of its very simplicity, substantial confusion has recently developed about the precise meaning of the definition, particularly in relation to parametric effects of stimulus and training variables. We will expand this point immediately below.

The other problem concerns failure to distinguish between type I and type II definitions of habituation. It is commonly treated both as an operationally defined phenomenon (type I) and as an inferred construct (type II) often withoug clear distinction. Even when the distinction has been made (e.g., see Davis and Wagner, 1968), type II habituation has been used as an "empty" construct, or at best one whose properties are implicit. To assert that repeated stimulation results in response decrement because habituation (type II) has occurred is of course circular and represents no significant advance over the assertion that it happens because God makes it happen. To be of use, a type II definition must include hypothetical properties permitting measurable consequences to be inferred or deduced. The dual-process theory (Groves and Thompson, 1970), and its further development here, represents an attempt to provide an explicit type II definition of habituation at both molar and molecular levels that is amenable to experimental test. We use response habituation to refer to the type I operational definition and habituation for the theoretical construct (Groves and Thompson, 1970).

In an earlier review (Thompson and Spencer, 1966), we summarized nine parametric effects of stimulus and training variables on response habituation. Most of these have been accepted by other workers. Hinde (1970) was perhaps the only authority to take serious issue, paying us the dubious compliment of devoting an extensive, and sometimes surprisingly polemic, article to criticism of the nine characteristics of habituation. His article appears to provide illustration of the confusion that results when type I and type II definitions are not distinguished. The nine characteristics of habituation we abstracted from the literature simply described the most commonly observed properties of behavioral response to repeated stimulation. In his critique, Hinde employed the term habituation both for behavioral responses and to mean an inferred process, often without distinction. Behavior, obviously, is measured as performance, which has only an inferred relationship to hypothetical explanatory constructs. Hinde reiterated the point that certain responses, particularly of individual animals, do not always clearly reveal a hypothetical process of habituation. Given all the

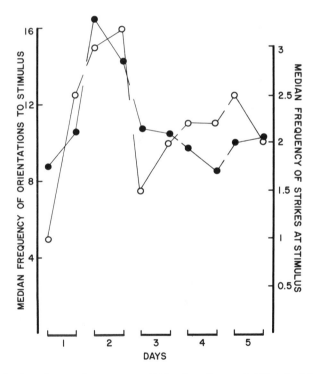

Fig. 2. Waning of aggressive responses [(●) orientations and (○) strikes] by the three-spined stickleback to male models, sampled at beginning and end of each daily 1-minute observation period. From Peeke *et al.* (1969).

variables that influence performance it would be most surprising if such were the case. It is unnecessary to go over Hinde's criticisms in detail—they are more than adequately covered by our earlier theoretical analysis (Groves and Thompson, 1970, which was completed prior to the appearance of Hinde's paper).

A more general issue appears to underlie Hinde's dissatisfaction: The real or natural behavior of animals is too rich and complex ever to be related to more elementary underlying processes or mechanisms. This in turn may reflect the aversion many ethologically oriented behaviorists have to more analytic approaches. Hinde emphasized natural behaviors in his discussion, particularly mobbing in the chaffinch (it is unclear, incidentally, why this is any more real or natural than rat startle). To counter this critique, we herewith provide further supporting examples for the dual-process theory drawn largely from more "natural" behaviors.

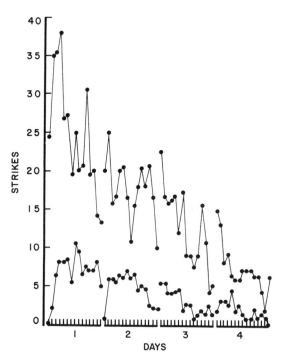

Fig. 3. Habituation of aggression (strikes) by three-spined sticklebacks to live conspecifics (top graph) and models of conspecifics (bottom graph) analyzed in successive 1-minute sessions for each day. From Peeke (1969).

In a series of studies on responses in natural environments by fish, Peeke, Herz, and associates (Peeke, 1969; Peeke *et al.*, 1969, 1971; Peeke and Peeke, 1970) have provided many striking examples of increments and subsequent decrements in responses to repeated stimulation beautifully consistent with our dual-process theory. Examples are given in Figs. 2–6 of responses to repeated presentations of live conspecifics and wooden models, measuring strikes, displays, and bites (see figure legends). As they noted, the periods of response measurement are critical—too large time blocks wash out initial

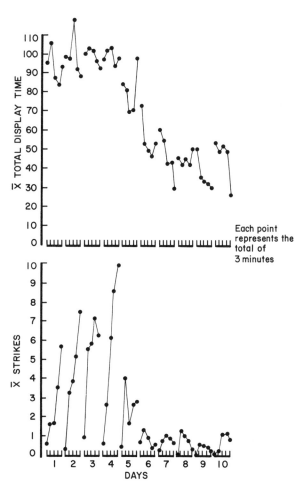

Fig. 4. Habituation of aggressive displays and strikes in Siamese fighting fish to a conspecific analyzed in successive 3-minute sessions for each day. From Peeke and Peeke (1970).

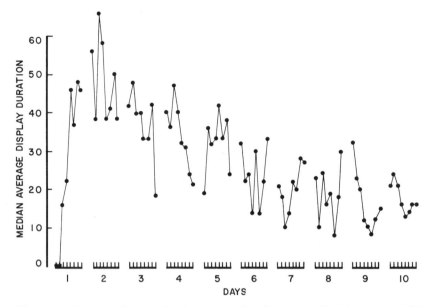

Fig. 5. Habituation of aggressive interactions in adjacently territorial convict cichlids analyzed in successive $2\frac{1}{2}$-minute sessions for each day. Replated from data from Peeke *et al.* (1971).

response sensitization. All of the data shown in these figures can be reconstructed by summating our two hypothetical processes of sensitization and habituation.

In another natural behavior, Ewert and Ingle (1972) presented clear evidence that sensitization occurs parallel with and independent of habituation of prey catching by frogs and toads. Ingle (1971) also made the important observation that alcohol weakened habituation and unmasked sensitization for the first test trial in this situation.

Human psychophysiological data provide many examples consistent with our dual-process theory. Data from hindlimb spinal flexion reflex of acute spinal cat (from Groves and Thompson, 1970) and intact human skin potential level (from Raskin *et al.*, 1969) to repeated stimuli of different intensities are compared in Fig. 7. The form and temporal course of response are strikingly similar. Strong stimuli yield lesser and shorter duration response sensitization followed by response habituation and weak stimuli yield virtually pure response habituation. These results are precisely what would be expected from the interaction of two independent processes of sensitization and habituation.

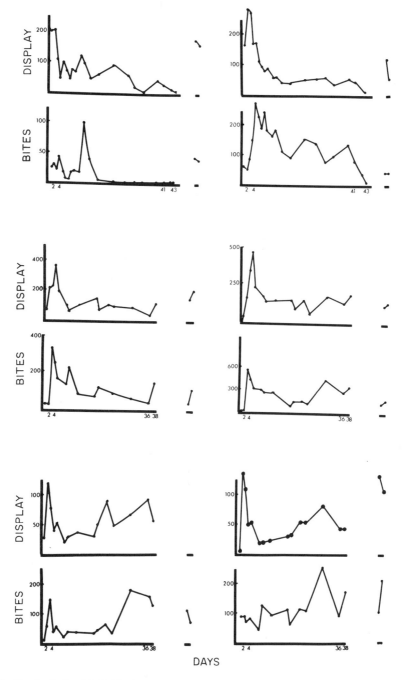

Fig. 6. Analysis of individual response patterns for displays and bites of cichlids, *op. cit.* in Fig. 5. Note the almost invarient initial sensitization, followed by habituation.

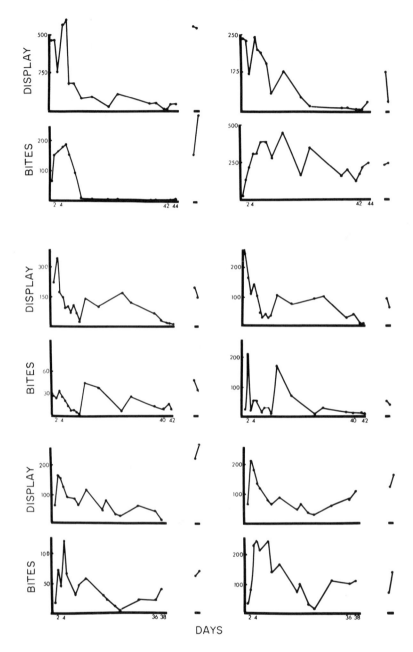

Fig. 6. (cont.)

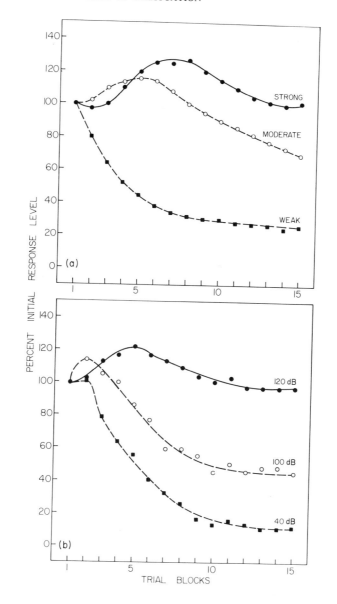

Fig. 7. Examples of behavioral response to repeated stimulation at different intensities illustrating net output of hypothetical habituation and sensitization processes suggested by our dual-process theory. (a) Hindlimb flexion reflex of acute spinal cat to skin shocks and (b) skin potential base level response of normal human *S*s to tones.

In an important recent paper, Amsel (1972) has developed a theory of partial reinforcement learning in terms of a construct he defined as persistence, closely related to habituation. Amsel analyzed the pronounced disrupting effects on learning of stimuli that interfere with ongoing approach behavior in appetitive partial reinforcement learning situations in animals. Occurrence of such stimuli results in marked disruption or sensitization, which rapidly habituates or decays, which in turn increases the resistance of the goal-approach behavior to disruption by the interfering stimuli. This treatment provides an interesting approach in which a view of habituation and sensitization resembling our dual-process theory is incorporated into a more general theory of reinforced learning.

A clear example of dishabituation by altered extraneous stimulation with rapid subsequent decay to habituated level was provided us in unpublished data (see Fig. 8) on pecking by pigeons from Miss Jo Edwards and Dr. Robert Isaacson, Department of Psychology, University of Florida, Gainsville. Animals were on a tandem FI 2 minutes after which a peck would yield food. A yellow light was on. They habituated to this situation (left portions of graphs). At the break in the graphs, the light was changed to blue and a tone given. Neither blue light nor tone had previously occurred. The immediate rise and rapid decay of response rate closely parallels the independent sensitization process we postulate.

Finally, Ratner (1972) has provided a lovely example of initial sensitization followed by habituation of anterior sucker release response to repeated light stimulation by the leech *Macrobdella decora* (see Fig. 9). The data for

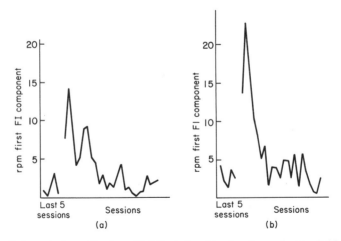

Fig. 8. Independent sensitization of habituated pecking by pigeons (see text). (a) Bird one and (b) bird two. Unpublished observations from Edwards and Isaacson.

initial sensitization and habituation were obtained in a single session with light presented 2 seconds and interstimulus interval of 10 seconds. A retention test was given 24 hours and second test 48 hours later. Note also the pronounced long-term persistence of habituation over days.

II. The Problem of Stimulus Intensity

The effect of stimulus intensity on response habituation poses interesting problems. It was asserted that "the weaker the stimulus, the more rapid and/ or more pronounced is (response) habituation. Strong stimuli may yield no significant habituation" (Thompson and Spencer, 1966, p. 19). More recently (Groves and Thompson, 1970) we demonstrated that repetition of very strong stimuli tend to yield increased response (i.e., response sensitization) rather than response habituation. Consequently, over a wide range of stimulus intensities the earlier described relationship must obtain for behavioral measures.

This general effect of stimulus intensity has been challenged in several recent studies where intensity of the stimulus is altered between initial presentations, habituation training, and final test presentations (e.g., Davis and Wagner, 1968; Wickelgren, 1967). The basic issue here concerns the type I operational definition of habituation (see above). According to this definition, the only required procedure, indeed the necessary and sufficient condition for habituation, if it occurs at all, is repetition of the stimulus. Alteration of any property of the stimulus, other than presenting it repeatedly, goes beyond the definition. Results of experiments where stimulus intensity is altered between habituation training and testing cannot therefore legiti-

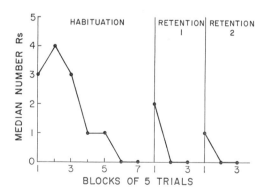

Fig. 9. Sucker release responses for a group of leeches given 2-second light every 16 seconds (habituation), and tested at 24 hours (retention 1) and 48 hours (retention 2). From Ratner (1972).

mately be used to characterize the effect of stimulus intensity on response habituation. Such experiments in fact provide measures of generalization of habituation along the dimension of stimulus intensity.

An analogy with conditioning clarifies the point. In a standard experiment CS intensity is held constant during training and testing. If the effect of stimulus intensity is studied, different groups (or conditions in within-subjects designs) are trained at different CS intensities and compared with control groups or conditions having corresponding (i.e., identical) CS intensities. If the intensity of the CS is altered between training and testing, the experiment becomes a study of stimulus intensity generalization; the degree of generalization is measured by comparing strength of conditioning to the altered test intensity against strength of conditioning to the training intensity (see, e.g., Hovland, 1937).

In an exactly analogous manner, if the intensity of a habituating stimulus is altered between habituation training and testing, the difference in response strength provides some measure of generalization along the dimension of stimulus intensity and *not* a measure of effect of stimulus intensity on degree of response habituation. It may of course be related, but only to the degree and in the form that generalization occurs. This point is of critical importance. As will be shown below (see also Thompson, 1965, 1969; Thompson and Spencer, 1966) the characteristics of generalization of response habituation permit inferences about possible underlying mechanisms.

An interesting study by Davis and Wagner (1968) illustrated the point. All animals (intact rats—acoustic startle response) were tested at four stimulus intensities, then given habituation training at one or another of two of the intensities, and tested at all four intensities. The overall finding was that groups given the more intense tone during habituation showed lower response strength, measured as percent of startle responses, than groups habituated to the less intense tone. From this, the erroneous conclusion might be drawn that habituation training to stronger stimuli produces greater response habituation. Such is not the case. For the two groups trained and tested at constant intensities of 108 or 120 dB, the final response level is much lower for the 108-dB group. When the difference in initial response resulting from stimulus intensity is factored out by computing response decrement relative to initial response level, the degree of response habituation exhibited by the two groups is about the same, a not too surprising finding in view of the relatively small difference in intensity.

III. Properties of Habituation

The assumptions of the dual-process theory given above are somewhat less than precise; the properties of habituation and sensitization are not clearly defined. In this section we will attempt further specification of habituation and deduce testable consequences. To simplify, the process of sensitization will be ignored here. Depending on the response system, it is possible to minimize or exclude sensitization by using stimuli that are not too intense, giving extensive habituation training to asymptotic response levels, and using measures such as percent response occurrence that are insensitive to sensitization.

A. Effect of Stimulus Frequency on Habituation

As noted above, habituation was assumed to develop exponentially (i.e., reach an asymptote), exhibit generalization, and recover spontaneously. These characteristics are widely accepted. We made the further assumptions that habituation was directly (and strongly) related to stimulus frequency and inversely (and weakly) related to stimulus intensity. There is, of course, nothing imperative about these assumptions—they seemed most reasonable in terms of the behavioral literature. Simpler assumptions can be made. Thus, for stimulus frequency, unless the total number of stimuli is held constant, number of stimuli and rate of presentation are confounded. Under limited conditions where (1) stimulus rate is slower than about 1 per second, (2) no sensitization occurs, i.e., weak stimuli and low to intermediate frequency, (3) significant spontaneous recovery does not occur between stimuli, and (4) other processes such as refractoriness and receptor fatigue are not present, habituation may be determined primarily by the number of stimuli given, independent of stimulus frequency. Many examples can be found where this does seem to be approximately true. Data from Thompson and Spencer on effect of stimulus frequency are plotted in terms of real time—the "frequency effect"—and in terms of number of stimuli in Fig. 10. Number of stimuli is clearly the significant variable here. (We are indebted to Dr. Fred Abraham, Department of Psychiatry, UCLA, for pointing this out to us.) In studies of habituation of flexion reflex in spinal frog, Farel (1972) has shown that over a frequency range of 1 per 10 minutes to 1 per 30 seconds habituation is determined solely by the number of stimuli given (see Fig. 11). Care must be taken not to overgeneralize this effect. Even in the absence of sensitization, at slow frequencies spontaneous recovery may occur between stimuli, yielding relatively less decrement, and with rapid frequencies refractory phenomena may augment the decrement. Nonetheless this critical effect of absolute number of stimuli, even under very limited conditions, suggests a relatively simple underlying mechanism, perhaps a slowly reversing chemical reaction at postsynaptic receptor sites.

There appears to be a clear discontinuity in the function relating habituation to stimulus frequency for stimulus rates faster than about 1 per sec, at

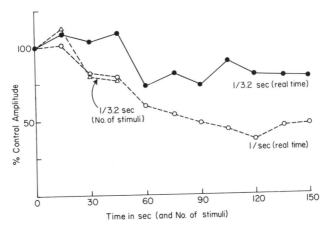

Fig. 10.   Dependence of habituation on number of stimuli: (●) and (○) plot response amplitude (hindlimb flexor reflex of acute spinal cat) in real time for two frequencies of stimulation. When response to slower frequency is replotted in terms of number of stimuli (△), development of habituation agrees closely for both rates of stimulation. Data from Thompson and Spencer (1966).

least in certain systems. As shown in Fig. 12, hindlimb flexion reflex of acute spinal cat exhibits a progressive increase in the amount and rate of relative response habituation for the same constant number (200) of stimuli at rates faster than 1 per second. In a quite different spinal preparation, isolated frog spinal cord (described in more detail below) ventral root response to dorsal root stimulation shows the same dependence on frequency, independent of stimulus number, over a range of 1 per 10 to 1 per 2 seconds (see Fig. 13). This discontinuity could most easily be explained by recruitment of an additional process at faster stimulus rates, e.g., decreased presynaptic mobilization and release of transmitter.

B. Effect of Stimulus Intensity on Habituation

The assumption concerning effect of stimulus intensity may also be simplified. Indeed the simplest possible view is that stimulus strength, rather than having a weak effect on habituation, has no effect. We tentatively adopt this extreme assumption here. It is important to distinguish carefully between inferred habituation and response habituation. Stimulus intensity has a very potent effect on the latter because of the sensitization produced at higher intensities.

In the dual-process theory, habituation is in essence a "common elements" construct. Some proportion of the elements in the S-R pathways are as-

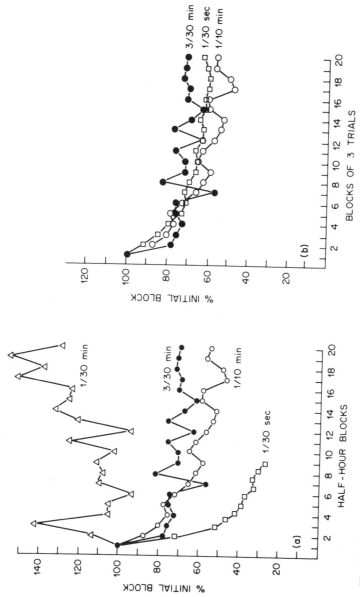

Fig. 11. Development of habituation of hindlimb flexor reflex in chronic spinal frog is dependent on number of stimuli rather than stimulus frequency over a wide range. Dots are plotted in real time in (a) and for number of stimuli in (b). The effect holds over the range from 1 per 30 seconds to 3 per 30 minutes stimulus rates, but not for 1 per 30 minutes. From Farel (1972).

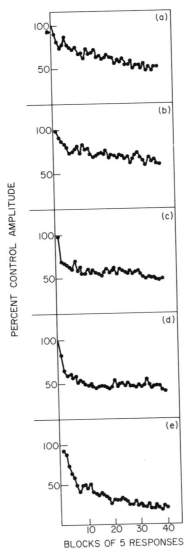

Fig. 12. Habituation of hindlimb flexion reflex to weak cutaneous stimuli as a function of frequency in acute spinal cat. Frequencies are expressed in terms of interstimulus interval: (a) 2 seconds (b) 1 second (c) 500 msec, (d) 250 msec, and (e) 130 msec. Spontaneous recovery was obtained in all cases but is not shown. Note that habituation is more rapid and more pronounced as the frequency of stimulation is increased for the same constant number of stimuli (200). From Groves *et al.* (1969).

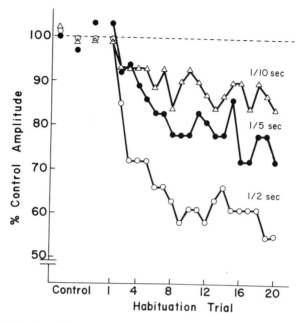

Fig. 13. Habituation of ventral root response to dorsal root stimulation in isolated frog spinal cord for stimulus rates of ! per 2, 1 per 5 and 1 per 10 seconds. Note that in each case 20 stimuli were presented. Farel and Thompson (1972).

sumed to develop habituation. Not all elements participate in habituation—in neural terms primary sensory systems and motoneurons do not appear to be involved—but some subset of S-R elements are plastic-type H neurons.

In order to deduce testable consequences, and thereby make disproof possible, it is necessary to be quite precise in stating that stimulus intensity has no effect on habituation. In particular, absolute and relative decrements must be distinguished. Over a wide range, stimulus intensity has a direct monotonic effect on the magnitude of unconditioned responses and hence on the elements of the S-R pathway. Assume that at intensity X, a plastic-type H element responds initially with a magnitude (i.e., number of nerve spike discharges or size of depolarizing response) of 4 and habituates to 2. If stimulus intensity is increased to $2X$, the element may respond with a magnitude of 8 and will habituate to 4. These simple results are plotted in Fig. 14. The relative amount of habituation, the decrement in response in relation to the initial control level, is 50% for both intensities. This is our assumption: Stimulus intensity has no effect on relative habituation. However, the absolute decrement is 4 units for intensity $2X$ and 2 units for intensity X.

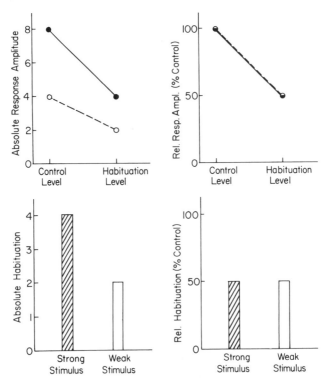

Fig. 14. Hypothetical effects of (○) weak and (●) strong stimuli on habituation. Strong stimulus might yield greater absolute decrement but relative decrements might be approximately the same.

The relative decrement may differ for different elements but is assumed to be constant for any given element. Current and very preliminary data from our laboratory indicate that this may indeed be the case for type H interneurons in the spinal cord of acute spinal cat.

We recently developed a model system that permits a more precise test of this somewhat unexpected prediction that relative habituation is independent of stimulus intensity in the absence of sensitization. The system is ventral root response to dorsal root stimulation in the isolated frog spinal cord removed from the animal and maintained *in vitro* in a small chamber perfused with oxygenated Ringers (Farel and Thompson, 1972). This preparation shows relatively little sensitization, never above initial control response level. When it does occur it is extremely brief, decaying spontaneously in a few seconds. When habituation is compared for two different stimulus intensities, absolute habituation is directly related to stimulus intensity and relative habituation is independent of stimulus intensity, as predicted (see Fig. 15).

That the total number of elements activated is directly related to the strength of a simulus is a truism for the real CNS. However, there is a very important qualification. Stimuli also induce inhibition and strong stimuli quite typically inhibit some elements that are activated by weaker stimuli (see, e.g., Rose *et al.*, 1963, for clear examples in the auditory system). Consequently, the elements activated by a weaker stimulus are not entirely a subset of the elements activated by the strong stimulus. This critically important fact was emphasized earlier in relation to stimulus generalization (Thompson, 1965) and in relation to habituation studies such as those of Sokolov (1963) where a decrease in stimulus intensity leads to an increase in a habituated response (Thompson and Spencer, 1966).

Another qualification, of no particular relevance here but of great impor-

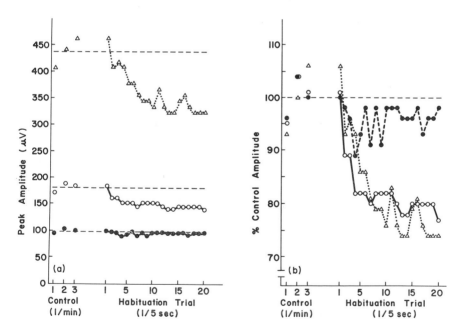

Fig. 15. Effects of stimulus intensity on habituation of ventral root response to dorsal root stimulation in isolated frog spinal cord: (●) 100, (○) 200, and (△) 500 mV pulse. (Weakest stimulus, 100 mV, is just threshold, shows no habituation, and may represent monosynaptic component.) For the two stronger stimuli, (a) absolute habituation is directly related to stimulus intensity, but (b) relative habituation is independent of stimulus intensity. Farel and Thompson (1972).

tance in relation to phenomena of increased responsiveness such as sensitization and conditioning, is that a given stimulus will activate some neurons to discharge spikes but will activate others below spike threshold, the so-called "subliminal fringe." Consequently, a weaker stimulus may influence a relatively larger subset of the elements activated by a stronger stimulus than would be indicated by the relative numbers of elements discharging spikes and hence acting through the CNS to generate behavioral responses.

1. INTENSITY GENERALIZATION OF HABITUATION

In an earlier discussion (Thompson, 1965) stimulus generalization was analyzed in neural terms by assuming that "amount of behavioral stimulus generalization . . . is a monotonic increasing function of the degree of overlap of excitation in the [interneurons] resulting from the training and test stimuli" (p. 159). This view was developed in relation to generalization of learned responses and later applied to an anaylsis of habituation (Thompson, 1969). The hypothesis, incidentally, is a simple restatement of the very old idea of common elements (Guthrie, 1930; Hull, 1920; Thorndike, 1913). Brown developed a similar view at the behavioral level that "equates generalization with transfer of training and attributes transfer to the presence of stimulus components or dimensions common to both conditioned and test stimuli" (1965, p. 22).

Generalization of habituation along the dimension of stimulus intensity appears to provide opportunities for critical tests of our hypothesis. The population of elements activated by a stronger stimulus will include most, but not all, of the elements activated by the weaker stimulus, but the weaker stimulus will activate a relatively smaller portion of those elements activated by the strong stimulus. Furthermore, after habituation to asymptote, the absolute amount of decrement in the elements will be greater for the strong stimulus than for the weak (see Fig. 14).

A simple prediction from this view concerns the effect of altering stimulus intensity in test trials following habituation to a given intensity. If intensity is decreased or increased the same psychophysical distance from the habituating level, the increased intensity ought to have a relatively much greater effect on response strength than the decreased intensity since a relatively much greater proportion of elements will not have been habituated to the increased than to the decreased intensity. Increased intensity will, of course, yield a larger response. Decreased intensity will produce either a small increase in response (because of the small percentage of elements activated by the weaker stimulus that were not activated and hence habituated by the stronger training stimulus; see discussion in Thompson and Spencer, 1966), no change, or a decrease, depending on conditions such as amount of habituation training and magnitude of stimulus change.

This prediction, although seemingly very elementary, is rather critical because Sokolov's theory of habituation (1963) would seem to predict the same amount of increase in response for changes in both directions. Bernstein (1968), using human GSR to tone, found that following habituation to a constant intensity, a 15-dB change to a stronger intensity caused a much greater response than a 15-dB change to a weaker intensity. Grings (1960) and Kimmel (1960) earlier reported analogous results in the context of autonomic conditioning. Using smaller stimulus changes and a somewhat different design, James and Hughes (1969) reported a slight decrease in human GSR response to tone when Ss were habituated at 76 dB and tested at 73 or 70 dB but a substantial increase in response for Ss habituated at 67 dB and tested at 70 or 73 dB (see Fig. 16). This is a particularly satisfying result since the test intensities were the same for both groups. It follows directly from our common elements model.

Less expected and perhaps more intriguing predictions concern relative generalization of habituation along the dimension of stimulus intensity. Assume, again, that sensitization and spontaneous recovery do not occur. If separate groups are habituated to two stimuli differing somewhat in intensity, then (1) the absolute level of response after habituation for the stronger stimulus will be greater, (2) the absolute amount of response decrement for the stronger stimulus will be greater, and (3) the relative amount of response habituation will be approximately the same for both groups. Assume now that additional groups are given the same treatments and then tested at the opposite intensity: (4) The group habituated at the lower intensity and tested at the higher intensity ought to show little relative response habituation (i.e., little decrement relative to initial control level of response to the stronger

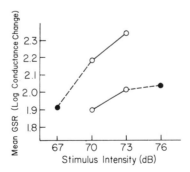

Fig. 16. Generalization gradients for separate groups of human subjects trained at 67 or 76 dB and both tested at common intensities of noise: (●) habituation and (○) test stimuli: Note that the group tested at intensities higher than training give substantially greater responses. From James and Hughes (1969).

stimuli) because many of the elements activated by the stronger stimulus were not activated and hence not habituated by habituation training to the weaker stimulus. In contrast, the group habituated to the stronger stimulus and tested to the weaker stimulus should exhibit greater relative habituation (i.e., more decrement relative to initial control level of response to the weaker stimulus) because most, although not all, of the elements activated by the weaker stimulus were activated and hence habituated by habituation training to the stronger stimulus.

We can also predict the relative amount of stimulus generalization of habituation across intensity: (5) The group habituated to the weaker and tested to the stronger stimulus ought to show less relative habituation than the group habituated and tested to the strong stimulus. This follows from the argument for (4) above. The ratio of these two measures is the index of generalization—actually the relative generalization of relative habituation. It ought to be substantially less than 100%. (6) Finally, and most important, the group habituated to the stronger stimulus and tested to the weaker stimulus ought to show greater relative response habituation than the group habituated and tested to the weaker stimulus. This follows from the fact that the stronger stimulus induces a greater absolute decrement in the elements during habituation than does the weaker stimulus; hence, most of the elements activated in the test to the weaker stimulus are those activated and habituated by the stronger stimulus. The ratio of these two measures is the index of generalization. Under these conditions it ought to be greater than 100%. Our theory has resulted in a seemingly paradoxical prediction.

Not entirely by coincidence, the hypothetical experiment we have described is that done by Davis and Wagner (1968). Since they did not conceptualize it in these terms and did not analyze for the measures discussed above, we have taken the liberty of doing so. The results for each of the six predictions are shown in Fig. 17. In all cases the results are in agreement with predictions.

The results for relative stimulus generalization of response habituation across intensity are particularly crucial. In spite of the fact that the same relative response habituation develops for the group trained and tested at the weaker intensity and the group trained and tested at the stronger intensity, our theory predicts, and the data verify, substantially less than 100% generalization of response habituation for the group trained to the weaker and tested to the stronger stimulus and greater than 100% generalization for the group trained to the strong and tested to the weak stimulus. Preliminary studies in our laboratory using hindlimb flexion reflex of acute spinal cat are yielding similar results, thus providing further general validity for the common elements model.

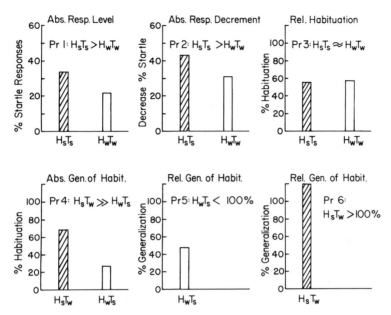

Fig. 17. Predicted (Pr) and actual (bar graphs) test outcomes in an experiment where rat startle was measured in different groups habituated (H) and/or tested (T) to stronger (subscript S) and/or weaker (subscript W) tones. Key: Abs., absolute; Rel., relative; Resp., response; G., generalization, and Habit., habituation. See text for further clarification. Data from Davis and Wagner (1968).

IV. New Evidence for the Dual-Process Theory

The fundamental assumption of the dual-process theory is that the amplitude of behavioral response is the net outcome of two processes, habituation and sensitization, which develop as a result of repeated stimulation. The extent to which these two hypothetical processes develop depends on the response system and on stimulus and training parameters as indicated at the beginning of this paper. Habituation was treated separately in the previous section by assuming experimental conditions that minimize sensitization, i.e., stimulus not too intense and given at moderate frequency. It is also possible to maximize sensitization and minimize habituation by giving very strong stimuli at slow frequencies such that spontaneous recovery of habituation can occur between trials. Much of the evidence for these parametric differences is based on data we have obtained on hindlimb flexion reflex in acute, barbiturized spinal cat (Groves *et al.*, 1969; Groves and Thompson, 1970; Thompson and Spencer, 1966).

In a most important recent study, sensitization was reexamined using hindlimb flexion reflex of chronic unanesthetized spinal rat (Pearson and Wenkstern, 1972). As these authors noted, barbiturates, which appear to interfere with habituation in systems involving the reticular formation, might act partially to damp habituation in acute spinal cat, thus resulting in sensitization being merely a consequence of anesthesia masking habituation. Another potential problem with the acute preparation concerns possible short-term effects of spinal transection. In this study rats were spinalized under ether, allowed 1, 3, or 5 days to recover, and tested using conditions that ought to maximize sensitization and minimize habituation—a very strong shock (35 V, 5 msec, 20 mA) given once every 10 seconds. The response measure was the integrated reflex EMG.

Results of the Pearson and Wenkstern study are beautifully consistent with the dual-process theory. Groups tested at 1, 3, or 5 days all showed significant sensitization. The results of the 5-day group are given in Fig. 18. Data are the means of consecutive averages of blocks of five responses; all responses were significantly greater than the initial response level. We have added the smooth line through their data points. It bears a striking resemblance to our hypothetical sensitization process shown in Fig. 1 which was inferred from studies on flexion reflex of acute barbiturized spinal cat and startle responses of intact rat. This clear correspondence further validates our parametric findings across species and indicates independence of anesthesia and acute transection.

We initially chose spinal reflexes for the study of habituation not because of a particular interest in spinal cord, *per se*, but as a model system where neuronal mechanisms could to some extent be analyzed. The current status of this analysis is indicated in Chapter 6 of Volume II of this series (Groves and Thompson, 1972) and in Thompson *et al.* (1972). There are two critical issues in the use of a model biological system for the study of behavioral plas-

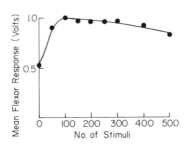

Fig. 18. Sensitization of hindlimb flexor EMG response in 5-day chronic spinal rats given strong infrequent shocks. Note resemblance to hypothetical sensitization curve in Fig. 1. Data from Pearson and Wenkstern (1972).

ticity in addition to its amenability to analysis. One concerns the degree to which the behavioral characteristics of plasticity in the model system parallel those of the intact behaving animal, particularly higher vertebrates. This has been a major thrust of our previous behavioral studies. Parametric effects of stimulus and training variables were shown to correspond for the spinal flexion reflex and responses of intact animals (Thompson and Spencer, 1966). The critical assumption of independence of habituation and sensitization, first demonstrated on spinal cord (Spencer et al., 1966; Thompson and Spencer, 1966) was shown to hold for startle response of intact rat (Groves and Thompson, 1970). The effect of ascending stimulus intensity, the fact that a stimulus of gradually increasing intensity results in substantially more habituation than a constant intense stimulus, first demonstrated by Davis and Wagner (1969) for startle response in intact rat, was shown to hold as well for the spinal flexion reflex (Groves and Thompson, 1970). Finally, as indicated earlier in this paper, the more specific common elements characterization of habituation based initially on spinal data was shown to have considerable predictive value for stimulus intensity generalization of habituation applied to the startle response of intact rat and the orienting response of intact human. These various predictive correspondences constitute strong evidence validating use of the spinal flexion reflex as a model system for the study of habituation.

The other critical issue in the use of a model system concerns the extent to which the mechanisms underlying plasticity in the model system also act in the intact organism. Correspondence of behavioral properties of plasticity for the model and the behaving animal is perhaps a necessary condition but unfortunately not a sufficient condition to demonstrate correspondence of mechanisms. A behavioral phenomenon can be produced by alternative neurophysiological substrates. It is necessary to develop intact preparations where mechanisms can be studied.

Experiments in intact behaving animals by Ursin and associates (1967, 1969) and Wester (1971) provide very strong support for the dual-process theory. Stimulating electrodes were implanted chronically in various brain sites in cats. Electrical stimulation (1-msec pulses at 100 per second for 5 seconds) characteristically yields a head-orienting response that closely resembles head orienting to novel peripheral stimuli (see Thompson and Welker, 1963). When stimulation was repeated at about half minute intervals, orienting responses from stimulation of many brian sites exhibited varying degrees of habituation. Wester's work on thalamic stimulation is particularly relevant to the dual-process theory. Repeated stimulation of lateral sensory nuclei always yielded marked and rapid habituation of evoked orienting behavior. On the other hand, orienting responses elicited by repeated stimulation of the intralaminar nuclei were highly resistant to habituation (Wester, 1971). Furthermore, marked sensitization of orienting was often obtained from intralaminar stimulation sites but *never* obtained with lateral stimulation (Wester, 1971). The correspondence of these findings with the dual-process theory is striking—it is almost as though lateral thalamic stimulation taps into the S-R pathways to yield only habituation while medial stimulation activates the state system to yield varying degrees of sensitization.

Other recent studies provide additional support for the dual-process notion and extend the generality of its applications. In an important paper by Cain *et al.* (1972), gnawing behavior in prairie dogs elicited by hypothalamic stimulation was shown to exhibit habituation to repeated stimulation and sensitization to strong peripheral stimulation. Indeed, as they pointed out, the functional plasticity of behavioral patterns elicited by hypothalamic stimulation (see, e.g., Valenstein *et al.*, 1968) can be explained very neatly by our dual-process views of habituation. The probability that a given behavioral pattern will be elicited is a joint function of the relative effectiveness of the hypothalamic stimulus, the degree of habituation of the elicitation resulting from prior stimulation and the degree of sensitization that exists. When habituation of the behavioral pattern has developed and sensitization is low or itself habituated, the same hypothalamic stimulus would more likely elicit an alternative behavioral pattern.

In a quite different context, Glaser and Griffin (1960) hypothesized that frontal cortex is essential for habituation, a view that contrasts with our own. They reported that frontal lesions abolished habituation of heart rate increment to cold tail pressor stimulation. In a careful recent study, Roydes (1970) demonstrated that frontal lesions in rats, although impairing habituation (a general effect of brain lesions on habituation, see Thompson and Spencer, 1966), did not prevent habituation of head shake response to air puff. Indeed frontal animals were more responsive throughout habituation training, as might be expected from the generally increased responsiveness following frontal lesions. This result is entirely consistent with the dual-process theory. There is considerable evidence that frontal cortex in rat exerts an inhibiting influence on reticular arousal (Clemente and Sterman, 1967; Lynch *et al.*, 1969; Lynch, 1970). Consequently, frontal lesions should yield a chronically increased behavioral state of sensitization, which should increase responsiveness to repeated stimulation but not prevent some degree of habituation. These are precisely the results obtained by Roydes.

Finally, in other recent work consistent with the dual-process notion, Jaffe *et al.* (1969) mapped the entire forebrain of the unanesthetized cat in terms of habituation of auditory evoked potentials and found two general functional categories: responses that habituated completely and responses that habituated only partially.

In current studies we are using the relayed pyramidal discharge (RPD) of the immobilized cat to study habituation and sensitization in the intact preparation. Procedures will be described briefly here, they are given in more detail elsewhere (Teyler et al., 1972). Cats were prepared under ether exposing motor-sensory cortex in the area of the forepaw. A recording electrode was placed in the medullary pyramids by moving the electrode to the position giving the largest direct response to a surface stimulation of the forepaw region of the ipsilateral motor-sensory cortex. The animal was then fixed to an atraumatic head holder (Teyler and Biela, 1972), given a local anaesthetic, and paralyzed with Flexedil, allowing time for recovery from the ether anesthesia.

That the preparation was truly atraumatic was demonstrated by (1) pupillary constriction and (2) sleep spindles in the EEG in the prolonged absence of peripheral stimulation. The stimuli to which the animal was habituated were a contralateral foot shock and a free-field click. The habituation runs employed an interstimulus interval of $\frac{1}{2}$, 1, 2, or 5 seconds and independent runs were separated by at least 30 minutes. Prior to each run a control baseline level was obtained, against which responses to repetitive stimuli were compared. The interstimulus interval during the control runs was either 1 or 5 minutes.

The data collection and analysis was completed in two phases. The first, data collection, was performed by a PDP-12 computer on-line, with an FM magnetic tape backup recording system. The neural activity of the pyramidal tract was sampled at 1-msec intervals for 256 msec subsequent to a stimulus presentation. Each 256-msec sample was recorded on computer tape for later analysis. In addition, the computer calculated an average for every eight responses and stored these on tape. Both the individual and the averaged responses were analyzed off-line. The evoked wave form was rectified, i.e., the absolute value of the voltage was computed, and two integrals were calculated. (For a more complete discussion of the techniques involved, see Roemer et al., 1971). The first integral was formed from the rectified wave form for the time period 25–75 msec after stimulus presentation. The first 25 msec of the wave form was excluded from analysis to avoid contamination by primary sensory activity in adjacent afferent tracts. The second integral was formed from the 75–250-msec time period. The two time periods will be termed early and late components of the response.

The early and late components were initially separated for analysis on the basis of visual inspection of individual responses, i.e., there appeared to be a relatively clear response complex in each time range. At very low stimulus intensities both components exhibit response habituation. However, increasing stimulus intensity has a clear differential effect with two components. Examples are given in Fig. 19 for two intensities of stimulation.

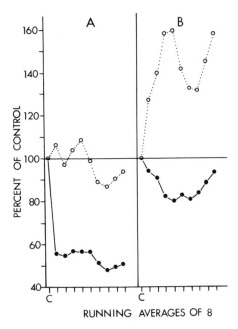

Fig. 19.   Effects of repeated (1 per sec) weak (A = 4 V) and strong (B = 60V) tactile stimuli on (●) early (25–75 msec) and (○) late (75–200 msec) components of the relayed pyramidal response in unanesthetized cat. Responses compard to control level (C) stimulation of 1 per 60 seconds. See text Data from Teyler *et al.* (1972).

At the lower intensity the early component shows response habituation and the late component shows no change. At the higher intensity the early component again shows habituation, but the late component shows clear and significant sensitization.

There are thus two processes exhibitied by the relayed response of the pyramidal tract to repeated peripheral stimulation, one a short latency decremental process and the other a longer latency process that exhibits sensitization at higher stimulus intensities. In our preliminary findings to date the parametric effects of stimulus and training variables on the early and late components closely parallel effects reported earlier for type H and type S neurons in spinal gray (Groves and Thompson, 1970) and are consistent with the hypothetical processes of habituation and sensitization. The pyramidal tract is a major output system from the cerebral cortex in higher mammals. In cat, neurons of the pyramidal tract are at least two synapses removed from the final common path, the motoneurons. At this level in the output from the major integrating system of the brain two distinct processes are seen which strikingly parallel hypothetical habituation in the S-R pathway and sensitization of state.

These findings provide further verification of our theoretical approach in a response system of the intact animal. Perhaps even more important, they provide a behavioral output measure from the intact brain where the two hypothetical processes can be characterized and differentiated, which makes feasible identification and analysis of the neuronal mechanisms underlying habituation and sensitization in the intact, behaving central nervous system.

References

Amsel, A. (1972). Behavioral habituation, counterconditioning, and a general theory of persistence. In "Classical Conditioning" (A. H. Black and W. F. Prokasy, eds.), Appleton, New York (in press).

Bernstein, A. S. (1968). The orienting response and direction of stimulus change. Psychon. Sci. 12, 127–128.

Brown, J. S. (1965). Generalization and discrimination. In "Stimulus Generalization" (D. I. Mostofsky, ed.), pp. 7–23. Stanford Univ. Press, Stanford, California.

Cain, R. E., Skriver, C. P., and Carlson, R. H. (1972). Habituation of electrically induced readiness to gnaw. Science (in press).

Clemente, C. D., and Sterman, M. B. (1967). Basal forebrain mechanisms for internal inhibition. In "Sleep and Altered States of Consciousness" (S. Kety, E. Evarts, and H. Williams eds.), pp. 127–147. Williams & Wilkins, Baltimore, Maryland.

Davis, M., and Wagner, A. R. (1968). Startle responsiveness after habituation to different intensities of tone. Psychon. Sci. 12, 337–338.

Davis, M., and Wagner, A. R. (1969). Habituation of startle response under incremental sequence of stimulus intensities. J. Comp. Physiol. Psychol. 67, 486–492.

Ewert, J.-P., and Ingle, D. (1972). Excitatory effects following habituation of prey catching activity in frogs and toads. J. Comp. Physiol. Psychol. (in press).

Farel, P. B. (1972). Post-transectional hyperexcitability and centrally mediated response decrements in the chronic spinal frog. Physiol. Behav. (in press).

Farel, P. B., and Thompson, R. F. (1972). Habituation and dishabituation to dorsal root stimulation in the isolated frog spinal cord. Behav. Biol. (in press).

Glaser, E. M., and Griffin, J. P. (1960). Changes of Habituation induced by lesions and stimulation of the brain in rats. J. Physiol, (London) 155, 54–55.

Grings, W. W. (1960). Preparatory set variables related to classical conditioning of autonomic responses. Psychol. Rev. 67, 243–252.

Groves, P. M., Lee, D., and Thompson, R. F. (1969). Effects of stimulus frequency and intensity on habituation and sensitization in acute spinal cat. Physiol. Behav. 4, 383–388.

Groves, P. M., and Thompson, R. F. (1970). Habituation: A dual-process theory. Psychol. Rev. 77, 419–450.

Groves, P. M., and Thompson, R. F. (1972). A dual-process theory of habituation: Neural mechanisms. In "Habituation: Behavioral Studies and Physiological Substrates" (H. V. S. Peeke and M. J. Herz, eds.), Vol. II. Academic, New York (in press).

Guthrie, E. R. (1930). Conditioning as a principle of learning. Psychol. Rev. 37, 412–428.

Harris, J. D. (1943). Habituatory response decrement in the intact organism. Psychol. Bull. 40, 385–422.

Hinde, R. A. (1970). Behavioural habituation. In "Short-term Changes in Neural Activity and Behaviour" (G. Horn and R. A. Hinde, eds.), pp. 3–40. Cambridge Univ. Press, London and New York.

Hovland, C. I. (1937). The generalization of conditioned responses. II. The sensory generalization of conditioned responses with varying intensities of tone. *J. Genet. Psychol.* **51**, 279–291.

Hull, C. L. (1920). Quantitative aspects of the evolution of concepts. *Psychol. Monogr.* **28**, No. 123.

Humphrey, G. (1933). "The Nature of Learning." Harcourt, New York.

Ingle, D. (1971). Personal communication.

Jaffe, S. L., Bourlier, P. F., and Hagamen, W. D. (1969). Adaptation of evoked auditory potentials: A midbrain through frontal lobe map in the unanesthetized cat. *Brain Res.* **15**, 121–136.

James, J. P., and Hughes, G. R. (1969). Generalization of habituation of the GSR to white noise of varying intensities. *Psychon. Sci.* **14**, 463–464.

Kimmel, H. D. (1960). The relationship between direction and amount of stimulus change and amount of perceptual disparity response. *J. Exp. Psychol.* **59**, 68–72.

Lynch, G. (1970). Separable forebrain mechanisms controlling different manifestations of spontaneous activity. *J. Comp. Physiol. Psychol.* **70**, 48–59.

Lynch, G., Ballantine, P., and Campbell, B. A. (1969). Potentiation of behavioral arousal following cortical damage and subsequent recovery. *Exp. Neurol.* **23**, 195–206.

Pearson, J. A., and Wenkstern, B. (1972). Sensitization of flexor-withdrawal reflex in conscious spinal rats. *Physiol. Behav.* (in press).

Peeke, H. V. S. (1969). Habituation of conspecific aggression in the three-spined stickleback (*Gasterosteus aculeatus L.*). *Behaviour* **35**, 137–156.

Peeke, H. V. S., and Peeke, S. C. (1970). Habituation of conspecific aggressive responses in the Siamese fighting fish. *Behaviour* **36**, 232–245.

Peeke, H. V. S., Wyers, E. J., and Herz, M. J. (1969). Waning of the aggressive response to male models in the three-spined stickleback *(Gasterosteus aculeatus L.)*. *Anim. Behav.* **17**, 224–228.

Peeke, H. V. S., Herz, M. J., and Gallagher, J. E. (1971). Changes in aggressive interaction in adjacently territorial convict cichlids (*Cichlasoma nigrofasciatum*): A study of habituation. *Behaviour*.

Prosser, C. L., and Hunter, W. S. (1936). The extinction of startle responses and spinal reflexes in the white rat. *Amer. J. Physiol.* **117**, 609–618.

Raskin, D. C., Kotses, H., and Bever, J. (1969). Autonomic idicators of orienting and defensive reflexes. *J. Exp. Psychol.* **80**, 423–433.

Ratner, S. C. (1972). Habituation and retention of habituation in leech, *Macrobdella Decora*. *J. Comp. Physiol. Psychol.* (in press).

Roemer, R. A., Teyler, T. J., and Thompson, R. F. (1971). A technique for the quantification and analysis of evoked potential activity. *Behav. Res. Meth. Instnu.*, 1971, **3**, 317–318.

Rose, J. E., Greenwood, D. D., Goldberg, J. M., and Hind, J. E. (1963). Some discharge characteristics of single neurons in the inferior colliculus of the cat. I. Tonotopical organization, relation of spike-counts to tone intensity, and firing patterns of single elements. *J. Neurophysiol.* **26**, 294–320.

Roydes, R. L. (1970). Frontal lesions impair habituation of the head shake response in rats. *Physiol. Behav.* **5**, 1133–1139.

Sokolov, Y. N. (1963). "Perception and the Conditioned Reflex" (S. W. Waydenfeld, translator). Pergamon, Oxford.

Spencer, W. A., Thompson, R. F., and Neilson, D. R., Jr. (1966). Response decrement of flexion reflex in acute spinal cat and transient restoration by strong stimuli. *J. Neurophysiol.* **29**, 221–239.

Teyler, T. J., and Biela, J. (1972). An acute atraumatic stereotaxic headholder for cat. *Physiol. Behav.*, 1972, **8**, 543.

Teyler, T. J., Roemer, R. A., and Thompson, R. F. (1972). Habituation and sensitization of the relayed pyramidal discharge in immobilized cat., *Physiol. Behav*, **8**, 201–205.

Thompson, R. F. (1965). The neural basis of stimulus generalization. *In* "Stimulus Generalization" (D. I. Mostofsky, ed.), pp. 154–178. Stanford Univ. Press, Stanford, California.

Thompson, R. F. (1969). Neural mechanisms of stimulus generalization. *In* "Stimulus Generalization" (D. I. Mostofsky, ed.), p. 1965. Stanford Univ. Press, Stanford, California.

Thorndike, E. L. (1913). "Educational Psychology. II. The Psychology of Learning." Teachers

Thompson, R. F., Patterson, M. M., Teyler, T. J. (1972). The neurophysiology of learning. *Annu. Rev. Psychol.* **23**, 73–104.

Thompson, R. F., and Spencer, W. A. (1966). Habituation: A model phenomenon for the study of neuronal substrates of behavior. *Psychol. Rev.* **173**, 16–43.

Thompson, R. F., and Welker, W. I. (1963). Role of auditory cortex in reflex head orientation by cats to auditory stimuli. *J. Comp. Physiol. Psychol.* **56**, 996–1002.

Thorndike, E. L. (1913). "Educational Psychology. II. The Psychology of Learning." Teachers College, Columbia University, New York.

Ursin, H., Wester, K., and Ursin, R. (1967). Habituation to electrical stimulation of the brain in unanesthetized cats. *Electroencephalogr. Clin. Neurophysiol.* **23**, 41–49.

Ursin, H., Sundberg, H., and Menaker, S. (1969). Habituation of the orienting response elicited by stimulation of the caudate nucleus in the cat. *Neuropsychologia* **7**, 313–318.

Valenstein, E. S., Cox, V. C., and Kakolewski, J. W. (1968). Modification of motivated behavior elicited by electrical stimulation of the hypothalamus. *Science* **159**, 1119–1121.

Wester, K. (1971). Habituation to electrical stimulation of the thalamus in unanesthetized cats. *Electroencephalogr. Clin. Neurophysiol.* **30**, 52–61.

Wester, K. (1971). Personal communication.

Wickelgren, B. G. (1967). Habituation of spinal motoneurons. *J. Neurophysiol.* **30**, 1404–1423.

Author Index

Numbers in italics refer to the pages on which the complete references are listed.

A

Abraham, F. D., 3, *53*, 127, *134*
Ackerman, P. T., 170, 176, *213*
Allabach, L. F., 24, *53*
Allen, C. K., 191, *212*
Amsel, A., 250, *269*
Anchel, H., 134, *134*
Anne, E., 110, *139*
Applewhite, P. B., 13, 14, 15, 16, 18, 25, *53*, *54*
Arechiga, H., 119, *134*
Arezzo, D. A., 177, 179, 180, *212*
Asafov, B. D., 176, *212*
Austen, B. G., 173, *212*

B

Babskii, E., 130, *134*
Badia, P., 176, 184, 189, 191, *212*
Baenninger, R., 64, 67, *81*
Baerends, G. P., 63, 74, 76, 79, *81*, *82*
Bagacz, J., 225, *237*
Bagshaw, M. H., 190, 196, *212*
Balderrama, N., 9, 28, 44, 51, *53*
Ball, T. S., 173, 192, *214*
Balvin, R. S., 122, *135*
Barham, E. G., 131, *134*
Barlow, G. W., 66, 70, *82*
Barrass, R., 10, *53*
Benjamin, L. S., 169, *212*
Benzies, S., 190, *212*
Berg, K. M., 172, 176, 178, 179, 180, 181, 184, *212*
Berg, W. K., 172, 176, 179, 181, 182, *212*, *215*
Beritov, I. S., 123, *134*
Berlyne, D. E., 191, *212*
Bernstein, A. S., 169, 173, 193, *212*, 261, *269*

B (cont.)

Bever, J., 168, 169, 170, 172, 177, 179, 181, 184, 185, *217*, 246, *270*
Biela, J., 267, *270*
Bindra, D., 200, *212*
Birukow, G., 91, 92, 125, *134*, *135*
Bishop, G. H., 86, 113, 122, *139*
Bishop, P. D., 186, 187, *212*, 223, 229, *236*
Björkvall, C., 186, *214*
Blair, M. W., 194, 202, *218*
Bloch, R. M., 185, *212*
Bohn, G., 28, 29, *53*
Bolles, M. M., 170, 176, 190, *214*
Bourlier, P. F., 266, *270*
Bower, G. H., 141, *160*
Breder, C. M., 62, *82*
Breland, B., 86, *134*
Breland, K., 86, *134*
Brotsky, S., 172, *213*
Brown, C. C., 169, *213*
Brown, J. S., *269*
Brunswik, E., 156, 157, 158, 159, 160, *160*
Buchwald, A. M., 172, 173, 177, 178, 179, *213*
Buchwald, N. A., 111, *134*
Bullock, T. H., 127, 128, *135*, *137*
Burch, G. E., 173, *213*
Burch, N. R., 182, 187, *217*
Bures, J., 110, *135*
Burns, B., 131, *134*
Buser, P., 108, *140*
Butz-Kuenzer, E., 92, *135*

C

Cain, R. E., 266, *269*
Campbell, C. B. G., 132, *137*
Campbell, D., 108, *135*
Carew, T. J., 33, 34, 35, 53, *53*

273

Subject Index